GRAPHIC NOVELS
BEYOND THE BASICS

GRAPHIC NOVELS
BEYOND THE BASICS

INSIGHTS AND
ISSUES FOR LIBRARIES

Martha Cornog and Timothy Perper, Editors

LIBRARIES UNLIMITED
An Imprint of ABC-CLIO, LLC

A B C 🙢 C L I O

Santa Barbara, California • Denver, Colorado • Oxford, England

Library of Congress Cataloging-in-Publication Data

Graphic novels beyond the basics : insights and issues for libraries / edited by
Martha Cornog and Timothy Perper.
    p. cm.
  Includes bibliographical references and index.
  ISBN 978-1-59158-478-0 (acid-free paper)
  1. Libraries—Special collections—Graphic novels.   2. Graphic novels—History
and criticism.   3. Libraries—Special collections—Comic books, strips, etc.
4. Comic books, strips, etc.—History and criticism.   I. Cornog, Martha.
II. Perper, Timothy, 1939–
  Z692.G7G73   2009
  025.2'89—dc22   2009016189

13   12   11   10   9   1   2   3   4   5

This book is also available on the World Wide Web as an eBook.
Visit www.abc-clio.com for details.

ABC-CLIO, LLC
130 Cremona Drive, P.O. Box 1911
Santa Barbara, California 93116–1911

This book is printed on acid-free paper ∞
Manufactured in the United States of America

This book is dedicated to
Joe Murray
of Captain Blue Hen Comics in Delaware,
who dared to talk manga to his new father-in-law,
and to
Bob Francoeur,
the father-in-law and our first comics co-conspirator.

CONTENTS

ACKNOWLEDGMENTS

We heartily thank our mentors and co-conspirators in comics from around the world. This book owes all to its chapter authors, who have all read many more comics than we have. The concept itself comes from our patient and craftful editor, Barbara Ittner, who helped us balance words and ideas—our own and everyone else's.

Throughout, we drew on information and goodwill about our favorite subject from the stalwart staff at Philadelphia's Atomic City Comics (aka Showcase Comics), who spoon-fed our addiction early. For camaraderie, good advice, and wellsprings of experience, we thank Steve Raiteri, John Shableski, Karen Green, David Serchay, Sandy Berman, and fellow illuminati on the Graphic Novels in Libraries e-list, the Anime and Manga Research Circle e-list, and the editorial board of *Mechademia*.

For actually hiring us to write about comics in one way or another, we are extravagantly grateful to *Library Journal* and TOKYOPOP, with special thanks to *LJ*'s Ann Kim and TOKYOPOP's Hope Donovan, Bryce Coleman, Kasia Piekarz, and Mike Kiley as well as veteran translator/adaptor Kathy Schilling. For their determined and successful media mastery, we thank the staff at *Publishers Weekly*'s PW Comics Week and at ICv2. For putting on the conventions that enliven our year, a big thanks to the hardworking people behind the New York Comic Con, Book Expo America, and the East Coast Black Age of Comics Convention. We are very appreciative of the behind-the-scenes work in public libraries that has and will put graphic narratives into the hands of so many people, including us, with a special thanks to the team in the Free Library of Philadelphia's Materials Management Division as well as the staff at its Independence Branch.

Finally, we thank the professors in our long-distant past who taught us French and Chinese, little knowing that much later we would seize upon what was left of our familiarity to gain access to Japanese comics not yet available in English.

INTRODUCTION: ORIGIN STORIES

Martha Cornog and Timothy Perper

We revere words; we devote libraries to housing them. We adore pictures; we build museums to house them. And when you combine the two, you can get something quite extraordinary![1]

The two of us grew up with the comics of the 1950s—*Archie, Brenda Starr, Mickey Mouse* and *Mighty Mouse, Pogo* and *Li'l Abner,* the pastel Hamlet of *Classics Illustrated.* We tarried briefly with a few 1960s counterculture favorites such as *Mr. Natural.* Then seduced by the Great Minds and Ideas of Literature and Science, we dropped comics from our radar for the next 30 years. We did not miss them. So many books, so little time.

Then our friend Bob plopped a couple of Japanese manga titles on our kitchen table. His daughter had married a comics shop owner, and what did we think of *Oh My Goddess!* and *Ogenki Clinic?*[2] Good question! We had never seen anything like them, and we were mesmerized. Between them—one, a romantic comedy and the other, wacko and explicit erotic humor—the complex and quirky plots, captivating characters, and consummate artistry were totally unlike what we remembered of American comics. We had not been looking for a new obsession, but this one adopted us. We were card-carrying AARP members—were we regressing to childhood or awakening to an equally mature medium? Easy decision. These comics certainly were not for children, and we wanted to know a good deal more about them. In the next decade, we hoarded a manga collection of over 500 series, with about 2,500 paperbacks and 600 comic books plus easily 200 books about manga, anime, comics, and Japanese culture. And gradually we discovered that American comics were not what we remembered either. We fell in love with *Courtney Crumrin* and *Dykes to Watch Out For.*

We invite librarians to take the same journey or to continue if you have already begun. But you do not have to love comics or adopt them as an obsession to see their value in library collections. It is enough to realize that comics are a medium—not a genre—for stories and information and that millions of Americans enjoy graphic narrative. It then becomes a matter of integrating comics and graphic novels into the collection as simply one more medium—books, magazines, talking books, DVDs, graphic novels—and a medium with amazing variety, reach, and flexibility yet still evolving around the world.

A QUICK HISTORY OF COMICS AND GRAPHIC NARRATIVE

Worldwide Origins

Stories told in sequences of pictures, with or without words, have developed and persisted across history and culture.[3] In the eons before writing, printing, and television, Paleolithic cave paintings depicted hunting expeditions. Egyptian tomb paintings from 1300 B.C.E. show stages in agrarian and domestic tasks, and cartoon-like Chinese stone reliefs date to the 11th century B.C.E. Early Aztecs and Mayans also produced sequential art. The 11th-century French Bayeux Tapestry illustrates the Norman Conquest, battle by battle with marginal commentary, and in both China and Japan, humorous scrolls dating to the 12th century and earlier tell satiric stories, even wacko and explicit erotic humor recalling the modern *Ogenki Clinic*.

The printing press only increased the reach and variety of graphic narrative. Surviving British, European, and American caricature work from the 15th through 19th centuries show similarities to modern comics. More directly, satirical drawings and political cartoons in 19th-century European, British, and North American periodicals led to short plots depicted through pictures and words together. Swiss academic Rodolphe Töpffer's amusing "picture stories" even diverted German writer Goethe from grief over his late son (Kunzel 2007, 52). We forget today that in the 19th century, adult fiction as well as children's books relied heavily on illustrations. Charles Dickens's *Pickwick Papers* was originally commissioned simply as text for Robert Seymour's drawings, and the original printing of William Makepeace Thackeray's *Vanity Fair* included 188 illustrations by the author (Klinkenborg 2004).

Favorite Homegrown Fare

American newspaper comics began in the late 1800s, and in the early 20th century, *Mutt and Jeff, Little Nemo in Slumberland,* and *Little Orphan Annie* all took root. By the 1930s, Disney favorites Mickey Mouse and Donald Duck had strips. Now most American dailies ran comics, not for a change of pace but to sell papers. Hooked on favorite characters, everyone ponied up their spare change to see what Dick Tracy or Flash Gordon might be up to. Across the Atlantic, British comics magazines had started up as well, German newspapers ran strips, and Belgian artist Hergé began his stories about boy reporter Tintin in 1929. (All 24 volumes of *Tintin* are still in print.) But not all instances of developing sequential art took comic strip form. Occasional woodcut artists such as Lynd Ward produced wordless, book-length stories in art alone—forerunners to the more artistic and literary graphic novels of the last 25 years.[4]

"Comic books," those familiar slender pamphlets, grew out of newspaper comics in the 1930s but soon introduced new material, especially for boys. Superman debuted in 1939 in *Action Comics* #1, opening the so-called "Golden Age" of comics, with superheroes and heroines who supported the Allies' efforts in World War II. Meanwhile, teen-protagonist comics such as *Archie* entered the stage. *Walt Disney's Comics and Stories* began in 1940 and, still published, takes honors as the longest-running American comic book.

When after the war the soldiers came home, they looked to find comfort in illustrated fantasies and plots appropriate to their age and experience. New genres became popular: detective, horror, and science fiction stories, many with bodacious babes as partners, mates, victims, and eye candy. Comic art versions of classic literature also date from this period, including *The Jungle Book* and *Hamlet.* But many people still saw comics as a youth-only medium—not completely without justification, given that in 1953 around 90 percent of kids were reading them (Comics in the Classroom 2006). Psychiatrist Fredric Wertham, similarly to 19th-century arch-censor Anthony Comstock, saw in comics a scapegoat for rising juvenile crime. Indeed, Wertham's 1953 *Seduction of the Innocent,* which blamed superhero, horror, and crime comics for ruining young minds, mushroomed into a nationwide crusade against the "evils" of comic books. Backed into a corner, U.S. comics publishers established a Comics Code Authority (CCA) that gutted comics of controversial themes, realistic plots, and sex. With focus changed to funny animals, sanitized heterosexual romances, teen humor, and television show adaptations, comics had lost their social relevance (Hajdu 2008).

But Across the Pacific . . .

Although unnoticed in the United States, things went differently in Japan. Growing out of the interaction of Japanese graphic traditions with modern Western comics, Japanese "manga" comics developed into an economic and aesthetic powerhouse. Bound folios of sequential woodblock prints began in the 1700s, continuing a graphic narrative tradition that was later influenced by Western cartoons in the 1800s and specifically American work starting in the 20th century. Like American comics, Japanese comics supported their own side of the war machine through the 1940s. And postwar also, the Japanese turned to comics to soothe and entertain them. Artist Osamu Tezuka, later honored as the "God of manga," debuted in 1947 with the cinematographic *New Treasure Island,* inspired by the Robert Louis Stevenson story.

As Tezuka matured, he produced a phenomenal output of derivative and original plots with innovative graphic design, taking inspiration from Disney, American films, and the Takarazuka Review.[5] A cultural icon in Japan since 1913, the Takarazuka troupe draws on an all-female cast to play both men's and women's roles, and their elaborate musical productions have been as beloved in Japan as the older all-male Kabuki theater.

Tezuka created wonderful characters—including Princess Sapphire, who passes as male for much of the plot of *Ribon no Kishi,* "Knight in Ribbons," usually translated as *Princess Knight* (1953). Ever since, breakout graphic design, magical girls and warrior women, and gender ambiguities have been staples of Japanese manga. Plots developed untrammeled to embrace realistic and fantastic stories of all kinds, with strong appeal to both sexes and all ages. By 2002, manga accounted for nearly 40 percent of Japan's print output in volume and over 20 percent in value. Female-oriented manga alone employs over 400 women *mangaka* (artists) (Gravett 2004, 13, 74).

American Comics Change

In the 1960s, animated television series ("anime") such as Tezuka's *Astro Boy* won fans in Japan and migrated to America—sometimes with their roots disguised—paving the way for later popularization of manga in this country. Meanwhile, a new breed of underground "comix" tunneled under the CCA with sometimes hilarious, sometimes savage, and sometimes poignant tales of sex, drugs, and anti–Vietnam War sentiment. Originally niche-marketed in "head shops," the work of Gilbert Shelton, S. Clay Wilson, and especially Robert Crumb lives on today, even as their sometimes-misogynistic comix paved the way for franker women's comics such as the art of Trina Robbins, Roberta Gregory, and several series including *Wimmen's Comix* (Robbins 1999). Gradually, the superhero genre revived in the 1960s and 1970s with new, more realistic, diverse, and even fallible characters, sometimes working in teams and including more women. Comics fan conventions began as a way to relax with fellow fans, still mostly male, and meet the artists. New publishers like Kitchen Sink, Fantagraphics, and NBM sprang up to showcase more contemporary and less mainstream plots, including many imported titles. Now well after the sexual revolution and post-Watergate, even newspaper comics, led by Gary Trudeau's *Doonsbury,* started focusing on real problems and lives of real people.

Enter the Graphic Novel

In 1978, Will Eisner's *A Contract with God* appeared, and Eisner popularized the term *graphic novel* as a way to differentiate his own serious and substantial work from what people thought of as "comics."[6] Graphic novels, unlike serialized newspaper strips and many comic books, had stories with a beginning and end. Moreover, they looked like meaty trade paperbacks, not flimsy mini-magazines. Eisner's work led to a comics award in his name and to a flowering of non-superhero graphic novels, artistic and literary with more realistic and controversial plots. As new work emerged, comics specialty shops sprang up, growing out of the comics conventions and head shops of the 1960s. Comics publishers began selling directly to these shops rather than to newsstands and drugstores as had been traditional. By the end of the 1980s, comics publishers had begun backing out of the CCA.

Mainstream publishers had been putting out occasional collections of comic books and popular newspaper strips. After *A Contract with God* appeared from small publisher Baronet Press, the larger publishing houses took interest in these new graphic novels. Comics content was now broader, and American culture more pluralistic, and distribution to comics readers could be more easily managed through the specialty stores as well as bookstores—which were now stocking the most popular and most literary graphic novels as well as paperback collections of comics like *Elfquest,* a popular fantasy series with a large female readership. In 1987 and 1992, Pantheon published Art Spiegelman's two-volume story of the Holocaust, *Maus: A Survivor's Tale.* Spiegelman won the 1992 Pulitzer Prize for Literature, the first cartoonist so honored. Graphic novels began attracting advocates, including then-Doubleday editor Jackie Kennedy Onassis, who honchoed publication of the first collection of Larry Gonick's *Cartoon History of the Universe* in 1990 (Skinn 2004, 272). Abroad, French and Belgian artists thrived, contributing local talent to the European scene, which also welcomed numerous imports, including manga. Overall, European comics have blossomed with adult, sophisticated titles that explore diverse themes.

Japan Converts America to Manga

In the 1990s, the power of Japanese graphic storytelling swept into the United States—and we loved it. Hiroshima survivor tale *Barefoot Gen,* imported in 1978 as the first translated manga, was only the beginning. With anime fans on campuses and elsewhere in support, a trickle of manga and anime throughout the 1980s soon became a torrent. The American comics industry reeled from a new wake-up call, as different from Fredric Wertham's as possible: In Japan, girls read comics! Women read comics! Adults read comics! Wow! Torn between threat and opportunity, comics publishers took notice. Some started publishing manga; others produced new series for girls, such as Disney's *W.I.T.C.H.,* that was imported from Italy. The American success of manga proved that people liked comics bound as trade paperbacks. Not only could you read more of the plot at a time, but also bookstores would sell them. Everyone was excited, if nervous. Was the "manga revolution" a mere fad? Would American girls and women read comics like the Japanese? Would manga fans cross over to American titles? Would they read manga-style comics if drawn by Americans?

The Expanding Universe of Graphic Narrative

As of 2008, manga remains wildly popular despite fears of over-diversification and occasional belt-tightening within the industry. Girls and women *are* reading comics—not just shōjo (girls) manga but other manga and American comics too. Who knew? As boy and girl comics readers grow up, the industry has begun to put out a wider line of young children's comics to grow new readers as well as publishing more comics for young and older adults, especially for the older teen readers who will soon want mature plots. The potential market really is as large as "all ages." Superheroes, manga, and a variety of different genres thrive, readership hyped by tie-ins with films and television series and numerous titles sold as graphic novels in bookstores. DC Comics' *Watchmen* has been jumping off the shelves due to the 2009 film, and DC reportedly printed one million copies to meet demand (Gustines 2008). And as for newspaper comics? Still popular. Even the *New York Times,* ever the comics holdout, bowed to the new respectability of graphic novels and added a "Funny Pages" section to its Sunday magazine in 2005 and then a "graphic books" category to its best seller list in 2009.

Why have comics persisted so vigorously across time and place, despite competition from other media and despite flurries of censorship? We know that humans love pictures and art of all kinds, but let's give some of the credit to the comics artists, also. People *want* to make comics, at least partly because comics offer the purest and most personal control of artistic vision ever invented. With text-only, readers interpret the action in their own way, independent from author intent. With video and even animation, an army of other people—actors, directors, animators—dilute, expand, and sometime pervert the original creative concept. But with comics, the artist/creator has indeed complete control. Said *Cancer Vixen*'s Marisa Acocella Marchetto: "You're the writer, producer, casting agent, the whole world."[7] Moreover, comics are easy and inexpensive to make in comparison with other visual storytelling. So we need have no fear that graphic narrative will ever disappear.

COMICS, GRAPHIC NOVELS, AND LIBRARIANS

From Disdain to Discovery

American libraries must have virtually ignored comics initially—only in 1943 did the word first appear as a subheading of "Children's literature" and "Children's reading" in the venerable Wilson index, *Library Literature.*[8] Throughout the 1940s, librarians flirted cautiously with comics, clearly intrigued but reserved. Several libraries tried various ways of using them as a bridge to lead youngsters over to "real books." However, the main theme of this period was reflected in library literature with articles such as "Comics Aren't Good Enough" and "Good Reading vs. Comic Book Reading." But by 1950, a California librarian proposed, "Make Friends with the Comics!" while a New York state library mounted an exhibition of comics history. With increased library interest, Wilson index staff turned "comics" into a main heading in 1952.

In 1955, Fredric Wertham spread his anti-comics message via *Wilson Library Bulletin.* Librarian articles about comics dropped off sharply as a result but picked up again in the late 1960s. The flirtation continued. A 1968 list of comics in *Library Journal's* magazine column reflected a bemused disdain on the part of both author and column editor. But by 1972, the second edition of *Magazines for Libraries* had an entire section on comic books and related publications, and in 1974, artist Will Eisner contributed a much more positive article about comics to *Library Journal.* Major collection development essays followed in *Choice* (1975) and *Serials Review* (1982). The heading "Comics" expanded to "Comic books, strips, etc." in 1978.

The Bandwagon Gathers Steam

Since the 1980s, the question for librarians has not been "do we?" but "how do we?" In 1985, artist Art Spiegelman wrote about his *Maus* for *Behavioral and Social Sciences Librarian.* Other articles had titles such as "Comics Bring 'Em in to Kansas City Libraries" (1988), "Comic Books for Grown-Ups: Introducing the Graphic Novel" (1989), "Picture This: Graphic Novels in Libraries" (1990), and "Get the Picture? A Serious Look at Comics in Libraries" (1991). *Library Literature* added "Graphic novel" as a see-reference to "Comics" in 1994 and then elevated the new term to main heading status in 1996.

In the mid-1990s, *Voice of Youth Advocates* began graphic novel reviews, in 1998 *School Library Journal,* and in 2000 *Publishers Weekly.* In breakthrough year 2002, *Library Journal* began reviews, and the Young Adult Library Services Association (YALSA) chose "Get Graphic @ Your Library!" as its theme for Teen Read Week, underscoring its endorsement with a preconference on the same theme at the annual meeting of the American Library Association (ALA). "Comics" had been a bad word, but "graphic novels" had credibility, even panache: finally librarians and comics, aka graphic novels, could get along. Books for librarians about comics and graphic novels followed the trend. Only one title had appeared in the 1980s: J. L. Thomas's *Cartoons and Comics in the Classroom: A Reference for Teachers and Librarians.* During the 1990s, Randall Scott's *Comics Librarianship: A Handbook* and D. Aviva Rothschild's *Graphic Novels: A Bibliographic Guide to Book-Length Comics* embodied the shift in terminology. But in 2003, two books came out, another in 2004, and at least 10 since 2005 (see Appendix C).

A Developing Synergy

Now 20-some years after Thomas's book, let's eavesdrop at the 2006 New York Comic Con, the first sizeable New York comics convention in many years.[9] *Publishers Weekly, Library Journal,* and *School Library Journal* shone among the show's sponsors. Some 35,000 mobbed the suddenly-too-small conference space, including numerous librarians. Exhibit booths plus panels for professionals offered extensive opportunities to meet the artists, writers, publishers, distributors, and stores committed to comics and graphic novel publishing. It was all about dialogue. Asked librarians, "The bindings fall apart—can you make them stronger?" "Will you provide descriptions along with age ratings so we can shelve this in the best place?" "Do you have more titles for younger readers?" Because many library systems still pigeonhole comics into children's and young adults' collections, age-grading is a challenge, and librarians lack places to put graphic novels with adult content and themes. Although convention attendees could all chant the comics mantra "It's a format, not a genre!" American culture and bureaucracy have not fully accommodated yet. Moreover, librarians revealed, it has sometimes been not parents but other library staff who offer the most resistance to graphic novels in library collections. And at the 2007 and 2008 New York Comic Cons, librarian interest and dialogue have only intensified.

For their part, comics industry staff show considerable interest in librarian input. John Shableski, formerly of Brodart and now of Diamond Comics, has compared librarians' role with graphic novels to that of radio stations playing the songs: both connect the product with the market.[10] Indeed, the industry recognizes that libraries constitute a major gateway to readers and is taking active steps to reach librarians and work with them. Publishers TOKYOPOP, VIZ, Marvel, and DC Comics, plus comics distributor Diamond, all exhibit at library conventions as well as comics conventions and have sections on their Web sites for librarians or brochures designed to tell library staff about comics and graphic novels.

Today, opportunities for librarian and industry collaboration are rich and growing. It is a win-win situation because librarians can provide the industry with not only readers and potential buyers but also valuable and articulate feedback about titles, product lines, packaging, and marketing. On the other hand, the industry can provide librarians with new readers—comics and graphic novel fans who may be drawn to the library only because the comics are (now) there. How many might these be? Potentially in the millions. At the Graphic Novel Conference held just before 2008's New York Comic Con, Milton Griepp of the pop culture watch organization ICv2 reported that the total graphic novel plus comic books market totaled $705 million in 2007, and the graphic novel market alone reached $375 million (Griepp 2008). If each buyer spends $100 per year on average, that comes to 4 to 7 million readers. Many of them probably have not used libraries. But they might use them now.

ABOUT COMICS TODAY

In the last few years, everything about the comics industry, and comics in libraries, has changed and is still changing. Every facet of graphic storytelling is diversifying and exploding as old and new creators and readers expand their visions. Once sadly contracted to mainly superheroes, funny animals, and sanitized domestic dramas, American comics have expanded and now cross-fertilize with manga and comics around the world, which themselves expand and cross-fertilize.

Size and Shape of the Market

The graphic novel explosion is indeed big news, and a sampler of statistics carries the message (Griepp 2008):

- The 2007 North American graphic novel market of $375 million shows a 12 percent increase from 2006 and quintuple the $75 million figure of 2001. Bookstore sales of graphic novels run double the sales through comics shops and other channels.
- Of titles released in 2007, manga constituted 46 percent and "American genre" titles (predominantly superheroes) 37 percent. The remaining 17 percent included non-genre fiction and nonfiction, titles for kids and tweens, humor, and "other." All categories except "other" have shown 40 percent or better growth in new titles over the last two years. The major distributor Diamond tracks over 11,800 titles.
- Graphic novels constitute over 11 percent of the overall book business. About 8 percent of online book buyers purchase graphic novels (ICv2 2008).
- In the 2007 total comics market of $704 million, the graphic novel market, at $375 million, passed the periodical comics market ("comic books"), at $330 million, for the first time. Previously, the periodical comics market had always been larger than the graphic novel market.
- For manga, a sizeable percentage of readers are women. In the "top 50 manga" best-seller lists compiled by ICv2, the number of shōjo titles appearing on the lists went from some 36 percent of titles in 2005 to over 50 percent for the first time in 2008.[11]
- Beyond the trade market, the library market for graphic novels is now $30 million, over 7 percent of the total.

Literacy

More big news: comics can enhance literacy, not erode it. Generations of misguided "wisdom"—that comics would seduce kids away from "real" books—have been proven wrong. Research now shows that children who read comics also read more for pleasure, period (Krashen 2004, 91–110). But what is so special about reading for pleasure? Plenty, as it turns out. Study after study shows that people who read more for pleasure are better readers, and better readers are more likely to be employed, to attain better professional positions and higher salaries, to volunteer more in their community, and even to vote more. *Reading correlates to almost every measurement of positive personal and social behavior surveyed—including exercising and playing sports* (National Endowment for the Arts 2007).

> Literacy is the most basic currency of the knowledge economy that we're living in today. . . . Reading is the gateway skill that makes all other learning possible, from complex word problems and the meaning of our history to scientific discovery and technological proficiency. (Obama 2005)

The word leads to the world, and so comics can be a gateway to literacy and success in life.

Beyond these studies, dozens of anecdotal reports have surfaced on comics blogs, discussion groups, and Web sites, with a common theme: I (or my spouse/sibling/kid) shied away from reading until my friend (or parent or uncle) gave me some comics. I couldn't stop reading them, and now I'm a writer/librarian/teacher/editor/other respected professional (Krashen 2004, 91–110, reports several such anecdotes). One former Marvel Comics editor-in-chief told how he won a first-grade spelling bee with the word *bouillabaisse,* encountered originally in a Disney comic book.[12] Text analysis shows that the average comic book uses more uncommon words than children's books and even adult television—and far more uncommon words than typical adult–adult as well as adult–child conversations (Krashen 2004, 104) and thus can serve as a conduit to more challenging reading.

As the news about comics and literacy has spread, interest has increased among the educational establishment (Thompson 2008). The National Council of Teachers of English scheduled 11 graphic novel panels at its 2008 annual conference. A number of organizations have sprung up to spread the gospel of comics and get kids interested in reading, such as the Comic Book Project of Teachers College at Columbia University (www.comic bookproject.org) and the Maryland Comic Book Initiative of the Maryland State Department of Education (Maryland State Department of Education 2008).

What's in It for Libraries?

For libraries, this is an unprecedented opportunity to expand the vibrancy and reach of their collections and attract these readers, children through older adults. Romance and action manga just fly off the shelves in school and public libraries, mirroring bookstore sales at a time when a single volume of the girls' manga *Fruits Basket* sold 12,000 copies during one pre-holiday week in December 2007. Another wildly popular series is *Kingdom*

Hearts, a Japan-Disney collaboration for ages 10 and up based on a video game. Superheroes are not what they used to be either: in 2008, DC Comics published manga artist Yoshinori Natsume's *Batman: Death Mask.* Even Latino kids and minority urban teens love manga. Have we ever seen globalization like this? Yet libraries can now offer comics of so many genres and for so many reasons. This includes leisure reading of romance and adventure stories, of course. In addition, comics in French such as *Tintin, Astérix,* and the Japanese manga *Rose of Versailles* (translated into French but never completely into English) can help with language learning. For those new to Marcel Proust, the French graphic novel adaptation by Stéphane Heuet of *A la Recherche du Temps Perdu,* plus the English translation, can ease entry into Proust's lush and complex drama. So much is available, and so much more is to come. At least six different series adapt Shakespeare plays to help students from middle school up actually see the action.

Can librarians imagine being really popular? Graphic novels can take you there:

- "Most [of the librarians we surveyed] reported that graphic novels circulate *more often* than other books" (Lyga and Lyga 2004, 81).
- "The boys scramble to get them. . . . They go beyond the class requirements . . . and come in before school and during lunch to get them!" (Lyga and Lyga 2004, 81).
- A survey of adult graphic novel readers at the Octogone Public Library in Montreal found that "the adult sequential art collection represents about 5 percent of the overall adult collection, but as a component of our circulation, it accounts for 13 percent of the adult and 11 percent of the overall (adult and children) borrowing" (Charbonneau 2005).
- "The presence of comics in a junior high library resulted in a dramatic 82% increase in library traffic and a 30% increase in circulation of non-comic books" (Dorrell and Carroll 1981).
- "At least half the students checking out graphic novels usually check out other fiction novels at the same time. Girls are reading the graphic novels, and I hope to attract more" (Lyga and Lyga 2004, 81).
- "How did library media teacher Alison Steinberg increase circulation at her school library by 50 percent this past year? She did it by investing $1,000 in a collection of graphic novels and a few beanbag chairs" ("Adding Comic Books" 2004).
- "I have kids in a piranha pack coming upstairs, clawing their way to the [graphic novel] collection."[13]

Both the comics industry and the millions of comics readers *want* to be library fans. And at meetings of YALSA and ALA, at comics conventions, and on the Graphic Novels in Libraries e-mail list, librarians are saying *that's just fine.* It is a whole new world, and it is ours.

ABOUT THIS BOOK

As of 2008, most librarians are on board with graphic novels. With new literacy information, there are even more reasons for beginning and enhancing a collection for all ages, ethnicities, and interests. With a basic roster of excellent books out there about getting started with graphic novels in your library (see Appendix C), we thought it was time for the graduate-level course: in-depth information about superheroes, manga, comics for girls and women, international comics, censorship, and more—and that is what this book is all about. It is also designed to fill in the gaps for librarians who may be serious manga otaku (extreme fans) but clueless about superheroes, or who may know their superhero Infinite Crisis plots down pat but cannot get into "that Japanese stuff," or who may devour the European imports from Fantagraphics and NBM but are less familiar with American non-superhero titles—even if some are regarded well enough to be republished successfully in Europe.

Part 1 looks at the graphic novels themselves, by broad category. How can we make sense of the bewildering universe of titles and content? It is common to think of three major subclasses—superheroes, manga, and everything else—so part of our study is organized around this simple classification.

In this country, comics have been strongly associated with superheroes since the 1950s, and so we begin with these caped charismastics. In chapter 1, Michael Niederhausen unpacks the background and appeal of the genre and introduces us to a varied selection of classic series to consider for library collections. Manga takes the stage in chapter 2, emceed by Robin Brenner. Why has manga taken America by storm and reached reader groups—such as girls—who are supposedly just not comics fans? For chapter 3, we continue the "girls" theme and take a short break from the three major subclasses. As Trina Robbins tells us, girls have always liked comics, but only recently have comics been available that appeal to them strongly. Girls and women are heavier library users than men,[14] so appealing to them is important.

It used to be that "everything else"—comics other than superheroes—were gingerly labeled "alternative" and occupied only a small market niche. But no longer, and Michael Lavin needed two chapters to characterize the rich variety now available among American comics alone. Chapter 4 introduces graphic novels falling into the usual library-recognized genres: science fiction, fantasy, Westerns, romance, and so on. Chapter 5 reviews graphic novels that are adaptations, realistic fiction, autobiography, and other nonfiction such as history, current events, science, and philosophy.

But there is a whole world of comics outside the United States, even excluding Japan. Franco-Belgian Europe has a long and rich tradition, and other parts of the world produce noteworthy graphic novels as well. Many of these titles are now available in English and can be important assets in library graphic novel collections. In chapter 6, John Lent provides a brief introduction to comics development in a number of world areas, which is followed by suggestions for titles that librarians can consider.

Part 2 looks at graphic novels in libraries from perspectives not relating to the literature. Francisca Goldsmith reviews in chapter 7 how librarians can give graphic novel collections a warm welcome in terms of purchasing, cataloging, processing, and access. In chapter 8, Lorena O'English lays out the special interests and perspectives of academic librarians, with many references and referrals to programs and resources. Gilles Poitras's chapter 9 returns us to Japanese pop culture as he summarizes the role and appeal of anime (Japanese animated cartoons) and their relationship to manga in the library.

Libraries and their collections live in a community of people with varying interests and perspectives, and some of these perspectives can be at cross purposes with library materials. Library materials of all types have been censored and challenged over the years. First, it was books and periodicals, and then as new formats became accepted for library acquisitions, some of these have been challenged also. It is no different for graphic novels in that not all of a library's collection will seem acceptable to all of its patrons all of the time. But challenges to graphic novels raise certain issues, and we discuss these in chapter 10 with the help of Erin Byrne. If much of the book is about what to collect and why it is good, chapter 10 centers on how to retain materials when others do not agree.

The appendices address briefly "need to know" information not always easily findable elsewhere. Appendix A, by Robin Brenner, introduces the subject of gaming in the library and how gaming relates to graphic novels, plus she provides useful resource lists of further reading, games linked to graphic novels, and graphic novels linked to games. Appendix B contains pathfinders for graphic novels of interest to African Americans, Latinos, LGBT (lesbian, gay, bisexual, and transgendered) patrons, and those interested in religious-themed content. Appendix C lists and annotates all known books published to date relating to graphic novels in libraries, and Appendix D lists selected online resources.

Editing this book has been an educational journey for us. Beginning with manga as we did, we found ourselves awed and inspired by the variety of fascinating and intriguing graphic novels we learned about in addition to Japanese work. An increasing number of librarians have taken the same journey, and we encourage those new to graphic novels to join us. But you do not have to be a fanboy, fangirl, or otaku to understand and appreciate the direct appeal of comics formats, the draw of good stories—how they stick to you—and the wonder in seeing a creative artist's mind's eye laid out like a banquet on a page. Perhaps superhero stories have been so appealing partly because the characters can fly, and some of the most compelling graphics take the reader swooping with Superman or Hawkgirl up among city skyscrapers. With comics, we can see Stéphane Heuet's vision of Proust's Combray and Nikolai

Maslov's Siberian tundra, tag along with Ted Naifeh's Polly as she fights pirates, shrink at the unspeakable horror in Kyle Baker's depiction of the slave trade, chuckle at Joann Sfar and Emmanuel Guibert's sweet and so unlikely vision of romance between a British girl and an Egyptian mummy, and appreciate the swirling beauty of Kosuke Fujishima's goddess Belldandy.

Even if graphic stories go back to cave paintings, comics are a whole new world for libraries. Offer the full richness of this world to your patrons.

NOTES

1. This idea is based on a quotation from Harvey Pekar, paraphrased by Rory Root and quoted in Lyga and Lyga 2004, 100.

2. These titles are both classics of their type, although we did not know it then. Kosuke Fujishima's *Oh My Goddess!* has reached 34 volumes and is still coming out in Japan, is still in print from Dark Horse Comics, and has been translated into numerous languages besides English. Haruka Inui's sexplicit burlesque of sex therapy, *Ogenki Clinic,* was originally published in English by the now-defunct Studio Ironcat but is being reissued by NBM as part of its Eurotica line as well as serialized in NBM's anthology magazine *Sizzle.*

3. These history sections are based on information from Gravett 2004; Koyama-Richard 2007; McCloud 1993; Sabin 1993, 1996; Schodt 1983; and Weiner 2003.

4. Lynd Ward, *Gods' Man: A Novel in Woodcuts.* New York: Jonathan Cape and Harrison Smith, 1929. See Michael Rhode, Tom Furtwangler, and David Wybenga, "Stories without Words: A Bibliography with Annotations." *International Journal of Comic Art* 2, no. 2 (Fall 2000): 265–306. Of my (Martha) parents' book collection, their copy of *Gods' Man*—long relegated to the attic and discovered by me covertly as a teen—was one of the few titles I kept.

5. For background about Tezuka, see Paul Gravett, "The Father Storyteller," in *Manga: Sixty Years of Japanese Comics* (London: Lawrence King/Harper Design, 2004), 24–37; Natusu Onoda, "Drag Prince in Spotlight: Theatrical Cross-Dressing in Osamu Tezuka's Early *Shojo* Manga," *International Journal of Comic Art* 4, no. 2 (Fall 2002): 124–38.

6. "Contrary to popular belief, Will Eisner didn't invent the graphic novel or even coin the term. The phrase 'graphic novel' was believed to have been coined by Richard Kyle in 1964 in the pages of the Comic Amateur Press Alliance's newsletter, *Capa-Alpha* #2" (Kaplan 2006, 13–14).

7. Marisa Acocella Marchetto, panelist, "Pictures of a Life: Comics and the Memoir" (Book Expo America, Washington, D.C., May 20, 2006).

8. This section draws on Martha Cornog's research in March 2006 through bound issues of Wilson's *Library Literature,* 1940s through 1990s.

9. Based on notes taken on-site by Martha Cornog at the New York Comic Con, New York City, February 24–26, 2006.

10. John Shableski, moderator of panel "Helping Libraries Buy and Shelve Comics for Teens" (New York Comic Con, New York, April 18, 2008).

11. Compiled by Martha Cornog from lists of the top 50 manga published in the *ICv2 Guide to Manga,* issues 13, 48, 50, 51, 54, 57, and 59, 2006–2008.

12. Jim Shooter, "Marvel and Me," in *The Comic Book Price Guide,* ed. R. Overstreet (New York: Harmony Books, 1986), A85–A96, qtd. in Krashen 2004, 91–92.

13. Overheard by Martha Cornog from audience member during the panel "Helping Libraries Buy and Shelve Comics for Teens" (New York Comic Con, New York, April 18, 2008).

14. According to a Harris Poll released September 22, 2008, 73 percent of U.S. women have a library card, compared to 62 percent of men (American Library Association 2008).

REFERENCES

"Adding Comic Books Leads to Super School Library Circulation Gains." *Curriculum Review* 44, no. 1 (September 2004): 8.

American Library Association. "New National Poll Shows Library Card Registration Reaches Historic High." Chicago: ALA, September 23, 2008. http://www.ala.org/ala/newspresscenter/news/pressreleases2008/September2008/ORSharris.cfm.

Charbonneau, Oliver. "Adult Graphic Novel Readers: A Survey in a Montreal Library." *Young Adult Library Services* 3, no. 4 (Summer 2005): 39.

Comics in the Classroom. "Comic Timeline." Comics in the Classroom, 2006. http://www.comicsintheclassroom.ca/timeline.htm.

Dorrell, Larry, and Ed Carroll. "Spider-Man at the Library." *School Library Journal* 27 (1981): 17–19.

Gravett, Paul. *Manga: Sixty Years of Japanese Comics.* New York: Harper Design International, 2004.

Griepp, Milton. "ICv2 White Paper: Inside a Growing Category." Keynote talk, ICv2 Graphic Novel Conference: "Breaking Out," New York, April 15, 2008. PowerPoint slides.

Gustines, George Gene. "Film Trailer Aids Sales of 'Watchmen' Novel." *New York Times,* August 14, 2008, E2.

Hajdu, David. *The Ten-Cent Plague: The Great Comic-Book Scare and How It Changed America.* New York: Farrar, Straus and Giroux, 2008.

ICv2. "Graphic Novels Well Represented among Online Book Buyers." ICv2.com, June 8, 2008. http://www.icv2.com/articles/news/12706.html.

Kaplan, Arie. "Neal Gaiman." In *Masters of the Comic Book Universe Revealed!* 169–96. Chicago: Chicago Review Press, 2006.

Klinkenborg, Verlyn. "Editorial Observer: Reading Thackeray's 'Vanity Fair' with the Illustrations Intact. *New York Times,* August 30, 2004. http://query.nytimes.com/gst/fullpage.html?res=9C04EEDC1631F933A0575BC0A9629C8B63&sec=&spon=&pagewanted=all.

Koyama-Richard, Brigitte. *One Thousand Years of Manga.* Paris: Flammarion, 2007.

Krashen, Steven D. *The Power or Reading: Insights from the Research.* Westport, CT: Libraries Unlimited, 2004.

Kunzel, David. *Father of the Comic Strip: Rodolphe Töpffer.* Jackson: University Press of Mississippi, 2007.

Lyga, Allyson A. W., and Barry Lyga. *Graphic Novels in Your Media Center: A Definitive Guide.* Westport, CT: Libraries Unlimited, 2004.

Maryland State Department of Education. "Maryland Comic Book Initiative." Maryland State Department of Education: Programs. http://www.marylandpublicschools.org/MSDE/ programs/recognition-partnerships/md-comic-book.htm (accessed September 30, 2008).

McCloud, Scott. *Understanding Comics.* New York: Paradox Press/DC Comics, 1993.

National Endowment for the Arts. *To Read or Not to Read: A Question of National Consequence; Executive Summary.* Washington, D.C.: NEA, 2007. (Research Report #47, also available at http://www.arts.gov)

Obama, Barack. "Bound to the Word." *American Libraries,* August 2005, 48–52.

Robbins, Trina. *From Girls to Grrrlz: A History of Women's Comics from Teens to Zines.* San Francisco: Chronicle Books, 1999.

Sabin, Roger. *Adult Comics: An Introduction.* New York: Routledge, 1993.

Sabin, Roger. *Comics, Comix & Graphic Novels: A History of Comic Art.* London: Phaedon, 1996.

Schodt, Frederik L. *Manga! Manga! The World of Japanese Comics.* New York: Kodansha, 1983.

Skinn, Dez. *Comix: The Underground Revolution.* New York: Thunder's Mouth Press, 2004.

Thompson, Terry. *Adventures in Graphica: Using Comics and Graphic Novels to Teach Comprehension, 2–6.* Portland, ME: Stenhouse, 2008.

Weiner, Stephen. *Faster Than a Speeding Bullet: The Rise of the Graphic Novel.* New York: NBM, 2003.

PART I

THE LITERATURE

1

THE ALLURE OF THE SUPERHERO

Michael Niederhausen

Superheroes have been around for 70 years, dominating the comics medium for most of them. What has helped these characters endure even into the 21st century? Take Spider-Man. Why have we been drawn to this character since we were kids? Is it the mask? The bright-colored outfit? (However, I've always favored the black costume.) Did we identify with him because Peter Parker had to deal with real problems and did not always end up on top like the god-like heroes such as Superman? Perhaps it is our wish to reach beyond normal humanity to save the world or just the appeal of following the endless adventures of a larger-than-life group of people. As one comics shop manager put it, "superheroes are soap operas for guys."[1]

The comics medium has had its financial ups and downs, but comics—and with them, superheroes—keep thriving. Librarians who understand the allure of the superhero can attract new patrons by stocking favorite series and keeping an eye on trends within the genre.

WHAT IS A SUPERHERO?

A Definition of the Superhero

Because superheroes have historically dominated U.S. comics, superheroes have been associated with all comics. However, superheroes are merely one genre within the medium—a highly influential one given that many non-superhero titles play off superhero traits and tropes. In *Superhero: The Secret Origin of a Genre,* Peter Coogan (2006) establishes three pivotal criteria: mission, powers, and identity.

- Mission means selflessness and intent to right any wrongs in society. Spider-Man initially does not have this mission, until his selfishness causes his Uncle Ben's death. Only then does he decide to fight evil.

- Powers are abilities beyond those of average people. Superman has super-strength, leaping and flying abilities, and invulnerability. Spider-Man has his spider-sense to anticipate danger, the ability to climb walls, and increased strength.
- Identity refers to a special persona different from the normal identity, plus a unique costume, usually with a symbol or icon. Superman has the very well-known "S," and Spider-Man sports the spider icon on his webbed outfit. When Marvel changed Spider-Man's costume from red to black in 1984, the spider icon was retained, and so the black costume is still associated with Spider-Man even though the red costume returned in 1988.

Coogan acknowledges that "superheroes can exist who do not fully demonstrate these three elements, and heroes from other genres may exist who display all three elements to some degree but should not be regarded as superheroes" (2006, 39–40). For example, the most recent incarnation of Starman written by James Robinson does not have a costume or a secret identity. (See discussion of Starman later in this chapter.) But he is still considered a superhero because he fulfills the other two criteria and does not fit well into another genre. His mission is protecting Opal City, and his powers come from his cosmic rod, which his father invented. Other writers such as Richard Reynolds (1992) have suggested additional characteristics that define a superhero, such as believing in justice more than the law.

One further element is the concept of continuity, the understanding that the current issue of any series should reflect what has happened in past stories. This concept has proven quite important to superhero fans, as they note any type of mistake and report it to editors. Marvel started giving out "No-Prizes" to those who find errors in a story but invent ways for the mistakes to make sense. Readers want to believe in their superheroes, and "the continuity of an individual character, and the relationship of that character with the entire 'universe' which they inhabit, provides a guarantee of the authenticity of each individual story" (Reynolds 1992, 45).

Types of Superheroes

Many writers over the years have classified superheroes. One way is by how a character has acquired the powers integral to being a superhero. Most superheroes could qualify as one of the following:

- *Science.* This type of hero was a big part of the Silver Age of comics. Most of the Marvel and DC superheroes acquired powers from science. The Hulk's powers come about from a bomb testing accident, whereas the Flash acquires his speed from exposure to a random combination of chemicals.

- *Mutant/Alien.* Some superheroes are born with their superpowers. Most recognizable are Marvel's mutants from *X-Men* whose special powers appear after puberty. (This category originally was an offshoot of Science heroes because these mutants were created as a result of all of the radiation testing done in the 1950s.) Aliens would fall into this category as well because it is their different natural physiology that gives them powers, such as Superman from the planet Krypton.
- *Highly Skilled.* This is the exact opposite of the Mutant/Alien; this type of superhero has no special powers except through extensive self-discipline and training. Batman is a good example, in that he trained his whole life to become a perfect fighting machine.
- *Magic/Myth.* This hero derives his or her powers from magical or mystical forces. For example, Captain Marvel acquired his powers from many gods. Also, heroes based on myths, such as Namor the Sub-Mariner who lives in Atlantis, or Thor who is literally the Norse god of thunder, would fall in this category.

SUPERHERO HISTORY

Predecessors to the Superhero

Superman is widely accepted as the first "superhero," but depending on how you view their lineage, the general concept can be traced back to the Greek and Roman gods and heroes. Superman has always been associated with Hercules, the biblical Samson, and particularly Achilles. The original Captain Marvel received his powers directly from Solomon, Hercules, Atlas, Zeus, Achilles, and Mercury. Thor has proven to be the most successful superhero to be completely based on a mythological god. In fact, Thor's costume is "half traditional, half super-heroical" (Reynolds 1992, 54). So a connection with gods of myth is well established.

Epic poems such as *The Epic of Gilgamesh* (second millennium B.C.E.) center on heroes with traits prevalent in the superhero genre. Besides such obvious characteristics as super-strength and heroic goals, Gilgamesh rejects sexual temptation with Ishtar, just as Superman originally did with Lois Lane.[2] The epics tend to match the American monomyth, in which a calm, peaceful community is threatened by evil, and a hero saves the day and restores peace (Coogan 2006).

The superhero has ancestors in folklore as well. In American folklore, Paul Bunyan and Pecos Bill stand out as precursors to the superhero as examples of characters with special powers. Robert E. Walls's description of Paul Bunyan is quite similar to the general definition of a superhero: "Giant, fictitious logger capable of Herculean deeds and . . . a demigod symbolic of American aspirations and identity" (1996, 105). The journalist-created "fakelore" hero Pecos Bill also shows larger-than-life attributes with superhero overtones. For example, Pecos Bill was raised by coyotes, which gave him skills beyond those of ordinary people.

International stories such as "The Seven Chinese Brothers" and the Russian tale "The Flying Ship" can be seen as precursors to the superhero team (Mahy 1990; Ransome 1968/1916). In "The Flying Ship," the Fool of the World (sometimes called Ivan the Fool) acquires a flying ship from a mysterious old man. He then picks up as companions many men who have specialized talents in eating, drinking, speed, and other areas. Their skills allow the Fool to overcome obstacles and win the hand of the Czar's daughter. This collaboration among individuals who each have a special talent presages the original superhero team, the Justice Society of America (JSA). Each JSA member adds his or her powers to make the team a superior fighting machine. The seven Chinese brothers are also a team, yet they are a family as well. This shows similarities to the Fantastic Four, the first superhero team based on family ties.

Frankenstein's monster, Nick of the Woods, and Tarzan are three literary predecessors to the superhero. Frankenstein's monster (1818) has enormous powers due to scientific experimentation, is an outcast, and wreaks revenge on humans. One can see the roots of Superman, yet Superman decides to use his powers for good. Nick of the Woods (from Robert Montgomery Bird's 1937 novel) is a Quaker who sees his family killed by Native Americans, and with a hidden identity he takes revenge. Nick can be seen as a predecessor of the Batman-type vigilante who has more interest in revenge than in protecting society (Coogan 2006). But again, the difference lies in Batman symbolically avenging his parents' murder on all criminals, which in effect does protect society. Tarzan (1912) is a clear example of the pulp Übermensch, "a physically and mentally superior individual who acts according to his own will without regard for the legal strictures that represent the morality of society" (Coogan 2006, 162–63). Tarzan has the ability to adapt in the wild and is physically superior to other humans.

A few comic-strip characters with superhero characteristics did appear before Superman, including Hugo Hercules, Popeye, and Alley Oop. However, none exhibits all the conventions since associated with the genre. For example, Popeye does not have a mission; he "uses his strength to earn a living as a prizefighter or to search for treasure" (Coogan 2006, 179).

The Superhero in Comic Books

Within a few years of Superman's 1938 debut, comics were full of superheroes, most notably Batman, Wonder Woman, Captain America, and Captain Marvel. Also, the first superhero team, JSA, began in 1940. The era spanning the 1930s to the early 1950s is known as the Golden Age of comics. Although Superman falls into the Mutant/Alien category, the type dominating this era was the Magic/Myth superhero. Most of the JSA acquired their powers from magic (e.g., Green Lantern and Doctor Fate) or myth (e.g., Wonder Woman). Superheroes held the top spot in comic book sales in the 1930s and 1940s, but by the 1950s, horror, romance, and real crime stories outsold the genre (Gerber and Gerber, 1990). The EC Comics line of horror comics is considered one of the best products of that era and was geared toward a more adult audience.

By the late 1940s, the superhero was all but extinguished but ironically was revived as a result of Dr. Fredric Wertham's 1954 *Seduction of the Innocent,* which claimed that comic books led to juvenile delinquency. In response, the comics industry created the Comics Code Authority to forestall the federal government from imposing standards on the medium (Nyberg 1998). The new Comics Code limited explicit and objectionable content but did allow good–versus-evil stories to prosper—if good always won. It was easy for simplified superhero stories to fill the bill. These restrictions, however, did limit more adult-themed stories such as the EC titles, given that they were not approved by the Comics Code.

In the early 1950s, DC Comics editor Julius Schwartz led a superhero revival, but with a contemporary spin, adding more emphasis on personal conflict and character development. His first resurrection was the Flash, and he gave the character a different origin story and costume, as well as a new identity as a police scientist. These recreated heroes established the Silver Age of comics. The other key event was in 1961 when Stan Lee and Jack Kirby resurrected Timely Comics, the home of the original Human Torch, Captain America, and Sub-Mariner, by starting a new line of superhero comics under the name of Marvel Comics Group.[3] Most notably, the Fantastic Four and Spider-Man were created during this time and became strong competition for Superman and his companions. Ever since, Marvel and DC have been the main publishers of superhero comics (see Daniels 1991, 1995). This age of superheroes was primarily of the Science type. The reworked versions of JSA with the Flash and Green Lantern had more scientific than magical underpinnings. This also includes the Marvel Silver Age, as Spider-Man was bitten by a radioactive spider, and Daredevil's heightened senses came from the radioactive isotopes that blinded him.

The only other accepted "age" is the Bronze Age, when superhero comics began to grow up—the stories became more reality-based and did not always end happily. It is still argued which single story started the trend, but certainly the following were key:

- The 1971 issues of *Amazing Spider-Man* revealing that Peter Parker's roommate was addicted to drugs
- The 1971 revelation that Green Arrow's sidekick was addicted to heroin
- The 1973 death of Spider-Man's girlfriend, Gwen Stacy
- Captain America's quitting in 1974 upon finding that the President of the United States was behind an evil organization

This age was not dominated by a specific type of superhero because it was a time of great experimentation.

What will the next stage and age be? This issue is still under debate—Peter Coogan (2006) refers to the Iron Age and the Renaissance Age. Simply put, in the Iron Age superhero comics became darker, with more analysis of the characters and more violence, beginning in 1985 with DC's *Crisis on Infinite Earths.* For example, Batman was established as being as psychologically deranged as his villains. Also gritty, violent characters such as the Punisher and Wolverine became popular. That trend has slowly waned, but remnants remain today. The recent Renaissance wave has brought a nostalgic return to both the Golden and the Silver Ages' traits of classic good versus evil, but continuing with realistic events and characters. The dark side of superheroes has slowly diminished with a shift to the concept that superheroes are good people. Most notably James Robinson's *Starman* and the JSA stories written by Robinson, David S. Goyer, and Geoff Johns exemplify more an adoration of the superhero than a deconstruction. Because of this nostalgia, the dominating type of superhero varies.

WHO LOVES SUPERHEROES?

Reader Demographics

The 1930s readers of superheroes were mainly children, but after the United States joined World War II, GIs swelled the ranks of fans. An article in 1945 concluded that 70 million people, then half the U.S. population, read comic books (Wright 2001). Adult readership continued into the 1950s, which led to more explicit content in EC Comics and other series. The Comics Code of the 1950s made comic books into kids' stuff again. Comics grew up a second time in the 1970s, but it was not as great a leap as in the 1950s. Ever since the 1970s, comics have slowly become more relevant, with realistic themes. In the mid-1980s, Moore and Gibbons's *Watchmen* stood out as an exploratory superhero story for adults that many writers since have tried to emulate. Today the average comic book reader is between 18 and 34 years old.

Actual sales of superhero comics have varied greatly over the years. Comic books in the 1930s averaged 200,000 to 400,000 copies each, whereas the top-selling Superman title *Action Comics* sold 900,000 and *Superman* 1,300,000 (Wright 2001). However, *Superman* was outsold by *Captain Marvel* comics, peaking at 2 million copies per issue in the mid-1940s (Lupoff 1970). By 1984, *Marvel Super-Heroes Secret Wars,* a crossover series featuring many heroes and villains, sold an average of 800,000 copies (Wright 2001). In 1990 the new Spider-Man series by Todd McFarlane sold 3 million, a new record, until a new *X-Men* #1 (1991) sold 8 million, mainly because of six different covers (Wright). These are, of course, major exceptions. In August 2006, DC released a new *Justice League of America,* which was #1 for the month but

sold only 212,000 copies (John Jackson Miller 2006). Compare this to the millions *Captain Marvel* sold in the 1940s, and it is obvious that superhero readership is down by comparison. Still, superheroes remain a major portion of the market, even if no longer the vast majority, and the graphic novel-format collections of series and miniseries sell well.

Audience Appeal

The superhero story allows readers to fantasize about having superpowers—abilities beyond those of average people—and thus becoming a powerful and special person. Obviously, reading about superheroes is a way to escape the drudgery of an ordinary life and the daily frictions and demands from family, employers, neighbors, and the world in general. Certainly U.S. soldiers being a big part of the early readership testifies to how the stories helped in the mental escape from a potentially life-threatening day-to-day existence. In general, young readers were for many years the largest part of the market, being at the bottom of the social hierarchy and naturally craving increased power and status. The fact that most creators have been men, most superheroes have been men, and superhero exploits have emphasized physical combat no doubt led to a majority of young males among fans. However, superheroes have always had women fans too, probably more so after the reality-based stories became popular starting in the 1970s and 1980s, and more women and couples entered the picture as characters. Now that Americans have discovered Japanese manga, much of it quite popular with female readers, it is likely that some of these readers are enlarging their appreciation of the comics medium to include superheroes in addition.

Comics in general and with them superheroes have had "in-group" appeal for decades, given that the culture at large considered them below literature and the next thing to trash. Thus another reason that superheroes have maintained their popularity is the sense of rebellion associated with reading superhero comics. Any authority figure denouncing comics would just inspire rebellious readers to read more of them. Moreover, over the years the superhero stories have coalesced into a complex set of interlocking universes with its own epics and traditions that keep fans involved in learning and relearning characters, relationships, skill hierarchies, and details of an awe-inspiring magnitude.

Finally, superhero comics have retained appeal because the comics creators slowly grew up with audiences, and so did the characters and plots. So when comic book readers matured to the point where clichéd good-versus-evil stories were not as exciting as before, more mature stories appeared somewhere in the comics medium. Sometimes these were superhero stories and sometimes not, but the reader maintained allegiance to the medium and often to superheroes as well.

SIGNIFICANT SUPERHEROES

There have been hundreds, perhaps thousands, of superheroes over past decades, and fans debate endlessly the fine points of their importance, as well as which plot arcs have proven most significant or have helped the genre progress into new levels. This chronological introduction to names and recommended works is by no means complete. (For much longer lists of series and titles, see Pawuk 2007, chapter 1.)

Icons and Individual Heroes

Superman

Perhaps the most important figure in comic books, Superman, with his instantly recognizable blue and red costume and "S" symbol, has always been a leading force for the superhero. As an alien from the planet Krypton, he has advanced powers beyond anyone on Earth, including flight, invulnerability, and super-strength, among many others. Superman, with his "real" persona, Clark Kent, has weathered countless battles with new and recurring villains and is now married to longtime crush Lois Lane. Of the many important Superman storylines, none stand out so much as the Silver Age stories, which became more fantastic with better supporting characters. These stories are available in the *Showcase Presents Superman* collections (2005–). Lois Lane, Perry White, and Jimmy Olsen were always a good supporting cast, but during the 1950s, DC put out additional titles with Lois Lane or Jimmy Olsen as the main character, and Superman was used to move along the plot, usually as savior. More Kryptonians were introduced, such as Krypto, Superman's dog; Kara Zor-el or Supergirl, Superman's cousin; and finally Kandor, a miniaturized Kryptonian city that Superman vowed to restore to normal size. Other stories introduced different types of Kryptonite having alternative effects on Superman. These characters and devices led to interesting stories for all ages.

Batman

Created in 1939, Batman has been perceived as the dark opposite of Superman in many respects. He is an average human with no powers bestowed by outside forces, he works at night in his gray and black costume with sweeping cape, and he uses fear to capture criminals. Batman is one of the few superheroes who acquired his exceptional achievements from his own hard training and from expert use of an arsenal of gadgetry. He is a master at detective skills and combat, going up against the urban criminal world as well as recurring villains with bizarre skills, such as the Joker. Some suggest that the earliest adventures of Batman are the ones most true to the character—once his younger sidekick Robin was introduced, the character became less dark. Frank Miller resurrected the original approach

in *Batman: The Dark Knight Returns* (1986), in which a 10-years-retired Batman returns to rescue society from criminal evil. Initially, Batman's main mission is to conquer a gang called the Mutants. Eventually, the U.S. government orders Superman to put Batman down because his activities have become too controversial. This plot has several political threads, but the title's success stemmed from Miller's skill in bringing Batman back to his roots as well as adding a female Robin, which would dismiss any suggested homoeroticism in the series.[4]

Captain Marvel

The original red-suited Captain Marvel was the best-selling superhero of the Golden Age. When young Billy Batson spoke the name "Shazam!" he became a superhuman with powers similar to Superman. He acquired his powers from seven gods, so he would fit in the category of a Magic/Myth hero. With fantastic plots and superhuman villains, the stories have a purity that many find give special luster to the 1940s. Peaking with the work of Otto Binder and C. C. Beck, Captain Marvel stories "took on a new dimension of complexity, marvelous strains of satire, and growing sophistication" (Lupoff 1992, 7) and had a "whimsical, almost fairy-tale quality" (Harvey 1999, 5). Certainly the fact that Captain Marvel's alter ego is a boy of 12 has helped kids identify with him and has hyped his popularity. The series taps a classic adolescent power fantasy: a kid changes into an adult with superpowers. Captain Marvel stories are available in the *Shazam! Archive* series and in *Showcase Presents Shazam!* (O'Neil et al. 2006). Recently, Jeff Smith, creator of *Bone,* wrote and illustrated *Shazam: The Monster Society of Evil* (2007). This version encapsulates the stories by Binder and Beck more so than anyone else since then.

Captain America

The quintessential American/government-sponsored superhero, Captain America punches out Adolf Hitler on the cover of his legendary first issue in 1941, some months before America entered World War II (Simon and Kirby 2005). Steve Rogers was a skinny young man who just wanted to help his country. So the military asked if he would be willing to be a part of a superhuman project where they would inject him with a formula to make him more powerful than any other soldier. This would make him a Science hero. In a key event of the Silver Age superhero revival that helped establish the young Marvel Comics Group, the Avengers discover a frozen Captain America and revive him (*Avengers* #4, 1964).

As a superhero representing the United States, even to his red, white, and blue costume with star and stripes, Captain America has had conflicts with the government because his creators wanted to show him as not just one-dimensional and blindly following orders. In 1974, against the backdrop of the Watergate scandal, Captain America discovers that the leader of an evil organization is a man in "high political office" and decides to resign his Captain America role for a while (Englehart and Friedrich 2006). Most recently, Captain America led the group opposing mandatory superhero registration in Marvel's *Civil War* crossover. After surrendering to the pro-registration side, Captain America was assassinated "Manchurian candidate" style.

Wonder Woman

Created in 1941, Wonder Woman, in her patriotic bathing suit–style costume and high boots, is an important figure as the first major female superhero. She was created from clay by the Queen of the Amazons, Hippolyta, with the blessing of the goddess Aphrodite. Thus she has powers above others because she was brought to life by the gods. She has had many incarnations and characterizations; perhaps most interesting was the ninja phase during the late 1960s (Daniels 2000, 126). Her importance as an icon for women everywhere was exemplified in her 1972 appearance on the first cover of *Ms. Magazine.* Throughout Wonder Woman's long and storied career, Greg Rucka's writing (2004) stands out as some of the best in recent memory. Rucka sets a nice balance of Wonder Woman as both warrior and ambassador of peace. In a plot more political than anti-villain, she establishes an embassy for her native Themyscira. She plays a pivotal role in the *Infinite Crisis* crossover as she kills a man who can control Superman, and his death at Wonder Woman's hands is used to subvert people's trust in superheroes. In 2007 Gail Simone took over the series as the first woman ongoing writer.

Spider-Man

First appearing in 1962, Spider-Man ranks as highly important on a number of grounds. Although neither the first superhero nor the first teen superhero, Spider-Man, with his saga, has proven one of the most innovative in terms of superhero stories and conventions. He was the first to be an outcast and loser in his secret identity, as well as in his superhero guise. He was the first superhero to quit, which he did because being Spider-Man caused more trouble than it was worth and led to grave doubts about his purpose. Also, Spider-Man sees girlfriend Gwen Stacy die partly as a result of his own actions. He was also one of the first major superheroes to completely change his costume, which he did in 1984, switching from his traditional red and blue to an all black costume with white spider webbing. This lasted a few years, but the costume developed an evil doppelgänger connotation. Spider-Man was also the first major superhero with a secret identity to get married, tying the knot with Mary

Jane Watson in 1988. (Superman and Lois Lane married in 1996.) Finally, *The Amazing Spider-Man* was the first superhero comic to deal with 9/11—ever since World War II ended, superheroes had been nonpolitical. All of these innovations helped the superhero genre continue in a progressive way.

Salvatore Mondello concludes, "The Amazing Spider-Man had helped to shape and reflect the American character and deserved special attention from students of American history" (1976, 237). Donald Palumbo (1983) researched the existentialist ideology prevalent in the 1970s stories, especially issues in which Spider-Man fights a clone of himself. These are but a few of the reasons that Spider-Man is one of the most important superheroes in comics.

All the *Amazing Spider-Man* stories are available in the DVD-ROM *Amazing Spider-Man: The Complete Collection* (2006). This is one of many DVD-ROMs that have every issue of a series scanned as a PDF file. These DVD-ROMs have literally hundreds of issues on one disc, which saves space, and they are relatively inexpensive considering the extensive content.

Black Panther

The Black Panther (T'Challa) was the first black superhero in mainstream comics, debuting in Marvel's *Fantastic Four* in 1966.[5] He is ruler of the technologically superior African nation Wakanda, located over deposits of the extraordinary meteorite metal vibranium. Special local herbs plus vibranium technology give the black-cloaked Black Panther his adept powers in combat, making him a Science hero. He has had several series since, including an Indiana Jones character-style from co-creator Jack Kirby (Ro 2004, 196). Since the Black Panther's debut, other black superheroes have included the Falcon (Marvel, 1969–), Luke Cage (Marvel, 1972–), and John Stewart in his role as Earth's Green Lantern after Hal Jordan resigned in the mid-1980s (DC Comics). The most recent series from Reginald Hudlin and Scot Eaton shows the Black Panther in a more serious characterization, facing his father's killer, Klaw, among other enemies, and facing numerous political complexities in a world where his superhero colleagues are at odds because of the crossover event *Civil War.* During this story arc, mutant superhero Storm from *X-Men* marries the Black Panther, and they become the world's number one power couple (2006).

Jack Kirby's Fourth World

Co-creator of Captain America and most of the original Marvel line, including the *Fantastic Four* and *Thor,* Jack Kirby and his work hold a special place in superhero history because of the many legendary superheroes he has created. Kirby worked for DC in the 1970s, where he created four interlocked adventure series known collectively as the Fourth World, originally intended as a sequel to *Thor.* DC reprinted all Fourth World stories in *Jack Kirby's Fourth World Omnibus* Volumes 1–4 (2007–2008), collecting the following four series: *Superman's Pal Jimmy Olsen, The New Gods, The Forever People,* and *Mister Miracle.*

In one standout story, "The Glory Boat" from *The New Gods,* a family in crisis finds themselves caught in a war between the heroes of New Genesis and the villains of Apokalips. When the family is threatened, it is the pacifist son who rushes to defend them, while the war-veteran father shirks in cowardice. The son dies, but he is transformed by Lightray, a god for New Genesis, into a beautiful being who will help end the battle. Although the interlocking series deal with the universal and often simplified battle of good versus evil, this type of more complex plotting is new in Kirby's work.[6]

Crossover Events

Since 1984, comics publishers have produced crossover events: story arcs that involve all or most of the characters with titles in their line at the time. A crossover event usually consists of a main mini-series, with ongoing titles continuing with an individual crossover issue. *Marvel Super-Heroes Secret Wars* (Shooter, Zeck, and Layton 1999) was the first crossover event, in which a god-like entity called the Beyonder pits hero against villain in an ultimate winner-take-all situation. The following year, DC followed with *Crisis on Infinite Earths* (Wolfman and Perez 2001), which was the story of the end of DC's multiverse. The idea was to create a simpler universe for readers in which there were not alternate dimensions of Earth. The crossover phenomenon has become almost an annual event with the two companies. Recently, DC produced a sequel to *Crisis of Infinite Earths* called *Infinite Crisis* (Johns and Jimenez 2007), and Marvel produced *Civil War* (Millar and McNiven 2007).

Today's crossover events generate many more issues—both *Infinite Crisis* and *Civil War* had well over 100 crossover issues each. These stories are critical for ongoing series because events occur that can affect particular characters. For example, Superman lost his powers for a year after *Infinite Crisis,* and readers of Superman comics can find out how this happened only by following the crossover story. So these events, even if the stories are not done well, are necessary reading for superhero fans. In 2008, Marvel drew together years of hints and subplots with *Secret Invasion* (by Brian Michael Bendis and Leinil Francis Yu; collections expected in 2009), in which the alien Skrulls initiate their attack on Earth. For its part, DC put out the third part of their Crisis trilogy with *Final Crisis* (Grant Morrison and J. G. Jones; collections expected in 2009). This is proving to be Morrison's take on Jack Kirby's Fourth World group of characters.

Watchmen

Watchmen (1986) is Alan Moore and Dave Gibbons's masterful examination of superheroes, considered one of the most important works in recent superhero history. Moore stripped the godliness out of superheroes and focused on their very human flaws. For example, the Comedian is a state-sponsored superhero, but he is far more psychotic than Captain America. The most interesting character is Rorschach, the gritty, vigilante sort of superhero that had just begun its dominance of the genre in the mid-1980s. Moore brings out the psychological damage behind these gritty superheroes in scenes such as when Rorschach meets with his state-appointed psychiatrist. Notably, only one is a Science-type with real superpowers. The rest fit the Highly Skilled category. Not a team, they act as individuals throughout the story. Altogether, the interaction among multiple plots, subplots, psychological subtext, symbolism, and graphics gives *Watchmen* "a richer, more complex, and more ambitious narrative infrastructure than serial comics had seen before" (Spurgeon 1999, 40).

Animal Man

Costumed in orange with a big blue "A," Animal Man debuted in 1965 but was not given his own series until the late 1980s as written by Grant Morrison. A human caught in the vicinity of an exploding alien spaceship and thus a Science type, Animal Man can mimic the powers of any animal to fight crime and injustice. The series championed vegetarianism and animal rights and featured the hero, Buddy Baker, as an "everyman" with wife and son, unusual at the time. In a recurring theme, Morrison played with the imaginary barrier that separates readers from the story. In a sequence in which Animal Man takes peyote, he "sees" the reader looking at him. The series culminates when Animal Man meets his maker, that is, Grant Morrison. This type of postmodern writing had not been done in a superhero story before. Morrison's complete run can be found in *Animal Man* (2001), *Animal Man: Origin of the Species* (2002), and *Animal Man: Deus Ex Machina* (2003).

Other comics have also shown characters meeting their creators-as-gods. When superheroes realize they are only comic book characters, they can feel as if their lives are meaningless. But Morrison shows his love and appreciation for superheroes in *Animal Man,* when his characters learn that they actually outlive their creators and live forever as a story in comics.

Starman

Starman is possibly the most notable superhero series of the 1990s; it is the story of Jack Knight, a dealer in popular culture artifacts. His older brother David inherited the Starman legacy from their father (who was lead in a predecessor series beginning in the 1940s), but David is killed. An unwilling

Jack must become the new Starman, avenge his brother, and save Opal City. He does so—although, unusually, he refuses a secret identity or his predecessors' costume—and slowly learns to appreciate what being Starman means to the city and to his family. The Starman superheroes obtain powers to fly and manipulate energy from a cosmic rod or staff that harnesses energy from stars, based on the scientific inventions of the original Starman. DC is currently reprinting the entire series in a six-volume *Starman Omnibus* (Robinson and Harris 2008–).

The series has a strong supporting cast that includes the earlier versions of Starman in the DC canon and the city itself. The O'Dares, a family of police officers, also play a significant part in the series. This historical-generational view is important to comics readers, who value story continuity.

Marvels

Marvels is considered one of the best works of the 1990s, a retelling and redrawing of the most infamous events in more than 35 years of the Marvel universe from the viewpoint of an everyman, news photographer Phil Sheldon. The series showcases Alex Ross's incredible painting style as well as writer Kurt Busiek's amazing knowledge of Marvel canon history (1994). Revisited incidents include Captain America and other superheroes fighting the Nazis, the arrival of the X-Men and anti-mutant prejudice, the battle between the Fantastic Four and Galactus, and the death of Gwen Stacy. Ross pays homage to Jack Kirby's original art while stripping away any cartoonish quality to make these unbelievable-looking characters seem to belong in the real world. Throughout, Sheldon's changing feelings about superheroes become part of the story.

Promethea

Published in 2000–2006 as one of the first titles in Alan Moore's superhero imprint, America's Best Comics (ABC), *Promethea* is the story of an entity that merges with people throughout history as a living embodiment of imagination. The most recent avatar, Sophie, is expected to fulfill Promethea's final goal, the end of the world. But to Promethea, ending the world is really simply merging reality with the Immateria, the world of imagination where all the Prometheas live. The series follows Sophie, whose Promethea persona comes with a Greek-like costume and magical caduceus staff, as she learns how to cope with her powers and responsibility and debates whether ending the world is a good thing. Moore ends the series like a classic crossover where all of the ABC superheroes unite to stop her from harming the world. The various Promethea incarnations mirror the many faces of the superhero, from the pulp heroine to a gritty urban warrior crime-fighter. Throughout, superhero action blends with metaphysical theory, spiritual symbolism, and psychedelic imagery, with inquiry into the nature of consciousness underlying all. Promethea "teaches us to deepen our experience by *deepening our awareness of experiencing*. Promethea lovingly lifts the screen to reveal the truth of existence" (Stuller 2006, 17). This reading of the Magic/Myth-type character brings a new level to the superhero: superhero as spiritual guide.

Ex Machina

Brian Vaughan's *Ex Machina* (2005) takes place in a world like ours—no superheroes—except when one man acquires the ability to talk to machines through a scientific, possibly alien explosion and decides to become a superhero, dubbing himself the Great Machine. Much like Spider-Man, the Great Machine is at first hunted by police as a menace. Eventually, he decides to quit the superhero role, announce his identity, and run for mayor of New York City. Before the primaries have concluded, the attacks of 9/11 occur, but the Great Machine actually stops one of the planes from colliding with a tower. The current setting of the series is his term in office and the many things he has to deal with as a civil servant and as an independent man. This series is possibly one of the first in a new wave of titles in which the super-heroics of the main character are not emphasized so much as his work as an individual—here, his good deeds as mayor of the city. By definition, it is a superhero story, but complex and sophisticated in execution.

Teamwork

Superhero teams began with DC's Justice Society of America in the 1940s, made up of existing superheroes without their own series including the Atom, Sandman, the Spectre, Doctor Fate, Hourman, Flash, Hawkman, Green Lantern, and Johnny Thunder. Beside the teams described in this following section, other noteworthy teams over the years include the Justice League of America (DC, 1960s–) and, for younger readers, *Teen Titans* (DC, 1960s– but especially 1980s–) and *Runaways* (Marvel, 2004–). The superhero team series are just as popular as the individual superhero titles. The creators can utilize the dynamics among several superheroes and sometimes set up romances that lead to marriages.

Fantastic Four

In the early 1960s, Marvel's Stan Lee and Jack Kirby created all-new characters to pioneer the Fantastic Four as the first family-based superhero team. Composed of the married couple Reed and Susan Storm Richards, plus Sue's brother Johnny Storm and their friend and colleague Ben Grimm, the blue-suited team all gained super powers after exposure to cosmic rays during a scientific space mission. The initial run lasted 102 issues and is considered one of the best in the genre, due in large part to strong, believable characters with real-life qualities and problems suggesting a loving but somewhat dysfunctional family.[7]

One of the most lasting stories in the run is "The Coming of Galactus" (*Fantastic Four* #48–50), basis for the 2007 film *Fantastic Four: Rise of the Silver Surfer.* Galactus and his servant, the Silver Surfer, initially both enemies to humans, pose a truly world-ending threat. But the Fantastic Four stop Galactus and convince the Silver Surfer to switch sides. Besides the Lee and Kirby stories, those from John Byrne (reprinted in *Fantastic Four Visionaries: John Byrne,* 2001–2007) and the team of Mark Waid and Mike Wieringo (reprinted in *Fantastic Four* vol. 1, *Imaginauts,* 2003) stand out as excellent Fantastic Four sagas by bringing back the quality original fantasies that Lee and Kirby created.

The X-Men

In the early 1960s, Marvel's *X-Men* debuted as a team of five mutants with different abilities, fighting evil. Through numerous additions and changes in team members, the current concept took shape in the 1970s as an international, multicultural, and multiethnic group, an approach not done successfully before. Team members Wolverine (Canada), with retractable claws and enhanced senses, and Storm (Kenya), who can fly and control the weather, have proved especially popular. This diversity was key to establishing these mutant superheroes as a new minority that would be discriminated against simply for being different, leading to savage attacks comparable to the Holocaust.

In the crossover story arc of *Mutant Massacre* (Claremont and Romita 1996), certain mutants are hired to eliminate other mutants living underneath the streets of New York. The X-Men come to the aid of the underground dwellers, but there are many consequences, including death for some of the mutants. This discrimination theme continues in the series today.

Recently, Peter Milligan and Mike Allred, writers for the X-Men spin-off *X-Statix* (2003–2004), completely changed the convention of angst-ridden mutant outcasts. The mutant superheroes in this new group are worshipped like celebrities, and they in turn act like the most conceited idol stars. X-Statix stops crime only when it benefits the team's publicity and merchandising. Other series have since explored the superhero-as-celebrity theme but none so well.

Birds of Prey

Beginning in 1996 as a collaboration between Barbara Gordon and Dinah Lance, the all-female Birds of Prey has relied on both enduring and new DC Universe characters. Formerly librarian by day and Batgirl by night, Gordon becomes paraplegic after being felled by the Joker's bullet in *Batman: The Killing Joke,* so she reinvents herself as all-seeing hacker-mistress Oracle. Lance had been a Justice League regular and on-again, off-again romantic partner to Green Arrow, with a superheroine persona named Black Canary. With Canary the passionate, martial-artist partner to Oracle's more cerebral and tactical talents, the pair takes on various assignments, expanding their team to include regulars Huntress, Lady Blackhawk, and Big Barda, plus numerous drop-ins.

The seven collections written by Gail Simone have been commended by fans for their strong characterizations, fine plotting, and well-contextualized action. Simone's collections begin with *Birds of Prey: Of Like Minds* (2004) and end with *Birds of Prey: Dead of Winter* (2008). In this last volume, Katrina "Spy-Smasher" Armstrong directs them in an anti-Soviet op that leads to a dramatic and sometimes-comic confrontation with the Secret Six, a team of not-quite-villains.

The Authority

The Authority (Ellis and Hitch 2000; Ellis et al. 2000) is a contemporary superhero group whose members decide to make things right, given that the world cannot behave, by deposing leaders, helping end starvation, and so on. The team begins with seven people, including three women and a gay couple, with varying abilities derived from different sources. The series is known for dramatic, universe-wide action, uncompromising attitude, and extreme violence as well as slower, more manga-style pacing. The edgier series is sometimes considered an over-the-top satire of the genre (Groenewegen 2000, 47). This is a popular title, possibly because of its violence, but it still depicts a superhero team that seeks to change the world for the better.

KEEPING CURRENT

With the advent of the Internet, there are many ways to keep current with superheroes and with comics in general. Three online sites notable for superhero titles are http://www.newsarama.com, http://www.comicbookresources.com, and http://www.wizarduniverse.com. All of these Web sites have op-ed columns and press releases about new titles and changes in creative teams. You can also access any of the publishers' Web sites, which should include their schedule of new releases. (For the "big two" publishers, see http://www.dccomics.com and http://www.marvel.com.)

A more active way of staying involved is attending conventions. Depending on how large the convention is, you can sometimes meet some of the creators or publishing company representatives as well as sometimes find material not in the local store—or find a title at lower cost. The big conventions include the mega-scale San Diego Comic-Con in July, the New York Comic Con in the spring, and Wizard World conventions in various cities throughout the year. But there are many more. For a lengthy list of comics conventions with dates and locations, see the "Conventions" link at http://www.comicbookconven tions.com.

Of course, one's local comic book shop is a wonderful place to find out about all kinds of comics. These retailers know their products, and a good employee will ask what kinds of titles are of interest and make suggestions. Finally, there are quite a few online comics outlets where you can find hard-to-find titles and volumes without having to travel. Some nationally known online stores good for superhero series include http://www.milehighcomics. com, http://www.mycomicshop.com, and http://www.talesofwonder.com.

SUPERHERO PROGRAMS IN LIBRARIES

There are many things a library can do to encourage patrons to discover superhero comics and welcome current fans of the genre. Groups of readers to reach include children and teens already familiar with comics, adults who may or may not have previously read comics, and adults who read comics as an active hobby.

For children and teens, libraries could have an art contest. Young people can create their own superhero or draw an existing superhero. Either way, a contest encourages patrons to consider continuing with drawing comics as a career or hobby. Of course, a library would give prizes by age group.

Another program would involve partnering with a local comics shop for Free Comic Book Day. A few years ago, the industry established an annual Free Comic Book Day, normally the first Saturday in May, to promote comics and broaden readership. Shops are sent supplies of special free issues from distributors, just to give out to customers. Overall, the day has been a success for comic shops, which find their sales increasing every year. (See http:// www.freecomicbookday.com.) Certainly the event has triggered interest from young readers and exposed adult readers to the more sophisticated comics. A library could give away comic books from a local shop and showcase its own comics materials. For example, on the sixth annual Free Comic Book Day in 2007, Mike Pawuk of the Cuyahoga County Public Library (Ohio) joined with York Comics and Cards to give away free comic books at the library. Pawuk also set up viewings of the first two Spider-Man movies, Spider-Man trivia, and superhero video games for patrons.

A library could also have a program about a selected comic book character, title, or series. Some superheroes have quite convoluted histories. You might invite a local comics shop employee or any expert on a given character to discuss the history of a particular superhero or group. This could help new readers get started. For example, someone new to the X-Men might have no idea where to begin because there are so many X-Men titles to choose from.

A new reader might pick up a collection in the middle of a major storyline and become confused and even lose interest. (It would be similar to starting a novel in the middle.) So someone new to the series might need someone to help them along and make proper suggestions.

Finally, sponsor discussion groups for active fans of the genre. Although there are Internet bulletin boards and blogs out there, fans generally enjoy give and take outside the Internet. After all, fans go to conventions to talk comics as much as to see them. Discussion groups can be modeled after discussion groups and book clubs centering on novels, but the topic would be on a specific superhero character or on a volume or story arc of a particular series.

Regardless of how your library encourages superhero readers or finds a place for superhero comics, superheroes are here to stay. Even though U.S. comics readership has expanded with strong interest into manga and non-superhero genres, there is still plenty of interest in superheroes, and it is a good idea to welcome these readers at the library.

NOTES

1. Editor's note: See Douglas Wolk's perceptive analysis of the structure, function, and appeal of superhero comics as well as outsiders' problems in understanding the sagas (2007, chapter 4).

2. The Superman of the Golden Age and Silver Age always refuted Lois's love because he did not want her to come to any harm as his wife. When *Superman* was revamped in the 1980s, that concept was put to rest, and they eventually married in 1996.

3. Stan Lee was recently awarded a National Medal of Arts "for his innovations that revolutionized American comic books." The medal was presented by President Bush in November 2008. The National Medal of Arts program is a presidential initiative managed by the National Endowment for the Arts. See http://www.nea.gov/news/news08/medals/Lee.html.

4. The homoeroticism was suggested in Fredric Wertham's *Seduction of the Innocent* (1954); see York's (2000) discussion of DC Comics' attempt to make Batman more noticeably heterosexual. In the comic book series *Supreme: The New Adventures,* an homage to *Superman* Silver Age stories, Alan Moore introduced a re-visioned Batman named Professor Night, with a female sidekick (vol. 3, #43, 1996).

5. See Appendix B-1, African American–Interest Graphic Novels: Resources.

6. Wells (2002) writes that Kirby may have had coauthors for his Marvel series; hence the DC Comics *Fourth World* reflects a more personal vision.

7. Volumes 1–10 of the Lee and Kirby *Marvel Masterworks: The Fantastic Four* (2003–) reprints up to issue 104. The *Essential Fantastic Four* series (1999–), black and white reprints, contains Lee and Kirby's entire run in the first five volumes. There is also a DVD-ROM of the entire series from 1961 to 2004 (Marvel Enterprises 2005).

REFERENCES

Amazing Spider-Man: The Complete Collection. DVD-ROM. Brooklyn, NY: Graphic Imaging Technology, 2006.

Busiek, Kurt, and Alex Ross. *Marvels*. New York: Marvel Comics, 1994.

Byrne, John. *Fantastic Four Visionaries: John Byrne*. Vols. 1–8. New York: Marvel Comics, 2001–2007.

Claremont, Chris, and John Romita. *X-Men: Mutant Massacre*. New York: Marvel Comics, 1996.

Coogan, Peter. *Superhero: The Secret Origin of a Genre*. Austin: Monkeybrain Books, 2006.

Daniels, Les. *DC Comics: Sixty Years of the World's Favorite Comic Book Heroes*. Boston: Little, Brown, 1995.

Daniels, Les. *Marvel: Five Fabulous Decades of the World's Greatest Comics*. New York: Abrams, 1991.

Daniels, Les. *Wonder Woman: The Complete History*. San Francisco: Chronicle Books, 2000.

Ellis, Warren, and Bryan Hitch. *The Authority: Relentless*. La Jolla, CA: Wildstorm, 2000.

Ellis, Warren, Bryan Hitch, Mark Millar, and Frank Quitely. *The Authority: Under New Management*. La Jolla, CA: Wildstorm, 2000.

Englehart, Steve, and Mike Friedrich. *Captain America and the Falcon: Secret Empire*. New York: Marvel Comics, 2006.

Gerber, Ernst, and Mary Gerber. *The Photo Journal Guide to Comic Books*. Vol. 2. Minden, NV: Gerber Publishing, 1990.

Groenewegen, David. "Smite Makes Right." *The Comics Journal*, no. 228 (November 2000): 46–47.

Harvey, R. C. "Foreword." In *Shazam Archives*. Vols. 2, 5–8. New York: DC Comics, 1999.

Hudlin, Reginald, and Scot Eaton. *Black Panther: The Bride*. New York: Marvel Comics, 2006.

Johns, Geoff, and Phil Jimenez. *Infinite Crisis*. New York: DC Comics, 2007.

Kirby, Jack. *Jack Kirby's Fourth World Omnibus*. Vols. 1–4. New York: DC Comics, 2007–2008.

Lee, Stan, and Jack Kirby. *Essential Fantastic Four*. Vols. 1–. New York: Marvel, 1999–.

Lee, Stan, and Jack Kirby. *Marvel Masterworks: Fantastic Four*. Vols. 1–10. New York: Marvel, 2003–2006.

Lupoff, Richard. "The Big Red Cheese." In *All in Color for a Dime,* ed. Dick Lupoff and Don Thompson, 58–83. Iola, WI: Krause Publications, 1970.

Lupoff, Richard. "Foreword." In *Shazam Archives*. Vols. 1, 5–7. New York: DC Comics, 1992.

Mahy, Margaret. *The Seven Chinese Brothers*. New York: Scholastic, 1990.

Marvel Enterprises. *44 Years of Fantastic Four*. DVD-ROM. Brooklyn, NY: Graphic Imaging Technology, 2005.

Millar, Mark, and Steve McNiven. *Civil War*. New York: Marvel Comics, 2007.

Miller, Frank. *Batman: The Dark Knight Returns*. New York: DC Comics, 1986.

Miller, John Jackson. "CBG Analysis: Third Straight August with Double-Digit Gains." *Comics Buyer's Guide,* August 2006. http://www.cbgxtra.com/Default.aspx?tabid=1737 (accessed July 13, 2007).

Milligan, Peter, and Mike Allred. *X-Statix*. Vols. 1–4. New York: Marvel, 2003–2004.

Mondello, Salvatore. "Spider-Man: Superhero in the Liberal Tradition." *Journal of Popular Culture* 10, no. 1 (Summer 1976): 232–38.

Moore, Alan, and Dave Gibbons. *Watchmen*. New York: DC Comics, 1986.

Moore, Alan, and J. H. Williams. *Promethea.* 5 vols. La Jolla, CA: America's Best Comics, 2000–2006.

Morrison, Grant, and Chas Truog. *Animal Man.* New York: DC Comics, 2001.

Morrison, Grant, and Chas Truog. *Animal Man: Deus Ex Machina.* New York: DC Comics, 2003.

Morrison, Grant, and Chas Truog. *Animal Man: Origin of the Species.* New York: DC Comics, 2002.

Nyberg, Amy Kiste. *Seal of Approval: The History of the Comics Code.* Jackson: University Press of Mississippi, 1998.

O'Neil, Denny, E. Nelson Bridwell, Elliot S. Maggin, C. C. Beck, and Kurt Schaffenberger. *Showcase Presents Shazam!* New York: DC Comics, 2006.

Palumbo, Donald. "The Marvel Comics Group's Spider-Man Is an Existential Superhero, or 'Life Had No Meaning Without My Latest Marvels!'" *Journal of Popular Culture* 17, no. 2 (Fall 1983): 67–82.

Pawuk, Michael. *Graphic Novels: A Genre Guide to Comic Books, Manga, and More.* Westport, CT: Libraries Unlimited, 2007.

Ransome, Arthur. *The Fool of the World and the Flying Ship.* New York: Farrar, Straus, and Giroux, 1968. [Originally published 1916.]

Reynolds, Richard. *Super Heroes: A Modern Mythology.* Jackson: University Press of Mississippi, 1992.

Ro, Ronin. *Tales to Astonish: Jack Kirby, Stan Lee, and the American Comic Book Revolution.* London: Bloomsbury, 2004.

Robinson, James, and Tony Harris. *Starman Omnibus.* Vol. 1–. New York: DC Comics, 2008–.

Rucka, Greg, and Drew Johnson. *Wonder Woman: Down to Earth.* New York: DC Comics, 2004.

Rucka, Greg, and Drew Johnson. *Wonder Woman: Bitter Rivals.* New York: DC Comics, 2005.

Shooter, Jim, Mike Zeck, and Bob Layton. *Marvel Super-Heroes Secret Wars.* New York: Marvel Comics, 1999.

Showcase Presents Superman. Vol. 1–. New York: DC Comics, 2005–.

Simon, Joe, and Jack Kirby. *Marvel Masterworks: Golden Age Captain America.* Vol. 1. New York: Marvel Comics, 2005.

Simone, Gail, and Ed Benes. *Birds of Prey: Of Like Minds.* New York: DC Comics, 2004

Simone, Gail, and Nicola Scott. *Birds of Prey: Dead of Winter.* New York: DC Comics, 2008.

Smith, Jeff. *Shazam! The Monster Society of Evil.* New York: DC Comics, 2007.

Spurgeon, Tom. "The Top 100 (English-Language) Comics of the Century." *The Comics Journal* no. 210 (February 1999): 34–108.

Stuller, Jennifer K. "Singing the Body Imaginative: The Elemental Flesh in Alan Moore's Promethea." In *Comic Arts Conference 2006.* CD. San Diego: Comic Arts Conference, 2006.

Vaughan, Brian K., and Tony Harris. *Ex Machina: The First Hundred Days.* La Jolla, CA: Wildstorm, 2005.

Waid, Mark, and Mike Wieringo. *Fantastic Four.* Vol. 1, *Imaginauts.* New York: Marvel Comics, 2003.

Walls, Robert E. "Paul Bunyan." In *American Folklore,* ed. Jan Harold Brunvand, 105–7. New York: Garland, 1996.

Wells, Earl. "For Once and for All, Who Was the Author of Marvel?" In *The Comics Journal Library*. Vol. 1, *Jack Kirby*. Seattle: Fantagraphics, 2002, 74–87.

Wertham, Fredric. *Seduction of the Innocent*. New York: Rinehart, 1954.

Wolfman, Marv, and George Perez. *Crisis on Infinite Earths*. New York: DC Comics, 2001.

Wolk, Douglas. *Reading Comics: How Graphic Novels Work and What They Mean*. Cambridge, MA: Da Capo, 2007.

Wright, Bradford W. *Comic Book Nation: The Transformation of Youth Culture in America*. Baltimore: Johns Hopkins University Press, 2001.

York, Chris. "All in the Family: Homophobia and Batman Comics in the 1950s." *International Journal of Comic Art* 2, no. 2 (Fall 2000): 100–10.

2

JAPANESE MANGA

Robin Brenner

Japanese manga have arrived in libraries, partly because teenage patrons clamor for their favorite titles but also because manga finally hit the right cultural moment to break through. As bookstores and libraries became purveyors of graphic novels, the audience shifted from the comic book collectors of previous generations to the avid readers of today's graphic novels. The graphic novel market in North America went from $75 million in 2000 to $375 million in 2007, and manga alone rose from $60 million in 2002 to over $210 million in 2007 (Griepp, "Graphic Novels" 2008). The manga market is robust, but the leap of only $10 million from 2006 to 2007, when in years past the increase from year to year had been closer to $25 million, has publishers and fans concerned about how the market will settle out. TOKYOPOP, long one of the major U.S. manga publishers, has decreased the number of volumes released per month significantly, signaling the industry's adjustments. As more and more titles arrive, fewer titles will be automatic hits, but the number of volumes hitting the shelves is holding steady (Griepp, "Manga Market" 2008). Around two-thirds of graphic novels are now sold in bookstores, versus one-third in comics specialty stores, and an estimated 80 percent of manga are sold in bookstores (Milton Griepp, e-mail, June 8, 2006). Japanese manga has gained a reputation and an avid following, and librarians are keen to understand this format and add it to their collections.

MANGA: A DEFINITION

The Japanese word for comics in print form. The word simply translates as "comics" and covers all printed matter from 300-page magazines issued weekly and monthly to the *tankobon,* or bound paperback volumes, available at newsstands, manga stores, and bookstores.

In Japan, the word *manga* may be used for comics of any origin—hence, the new Japanese International Manga Award, limited to "up and coming foreign manga artists" from outside Japan. In the United States, the word means comics from Japan as well as from Korea and China—and sometimes, by extension, comics from any country that are drawn similarly to Japanese titles. (Fans debate this last meaning.)

ORIGINS AND INFLUENCES

Manga as recognized today was not fully formulated until the 1950s in Japan, but the art draws its roots from traditional Japanese arts and practices.[1] The calligraphic line, humor, caricature, and sense of sequence can be traced back to illustrated scrolls created by 12th-century Buddhist monks. The *Chouju Giga,* or "animal scrolls," featured animals as clergy and noblemen in deft, elegant pen-and-ink portraits, parodying the religious and noble classes. During the relative peace of the Tokugawa Era in the 16th and 17th centuries, woodblock printing techniques inspired artists, and the quick reproduction built up mass-market appeal and availability. These *ukiyo-e,* literally "pictures of the floating world," were the most famous prints of the time and were avidly collected. The "floating world" referred to the pleasure districts of the capital city of Edo (now Tokyo), and the illustrations of courtesans, kabuki actors, and samurai remain some of the most indelible images associated with Japanese history and culture.

Katsushika Hokusai (1760–1849), the noted ukiyo-e artist who created the classic painting *The Great Wave off Kanagawa,* is credited with coining the term "manga"—literally, "whimsical pictures." Hokusai used the term to describe his own sketched caricatures observed from life or taken from folktales.[2] Bound collections of caricatures and drawings of humorous escapades appeared at the turn of the 18th century, selling by the thousands.

Western Comics Plus Japanese Style

Through the tumultuous decades after 1867 when Japan opened to the West, Western influences catching on among Japanese artists included cartoons and comic strips. Artists started by mimicking the political cartoons and jibes of London's famous *Punch* magazine and absorbed European influences also, but the Japanese artists soon mixed traditional Western comics features of panels, text bubbles, and sound effects with Japan's artistic and storytelling traditions. By the 20th century, a variety of Japanese periodicals included comics, which ranged from political commentary to *Fuku-chan,* a strip akin to *Dennis the Menace.* By the 1940s, comics drew enough interest to stand alone in magazines with hundreds of pages.

World War II changed everything. The prewar and wartime ultranationalist policies all but halted the booming comics industry because anyone in the industry was required to create governmental propaganda or be arrested. Postwar, the industry slowly built back up, due in no small part to Osamu Tezuka and his fellow innovators.

The God of Manga

Tezuka is rightly reputed as the god of Japanese comics: his influence on both comics and animation is still palpable today. He drew inspiration from theater, cartoons, animation, and most importantly, film; moreover, he set manga production standards that differentiate Japanese comic art from other national traditions. Strongly influenced by cinema, he began creating works using thousands of panels and pages, employing cinematic points of view and editing to shape his tales. He took character design cues from Western animators including Disney and the Fleischer brothers, setting the standard in style for the large eyes many new readers first notice upon opening a Japanese title. His landmark work set in motion the major genres and intended audiences for manga, from *Astro Boy*'s science fiction tale for boys to *Princess Knight*'s gender-bending heroism for girls. Tezuka originally wrote for children, but in the 1960s he was one of the first creators to recognize that the format could tell any kind of story. Tezuka began to push the boundaries again, with comics for adults.

Magazines, Audiences, and Diversification

By the 1970s, anthology magazines with hundreds, even thousands, of pages devoted to manga became the norm. Manga were soon found everywhere and read by everyone as a quickly digested, ephemeral distraction from school or work-time stress. The best stories were reprinted as bound paperbacks, called *tankobon,* and these were what readers collected. Merchandising around popular stories is rampant, but the Japanese market was and still is all about reading the story rather than collecting the first issue.

Manga continued to diversify. Female creators arrived in the 1970s, rejuvenating manga aimed at girls and women with innovative ideas and styles now standard in girls—or shōjo—comics. Manga about everything and anything hit the shelves, from *pachinko,* a favorite type of vertical pinball game, to famous figures such as Anne Frank and Beethoven. Today manga makes up almost 40 percent of Japanese publishing: 31 percent of the magazine market and a whopping 69 percent of the book market.

Manga Arrives in the States

U.S. audiences originally met Japanese comics through anime, or Japanese animation, though many never knew it: Tezuka's *Astro Boy* and *Jungle Emperor* (known here as *Kimba the White Lion*) were dubbed into English and aired on U.S. television in the 1960s. Anime feature films, most notably *Akira* in the late 1980s and *Ghost in the Shell* in the 1990s, shocked and intrigued U.S. audiences by animating complex, violent, and sophisticated science fiction stories for adults—the kind of tales U.S. audiences had never seen animated (Napier 2000, 3–14).

Manga arrived in the United States on the heels of these breakthrough anime titles. The first to appear were meant to appeal to the established comics market of the time: older teenage and adult men who were more collectors than readers. Thus, many of the vanguard—*Lone Wolf and Cub, Akira,* and *Adolf*—were intended both in Japan and in the United States for adult males. Although publishers worried that U.S. readers would need the manga "flipped" into English language left-to-right order, fans made it clear that they actually preferred the traditional right-to-left order. Flipping is arduous and expensive, so retaining the traditional format allowed publishers to issue more titles more frequently (Reid 2004). Once publishers introduced shōjo titles, as TOKYOPOP did in the late 1990s, the market exploded as girls and women, traditionally underserved by U.S. comics, latched on to these new arrivals written expressly for them.

THE MANGA BOOM

Today, more and more kinds of manga are being translated, with niche audiences and publishers gaining solid footholds in the U.S. market. Female readers continue to establish their presence, but now everyone from third graders to grandparents is discovering a manga out there to enjoy, just as many readers did with U.S. comics and graphic novels.

It is important to remember that for better or worse, the term "manga" is used not just for Japanese comics but also as an umbrella term for Korean comics (*manhwa*) and Chinese comics (*manhua*). Korean manhwa, featuring similar black and white art and stylistic choices, are recognizable as closely related to Japanese titles. Japanese genres are mirrored in Korean offerings, yet manhwa display subtle differences. Some mimic the Japanese visual style, whereas others distinguish themselves with more pronounced lips, intense blacks, and emphasis on outlines. Korean titles read left to right and reflect the Korean perspective on history, culture, and the greater world. More and more titles are arriving, especially as publishers specializing in manhwa have opened for business. Chinese comics are more obviously different from manga—most are in color, and the few titles currently translated are kung fu action/adventure titles. As recognition of Asian comics grows, more titles may be imported.

RECOMMENDED READING ON MANGA AS A FORMAT

Manga: 60 Years of Japanese Comics, by Paul Gravett (Laurence King Publishing/Collins Design, 2004). It looks like a coffeetable book, but the accompanying essays are pithy and incredibly informative. The book is intended for adults and includes some adult content. All in all, one of the best visual histories of the format.

Manga! Manga! The World of Japanese Comics, by Frederik L. Schodt (Kodansha, 1983). The first and still one of the best histories published in the United States about manga. Though dated in some ways, the history of the form remains solid and the enthusiasm for the format engaging.

Dreamland Japan: Readings on Modern Manga, by Frederik L. Schodt (Stone Bridge Press, 1996). Beyond a simple update, this book expands on Schodt's 1983 work plus includes essays about different aspects of manga.

Manga: The Complete Guide, by Jason Thompson (Del Rey, 2007). If you are looking for information and short reviews, this guide offers snapshots of individual titles and series plus background on themes, customs, and characteristics of manga.

One Thousand Years of Manga, by Brigitte Koyama-Richard (Flammarion, 2007). A visual documentary with commentary on manga's origins and forms.

Understanding Manga and Anime, by Robin Brenner (Libraries Unlimited, 2007). My own book introduces manga and anime to librarians: format, content, themes, traditions, fans, programs, and recommended title lists.

Publishers

Numerous U.S. publishers are diving into manga. Dominant industry powerhouses VIZ Media and TOKYOPOP may release as many as 30 to 40 new volumes every month. VIZ is well known for the top U.S. manga anthology magazines, *Shonen Jump* and the more recent *Shojo Beat,* as well as the wildly popular featured series that include *Naruto, Rurouni Kenshin, Absolute Boyfriend,* and *Nana.* TOKYOPOP has pursued teenage girls as a substantial audience since the end of the 1990s, though they release all types of manga. Both publishers tend to stick to a no-frills approach—there may be translation notes or occasionally sound effects indexes, but there are rarely extras, and the books are constructed according to standardized specifications. So libraries can count on almost all the titles being the same size and general thickness, and the fewer extras means a cheaper price.

Aside from the big two, a few other manga publishers have been around for at least as long, most notably Dark Horse Comics. Dark Horse has focused on *seinen*—men's—titles as well as preserving the original Japanese design and quality in their translations. Central Park Media is another veteran, though recent financial problems have them struggling to stay afloat. Vertical Inc. has carved out a niche publishing classic works by Osamu Tezuka, including *Buddha* and *Ode to Kirihito,* whereas Fanfare/Ponent Mon represents a combination of Japanese and Franco-Belgian talent, both companies putting out titles of excellent design and quality.

Besides manga-focus publishers, book publishers are also getting in on the act. Del Rey Manga, part of Random House, produces over 20 series distinguished by excellent translation notes, extras, and high-quality reproduction yet with relatively low price. A number of smaller publishers have arrived in the past few years, including Digital Manga, Go! Comi, Seven Seas, Broccoli Books, Yen Press, and Korean manhwa publisher Netcomics. All are attempting to catch part of the manga boom by offering something a bit further afield than the typical VIZ or TOKYOPOP titles. Digital Manga, for example, has become the one-stop shop for yaoi/BL manga with their Juné imprint (see "Themes and Genres" later in this chapter for more on BL). Go! Comi thoughtfully produces each of its titles with direct involvement of the Japanese creators whenever possible. Yen Press presents one of the most diverse arrays of manga and manga-style titles, from Japanese manga to Korean manhwa to U.S. creator manga-style tales. Netcomics offers instant reader gratification by making titles available for download long before the print hits the shelves. More and more companies are considering this tactic, as competition with illegal download sites featuring scanlations—fan translations of manga titles—threatens the industry.

MANGA AUDIENCES, SYMBOLS, AND LITERACY

Intended Audiences

In Japan, manga is divided and marketed to four defined audiences. *Shōnen* manga is aimed at boys up to about age 15 and emphasizes action, humor, and adventure. *Shōjo* manga, aimed at girls up to about age 15, highlights relationships, drama, and quests. *Seinen* manga is aimed at older teenage boys and adult men and plays out like shōnen manga grown up. There is still action and comedy, but there is also shadier morality and adult content, from sensuality and sexuality to more explicit action and violence. *Josei*—women's—manga follows in shōjo manga's footsteps but is more likely to have explicit sensual or sexual content or violence mixed with the melodrama. Within comics for either gender, there are *ero* (from erotic) and *hentai* (literally, perverted) manga, that is, erotic and pornographic manga intended exclusively for adults.

These categories are publisher-determined, and artists move from magazine to magazine and thus from audience to audience to try out different stories. However, target audience does not necessarily equal real audience, and VIZ remains the only U.S. publisher to label titles as shōnen or shōjo. Shōnen manga are avidly read by fans of both genders, and shōjo stories are read by everyone from teenage guys to businessmen, though they may not admit it. Even in Japan, there are many crossover titles that break down the presumed gender barriers: CLAMP's innovative and popular title *Chobits* was originally seinen, yet the series appeals to teenagers and adults of both genders.

Cracking the Code

Manga has its own unique code developed from Japanese words, cultural references, and visual traditions. The first adjustment is to flip how you read—to follow text and panels from right to left instead of left to right. This reversal is only the first step; trademark visual conventions are everywhere. Characters can be wildly exaggerated and shift into the simplified, squat "chibi" form when running through emotional highs and lows. People's personalities are defined by subtle but significant shifts in eye shape, body type, and dress. Symbols pop up, indicating anger, nervousness, embarrassment, or all three. The panel "camera" shifts between objects in a scene, forcing the reader to pause and consider the story's environment rather than continue with the action.

All these conventions build a steep learning curve for new readers. Just as most U.S. readers recognize a thought bubble, most Japanese know that a bloody nose means a character is aroused, or a giant drop hovering overhead refers to sweat and thus nervousness. As readers continue, they learn to recognize more nuances. Shades of respect and insult conferred by honorifics hint at relationships, and wearing a combination of swords in a historical drama indicates status. These symbols and references are frequently unexplained. Most manga readers decode whatever they do not understand by reading, asking fellow fans, and consulting online resources. (Resources about anime are often useful for deciphering manga—see chapter 9.)

DECODING GRAPHIC NOVELS AND MANGA

Making Comics: Storytelling Secrets of Comics, Manga and Graphic Novels, by Scott McCloud (HarperPerennial, 2006). McCloud's latest excellent volume, joining his *Understanding Comics* and *Reinventing Comics,* delves into how sequential art works for readers and creators and features substantial discussions of how and why manga works the way it does. Crucial reading for any librarian!

This secret language discourages many new readers, especially those less comfortable or familiar with visual storytelling. But for teen fans, the thrill of reading something that puzzles their parents is one of the appeals. The acquired knowledge of these elements of culture and language establishes a connection and reputation among fans. At the same time, the specialized expertise renders the medium itself inhospitable to many of their parents' generation, maintaining manga as a teen domain.

It's More Than Just Reading Right to Left

Whereas many U.S. comics stories begin as monthly 20- to 30-page comic books, in Japan manga stories are collected in sizeable weekly and monthly anthologies, each story episode taking up about 20 pages (Gravett 2004, 13). With relatively small studios and only a handful of assistants compared to the larger teams commonly involved in U.S. comics production (15–16), manga creators churn out from 40 to 140 pages a week (Lehmann 2005). The elements that define manga—longer storylines told with many panels per page, a constant soundtrack using thousands of sound effects, the leaps between panels—signal its strong connections to film. At the same time, the less familiar features, including permeable or nonexistent panel borders, frequent use of symbolic dividers such as flowers or feathers, and changing text-bubble shapes, demonstrate comic art's strengths. Extended pacing and high page counts allow readers to get to know characters over a period of time, similar to the best television shows and novels, and allow for real-time character growth and intricate plotting.

The format differences illustrate how manga is designed to engage readers' emotions above all. Symbols emphasize characters' internal lives as often as physical action. The high use of aspect-to-aspect transitions between panels, as Scott McCloud describes in *Understanding Comics,* challenges the reader to create the story from fragments and, by requiring active participation with the text, draws readers deeper into the experience (McCloud 1993, 60–93). This applies to every type of manga, from romances to action; drawing out a lingering goodbye and a deadly samurai duel use many of the same "you are there" techniques (McCloud 2006, 215–23).

Creator Control

Manga creators own and control their own work, plots, and characters. This approach is quite different from the dominant U.S. paradigm, where companies own the characters and bring in new writers and artists to reinvent a character or series. Thus Batman and Superman have been around for 60 years. With manga, creators work with editors to tell the stories they are inspired to tell, with their own original characters. Because of this setup, manga series also end. A few series seem to go on forever (as in *InuYasha*'s 50-some volumes), and popular series may have spin-offs and sequels, but readers expect each series to wrap up.

Themes and Genres

Manga does not have a dominant genre, in the way that the superhero genre has dominated in the United States, although genre tales including science fiction, fantasy, and mystery are prevalent. Given manga's rapid rise, creators quickly branched into more and more genres, many familiar to us: hero quests, adventure quests, dystopian futures, and complex mysteries. However, certain subgenres stand out as part of manga's canon: *mecha* tales featuring robots, cyborgs, and different variations on man versus machine and magical girl stories, which feature a "typical" girl gaining special powers and embarking on a quest to save herself, her friends, and the world. A subgenre recent in the United States and increasingly popular is boys' love, also known as BL or *yaoi,* focusing on romances between two male characters written by female authors for teen girls and women. (Editor's note: see also chapter 3 and Appendix B-3.) This subgenre has gained a loyal audience in the United States, filling an unanticipated gap in the market. All manga draws on Japanese history, religion, folklore, and legends and can reflect Japanese history and pop culture seriously or with bubbly irreverence.

Manga creators love to create genre mash-ups. It is par for the course to have an action/police/procedural/horror/comedy (*Descendants of Darkness*) or a mythological martial arts/romantic comedy (*Ranma 1/2*). Humor is one of the most common elements—even the most serious titles will use slapstick, puns, or practical jokes to lighten the mood. Flashes of humor, anger, and embarrassment barrel through manga, sometimes lasting for no more than a panel or two, and the rapid shift in mood can push new readers out of the story or disorient them if they pick up a romance, they want a romance, not a horror story, or if they pick up an action title, they want action, not deep thoughts about humankind's place in the world. However, once readers get used to the innovative genre combinations, the creative twists become part of the appeal.

Thematically, the samurai tradition and Japan's rich history still maintain a romantic allure. Tales contemplating war, conflict, and humanity's part in threatening the natural environment are common touchstones. Recent history zeroing in on the aftereffects of World War II, specifically the atomic detonations, is referenced again and again in fantasy and science fiction, though it is rarely shown outright in historical context. In numerous family and school dramas, manga cover the familiar territories of romance, peer pressure, family expectations, school life, bullying, and suicide. (The suicide rate in Japan in particularly high.)

Manga titles are never packaged for export, so even the simplest stories keep a Japanese point of view, from everyday school duties to idiosyncrasies of Japanese pop culture, music, and fashion. All the cultural references add yet another layer for readers to decode. At the same time, manga provides a window into a culture a world away; and though there are many similarities to make the view familiar, there are also differences. For fans, all this heightens the sense of being in the know as well as a feeling of global community.

Manga by Any Other Name

Given manga's growing presence in U.S. culture over the past 25 years, many of today's comics creators have been inspired by manga's style and dominant genres. This trend will only continue as legions of American fans become writers and artists themselves. Art style can be most obviously pegged to manga influence, but everyone from Frank Miller to Colleen Doran uses elements of manga's traditions without the work necessarily looking like manga.

A number of creators started incorporating manga elements in the 1990s, some adopting almost every visual cue, including Chynna Clugston (*Hopeless Savages*), Ben Dunn (*Ninja High School*), and Rod Espinosa (*Neotopia*). At the turn of this millennium, a whole new crop of manga-style artists started putting out books due in no small part to opportunities such as TOKYOPOP's Rising Stars of Manga contest. Creators from Bryan Lee O'Malley (*Scott Pilgrim*) to Becky Cloonan (*Demo, East Coast Rising*) to Fred Gallagher (*Megatokyo*) use bits and pieces of manga style while maintaining their own voice and flair. TOKYOPOP was the first publisher to dive in whole hog with a line of titles, including Svetlana Chmakova's *Dramacon,* Jen Lee Quick's *Off*beat,* and Christy Lijewski's *Re:Play.* Seven Seas has also released a number of U.S.-created titles.

A debate periodically flares up between strict manga fans and more inclusive comics readers over whether it is correct to call comics "manga" if they are not made in Japan. For our purposes, manga-style comics can be just as good as their inspirations. In the end, as with all forms of sequential art, they will succeed or fail on the strength of their storytelling.

CULTURAL ROAD BUMPS

Fantasy versus Reality

In manga, one storytelling rule governs everything: in fiction, anything can (and will) happen. In the United States, we believe that what happens in fiction or in our imaginations might happen in real life. This is why we debate whether violent video games (or music or fiction) will lead people to violence in reality. In Japan, however, there is much less fear that anything happening in fantasy will happen in real life. From the evidence in their own society, Japanese conclusions are more justified than not: despite playing as many violent video games as we do, Japan has a much lower violence rate (Etherington 2004). And for a country with an $80 billion sex industry (Shreve 2006), they have the least amount of sex of any country in the world ("Durex's Global Sex Survey" 2005).

In manga and inside the reader's head, all manner of taboos may be broken, and violence may occur; but bringing taboo actions into the real world is considered just as troublesome in Japan as it is in the United States. Similar artistic traditions reach all the way back to ukiyo-e prints featuring blood-soaked samurai battles and wide-ranging erotic subjects (Schodt 1996). Present-day creators of adult manga express little worry when covering the same territory. This sense of freedom on the page can unnerve people used to topics being considered out of bounds. Japanese creators merrily cross boundaries to explore the limits of human nature and imagination, for comic effect or for serious contemplation, content in the expectation that no one will take their worlds too much to heart.

The Schoolgirls and Samurai Myth

One of the most damaging stereotypes about manga (and its animated counterpart) is that it is all rife with violence and pornography. This is far from true. Like any other medium, manga contains all levels of content. Because manga has grown and diversified over that past 60 years, works cover the same range of topics that novels and films do here. Thus, although there are children's comedies and teen romances, there are also adult stories in all genres that contain explicit violence and sex, including erotic manga.

Confusion arises from the lingering impression among Americans that comics are for children—though in fact this has not been true for more than 30 years. Any reader expecting comics to cater to children is undoubtedly shocked by Otomo Katsuhiro's *Akira,* Takumi Koshun's *Battle Royale,* or Tateno Makoto's *Yellow,* each mature in its own way. Manga in Japan is not a cult product or a side market: it is ordinary, and it is everywhere. As simply another choice in the storytelling landscape, it covers the whole range of possibilities, as eventually graphic novels and comics will do here.

In Japan, explicit scenes of sexuality or violence are always intended for mature audiences. That being said, the Japanese public and manga readers do have a different sense of what is appropriate for various age ranges. For example, incidental nudity is not considered something to cover up because it is regarded as a natural part of life. As a colleague of mine once said, in American comics, if you are taking a bath, the water is opaque; in Japanese comics, the water is clear. In younger-age titles, slapstick jokes may involve nudity and subsequent embarrassment, but the images are not sexual. In teen titles, there may be more nudity and more sensuality to reflect the growing maturity of the audience and characters, but explicit depictions of sex are rare. Given that until the mid-1990s images showing genitalia were illegal, creators got very inventive in depicting sensual and sexual content inexplicitly, and that custom remains prevalent unless the title is expressly adult.

TOKYOPOP led the way in rating its titles to indicate intended audience, and their system was recently revised in collaboration with librarian and graphic novel advocate Michele Gorman. The revamped system provides content indicators similar to the television ratings system. Most manga publishers rate their series by age group, though there is currently no industry standard, and ratings can be very helpful in figuring out the intended audience at a glance.

Fan Service

One wrench in the works for evaluating manga's sensuality level is the tradition of fan service. Any manga content that is present only for fans, and that does not advance the plot or develop characters, is fan service. Fan service can include extensive shots of technology and robots in mecha tales, but it is most often the display of pin-up poses, sexy garments, and exaggerated anatomy for the reader to ogle.

Fan service changes dramatically depending on the audience. In teen boys' and men's comics, the women may be drawn to titillate with stupendous fantasy physiques confined by tight clothes that accentuate all the curves and allow frequent glimpses of panties and breasts. In teen girls' and women's comics, beautiful young men may be shown off, frequently shirtless and in pin-up poses.

U.S. comics are not strangers to fan service—just look at any title featuring a female superhero, and you will find similarly exaggerated anatomy and poses. Objectification is, for better or worse, a part of the deal in all media, from film and television to comics. At least manga shows equal opportunity: it is acknowledged that teen girls and women like to look at sexy men as much as teen guys and men enjoy looking at sexy women. Until the trend disappears from media altogether, there will always be some element of fan service in comics, manga, and other visual media, but fan service can be and is balanced out by strong characters, complex plots, and smart story twists. Knowing the tradition of fan service can help selectors to understand why these images are included and to make decisions in choosing titles. Fan service should not automatically exclude a title, or some of the best comics and graphic novels would never make it to the shelves. But a high ratio of fan service images may indicate that a title is best placed in an adult rather than teen collection.

COLLECTION DEVELOPMENT

Understanding Before Buying

Read manga! As with graphic novels in general, before you can successfully build, promote, and defend a manga collection, you must read manga. Reading titles from the major traditions is key to grasping the format. Everyone starting out should read at least one typical shōnen manga, one shōjo manga, one classic, one romance, and one mecha. Give yourself time to feel confused, but keeping reading—the more you read, the more you will get a sense of how manga works and why it is appealing.

RECOMMENDED READING: MAJOR MANGA TRADITIONS

Shōnen Manga

> *Bleach,* by Tite Kubo (VIZ Media, 2004–) (teen)
> *Death Note,* by Tsugumi Ohba and Takeshi Obata (VIZ Media, 2005–2007) (older teen)

Shōjo Manga

> *Fruits Basket,* by Natsuki Takaya (TOKYOPOP, 2004–) (teen)
> *Fushigi Yûgi,* by Yû Watase (also Romanized as Yuu; VIZ Media, 2003–2006) (teen)

Classics

> *Lone Wolf and Cub,* by Kazuo Koike and Goseki Kojima (Dark Horse, 2000–2002) (older teen)
> *Barefoot Gen,* by Keiji Nakazawa (Last Gasp, 2003–2004) (teen)

Romance

> *Mars,* by Fuyumi Soryo (TOKYOPOP, 2002–2003) (teen)
> *Only the Ring Finger Knows,* by Satoru Kannagi and Hotaru Odajiri (Digital Manga, 2004) (BL, teen)

Mecha

> *Ghost in the Shell,* 2nd ed., by Masamune Shirow (Dark Horse, 2004) (mature)
> *Battle Angel Alita,* by Yukito Kishiro (Dark Horse, 2004–2005) (older teen)

STATISTICS, COMMUNITY, AND POPULARITY INFORMATION

ICv2, http://www.icv2.com. This pop culture industry Web site follows the news in the manga and anime industries with daily updates. When you need statistics or market information, this should be your first stop. Watch for the most recent *ICv2 Insider's Guide,* a magazine featuring articles, market summaries, and reviews relating to graphic novels, anime/manga, and gaming.

Graphic Novels in Libraries e-mail list (GNLIB-L), http://groups. yahoo.com/group/GNLIB-L. Made up of librarians, publishers, educators, columnists, and bookstore staff, this e-mail list covers everything you ever wanted to know about graphic novels in libraries. As a network and resource, it is one of the fastest ways to get a prompt and reliable answer for everything, from where a series belongs age-wise to a quick review of a title.

· Mania: Beyond Entertainment—Manga Comparison, http://www. mania.com/manga_comparison.php. When you are trying to figure out how many volumes are in a series, these charts for manga, manhwa, and manhua are the place to look. They include the current number of U.S. volumes, the number of volumes in the country of origin, and whether the series is finished or continuing.

Anime News Network: Rating Stats: Top Ten Best Rated Manga, http://www.animenewsnetwork.com/encyclopedia/ratings-manga.php. Keep your finger on the pulse of manga's popularity! This site includes the best, worst, and most popular manga and similar lists for anime.

Building manga collections can be daunting. Although series do end, the number of volumes can discourage libraries from collecting entire sets. If you are just starting with manga, it is best to get the first few volumes of a core list of titles. You can buy more of just those that circulate. Remember that like all graphic novels, manga should be shelved by age: children, teen, or adult. Be sure to advertise the new collection. Give it its own shelving to show off the new section and the attractive covers. Create a short and sweet bookmark explaining what manga is and recommending starter titles. On the back of the bookmark, ask for patrons' input on what should be added. If your library already has a substantial graphic novel collection, those patrons may notice you have manga. However, manga fans and Western graphic novel fans are not necessarily the same people, so manga readers may not be aware that the library carries their favorite format.

CORE READING LISTS

Kids

> *Yotsuba&!* by Kiyohiko Azuma (ADV Manga, 2005–)
> *Cardcaptor Sakura,* by CLAMP (TOKYOPOP, 2003–2005)
> *Baron: The Cat Returns,* by Aoi Hiiragi (VIZ Media, 2005)

Teens

> *Bleach,* by Tite Kubo (VIZ Media, 2004–)
> *The Wallflower,* by Tomoko Hayakawa (Del Rey, 2004–2006)
> (older teen)
> *Tsubasa: RESERVoir CHRoNiCLE,* by CLAMP (Del Rey, 2004–)

Adults

> *The Push Man and Other Stories,* by Yoshihiro Tatsumi (Drawn
> and Quarterly, 2005)
> *Buddha,* by Osamu Tezuka (Vertical, 2003–2005)
> *To Terra,* by Keiko Takemiya (Vertical, 2007–)

> For more core lists, see my own *Understanding Manga and Anime*
> (2007), *Graphic Novels: A Genre Guide to Graphic Novels, Manga,
> and More* by Michael Pawuk (2007), and *Manga: The Complete Guide*
> by Jason Thompson (2007).

News and Review Resources

More and more manga titles are being reviewed in professional library journals, though the explosion in the manga market makes it extremely difficult to keep up with the sheer volume published. Manga are currently reviewed in *Booklist, Kirkus, Library Journal, School Library Journal,* and *Voice of Youth Advocates (VOYA). Library Journal* also offers free weekly Web-only reviews of graphic novels through their Xpress Reviews section, many of which are manga.

Outside of the library sphere, there are also industry sources for reviews. With its broad scope of all publishing, *Publishers Weekly* covers manga in reviews and articles and in its PW Comics Week E-newsletter (also available online at www.publishersweekly.com). *New Type USA* was one of the better magazines in terms of breadth of reviews and up-to-date articles, but it ceased publication in 2008. *Protoculture Addicts* and *The Comics Journal* both tend toward the academic but are both excellent resources on the history and background of manga. *The Comics Journal* can be particularly helpful in investigating classic and adult manga because many of their features focus on these categories. A new magazine has just arrived on the scene, *Otaku USA*, which is geared toward older teen and adult fans and which includes a range of articles, reviews, and features.

Currently, the reviews most in line with fan concerns and critiques can be found online. These reviews may not always synchronize with collection development concerns of librarians, but they do give a sense of how a title holds up to fan expectations and interests.

ONLINE SOURCES FOR REVIEWS

Anime News Network: Reviews, http://www.animenewsnetwork. com/review. Insightful reviews of manga and anime with a strong awareness of the fan's point of view.

Gilles' Service to Fans Page: The Librarian's Guide to Anime and Manga, by Gilles Poitras, http://www.koyagi.com/Libguide. html.

Gilles' Service to Fans Page: The Anime Companion Online Supplement, by Gilles Poitras, http://www.koyagi.com/ACPages/ ACmain.html.
Vocabulary, recommended lists, and collection development advice from librarian anime guru Gilles Poitras (see chapter 9).

Manga Life, http://www.mangalife.com. A substantive site of manga news, reviews, and features.

MangaBlog, by Brigid Alverson, http://mangablog.net. Features periodic reviews of manga from a parent and manga fan. Also one of the best blogs for keeping up with news about the manga world.

No Flying, No Tights, by Robin Brenner, http://www.noflying notights.com. My own site features graphic novel reviews of all kinds, including a substantial collection of manga reviews.

PopCultureShock, http://www.popcultureshock.com. This frequently updated site is a valuable one-stop shop for graphic novel and manga news, in-depth volume reviews, and insightful commentary.

MAKING MANGA'S APPEAL WORK FOR YOU: PROGRAMS AND YOUR COMMUNITY

The way fans express their love for manga has created a vibrant community. Fans collect favorite series and related paraphernalia, from buttons to bags to hats. They embrace group activities by attending conventions, screenings, and clubs; presenting panels; competing in cosplay (or costume play) events; and dancing the night away to their favorite Japanese music, from j-pop to j-rock. Online fan activity is even more diverse, as fans join online forums; create fan art, fan fiction, and anime music videos; and trade knowledge on everything from the latest trends in gaming to how best to achieve manga-inspired hair.

The key to attracting manga fans and encouraging new ones lies in acknowledging their love for the medium. Manga and anime fans are delighted when libraries include their favorites in their collection, and when they find staff members both knowledgeable and receptive, they jump at the chance to share their expertise. Few librarians can maintain the encyclopedic knowledge fans thrive on, but simply recognizing series titles and knowing what cosplay is will get you far.

Especially at the start of a collection, seek out fans' advice on what to add. Integrate manga into genre displays, and when the local anime and manga convention is gearing up, consider displays on costumes and costume-making, manga art and writing, and Japanese traditional and pop culture.

There are many program opportunities that will appeal to manga and anime fans. The simplest is a manga café, or providing a set time and place for manga fans to gather, read, and socialize. This can be even more fun with Japanese snacks like Pocky (chocolate-coated cookie sticks) and wasabi peas. Host a fan art contest, inviting fans to create homages to their favorite series or characters for display in the library—or, if possible, for a contest judged by their peers. More involved events include workshops for cosplayers, either by simply providing tailoring books and allowing cosplayers to network or perhaps by inviting in a local tailor to teach the basics of clothing production. Hold a cosplay masquerade or contest, so that fans can show off their hard work.

TITLES FOR ASPIRING MANGA ARTISTS

Mangaka America: Manga by America's Hottest Artists, by Steel-River Studio (Collins Design, 2006). Interviews, advice, instruction, and lush examples from today's top American creators in the manga style.

Shojo Beat's Manga Artist Academy, edited by Hiroyuki Iizuka (VIZ Media, 2006). Yû (also written as Yuu) Watase (*Fushigi Yûgi*) and Rie Takada (*Happy Hustle High*) are just a few of the Japanese manga artists who offer advice, techniques, and support for those who want to try shōjo art.

For more "how to draw manga" titles, see http://www.koyagi.com/recDrawingBooks.html.

Consider creating a workshop on how to draw manga, which can be as simple as providing pencils, pens, paper, and a selection of "how to draw manga" titles. Build on the keen interest in creating manga-style art by inviting local artists or writers to speak at the library or present comics and manga creation workshops.

Continuing events are also welcome, including manga and anime discussion clubs. (See chapter 9 for more on anime and anime clubs.) Manga and anime clubs can be as low-key as getting together to watch anime or discuss favorite series or genres. Once a club is started, members can determine whether the club will stick to regular meetings or branch out into one-shot events, the most logical being a day-long anime marathon or manga read-in. Clubs may also produce items for the library, such as recommended title lists, a club newsletter, or reviews for the library newsletter or Web site.

Once you know you have an audience, several events can be coordinated into a mini-convention. You could start with an anime marathon; add in art shows, title discussions, and special guests; and finish the event with a cosplay masquerade and party. Conventions require substantial planning and coordination and thus may be best attempted with the help of an already established club. Make sure to check with local businesses about sponsoring prizes and food to help keep costs down, and recruit fans to help set up and break down the convention.

PUTTING IT ALL TOGETHER

Japanese manga is a huge draw for teens and, more and more, for all kinds of readers, from older kids who love the anime-style *Avatar: The Last Airbender* and are looking for more to adults who have discovered the genius of Osamu Tezuka's *Ode to Kirihito*. Libraries can diversify their collections and attract new patrons by adding manga suitable for every age and taste to complement established graphic novels sections. Teen demand continues to dominate the market. Yet as more and more types of manga reach American shores, the variety and expressiveness of manga can lead readers to many worlds, from the urban landscape in modern Tokyo (Tatsumi Yoshihiro's *Abandon the Old in Tokyo*) to a new perspective on legends of the Arabian Nights (Jin-Seok Jeon's *One Thousand and One Nights*). We are limited only by the creative output of manga-makers on all shores, and we are far from hitting the end of innovation in the format.

NOTES

1. Background for this section is drawn from Schodt 1983, Schodt 1996, and Gravett 2004.

2. Although commonly credited with coining the term *manga,* it seems that Hokusai did not actually invent the word. Certainly his series titled *Hokusai Manga,* published

1814–1878, remains the most outstanding early example of a work with the word in the title. Kern (2006, 139–44) describes previous usage of the term by other artists and writers as early as 1771, including in a humorous haiku.

REFERENCES

Brenner, Robin E. *Understanding Manga and Anime.* Westport, CT: Libraries Unlimited, 2007.

"Durex's Global Sex Survey." Gavin's Blog. January 6, 2005. http://www.gavinsblog.com/2005/01/06/durexs-global-sex-survey/ (accessed April 25, 2009).

Etherington, Daniel. "Blaming the Dark Side of Gaming." BBC News, February 2004. http://news.bbc.co.uk/2/hi/technology/3466525.stm (accessed December 31, 2006).

Gravett, Paul. *Manga: Sixty Years of Japanese Comics.* London: Laurence King Publishing/Collins Design, 2004.

Griepp, Milton, ed. "Graphic Novels Hit $375 Million." *ICv2.com,* April 18, 2008. http://www.icv2.com/articles/news/12416.html (accessed August 25, 2008).

Griepp, Milton, ed. "Manga Market Growth Rate Slows, Title Count Likely to Flatten in 2008." *ICv2 Guide to Manga,* no. 57 (September/October 2008): 4.

Kern, Adam L. *Manga from the Floating World: Comicbook Culture and the Kibyōshi of Edo Japan.* Cambridge, MA: Harvard University Asia Center, 2006.

Lehmann, Timothy. *Manga: Masters of the Art.* New York: Collins Design, 2005.

McCloud, Scott. *Making Comics: Storytelling Secrets of Comics, Manga and Graphic Novels.* New York: HarperPerennial, 2006.

McCloud, Scott. *Understanding Comics: The Invisible Art.* Northampton, MA: Kitchen Sink Press, 1993.

Napier, Susan J. *Anime from Akira to Princess Mononoke: Experiencing Contemporary Japanese Animation.* New York: Palgrave, 2000.

Pawuk, Michael. *Graphic Novels: A Genre Guide to Comic Books, Manga, and More.* Westport, CT: Libraries Unlimited, 2007.

Reid, Calvin. "Manga Sells Anime—and Vice Versa." *Publishers Weekly* 251, no. 42 (October 18, 2004): 30–33.

Schodt, Frederik L. *Dreamland Japan: Writings on Modern Manga.* Berkeley: Stone Bridge Press, 1996.

Schodt, Frederik L. *Manga! Manga! The World of Japanese Comics.* Tokyo: Kodansha International, 1983.

Shreve, Jennifer. "Behind the Pink Door." *Wired* 14, no. 10 (2006). http://www.wired.com/wired/archive/14.10/play.html?pg=8 (accessed December 31, 2006).

Thompson, Jason. *Manga: The Complete Guide.* New York: Del Rey, 2007.

3

GIRLS, WOMEN, AND COMICS

Trina Robbins

WHAT? GIRLS READ COMICS?

For more than 30 years and until very recently, mainstream comics editors and publishers have suffered from collective amnesia, assuming and even insisting that girls and women never read or drew comics.[1] True, during that period, girls were not reading comics because there were no comics they liked. And women were not drawing comics either because women are not fond of drawing overly muscular guys with big chins, punching each other out. Comic books from the late 1960s through the 1990s were mostly superhero adventures aimed at young males. A 1994 study from DC Comics showed over 90 percent male readership and only around 6 percent females.[2] But there was a time when more girls than boys read comics because there were many more comics for girls.

WOMEN AND COMICS: A LONG TRADITION

Before there were comic books, Americans read their comics in newspapers, and a good many of those newspaper strips were read by and drawn by women. It was not considered unusual in the early 20th century for women to draw comics. As early as 1903, the amazingly prolific Grace Drayton was doing such popular strips as *Toodles, Dolly Drake and Bobby Blake, Dolly Dimples and Bobby Bounce, Dolly Dingle,* and *Dottie Darling.* All featured the misadventures of adorable chubby toddlers who bore an uncanny resemblance to the Campbell Kids—no coincidence, given that Drayton herself designed the Campbell Kids in 1906.

In 1909, Rose O'Neill's Kewpies debuted to the American public in the *Ladies Home Journal* and other women's magazines. Her Kewpie stories took the form of verse with illustrations—many early comics had no panels or speech balloons. Several decades later, O'Neill-drawn Kewpies were appearing in syndicated newspapers in traditional comics form.

Flappers and Independent Women

Other early women's comics featured older characters. In 1907, Nell Brinkley signed with the Hearst syndicate and produced a daily drawing with commentary for newspapers nationwide. By the 1920s, she was also drawing comics for Sunday paper color sections across the country (see Robbins 2009). The beautiful flappers she drew were called "The Brinkley Girls" and were so popular that at least three popular songs were written about Nell and her characters. Fans could even buy Nell Brinkley hair curlers for 10 cents a card. Brinkley's biggest fans were girls, who pasted her strips and cartoons into scrapbooks.

By the 1920s, comics about bright, young emancipated flappers had captured the public's hearts, and women following in Brinkley's footsteps included Ethel Hays, Virginia Huget, Gladys Parker, Sylvia Sneidman, Virginia Kraussman, Dorothy Urfer, and Dot Cochran. But when America entered the war in 1941, the country's women became women of courage and daring. They took over jobs vacated by men who had entered the military, following the wartime motto, "We can do it!" So women drove trucks and buses and made planes and flew them—and increasingly, they drew comics. During the 1940s, more women than ever before were drawing comics and now were drawing strong, courageous women heroes.

Dale Messick's *Brenda Starr, Reporter* first appeared in 1940. Born Dalia, Messick felt she had to adopt a sexually ambiguous name to sell her strip. Her heroine was a young woman reporter who proved that she was as good as the male reporters at her newspaper, *The Flash*. The stories combined fashion, romance, and action. Women loved them. From the same period came *Torchy Brown,* drawn by the pioneering African American woman cartoonist Jackie Ormes.

In 1941, woman cartoonist Tarpe Mills created *Miss Fury,* who disguised herself in a panther skin to become the first costumed action heroine. Like *Brenda Starr,* this strip about a beautiful woman who fought Nazis combined action and romance. *Miss Fury* lasted until 1950. Shortly after Miss Fury first donned her panther skin, pop psychologist William Moulton Marston proved that men could be as good as women at creating great superheroines. Marston and artist Harry G. Peter created the eternal Amazon Wonder Woman for comics. Wonder Woman was a role model for 1940s girls and even today remains an icon for grown women.

Teen and Romance Comics

In the early 1930s, collections of reprinted newspaper strips began to appear as "comic books." By wartime, these now-familiar pamphlets were at their peak of popularity, read by everyone from kids to GIs. A 1946 chart from *Newsdealer* magazine showed more girl comics readers than boys in ages 8 to 11 and 18 to 35.[3] These girls were reading the teen comics that had started several years earlier with *Archie* and related titles. The adventures of the redheaded teenager and his girlfriends Betty and Veronica were so popular that other publishers quickly jumped into the market. Soon adolescent girls all over America were devouring comics about vivacious Patsy Walker and Millie the Model and were sending in their own fashion designs for Katy Keene. Meanwhile, their big sisters read romance comics.

The first romance comics began in 1947 and sold over one million copies per issue. A 1948 survey showed comics readers to be made up of 43 percent men and 52 percent women in ages 21 to 30.[4] Undoubtedly, those women were reading romance comics. By 1950, romance titles constituted over a quarter of all comics published, and that year *Newsdealer* reported that girls aged 17 to 25 were reading more comics than boys.[5]

Comic books generally go through cycles of popularity. In the past, Westerns have been popular, and during another time the biggest sellers were crime comics. But teen and romance comics remained consistent sellers for decades, simply because they appealed to girls as well as many boys. Nevertheless, by the late 1960s, the mainstream comics industry had phased out their comics aimed at girls in favor of male-oriented superhero comics, thus losing 52 percent of the potential reading population. Comics-watchers speculate about why romance comics vanished, but vanish they did.[6]

Underground Comix and the Boys' Club

The late 1960s also saw the birth of a new kind of comic. Underground comics, or "comix," sprang up with the hippie movement, giving young aspiring cartoonists the opportunity to draw comics that reflected their emerging counterculture. But like the mainstream superhero books, the world of comix was a boys' club. Not only were women cartoonists almost nonexistent, but additionally, these comix were full of misogyny and anti-woman violence. In response, the few women cartoonists created their own space with women-only comix. The very first all-woman comic ever, *It Ain't Me, Babe,* came out in 1970. By 1972, a core group had met in San Francisco to form the Wimmen's Comix Collective and publish *Wimmen's Comix,* the first—and with 20 years in print, still the longest-lasting—ongoing all-woman anthology comic. *Wimmen's Comix* opened the door to aspiring female creators who finally had a venue for their work, including Melinda Gebbie, Roberta Gregory, Phoebe Gloeckner, and me. Soon more women were drawing comix, tackling subjects that men would not touch: lesbian relationships plus autobiographical stories about menstruation, childbirth, and abortion, all hitherto taboo. These comix were self-published or published by very small presses.

Japan Conquers American Girls

The number of women cartoonists continued to increase, and by the 1990s there were more women drawing comics than ever before. But their comics were *still* self-published or published by small presses. Women's comics were hard to find in comics shops, which carried mostly superhero titles. So, although many male mainstream superhero cartoonists earned good salaries, the women had to keep day jobs and draw comics part-time. This sorry state of affairs continued until the late 1990s, when a trickle of Japanese comics (manga), including the wildly popular *Sailor Moon,* arrived in America. By the beginning of the 21st century, the trickle had become a tsunami. Half of all manga published in the United States were shōjo manga, written and drawn by women. Long starved for appealing comics, American girls ate them up despite the black and white art and the traditional Japanese right-to-left format. The manga trade paperbacks sold like hotcakes in bookstores, and libraries could not keep them on the shelves. The runaway success of shōjo manga in America proved once again that girls do read comics when given comics they like. Ultimately, this format enabled women cartoonists as well as male creators of girl-friendly comics to bypass the dreaded comics shops that catered mainly to young male superhero readers.

SO WHAT DO GIRLS WANT?
COLLECTION DEVELOPMENT

If Sigmund Freud had read comics, he would not have had to ask what women and girls want. Comparing shōjo manga with teen and romance comics from America's Golden Age of comics shows that girls have enjoyed the same themes for decades: light, often funny romances involving high school girls and boys and just plain romances. Of course, girls and women want to see the female point of view on all aspects of life, funny or serious. Add a generous shake of gothic drama, fantasy, or science fiction, pepper it heavily with cute fashions, and there you have it. Here are some suggestions about categories and female-friendly titles for your collection.

Teens

Manga

The shōjo manga stories currently so popular with teen girls echo problems faced by their readers. Just as adolescents experience troubling and uncontrollable hormonal changes often triggered by the opposite sex, in Yukiru Sugisaki's *D.N. Angel,* middle-school Daisuke turns into the famous jewel thief, Dark, when he gets romantic feelings for the girl he likes. In Natsuki Takaya's wildly popular series, *Fruits Basket,* orphaned Tohru is adopted into a family that suffers from a hereditary curse: when they are hugged by the opposite sex, they turn into animals of the Chinese zodiac. A list of the hundreds of available shōjo manga would take up an entire book by itself, but consider some of the following outstanding titles, aimed at ages 13 and up. (Some boys will like these also.)

In Kosuke Fujishima's long-running and popular *Oh My Goddess!* college student Keiichi dials a wrong number and reaches the Goddess Tech help line. As a result, the goddess Belldandy comes to live with him "always." He tries to pass her off as a foreign exchange student but is kicked out of his all-male dorm.

Another popular series is Yuu Watase's *Absolute Boyfriend.* Lonely high schooler Riiko orders a boyfriend "figure" online in a "free trial" promotion and discovers that she got more than she bargained for. Because there is some humorous talk about sex and discreetly presented sex toward the end, the series is rated for older teens.

Princess Ai, with pop singer Courtney Love listed as coauthor with Misaho Kujiradou, tells of an other-world princess who winds up in modern-day Tokyo. The story is beautifully drawn and includes some great fashions.

Socrates in Love comes with my highest recommendation! Adapted by Kazumi Kazui from Kyoichi Katayama's best-selling Japanese novel, it is rather like a Japanese version of Eric Segal's *Love Story.* Keep a box of tissues handy when you read it—it is sad but very beautiful.

Girls who love sports will like Mitsuba Takanashi's *Crimson Hero.* Nobara's family wants her to be a traditional old-fashioned girl, but she is a shorthaired tomboy who lives for volleyball.

Keiko Suenobu's *Life* is about teenage self-mutilation: high school freshman Ayumi reacts to stress and depression by cutting herself. The story is aimed at older teens, but the important message is not too strong for girls under 16.

Manga from American Creators

Some U.S. manga publishers are now publishing manga-style graphic novels by Americans. All of the following graphic novels are rated for ages 13 and up and are read in the Western tradition, from left to right.

Nicole Hayes, the heroine of Amy Kim Ganter's *Sorcerers & Secretaries,* lives in two worlds: the real world, where she holds an after-school job as a receptionist, and her own fairy-tale fantasy world, which she chronicles in her private book. But when her fantasies intrude on her real world, which world is truly real?

Manga fans who attend conventions will enjoy Svetlana Chmakova's *Dramacon,* the lively tale of a teenage girl's first anime "con."

Penny, the heroine of Amy Reeder Hadley's *Fool's Gold,* is a young costume designer who makes her own cute clothing and sells some of her designs in a local boutique. When she sees her best friend made miserable by a two-faced boyfriend, she forms a club with her friends to expose those boys who seem to be good as gold but are really phonies, or "fool's gold." This is one of the best girls' graphic novels out there—it reads like a young adult novel, and the art is clear and attractive. Hollywood, are you paying attention?

Bettina Kurkoski's *My Cat Loki,* about a young man who adopts a shivering, rain-drenched stray cat, is another outstanding story. The art is attractive and accessible, the cat is adorable, and the ending is very moving. Animal lovers will enjoy reading about how a frightened creature learns love and trust.

Non-Manga Graphic Novels

Not all good graphic novels for girls are done manga-style. Jeremy and Robert Love's *Shadow Rock,* a combination ghost story and mystery, is printed in full color and a larger size and should appeal to both boys and girls.

Jane Fisher self-publishes *WJHC,* an attractively produced full-color graphic novel that revolves around a high school radio station and the kids involved with it. The art is cute, and the stories are satisfying and an easy read.

Artists and aspiring artists of all ages will love Nicholas Debon's *Four Pictures by Emily Carr.* Carr was a Canadian painter who has been compared with Georgia O'Keefe and Frida Kahlo. This enchanting, low-key graphic novel is fully painted in a style reminiscent of the *Tintin* books.

Older teens will laugh themselves silly over Lauren Weinstein's *Girl Stories,* more than 200 color pages of the artist's middle school and high school memories and mishaps. For younger readers, a charming series is Jimmy Gownley's *Amelia Rules,* relating the adventures of nine-year-old Amelia McBride and her friends. The three full-color *Amelia* hardcovers are in turn funny and touching. Younger readers will also love Jennifer and Matthew Holm's *Babymouse* graphic novels printed in black, white, and pink, with pink and silver covers. In the first title in the series, Babymouse is a sassy young mouse who dreams of being queen of the world but would settle for an invitation to Felicia Furrypaws's slumber party.

An enchanting read for young and old is Linda Medley's originally self-published *Castle Waiting* series, collected by Fantagraphics into a 456-page graphic novel. These are Medley's whimsical takes on the Grimm brothers' fairy tales. Beautifully drawn in a style reminiscent of classic fairy-tale artist Arthur Rackham, Medley's stories start where the Grimms leave off.

Adaptations: Television Shows, Books, Etc.

Some publishers have started adapting well-known books and television shows into graphic novel form with mixed success. *Buffy* fans who miss their favorite television series will be happy to discover that they can find full-color adaptations from Dark Horse Comics, featuring new *Buffy the Vampire Slayer* adventures created by Joss Whedon and various others.

Unfortunately, not all adaptations rate my recommendation. Dark Horse also publishes manga versions of Harlequin romances in two different editions: Harlequin Pink is for all ages, and Harlequin Violet is rated for ages

16 and up. The books are written by Americans and drawn by Japanese artists. But considering four titles—*A Girl in a Million, A Prince Needs a Princess, Never Kiss a Stranger,* and *Jinxed* (all pink)—the adaptations seem insipid, and the art is listless and lacking the sparkle of most shōjo manga.

Fan of the *Nancy Drew* books might expect high quality from the Papercutz graphic novel adaptations, but the coloring is dark and murky. And remember Bess, Nancy's chubby girlfriend? Thousands of overweight girls identified with Bess. But in the adaptations, she has become a babe dressed in hot pants and a halter top!

Emily the Strange was originally a glum, gothic little girl created to sell T-shirts, now packaged into comics by Dark Horse. But *Emily* is basically just commercially mass-produced rebellion, not my idea of recommended fare for kids who want to be different. Certainly the character's negativity is not funny or clever. So much better that kids emulate creative girls like Penny from *Fool's Gold* or the girls in *Amelia Rules* or *The Baby Sitters Club. The Baby-Sitters Club,* published by Scholastic's new Graphix line, is a much more fortunate adaptation than the titles previously mentioned. Amy Martin and Raina Telgemeier do a top-notch job adapting and drawing the popular series. It is a fast, enjoyable read with cute, clean art. Girls of all ages will love it.

Also part of the Graphix line but not an adaptation is Chynna Clugston's *Queen Bee.* This nicely drawn manga-style graphic novel is the tale of a girl nerd trying to belong to the high school in-crowd but with a difference: nerd-girl just happens to have psychokinesis.

Superheroes for Girls

Superhero fans are a minority among girl readers, but for that minority, Marvel Comics has targeted some stories now collected into graphic novel format. Two titles stand out as the best of the bunch. *Ororo: Before the Storm* is Marc Sumerak and Carlo Barberi's nicely told-and-drawn tale of the young Ororo before she became the *X-Men* superheroine Storm. Even better is Sean McKeever and Takeshi Miyazawa's *Spider-Man Loves Mary Jane.* This charmingly drawn and easy-to-read high school romance stars Spider-Man's alter ego, Peter Parker, and Mary Jane Watson. Mary Jane likes Peter but thinks *he* likes Gwen Stacy. Peter does like Mary Jane but thinks she does not like *him.* This is the closest of all the Marvel titles to shōjo.

A different kind of superhero comic is my own *Go Girl!* co-created with Anne Timmons. Back in her younger days, Lindsay Goldman's mother was a teenaged superheroine named Go-Go Girl. But she has retired, and Lindsay—who inherited her mom's ability to fly—now wears her mom's go-go costume and fights bad guys. Sometimes her mom teams up with her. The positive stories stress friendship and cooperation and downplay violence in favor of humor.

Older Teens and Adults

Libraries need not neglect mature readers—there are plenty of graphic novels out there for older teen girls and adult women. Some titles with good messages for older teens include Katherine Arnoldi's *The Amazing "True" Story of a Teenage Single Mom;* Catherine Doherty's *Can of Worms,* an adopted girl's story about seeking and finding her birth mother; and Bryan Talbot's *The Tale of One Bad Rat,* which deals with childhood sexual abuse.

Syndicated Strips, Collected

Women cartoonists are still comparatively underrepresented in syndicated newspaper strips, but they have come a long way since the 1980s when the only two women who could be found on the newspaper comics page were Cathy Guisewite (*Cathy*) and Lynn Johnston (*For Better or For Worse*). Rina Piccolo's strip, *Tina's Groove,* runs in over one hundred newspapers and has now been collected into graphic novels. The stories about café waitress Tina and her friends are clever and amusing, and the art is cute. How can you go wrong? For a taste of something different, Hawaii expat Deb Aoki, now living in Southern California, has collected her *Honolulu Advertiser* strips into a book titled *Bento Box.* Readers who have spent time in the Aloha State will especially enjoy this collection.

Manga

Manga for older teens and adult women are far more common in Japan than in the United States. Some translated titles suitable for the adult collection include *Paradise Kiss* and *Nana,* modern fashion-conscious romances from Ai Yazawa; delicately drawn relationship dramas from Erika Sakurazawa such as *The Aromatic Bitters* and *Angel;* sweeping romantic comedy *Maison Ikkoku* from Rumiko Takahashi; You Higuri's gorgeous Renaissance soap opera *Cantarella;* Kenichi Sonoda's *Gunsmith Cats,* a fast-paced shoot-'em-up about two women private investigators versus the Chicago drug mafia; and for the sweet-toothed, Fumi Yoshinaga's *Antique Bakery,* about the romances, gay and straight, of an endearingly goofy quartet of beautiful men who run a pastry shop.

Yaoi and Yuri

Yaoi is a more recent import from Japan, a genre also sometimes called *shōnen-ai,* or "boys love." Yaoi manga are homoerotic stories of young, pretty boys in love but are considered a subset of romance comics and aimed at female readers. Yaoi has its own active fandom, which attends conventions, or yaoicons. Although genitals or graphic sex are rarely shown, the books are still usually rated for older teens or for a mature audience because of the subject matter. Although the stories vary, yaoi manga tend to have certain elements in common. The stories often involve two teenage boys or young men, one tall, dark, long-eyed, brooding, and more dominant, the other smaller, blonde, rounder-eyed, more feminine, and less assertive.

Kazusa Takashima's *Wild Rock,* rated "mature," is a kind of prehistoric *Brokeback Mountain* mixed with a little *Romeo and Juliet.* Emba and Yuen, sons of the chiefs of two rival tribes, meet and fall in love. It is a fast, easy read with lovely art.

You Higuri's *Gorgeous Carat,* for older teens, takes place in *fin de siècle* Paris, where the impoverished noble Rochefort family is deeply in debt and in danger of losing their mansion. The mysterious Count Courland comes to the aid of Madame Rocheford, demanding in return that her pretty teenage son, Florian, be entrusted to his care. Florian arrogantly resists his legal captor, who is still a teenager himself. There is a pretty racy scene in which the Count has Florian chained and whipped in an attempt to break his spirit. The book is a traditional bodice-ripper, with boys' love and a little mild bondage and S&M thrown in.

The Japanese female equivalent of yaoi is *yuri,* girl-on-girl romantic manga. Some manga with yuri relationships include Akahori and Katsura's *Kashimashi,* Chiho Saito's *Revolutionary Girl Utena,* and Riyoko Ikeda's *Rose of Versailles* (untranslated, but available in French). Seven Seas Entertainment has announced a new imprint, Strawberry, to focus on these kinds of romances, such as the crushes and heartbreaks at a girls' boarding school. As with yaoi, these stories are aimed at female readers broadly. (For yaoi and yuri, see also Appendix B-3.)

Non-Manga Graphic Novels

In *Sexy Chix,* Diana Schutz's anthology of comics by 22 women, it is the comics creators who are the "sexy chix"—because creativity is sexy. *Naughty Bits,* the popular series by indie cartoonist Roberta Gregory about world-class kvetcher Bitchy Bitch, is now collected into one thick hilarious book, *Life's a Bitch.* But many graphic novels aimed at mature readers go beyond mere entertainment with smart stories that can be alarming, instructive, or sad. Jessica Abel's *La Perdida* tells the story of Carla, a young half-Mexican woman brought up in the United States who goes to Mexico looking for her roots and finds more than she bargained for.

Every woman will relate to *Cancer Vixen,* in which Marisa Acocella Marchetto deals with her cancer year, a frightening subject, with grace and humor. And if you do not already have *Persepolis* on your shelves, Marjane Satrapi's best-selling graphic novel about growing up in Iran, run out and get it. This great book is for ages 18 to 80.

Alison Bechdel, the best-known lesbian cartoonist, draws *Dykes to Watch Out For,* a series that appeals to many people regardless of their sexual orientation. (Yes, there are a goodly number of lesbian artists producing comics today.) Her new stand-alone graphic novel, *Fun Home,* is a movingly humorous and intensely literary memoir of growing up with a closeted gay father who died at age 44, possibly by suicide. *Fun Home* made "best of 2006" lists from *Time* magazine and the *Village Voice* and has been widely praised.

Diane DiMassa is the polar opposite of Bechdel. The art and writing in her collected *Complete Hothead Paisan: Homicidal Lesbian Terrorist* is wildly expressionistic, whereas Bechdel's is controlled; and whereas Bechdel's humor is low-key, DiMassa is violently gut-funny. But coincidentally, her latest book, *Jokes and the Unconscious,* written by performance-poet Daphne Gottlieb, is also about a father's death.

Paige Braddock's art and storytelling are closer to the style of Bechdel. Braddock publishes her comic, *Jane's World,* on the Internet before collecting it into graphic novels. For a good overview of at least seven other contemporary lesbian cartoonists (as well as seven very good gay male cartoonists), see Jennifer Camper's anthology *Juicy Mother.* All the graphic novels mentioned in this preceding discussion should appeal to intelligent straight women as well as lesbians.

ASSESSING INTEREST AND KEEPING UP: WHAT'S HOT?

How can you stay afloat in the tidal wave of graphic novels for girls and women? How do you know which titles are popular, and how do you avoid wasting your precious budget on a loser that will molder on the shelf?

The Local Comics Shop

If your local comic book store is girl-friendly (not all of them are), now is the time to stop in and introduce yourself. The owner or manager can tell you which are the best-selling titles for girls and women in your area. You can reciprocate by inviting staff from the store to participate in library programs about comics (see more on this in the next section of this chapter).

Comics-Savvy Patrons

Your patrons are another major source of information about what is new and popular. You can form a "consulting panel" of regular female patrons who are active comics readers. "Convene" them via e-email or brief events with refreshments. Ask them for recommendations and for brief reviews. Then post the reviews in the library and on the library's Web site. In addition, it is easy to build a feedback mechanism such as a mini-questionnaire into any patron program involving graphic novels.

Other Librarians

A terrific source of information from librarians is the GNLIB e-mail list (see http://groups.yahoo.com/group/GNLIB-L). You may feel free to ask for recommendations and opinions, in general or about specific titles, from this highly knowledgeable Web community of comics-savvy librarians and comics industry professionals.

Web Sources

On the Web, two good resources include Friends of Lulu (FoL) and Sequential Tart. Founded in 1994, Friends of Lulu (http://www.friends-lulu.org) encourages participation in comics by women, both as readers and as creators. Every year FoL gives out Lulu awards to outstanding women and men who produce work that reflects the group's aims. There are also a printed quarterly newsletter and an online review board that reviews the latest comics and graphic novels. *Sequential Tart* (http://www.sequentialtart.com) is a Webzine about the comics industry, focusing on women-oriented issues. It features exclusive interviews, in-depth articles, up-to-the-minute news and information, and reviews of the latest women-oriented comics.

For younger ages, Kids Love Comics (http://www.kidslovecomics.com) provides an excellent list of recommended comics that are free of violent or sexist images and usually girl-friendly. A more general site that can be mined for award-winning women comics creators is the Comic Book Awards Almanac (http://www.hahnlibrary.net/comics/awards/index.html). An array of U.S. and international comics awards are listed, with drill-down information on winners for years back.

Comics Publishers, Magazines, Etc.

All major graphic novel publishers have Web sites to inform you of their newest books—you can easily Google them—but of course they will tell you *all* their books are great. However, some sites contain links to useful reviews. In general, Googling a title and/or author (rather than the publisher) will often turn up some review or commentary or blog that will give you a better idea about the quality and content. The Internet community includes an enormous number of comics-based sites, not all intelligently critical but most enthusiastic and reasonably articulate.

Most comics magazines have a largely male focus. However, VIZ Media's *Shojo Beat* is written for young women. If your library subscribes, you may find it somewhat useful in its coverage of shōjo manga and girl-friendly J-pop. But keep in mind that it promotes VIZ titles only.[7]

Retrospectively . . .

Finally, my own book, *From Girls to Grrrlz,* is an illustrated history of comics for girls and women from the 1940s to the end of the 20th century. Because it dates from 1999, it leaves out manga, but it is the best place to learn all about the first 50 years of girls' comics.

YOUR COMMUNITY: HOW TO GET GIRLS INTO YOUR LIBRARY

Once comics-reading girls and shōjo fans learn that they can find their favorite graphic novels in the library, they will come. But how do you reach them? Here are some ideas for programs and publicity.

Comics Festival

If you have the space, hold a comics festival. I attended a comics festival given by the main branch of the Los Angeles Public Library, in their beautiful courtyard under blue skies and a warm sun. But if you have no courtyard and bad weather, a large indoor room will do fine. Invite staff from the local comics store, any local comic artists, and—if you are lucky enough to have one near your city—a comics publisher. If you have no comics shop nearby, see if a local chain bookstore has a staff member who specializes in manga and graphic novels. Encourage aspiring comic artists, especially girls, to bring samples of their work to show the publisher and display for attendees. Provide tables for everyone to sit and sell their wares. Feature at least one panel in which guests discuss comics, with at least one woman speaker. Then publicize the festival with flyers distributed not just at your library but also at the local comics shop and high school. With sufficient lead time, a local paper will probably be happy to promote it also.

Cosplay

For manga fans, hold a cosplay contest. This means inviting girls and boys to dress up as their favorite manga and anime characters. Invite the owner of the local comic book store—or editor from the local comics publisher or a famous local cartoonist, if you are lucky enough to have one in your city—to judge the contest. Have any extra manga? Give them away as prizes, and let the contestants know that they can find more of the same on the library shelves.

Other Program and Promotion Ideas

Nearly any program or outreach project can be adapted to encouraging girls and women to find great graphic novels at your library. In book displays, add female-friendly comics titles. For book talks, investigate bringing in a woman comics creator—sometimes publishers will fund travel. Hold a workshop on how to draw comics (find a local comics creator or art instructor to teach it), and display students' work—especially from girls. Search out commercial or noncommercial comics from women (and men) produced locally, add them to the catalog and collection, and display them.

If a local artist is interested, ask her to create single panels or strips about the library and post them in the building and on the library's Web site. Write mini-reviews of girl-friendly titles or obtain reviews from librarians and/or patrons (see earlier discussion) and post them in the library. Consider adding them to the online catalog or separately on the Web site. Hold parent education workshops such as "Comics and Your Kids: Good Reading!" and showcase girl-friendly titles for both genders.

GIRLS, WOMEN, AND COMICS: REPRISE

What is in store for the future? Graphic novels are obviously here to stay, and American mainstream publishers now know that girls and women will read them, thanks to manga.[8] DC Comics of *Batman* and *Superman* fame is publishing a new Minx line of graphic novels written and drawn by both male and female creators, but aimed at girl readers. So far, with only one exception—the dark and confusing futuristic Internet fantasy *Kimmie66*—the books are clear, readable, and enjoyable. However, the Minx line does not label their books for age, and librarians are advised to read the books before shelving them. Although most of them can be read by any age group, *Burn-out,* a sensitively written story that combines teen angst with eco-terrorism, contains some hot and heavy make-out scenes. And *Water Baby,* an amazing graphic novel about a surfer girl who loses her leg to a shark, contains rough language, girls in very brief underwear and bikinis, make-out scenes, lesbianism, and even scenes of urination! I loved it and immediately started casting the possible movie in my head, but I can imagine the outcry of some parents if their very young daughters got hold of the book.[9]

Women comics creators have definitely come into their own. In 2006, *Time* magazine put Alison Bechdel's *Fun Home* in first place on their list of the 10 best books of the year. Successful books like Bechdel's and like *La Perdida* and *Persepolis* are proving that women comics creators no longer need take a back seat to anything done by men. Putting comics that girls and women want into your library is an opportunity all around for matching better and more appealing collections with an expanding and increasingly enthusiastic readership.

NOTES

1. "I must admit to being utterly fascinated by Western comics publishers' inability to learn from the lessons offered by manga's current success. . . . 'Girls don't read comics, there's something in how their brains are wired that just doesn't respond to the way comics work.' I've actually heard people use that argument, believe it or not." Dirk Deppey, "Dallas Middaugh" (interview), *The Comics Journal* 277 (July 2006): 252.

2. DC Comics, Superman-Batman Group, *DC Comics Survey: Sex of Respondent* (New York: DC Comics, 1994), based on DC Comics Survey conducted by Mark Clements Research, 1994.

3. Untitled bar graph, *Newsdealer* (April 1946): page unknown.

4. Edward L. Feder, *Bureau of Public Administration, Comic Book Regulation* (Berkeley: University of California, 1955), 2. This document cited an earlier study: *Report on Comic Books* (New Orleans, LA: New Orleans, Public Relations Section, October 18, 1948), 5.

5. "Comics Sales Climb," *Newsdealer* (July 1950): 8.

6. John Lustig speculates that the romance market dropped off because the Comics Code restrictions installed in the mid-1950s made it difficult for writers to expand into franker treatment of sex and social issues or even depictions of realistic relationships. But other 1960s media exploded with much more sexual and socially relevant content aimed at women, including afternoon soap operas and Harlequin "bodice-ripper" novels. At the same time, television became more popular in general. So one factor may have been that romance comics simply could not attract readers in comparison with similar material in other media. See John Lustig, "The Terrible, Tragic (>Sob!<) Death of Romance (Comics!!)," *Back Issue* 1, no. 13 (December 2005): 16–23.

7. Unfortunately, VIZ Media announced in May 2009 that *Shojo Beat* will cease after the July 2009 issue.

8. Volume 15 of the shōjo manga *Fruits Basket* sold an astonishing 12,000 copies in the United States during one week in December 2006. See "'Fruits Basket' Tops Holiday Bookstore Sales," December 27, 2006, http://www.ICv2.com (accessed January 7, 2007).

9. Unfortunately, DC Comics announced in September 2008 that the Minx line is being shut down as of January 2009. (See Calvin Reid, "DC Folds Minx; Virgin Becomes Liquid Comics," *Publishers Weekly,* September 25, 2008, www.publishersweekly.com/article/CA6599653.html?rssid=192.)

BIBLIOGRAPHY

These titles barely scratch the surface. Some below are out of print but are worth buying used on Amazon.com or via other sources of used or out-of-print titles.

Able, Jessica. *La Perdida.* New York: Pantheon, 2006.

Akahori, Satoru, and Yukimaru Katsura. *Kashimashi.* Los Angeles: Seven Seas Entertainment, 2006–.

Alexovich, Aaron. *Kimmie66.* New York: Minx Books/DC Comics, 2007.

Aoki, Deb. *Bento Box.* North Hollywood, CA: Bento Box Press, 2006.

Arnoldi, Katherine. *The Amazing "True" Story of a Teenage Single Mom.* New York: Hyperion, 1998.

Bechdel, Alison. *Dykes to Watch Out For.* Vols. 1–9. Ann Arbor, MI: Firebrand, 1986–2000; Vols. 10–. New York: Alyson, 2003–.

Bechdel, Alison. *Fun Home.* New York: Houghton Mifflin, 2006.

Braddock, Paige. *Jane's World.* Sebastopol, CA Girl Twirl Comics, 2006–.

Campbell, Ross. *Water Baby.* New York: Minx Books/DC Comics, 2008.

Camper, Jennifer, ed. *Juicy Mother: Celebration.* Brooklyn, NY: Soft Skull Press, 2005.

Chmakova, Svetlana. *Dramacon.* 3 vols. Los Angeles: TOKYOPOP, 2005–2007.

Clugston, Chynna. *Queen Bee.* New York: Graphix/Scholastic, 2005–.

Debon, Nicholas. *Four Pictures by Emily Carr.* Toronto, ON: Groundwood Books, 2003.

DiMassa, Diane. *The Complete Hothead Paisan: Homicidal Lesbian Terrorist.* San Francisco: Cleis Press, 1999.

Doherty, Catherine. *Can of Worms.* Seattle, WA: Fantagraphics, 2000.

Donner, Rebecca. *Burnout.* New York: Minx Books/DC Comics, 2008.

Fisher, Jane Smith. *WJHC: Hold Tight.* Oceanside, NY: Wilson Place Comics, 2003–.

Fujishima, Kosuke. *Oh My Goddess!* 2nd ed. Milwaukie, OR: Dark Horse, 2005–.

Ganter, Amy Kim. *Sorcerers & Secretaries.* 2 vols. Los Angeles: TOKYOPOP, 2006–2007.

Goldstein, Nancy. *Jackie Ormes: The First African American Woman Cartoonist.* Ann Arbor: University of Michigan Press, 2008.

Gottlieb, Daphne, and Diane DiMassa. *Jokes and the Unconscious.* San Francisco: Cleis Press, 2006.

Gownley, Jimmy. *Amelia Rules!* 3 vols. Harrisburg, PA: Renaissance Press, 2006.

Gregory, Roberta. *Life's a Bitch: The Bitchy Bitch Chronicles.* Seattle: Fantagraphics, 2005.

Hadley, Amy Reeder. *Fool's Gold.* Los Angeles: TOKYOPOP, 2006–.

Higuri, You. *Cantarella.* Agoura Hills, CA: Go! Comi, 2005–.

Higuri, You. *Gorgeous Carat.* Los Angeles: Blu, 2006–.

Holm, Jennifer, and Matthew Holm. *Babymouse.* New York: Random House, 2005–.

Ikeda, Riyoko. *La Rose de Versailles.* 3 vols. Brussels: Dargaux Benelux, 2002–2005.

Katayama, Kyoichi, and Kazumi Kazui. *Socrates in Love.* San Francisco: VIZ Media, 2005.

Kujiradou, Misaho, Courney Love, and D. J. Milky. *Princess Ai.* 3 vols. Los Angeles: TOKYOPOP, 2004–2006.

Kurkoski, Bettina. *My Cat Loki.* Los Angeles: TOKYOPOP, 2006–.

Love, Jeremy, and Robert Love. *Shadow Rock.* Milwaukie, OR: Dark Horse, 2005.

Marchetto, Marisa Acocella. *Cancer Vixen.* New York: Knopf, 2006.

Martin, Amy M., and Raina Telgemeier. *The Baby-Sitters Club.* 2 vols. New York: Scholastic, 2006.

McKeever, Sean, and Takeshi Miyazawa. *Spider-Man Loves Mary Jane.* New York: Marvel, 2006.

Medley, Linda. *Castle Waiting.* Seattle, WA: Fantagraphics, 2006.

Piccolo, Rina. *Tina's Groove.* Kansas City, MO: Andrews McMeel, 2006.

Robbins, Trina. *The Brinkley Girls.* Seattle: Fantagraphics, 2009.

Robbins, Trina. *From Girls to Grrrlz.* San Francisco: Chronicle Books, 1999.

Robbins, Trina, and Anne Timmons. *Go Girl!* Milwaukie, OR: Dark Horse, 2002–.

Saito, Chiho. *Revolutionary Girl Utena.* 5 vols. San Francisco: VIZ Media, 2003–2004.

Sakurazawa, Erica. *Angel.* Los Angeles: TOKYOPOP, 2003.

Sakurazawa, Erica. *The Aromatic Bitters.* Los Angeles: TOKYOPOP, 2004.

Satrapi, Marjane. *The Complete Persepolis.* New York: Pantheon, 2007.

Schutz, Diana, ed. *Sexy Chix: Anthology of Women Cartoonists.* Milwaukie, OR: Dark Horse, 2005.

Sonoda, Kenichi. *Gunsmith Cats.* 9 vols. Milwaukie, OR: Dark Horse, 1996–2002. (Currently being reissued.)

Suenobu, Keiko. *Life.* Los Angeles: TOKYOPOP, 2006–.

Sugisaki, Yukiru. *D. N. Angel.* 10 vols. Los Angeles: TOKYOPOP, 2004–2005.

Sumerak, Marc, and Carlo Barberi. *Ororo: Before the Storm.* New York: Marvel, 2006.

Takahashi, Rumiko. *Maison Ikkoku.* 2nd ed. 14 vols. San Francisco: VIZ Media, 2003–2005.

Takanashi, Mitsuba. *Crimson Hero.* San Francisco: VIZ Media, 2005–.

Takashima, Kazusa. *Wild Rock.* Los Angeles: Blu, 2006.

Takaya, Natsuki. *Fruits Basket.* Los Angeles: TOKYOPOP, 2004–.

Talbot, Bryan. *The Tale of One Bad Rat.* Milwaukie, OR: Dark Horse, 1995.

Watase, Yuu. *Absolute Boyfriend.* San Francisco: VIZ Media, 2006–.

Weinstein, Lauren R. *Girl Stories.* New York: Henry Holt, 2006.

Whedon, Joss, creator. *Buffy the Vampire Slayer.* Milwaukie, OR: Dark Horse, 1998–. (Written and illustrated by various.)

Yazawa, Ai. *Nana.* San Francisco: VIZ Media, 2005–.

Yazawa, Ai. *Paradise Kiss.* 5 vols. Los Angeles: TOKYOPOP, 2002–2004.

Yoshinaga, Fumi. *Antique Bakery.* 4 vols. Gardena, CA: Digital Manga, 2005–2006.

4

AMERICAN COMICS: BEYOND THE SUPERHERO, PART ONE, GENRE FICTION

Michael R. Lavin

U.S. comics sales today are dominated by two categories: superhero titles and manga. According to monthly sales lists from *Publishers Weekly* and Diamond Comic Distributors, the best-selling graphic novels in bookstores and specialty comics stores alike remain almost exclusively superhero and manga titles. This chapter and the one following introduce the rest of the graphic novel landscape. When commentators today stress that comics are "not just for kids" anymore (not that they ever were just for kids), they are usually referring to some of the outstanding graphic novels beyond superheroes and manga—those that win prestigious literary awards outside the comics industry and speak to serious and timeless issues with unique art styles. Today, this broader vista of the comics landscape is attracting more and more aficionados to the medium, as well as more new creators.

This chapter looks at graphic novels in areas of traditional genre fiction, including such popular categories as science fiction, fantasy, and horror. The following chapter examines non-genre fiction as well as nonfiction comics. Both chapters focus on books from American publishers and created by American writers and artists, although some Canadian works are tossed for good measure. Foreign works translated into English, such as *Persepolis* or *The Rabbi's Cat,* are excluded (see chapter 6). Works by British writers and artists are excluded except for those issued first by American publishers for American readers. For the most part, the term "comics" includes both comic books and graphic novels. For both chapters, all titles cited are published in graphic novel format for some or all of the stories, and suggested age levels are provided.

INTRODUCING THE BROADER VISTA

Styles and Formats

Readers familiar with superhero comics usually know what to expect when it comes to storytelling conventions, artistic styles, and publishing formats, especially with titles from DC Comics and Marvel Comics. Graphic novels outside the superhero arena are much more likely to embody different styles and formats, so it makes sense to comment briefly about some of them.

The most striking difference relates to color. Full-color printing (actually, four-color printing, which uses mixtures of cyan, magenta, and yellow, together with black) is more expensive than black-and-white. As a result, graphic novels from smaller publishers, and those from larger publishers with smaller expected print runs, are not printed this way. We can expect to see superhero comics in full color, but not so with other graphic novel genres. Some of the titles described in this and the next chapter are indeed in color: *Conan, Fables, Amelia Rules,* and *Sandman,* among many. Most, however, are printed in black-and-white or some other monochromatic process such as with gray or sepia tones.

A second difference involves size. Most graphic novels featuring superheroes match the physical dimensions of a traditional comic book, typically 7″ x 10.5″. Non-superhero graphic novels employ these dimensions, but they are just as likely to appear in a range of other sizes, from digest to oversize to oblong.

Another difference deals with page layout. The traditional U.S. comic book layout involves multiple panels on a single page, averaging six panels per page. Although this is less true in superhero comics now, it remains the norm. Non-superhero graphic novels are much more likely to depart from the traditional page layout. Some may feature a single illustration on each page. Others may have nine or more smaller panels per page. In still another departure from traditional comic-book conventions, many do not utilize speech balloons for character dialogue. Instead, they may employ free-floating text within the panel or captions outside of the panel. In some cases, graphic novels have diverged from comic book conventions so far as to resemble a children's picture book. Examples include Gareth Hinds's *Beowulf* (Candlewick Press, 2007) and Jill Thompson's *Scary Godmother* (Sirius Entertainment, 1997).

Also, a number of graphic novels combine comics-style storytelling with standard prose. One of the first to do this was Mark Oakley, in his self-published ongoing fantasy series *Thieves and Kings* (I Box Publishing). An especially interesting project of this type is the fantasy series *Abadazad* from writer J. M. DeMatteis and artist Mike Ploog, which began as a highly acclaimed comic book from CrossGen Comics. But after the publisher declared bankruptcy, the Walt Disney Company acquired the rights and is publishing the series as graphic novels. *Abadazad* follows modern-day teenager Kate, who travels to a magical but dangerous realm in search of her missing younger brother Matty. To Kate's astonishment, this secret land completely replicates a beloved series of children's books she read as a young girl. The

Disney books, published by subsidiary Hyperion, provide a combination of illustrated prose together with pages of standard comics panels, all displaying Ploog's dazzling artwork. Two books have been published to date. Other creators combining prose and graphic novel formats include Ted Rall for journalism and Phoebe Gloeckner for autobiography.

One final comment relates to artistic style. Again, readers of superhero comics have a pretty clear notion of what the artwork in their favorite titles will look like. Of course every artist has an individual style, but the drawings in superhero comics always look heroic and larger than life. Artists in other graphic novel genres are much more likely to utilize distinctly different styles, whether cartoon-like, photo-realistic, childlike, folk art, or even intentionally ugly. They may also employ different media beyond traditional pen and ink or ink and brush, such as markers, gouache, watercolor, ink wash, and even collage or multimedia.

Publishers

Dozens of firms specialize in publishing graphic novels outside the areas of superheroes and manga, but most of these titles come from traditional comic book publishers. The two leading American publishers, Marvel and DC, issue a variety of non-superhero titles in book form each year, especially DC with its Vertigo as well as other imprints. Vertigo comics focus on stories for more mature readers, including such well-known series as *Sandman, Preacher, Transmetropolitan, Hellblazer, Fables,* and *Swamp Thing.*

Many mainstream book publishers release graphic novels also, but few offer an extensive list. Two houses with growing lists are Pantheon and Hill & Wang. However, a number of children's and young adult book publishers have plunged into the graphic novel world in a big way, including Lerner, Rosen, and Capstone Press.

Another significant characteristic of non-superhero graphic novels is the prominence of self-published work. Some of the very best titles published over the past two decades have come from creator-owned companies, including Jeff Smith's Cartoon Books (*Bone*), Dave Sim's Aardvark-Vanaheim (*Cerebus*), Batton Lash's Exhibit A Press (*Supernatural Law*), and Terry Moore's Abstract Studio (*Strangers in Paradise*).

Even when these writers and artists do not publish their own material, most have made a point of maintaining ownership rights to their creations. As a result, some series have switched publishing houses over the years. Stan Sakai's *Usagi Yojimbo* moved from Fantagraphics to Mirage and then to Dark Horse Comics in 1996. More recent examples include Eric Powell's *The Goon,* which moved from Avatar Press to Dark Horse, and Jeff Mariotte's *Desperadoes,* which moved from DC/Homage to IDW Publishing.

Although we have not the space here to profile all of the leading independent graphic novel publishers, a handful of firms deserve special mention.

Dark Horse Comics is one of the largest U.S. graphic novel publishers, founded in 1986. They are best known for their comics treatments of licensed characters, including movie and television franchises such as Star Wars, Predator, Alien, Conan the Barbarian, and Buffy the Vampire Slayer. Dark Horse publishes very few ongoing series, relying instead on recurring limited series. Genres include humor (Tony Millionaire's *Sock Monkey,* Sergio Aragones' *Groo*), crime (*Sin City*), horror (*Hellboy,* Steve Niles's *Criminal Macabre*), science fiction (Frank Miller's *Martha Washington,* Paul Chadwick's *Concrete*), and nonfiction (Harvey Pekar's *American Splendor*). Dark Horse does not publish traditional superhero comics, though several Dark Horse characters wear costumes, notably in Matt Wagner's *Grendel* (science fiction/crime blend) and *Nexus,* a science fiction series from the team of Mike Baron and Steve Rude. Dark Horse is also known for manga.

Drawn & Quarterly (D&Q) is an independent publisher in Montreal that is widely regarded as one of the best publishers of alternative comics in North America (see next chapter). One of the publisher's most acclaimed titles is Chester Brown's *Louis Riel: A Comic-Strip Biography*. Another impressive project is *Berlin,* Jason Lutes's ambitious look at pre–World War II Germany. Among D&Q's well-known artists are Adrian Tomine (*Optic Nerve, Shortcomings*), Seth (*Palookaville*), Joe Matt (*Peepshow*), and Julie Doucet (*Dirty Plotte*), all of whose work was first published as comic book anthologies with serialized stories that were subsequently collected into books.

Fantagraphics Books offers one of the most distinctive voices in American comics. Founded in 1976, the company is probably best known for the *Love and Rockets* comic books and graphic novels from the Hernandez brothers and for Chris Ware's *Acme Novelty Library*. For the most part, Fantagraphics publishes adult-oriented humor and non-genre fiction, but they recently picked up Linda Medley's fantasy series *Castle Waiting*. Like NBM, they carry a line of imports as well as North American creators.

First Second, an imprint of children's and young adult publisher Roaring Book Press, was founded in 2005 by editorial director Mark Siegel. First Second publishes a wide range of high-quality fiction and nonfiction graphic novels for all ages: children, young adults, and adults. For such a young publisher, the company has received an impressive number of industry awards and accolades. At the top of the list is Gene Yang's outstanding *American Born Chinese,* which won ALA's Michael Prinz Award as well as both Eisner and Reuben awards, to name but a few of its many honors. Other First Second titles range from Jessica Abel's highly original vampire romance, *Life Sucks,* to *Deogratias,* J. P. Stassen's heartbreaking tale of a young boy in Rwanda.

IDW Publishing, established in 1999, focuses on horror comics together with titles based on licensed characters from television, movies, and video games. IDW is generally considered the fifth largest U.S. comics publisher (after Marvel, DC, Dark Horse, and Image). One of IDW's best-known franchises is the vampire story *30 Days of Night* and its spin-offs. Other series include TV-based titles such as *Angel, The Shield,* and *24;* video-game stories, such as *Castlevania* and *Silent Hill;* and movie properties, such as *Shaun of the Dead* and *Scarface.* IDW currently holds the license for comics and graphic novels based on Hasbro's popular line of Transformers toys.

NBM Publishing, officially known as Nantier Beall Minoustchine Publishing Inc., was one of the first companies to publish "graphic novels" as such in America. The company was founded in 1976 by Terry Nantier, who had studied abroad and was a fan of French graphic artists. Most NBM titles are translations from Europeans such as Enki Bilal and Lewis Trondheim. Among NBM's American creators are Richard Moore (*Boneyard*) and Rick Geary (the *Treasury of Victorian Murder* true-crime series). NBM has reprinted many classic newspaper strips collections, including *Terry and the Pirates* and *Tarzan.* Nantier also founded Papercutz, an independent company not affiliated with NBM. Papercutz publishes graphic novels for younger readers, including the *Hardy Boys* series, *Nancy Drew,* and a relaunch of the *Classics Illustrated* line.

Oni Press was founded in 1997 and publishes both comic books (predominantly in limited series format) and graphic novels. Although their backlist is eclectic, Oni avoids "mainstream" superhero, fantasy, and science fiction titles. Instead, they focus on romance, drama, and action/adventure. One of their best-known titles is the espionage series *Queen & Country.* Other popular Oni series are Bryan Lee O'Malley's *Scott Pilgrim* and J. Torres's *Alison Dare.* Creators who publish with Oni include Ted Naifeh (*Courtney Crumrin* and *Polly and the Pirates*), Andi Watson (*Breakfast after Noon, Dumped, Love Fights*), and the team of Nunzio DeFilippis and Christina Weir (*Maria's Wedding, Once in a Blue Moon*). Oni recently announced a new imprint, Slaughterhouse, edited by best-selling novelist Karin Slaughter. Slaughterhouse was created as a vehicle for traditional prose authors to launch graphic novel projects.

Top Shelf Productions, though founded in the late 1990s and fairly young, has a number of award-winning titles in its backlist. One of its first releases was the widely acclaimed children's fable *Good-bye, Chunky Rice,* by Craig Thompson. Other notable titles include Thompson's *Blankets* and the collected edition of *Box Office Poison* by Alex Robinson. Well-known artists published by Top Shelf are James Kochalka and Jeffrey Brown. In 2000, Top Shelf reprinted *From Hell,* Alan Moore and Eddie Campbell's monumental reexamination of the Jack the Ripper mystery. Top Shelf is highly eclectic, with material ranging from the delightful children's series *Owly* by Andy Runton to the decidedly adult *Lost Girls* by Alan Moore and Melinda Gebbie.

Relationship between Graphic
Novels and Comic Strips

Before plunging into our whirlwind tour of genres, let us touch on newspaper comic strips. Long before most librarians had ever heard the term "graphic novel," many libraries actively collected book compilations of popular strips such as Charles M. Schulz's *Peanuts* and Jim Davis's *Garfield.* Comic strips are enjoyed by people of all ages, educational backgrounds, and reading tastes. Any newspaper editor will tell you that canceling a longstanding strip or adding a new one will generate more reader mail than any other editorial decision.

Except for their combined use of words and pictures, most comic strips, especially "gag-a-day" comics such as *Beetle Bailey* or *Blondie,* differ greatly from graphic novels in that they do not carry a sustained narrative. Nevertheless, both the Dewey Decimal and the Library of Congress classification systems group most graphic novels together with traditional newspaper comics. This chapter largely ignores newspaper strips, but their perennial popularity in libraries warrants a few brief comments.

The choice of comic strip titles in a library depends on community interests. Certain series such as *Garfield* are popular virtually anywhere, but every strip has its fans and foes. Despite widespread popularity of certain titles, many readers either do not enjoy them or simply do not "get" the jokes. Examples include *Calvin & Hobbes* by Bill Watterson, *The Far Side* by Gary Larson, and *Fox Trot* by Bill Amend, all published in book form by Andrews McMeel. Some titles, such as G. B. Trudeau's *Doonesbury* (also Andrews McMeel), can polarize readers with their stance on current events and politics.

Some newspaper strips do present ongoing stories in ways similar to comic books and graphic novels, except serialized in a few panels per day rather than 22 pages per month. Many such strips mix daily punch-line humor with ongoing human interest plots. Examples include *For Better or For Worse* by Lynn Johnston (another Andrews McMeel series) and *Funky Winkerbean* by Tom Batiuk (various publishers, including NBM). Comic strips with ongoing dramatic or adventure stories, though once popular, are increasingly uncommon in American newspapers. Two long-time strips still appearing today are *Prince Valiant* (created by Hal Foster in 1937) and *The Phantom* (created by Lee Falk in 1936).

An encouraging trend for libraries is that many classic strips of bygone years are being collected into books: some humor strips, some adventure, and others blends of the two. (See text box.) Fantagraphics has been a longtime champion of such collections. Other graphic novel publishers have jumped into reprints, including D&Q and IDW. All three are devoting loving care and attention to reproducing classic daily and Sunday comics with the highest-quality printing, intending in many cases to reproduce the entire series in chronological order. One of the most ambitious is the *Complete Peanuts,* a hardcover series launched by Fantagraphics in 2004 and projected to require 12 years to complete.

CLASSIC NEWSPAPER STRIPS CURRENTLY BEING REISSUED

Dick Tracy by Chester Gould (IDW)
Gasoline Alley by Frank King (D&Q)
Krazy Kat by George Herriman (Fantagraphics)
Little Nemo in Slumberland by Winsor McCay (Fantagraphics)
Little Orphan Annie by Harold Gray (IDW)
The Complete Peanuts by Charles Schultz (Fantagraphics)
Pogo by Walt Kelly (Fantagraphics)
Popeye by E. C. Segar (Fantagraphics)
Prince Valiant by Harold Foster (Fantagraphics)
The Spirit Archives by Will Eisner (DC Comics)

AN OVERVIEW OF GENRES

One of the most common and useful ways to organize information about graphic novels is by genre. To one degree or another, virtually every popular literary genre shows up in graphic novel form. Some genres are abundantly represented, such as horror-supernatural, action-adventure, and fantasy of all types. Other categories, though seemingly tailor-made for comics-style storytelling, are not yet as prevalent in this country as one might think: science fiction, Westerns, and war stories. A few genres, like romance fiction and children's humor, are only now becoming more widely available as American publishers are reaching out to new audiences. As the next chapter shows, non-genre fiction, as well as nonfiction, is also expanding into the market, riding the general wave of graphic novel popularity and the evolving tastes of comics readers. Readers looking to expand their horizons can find something suitable for almost every taste and level of sophistication. The remainder of this chapter focuses on broad groupings of graphic novel genre fiction: science fiction, fantasy, horror, action, Western, crime, historical fiction, romance, and humor.

A limitation of this genre-specific approach quickly becomes apparent: it is sometimes difficult to classify fiction into tidy pigeonholes. One reason is the popularity of stories that cross genre boundaries. Virtually every fictional genre represented in graphic novels boasts numerous examples of genre-mixing. In some cases, the blend represents an imaginative stew-pot of many ingredients. For example, Alan Moore's *The League of Extraordinary Gentleman,* vol. 1 (DC/America's Best Comics, 2002) combines characters and genre conventions from Victorian adventure novels, science fiction, and horror to create a wonderfully inventive action story. Traditional superhero comics cross genre boundaries also. Alan Moore's *Top Ten* series (DC/America's Best Comics) blends in standard elements of science fiction, and characters such as Deadman, the Spectre, and Dr. Strange all embody elements of the supernatural.

Science Fiction

Science fiction is a huge and sprawling genre with all manner of subgenres, including space travel, alien encounters, future societies, and much more. It is also a genre particularly suited to graphical treatment, and comics adapting movie franchises have been especially successful. Dark Horse Comics has been extremely aggressive in this area over the years, with an abundance of books based on the *Star Wars, Predator,* and *Alien* movies, among others.

One of the most original science fiction comics is Paul Chadwick's *Concrete* series (Dark Horse, ages 16+), beginning in 1986. Concrete is a man-shaped creature of solid stone, inhabited by the mind of former political speech writer Ron Lithgow. While hiking in the mountains, Lithgow is abducted by aliens, who remove his brain and transfer it to the Concrete body. This might sound like the origin story of a new superhero, but *Concrete* is not a superhero comic. In the comic, the gentle Lithgow learns to adjust to his new body and tries to live as normal a life as he can. After escaping from the aliens (who never return), he is studied by the government but eventually is granted his freedom. Concrete uses his newfound celebrity to finance his personal interests—art, natural history, and the environment. He lives with Maureen Vonnegut, a government biologist charged with keeping an eye on him, and Larry, a personal assistant hired to help with public relations. Chadwick is a skilled artist and writer; his stories often focus on the dual topics of celebrity and environmental protection.

A series about as different as possible from the gentle humanity of *Concrete* is *Transmetropolitan,* (DC/Vertigo, 18+), a futuristic political satire starting in 1997 from the acerbic pen of British writer Warren Ellis, with wildly imaginative and energetic art by Darick Robertson. The series features one of the most memorable characters in all of comics history: renegade reporter Spider Jerusalem, whom Ellis unapologetically modeled after the late Hunter S. Thompson. Spider gleefully stalks the politicians, cult leaders, and celebrities of this nightmarishly believable future, with journalism as his gun: "Aim it right and you can blow the kneecap off the world." Spider's anger takes special aim at the masses' obsession with heedless, hedonistic consumerism and, most of all, at their total oblivion regarding the political corruption and manipulation surrounding them. Much of Ellis's imaginative future is simply a logical extension of our current excesses, from drug use and mass entertainment to plastic surgery and body art. The adults-only series is profane, outrageous, furious, thought-provoking, and wildly entertaining.

Warren Ellis is a particularly inventive, versatile, and enthusiastic architect in the science fiction sandbox. His *Orbiter* (Vertigo/DC, 2004, 18+) combines mystery with space travel to create a more traditional, but gripping tale set in the near future. When a long-missing spacecraft returns to Earth with only one crew member surviving, a dedicated team of scientists must determine what happened. Here Ellis weaves science fact into a highly realistic ode to space exploration. Ellis's *Planetary* (Wildstorm/DC, 16+) combines elements of science fiction, pulp adventure, and superhero traditions to deconstruct conventions in all three genres. The story features three super-powered (but non-costumed) humans, headed by the mysterious centigenarian Elijah Snow. The team investigates unexplained phenomena and, in fine *X-Files* fashion, attempts to uncover a powerful worldwide conspiracy.

Astronauts in Trouble (AiT/Planet Lar, 16+) is, like *Orbiter,* a realistic space thriller. Three books make up the series, all by skilled storyteller Larry Young and artist Charlie Adlard: *Live from the Moon* (1999); *Space, 1959* (2000); and *One Shot, One Beer* (2000). All three feature intelligent, lively action involving man's exploration of the moon, mostly told from the point of view of a television news crew. The first two books are adventure/suspense stories with complex plots, whereas *One Shot, One Beer* is a collection of vignettes told by patrons of the moon's only bar, Cool Ed's. *Astronauts in Trouble* is a great trilogy for space buffs and lovers of traditional science fiction.

Black Hole (Pantheon, 2005, 18+) by artist/writer Charles Burns, combines science fiction, coming-of-age story, graphic body horror, and murder mystery. In 1970s suburban Seattle, a strange sexually transmitted disease, termed the "Bug," attacks teenagers. Afflicted kids develop bizarre deformities, like a second mouth appearing on the victim's trachea. Many with the most horrific symptoms flee into the woods, where they form a loose-knit community and attempt to survive. Amidst this already horrible situation, a serial killer stalks the vulnerable teens. The "Bug" is a blatantly direct metaphor for AIDS, but as many reviewers have pointed out, the disease and its effects also symbolize teenage alienation, the transition from childhood to adulthood, the jarring physical transformations of puberty, and the milestone of one's first sexual encounter. Burns is a prolific comics artist with a precise inking style, and this work is widely regarded as his masterpiece. Due to nudity, sexuality, and violence, it is not for younger readers.

Nearly every significant subgenre of science fiction is represented in graphic novels—often brilliantly so. A few final examples should suffice to make the point, all by coincidence from DC/Vertigo (all 18+). In the tradition of the very best science fiction stories, these examine important moral, political, and social issues. Artificial and enhanced life forms are a common science fiction theme, and *We3* (2006) is a heartbreaking variation from the brilliant team of writer Grant Morrison and artist Frank Quitely. Three house pets—a dog, a cat, and a rabbit—are transformed into high-tech killing machines by the military and now must escape captivity before they are euthanized by their masters. The recently ended *Y: The Last Man* from writer Brian K. Vaughan, with art primarily from Pia Guerra, presents an interesting variation on the end-of-the-world theme. In the near future, a mysterious plague wipes out every male on Earth, human and animal. The surviving women are left to reform the world's governments or cope in others ways by establishing renegade societies and cults. When Yorick Brown turns up as the only surviving man, scientists and leaders quickly realize that Yorick's biochemistry holds the key to the future of humankind. Finally, *V for Vendetta* from writer Alan Moore and artist David Lloyd presents an alternative dystopia of Great Britain controlled by a repressive fascist state. The protagonist, Codename V, is a masked anarchist who uses violence to undermine the ruling government. *V for Vendetta* is an intricate, challenging book that asks readers to examine the moral implications of revolutionary action.

Fantasy

Fantasy fiction of all types constitutes one of the most robust categories of non-superhero comics. In particular, the subgenre of heroic fantasy is a short hop from the themes and attraction of superhero stories. Sword and sorcery, beginning with 1930s pulp fiction magazines, remains enormously popular in graphic novel form. The character Conan the Barbarian, Robert E. Howard's most famous creation, was introduced into comics by Marvel in 1970 and is enjoying renewed popularity today. Today, the character is licensed by Dark Horse (16+), and its team of writer Kurt Busiek and artist Cary Nord has done an amazing job adapting the original stories, capturing Conan's fierce savagery, lust for life, heroic code of honor, and primal fear of the supernatural. Dark Horse is also reprinting the original Marvel run from the 1970s and 1980s (13+), from writer Roy Thomas and artist Sal Buscema.

Perhaps the most widely acclaimed fantasy comics series is Neil Gaiman's *Sandman* (DC/Vertigo, 18+), which quickly became Vertigo's flagship title. In a cast of seven siblings, god-like beings known as the Endless, each embodies an important aspect of human consciousness and existence. The lead character is Dream (also known as Morpheus), the entity responsible for our nightly dreams and nightmares. Dream's brothers and sisters are Destiny, Death, Destruction, Desire, Despair, and Delirium (formerly Delight). Throughout its seven-year run, starting in 1987, *Sandman* visited themes, characters, and archetypal stories from mythology, folklore, canonical literature, and history as well as numerous aspects of fantasy, horror fiction, and non-genre fiction. *Sandman* jumps seamlessly from one imaginative premise to the next: a convention of mass murderers, the source of Shakespeare's creative inspiration, what would happen if Lucifer gave up his claim on Hell, and so on. Gaiman's work on the series has won numerous awards, including winning a 1991 World Fantasy Award, the only comics title ever to have done so. A number of artists worked on the individual story arcs, with varied results. However, every issue featured a stunning, surrealistic cover by Dave McKean, who employed various techniques, including watercolors, photography, and mixed media collage. The covers alone were collected into a paperback from Vertigo in 1998.

Current graphic novels run the gamut of fantasy subgenres with an extensive array of wonderfully imaginative stories. Jane Irwin self-published the *Vogelein* series (10+), a lovely, highly original takeoff on the Pinocchio theme.

Created by a master clockmaker in 1671 Heidelberg, the tiny, fairy-like autom-
aton Vogelein is magically, mysteriously imbued with life, perhaps in response
to the widower's loneliness or perhaps by some spiritual recognition of his
monumental artistry. In order to retain her spark of life, Vogelein's clockworks
must be wound every 36 hours. For most of her 300-year existence, the doll-
like creature has been under the protection of "Guardians," a series of human
caretakers. When her latest Guardian dies of old age, the heretofore-sheltered
fairy decides to explore the world on her own. Vogelein is a wonderful heroine:
naïve, yet wise; vulnerable, but intrepid. Irwin's delicate painted art is a bit
inconsistent in quality, but at its best it is absolutely exquisite.

No discussion of fantasy comics could ignore Jeff Smith's masterpiece,
Bone (Cartoon Books, 1991–2004, 10+), one of the most award-winning
comics in recent history. The original black-and-white volumes were recently
reprinted in full color by Scholastic Books. Three cousins—Phoney Bone,
Smiley Bone, and central character Fone Bone—are chased from their Bone-
ville home by an angry populace defrauded by the greedy, always-scheming
Phoney. Mid-flight, the cousins stumble into a magical kingdom populated by
dragons, talking bugs, sorcerers, gigantic lions, and "Stupid, Stupid Rat Creatures." In a small town, they meet Thorn, a resourceful young farm girl who,
we later discover, is heir to the throne and key to the kingdom's survival in its
struggle against the unseen Lord of the Locusts. The Bone cousins resemble
Walt Kelly's Pogo character crossed with Casper the Friendly Ghost, and
former animator Smith is a brilliant visual storyteller. *Bone* is a sweeping tale
of high fantasy, seamlessly combining rollicking comedy, gentle sweetness,
and gripping suspense.

Among the very best of several critically acclaimed fantasy series drawing
on fairy tales is Linda Medley's *Castle Waiting* (13+). In a land reminiscent
of medieval Europe, pregnant Lady Jain flees her abusive husband. She stum-
bles upon an apparently abandoned castle, only to be welcomed by its odd
collection of misfits, outcasts, and mythical creatures. Among the creatures
who befriend her are Rackham, a major domo stork, and Sir Destrier, a muscular talking horse who walks upright. Writer and artist Medley incorporates
extensive research on medieval folkways, history, fairy tales, and nursery
rhymes to create a rich, thoroughly charming world like no other in graphic
fiction. Originally self-published starting in 1997, the series was relaunched
by Fantagraphics.

Another remarkable award-winning fantasy series with a fairy-tale theme
is Bill Willingham's full-color *Fables* (DC/Vertigo, 18+), ongoing since 2002
with a recent spin-off series, *Jack of Fables*. The complex saga of Fabletown
follows a hidden community of legendary characters from fairy tales, nursery rhymes, and folklore now living in the heart of modern-day Manhattan.
Among a massive cast, lead characters include Snow White and sister Rose
Red, Bigby Wolf (the Big Bad Wolf in human form), Prince Charming, Boy
Blue, and Jack of Fables (an amalgam of Jack and the Beanstalk, Jack Spratt,

and other famous Jacks from folklore). Centuries ago, the characters fled their various fantasy kingdoms to escape the conquering armies of the dreaded Adversary. As the plot slowly builds to a confrontation between Fabletown and the Adversary, storylines run from delightfully funny to deadly serious. But all are richly developed, highly imaginative, engaging, and enlivened by Willingham's masterful dialogue.

Horror and the Supernatural

One of the most popular non-superhero genres in comics today is the broad area of horror and the supernatural. This renewed interest has been fueled in part by the recent revitalization of horror movies. In fact, a number of horror-themed comics have lately been made into films: *Hellboy, Constantine* (from Vertigo's *Hellblazer* series), and *30 Days of Night.* Diverse subcategories include stories featuring traditional monsters (especially vampires and zombies), the demonic element, psychotic killers (including slasher stories and body horror), paranormal investigators and adventurers, and heroic sorcerers and magicians. Two of the leading publishers are IDW Publishing and Moonstone Books.

Vampire comics have always been popular, whether variations on Dracula or imaginative takeoffs. *Buffy the Vampire Slayer,* appearing first as a film and then as a long-running television series, has generated a huge number of volumes from Dark Horse (13+). Marvel's *Blade the Vampire Hunter* (13+) went in the opposite direction, beginning as a supporting character in early 1970s comics before jumping to a movie franchise and television series. One of the most original and intriguing titles is *30 Days of Night* (IDW, 2003, plus *Return to Barrow,* 2004, 18+), told with chilling realism and visceral horror by writer Steve Niles and artist Ben Templesmith. The premise is simple but ingenious: because the town of Barrow, Alaska, is located near the Arctic Circle, town residents experience 30 days of unending night during deepest winter. What would happen if the town were invaded then by bloodthirsty vampires?

Comics with a zombie motif have been especially popular recently, also inspired by cinematic successes. In many ways, zombie comics follow the conventions of postapocalyptic science fiction. One of the best of this type is *The Walking Dead* (18+), a highly realistic series from Image Comics since 2003, written by Robert Kirkman and with art primarily by Charlie Adlard. Southern police officer Rick Grimes wakes from a coma to discover almost all humanity has died, replaced by animated corpses. Grimes manages to reunite with his family and a small band of other refugees. As in all good postapocalypse stories, *The Walking Dead* is character-driven, exploring the interaction of the surviving humans and what they must do to carry on.

One of the most unusual horror comics characters is *Hellboy* (Dark Horse, 13+), creation of writer/artist Mike Mignola since 1993, together with spin-off series *B.P.R.D.* Though a good guy, Hellboy is an eldritch supernatural creature recalling H. P. Lovecraft. In the dark days of World War II, a Nazi attempt to retrieve an unspeakably powerful supernatural weapon is interrupted by a British commando team. What comes through from the "other side" is a cute baby demon, whom team leader Trevor Bruttenholm raises to become Hellboy. Following the war, the now-grown Hellboy becomes the lead field investigator for the U.S. government's Bureau for Paranormal Research and Defense. He is incredibly strong and largely impervious to injury, and he wields a gigantic stone fist that he uses against an assortment of demons and monsters. The tone of *Hellboy* stories varies from humorous to dramatic, often incorporating lesser-known myths and folklore from cultures worldwide.

No discussion of horror/supernatural comics would be complete without *Preacher* (DC/Vertigo, 18+), a late 1990s phenomenon starring Jesse Custer, a hard-drinking Texas preacher who finds himself infused with the spirit of an angel-devil half-breed. Accompanied by ex-girlfriend and erstwhile professional assassin Tulip O'Hare, as well as charming Irish vampire Cassidy, Jesse embarks on a quest to find God, who has apparently abandoned his role as the Almighty. The indescribable cast of supporting characters and villains include the Saint of Killers, a Clint Eastwood–style gunman from the Old West who is now a supernatural agent of vengeance, and the hilarious but poignant Arseface, a teenager with a horribly mutilated face from a failed suicide attempt. With graphic violence, high body counts, profane humor, sacrilege, and all-around bad behavior, *Preacher* is not for the young or faint of heart with its wild mixture of horror, action, crime, Western trappings, and black humor. At its core, *Preacher* is a sprawling commentary on late 20th-century America but also a thoughtful examination of friendship, loyalty, and faith written by Irish madman Garth Ennis and drawn memorably by Steve Dillon.

A flourishing horror subgenre blends supernatural themes with humor, based on the juxtaposition of seeming opposites: humor and fear. One title for teens and up is *Death Jr.* (Image Comics, 2005, 2007) by Gary Whitta, with art by Ted Naifeh. The title character was originally designed for a video game and was spun off into comics. "DJ" is the son of the Grim Reaper. He is eager to join Dad in the family business, but for now he attends middle school with a band of grotesquely hilarious misfits.

One of the longest-lived humor/supernatural blends is *Supernatural Law* (13+), self-published by creator Batton Lash's Exhibit A Press. Lawyers Alanna Wolff and Jeff Byrd represent monsters and other supernatural creatures wronged by mundane society. Collections include *Sonovawitch!* and *The Vampire Brat,* among others. Another hilarious horror title is Eric Powell's *The Goon* (13+), an award-winning series now from Dark Horse. The Goon is a hulking, scar-faced brute who happens to be the crime boss of a downtrodden town overrun by zombies. With diminutive friend Franky, the Goon uses his massive fists (and anything else he can lay hands on) to subdue the supernatural creatures sent by the evil Zombie Priest to wrest control of the town.

Not surprisingly, dark humor is a major feature of this subgenre (as the enduring popularity of *Preacher* attests), and titles with enthusiastic cult followings include *Johnny the Homicidal Maniac: Director's Cut* (1998, 18+), by Jhonen Vasquez, and *Lenore* (13+), by Roman Dirge (both Slave Labor Graphics). *Johnny the Homicidal Maniac* ("JTHM" to fans) features a sociopathic goth teenager who strikes back at his mocking neighbors by murdering them in ways so sadistically over-the-top that readers cannot help but laugh. In contrast, Lenore is a sweet little girl who has no moral compass, has no adult supervision, and happens to be dead. As with *Johnny,* the humor in *Lenore* lies in the ridiculously horrific levels of violence she inflicts so impassively on those she meets, including cute bunnies.

Action/Adventure

Most graphic novel genres include their fair share of action or adventure. However, when we speak of action/adventure as a genre, we mean titles that feature adventurers, whether amateur or professional, as their main characters. This means action heroes who are not superheroes, although lines often blur. Such popular characters as Doc Savage or James Bond may not have superpowers, but their abilities and exploits strain credulity to the point that they may as well be superheroes. In some cases, such non-super action heroes actually wear costumes, as does Lee Falk's the Phantom (Moonstone Books).

Action/adventure subgenres feature explorers, mercenaries, troubleshooters, jungle heroes, pirates, and spies. Literally hundreds of comics have starred Edgar Rice Burroughs's immortal Tarzan of the Apes (see Dark Horse reprints from the Joe Kubert years; 13+). Indeed, dozens of other comics titles over the decades have featured jungle adventurers of both sexes: men such as Ka-Zar and Ka'anga and women such as Sheena and Lorna the Jungle Girl. Comics starring "jungle girls" often provide pin-up artists such as Frank Cho and Bud Root with an opportunity to draw preposterously voluptuous women wearing scanty animal-skin bikinis. A recent example is Marvel's *Shanna the She-Devil* (2006, 16+), written and drawn by Cho. Although this is not Pulitzer Prize material, *Shanna* provides a satisfying action yarn, featuring the jungle girl stranded on a remote island with a small group of American military personnel. Before the story's conclusion, our intrepid adventurers encounter an abandoned Nazi scientific facility, an island filled with vicious dinosaurs, and enough violence to satisfy the most hard-core action fans. Marvel published a sequel called *Shanna the She-Devil: Survival of the Fittest* (2008). Without Frank Cho at the helm, this second outing was panned by most critics, not only for the absence of Cho's stunning artwork but for its derivative plot as well.

Spy stories seem well-suited to comics. One of the best is *Queen & Country* (Oni Press, 2001 on, 18+). This action-packed, realistic series features "The Minders," an elite clandestine unit within the British government's Secret Intelligence Service. Lead character Tara Chace, "Minder Two," is a tough, intelligent, highly professional agent who has suffered more than her fair share of mission failures and personal tragedies. Creator Greg Rucka draws on real-world events and settings when crafting his grim stories. And like the very best novels in the genre, *Queen & Country* explores the moral and political complexities and consequences associated with the world of espionage. Rucka, a prolific novelist beyond his comics work, has also penned two prose books featuring Tara and her colleagues.

Another popular action/adventure subgenre is the martial arts story. Many martial arts comics characters are really superheroes, costumed or not, like Marvel's Iron Fist, DC's Richard Dragon, and the ever-popular Teenage Mutant Ninja Turtles. One of the most interesting and unusual series is *Usagi Yojimbo* from Stan Sakai since 1984 (Fantagraphics, Dark Horse, 10+). Loosely based on the saga of legendary Japanese samurai Miyamoto Musashi, this comic features a large, varied cast of anthropomorphic animals. Main character Miyamoto Usagi is a rabbit *ronin* (masterless samurai) who travels throughout feudal Japan on a self-imposed quest for spiritual enlightenment. Violence, though present, is downplayed, making the stories suitable for all ages. Sakai has done considerable research on the history, customs, costumes, and folklore of feudal Japan, and his stories reflect that care and seriousness of purpose.

To show that action comics do not always follow genre formulas, consider *Elk's Run* (Villard, 2007, 16+), by writer Joshua Hale Fialkov and artist Noel Tuazon, about a small group of teenagers in the survivalist community of Elk's Ridge, West Virginia. The remote town was founded by the kids' parents, a band of Vietnam veterans and their wives who sought isolation from the modern world. With each passing year, the teens yearn to break free of the community's confines, if only to explore the wider world and meet other people. When an accident sets off an escalating wave of violence and overreaction by the repressive parents, the kids hatch a plot to escape. Although the actions of the adults are not always completely believable, the story is compelling and suspenseful, the dialogue is very realistic, and Tuazon's artwork is highly expressive.

Westerns

Throughout the early 1950s and 1960s, Westerns were nearly as popular in comics form as they were in movies and television. Even the cowboys' horses had their own comics: *Hi-Yo Silver,* starring the Lone Ranger's famous steed, and *Gene Autry's Champion* (both from Dell Publishing). Today, Western genre comics are somewhat rare. Those published in recent years are often genre blends, integrating horror, fantasy, or even humor.

One of the few enduring Western comics has been DC's *Jonah Hex,* introduced in 1972 (18+). A white man raised by Apache, Hex is an anti-hero bounty hunter and a Confederate veteran of the Civil War. His most distinctive physical characteristic is a horrible facial scar inflicted as punishment by his own tribe. DC has released five book-length compilations to date. Though Hex has always been violent and "gritty," the stories since 2005 are definitely aimed at a more adult audience.

An especially notable DC Western title is *The Kents,* first published in 1999 (13+). Skillfully written by the always reliable John Ostrander, with art by Timothy Truman and Tom Mandrake, this series story follows the lives of abolitionist Silas Kent and his family in Bloody Kansas in the years leading up to the Civil War and beyond. (Silas is an ancestor of Clark "Superman" Kent's adoptive father.)

Marvel has recently revived some of its classic Western characters. The creative team of John Ostrander (again as writer) and Leonardo Manco (artist) has produced two limited series collected into books (both 16+): *Blaze of Glory: The Last Ride of the Western Heroes* (2002) and its sequel, *Apache Skies* (also 2002). The first features most of Marvel's major Western heroes from the 1950s through 1970s, including Kid Colt, the Rawhide Kid, and the Two-Gun Kid. In stereotypical Western style, the heroes unite to save a small Montana town from violent raiders. In the sequel, notable for Manco's painted art, the Rawhide Kid sets out to avenge the death of his friend, the Apache Kid.

Horror-Western crossovers are surprisingly popular. The *Desperadoes* series beginning in 1998 features four gunslingers on the lam from the law who encounter an assortment of monsters, ghosts, and zombies in their travels (DC/Wildstorm, Image Comics, and IDW, 13+). Despite the supernatural angle, writer Jeff Mariotte—a fairly prolific author of young adult novels and a former comics editor—strives to make the Old West aspect of the series as believable as possible. Another horror/Western blend is *Billy the Kid's Old Timey Oddities* (Dark Horse, 2006).

A few humor titles have also visited Western landscapes, most notoriously *Rawhide Kid: Slap Leather* (Marvel Comics, 2003, 18+) by Hollywood writer (and *Howard Stern Show* refugee) Ron Zimmerman. This book answers the age-old question, "Why do cowboy heroes never marry the schoolmarm?" Here, Zimmerman looks to the Rawhide Kid's white gloves and impeccable wardrobe for answers, with an endless barrage of not-so-veiled jokes featuring the frontier townspeople questioning our dapper hero's sexual orientation. Adding to the fun, Marvel brought in 86-year-old John Severin, one of the character's original artists from the 1950s, to draw the story. Despite a firestorm of publicity, the title was generally well received by the gay and lesbian communities and is actually quite funny. (See Appendix B-3 for more on lesbian and gay comics.)

Westerns can also cross over with science fiction. Here, stories adopt Western themes, characters, and trappings but are set in other worlds or times. *Just a Pilgrim* (Titan Books, 2003, 16+), takes place in a postapocalyptic future, where the mysterious, shotgun-toting Pilgrim rescues a band of refugees from bloodthirsty pirates. As written by fan-favorite Garth Ennis with stark, moody art by Carlos Ezquerra, the Pilgrim wears a full-length duster and a hat that resembles a cross between a Stetson and a Puritan's headgear.

The Western's enduring powers of genre-blending shine in the unusual *Ballad of Sleeping Beauty,* from independent publisher Beckett Comics (2005, 16+). Written by Gabriel Benson, with effective artwork by Mike Hawthorne, the story retells the fairy tale of Sleeping Beauty in a Wild West setting, combining violent gunplay and an Indian curse to create a highly satisfying and widely acclaimed Western comic unlike any other.

Historical Fiction

Historical fiction remains fairly rare in graphic novels, excepting the afore-mentioned Western comics and excepting war-related fiction. Throughout the 1950s and 1960s, war comics even outnumbered cowboy titles. Some featured unstoppable action heroes, such as DC's Sgt. Rock or Marvel's Sgt. Nick Fury. A few series utilized bizarre cross-genre elements, like haunted tanks or soldiers battling dinosaurs, whereas others strove for grim realism. Some of the very best dramatic war stories have been reprinted in *The Mammoth Book of Best War Comics,* edited by David Kendall (Carroll & Graf, 2007, 16+), and the first two volumes of *The EC Archives: Two-Fisted Tales* (Gemstone Publishing, 2007, 16+). The latter feature art and stories by such industry giants as Harvey Kurtzman and Wally Wood.

Today's much sparser war comics present serious themes and messages, some of the more interesting being anthologies. Will Eisner's *Last Day in Vietnam* (Dark Horse, 2000, 16+) collects six short stories set during the Vietnam War. The two-volume *War Stories* (DC/Vertigo, 2004, 2006, 18+) presents eight realistic tales from various World War II combat theatres, all written by Garth Ennis with various artists.

Two historical titles deserving special mention also relate to World War II, both showing meticulous research. Jason Lutes's *Berlin: City of Stones* (Drawn & Quarterly, 2000, 16+) explores life in Weimar Germany during 1928–1929, prior to Hitler's rise to power, with journalist Kurt Severing and his lover, art student Marthe Muller, as the main characters. *Berlin* is meticulously detailed, both in story and in art, and demands much from its reader, but it offers a wonderful example of how the graphic novel medium can be used to tell complex and sophisticated tales. Two more volumes are planned. *Yossel: April 29, 1943* (16+), though fictional, is a deeply personal story for creator Joe Kubert, whose family came to America from Poland in the mid-1920s. In *Yossel,* Kubert imagines what might have happened to him had his parents not left their homeland. Here the Nazis force the family to leave their small village and relocate to the enclosed Jewish ghetto in Warsaw. Eventually, Yossel's parents die in the Treblinka concentration camp, while Yossel remains a prisoner in the enclosed ghetto because his remarkable skill as an artist has garnered favor with his Nazi captors. Eventually, Yossel joins the underground resistance movement in the ghetto and dies there when the Nazis attack the community with tanks and exterminate the remaining residents. In telling this tragic story, Kubert published his preliminary rough pencil sketches rather than finishing them in ink, making the pages appear as though drawn by "Yossel" himself.

Beyond war stories and Westerns, *The Golem's Mighty Swing* (Drawn & Quarterly, 2001, 16+) examines the barnstorming baseball leagues of the 1920s, focusing on the anti-Semitism facing the Stars of David, a Jewish team traveling throughout the Midwest. Though fictional, the story draws its inspiration from the House of David baseball teams popular during the era. (The story also appears in the trilogy *James Sturm's America: God, Greed, and Golems,* D&Q, 2007.) Outstanding as well is the award-winning *Kings in Disguise* (Norton reissue, 2006, 16+), set in the heart of Depression-era America by writer James Vance, with stunning art by Dan Burr. Twelve-year-old Freddie Bloch hops a cross-country freight car, hoping to find his father. Along the way, he becomes involved with labor organizers and socialists, providing a heart-rending personal look at key social movements of the day.

Crime and Detective

Comics have long embraced crime stories of all types: "whodunnits," police procedurals, lone-wolf private detective yarns, violent stories of underworld life, and innumerable Sherlock Holmes adaptations. One of the major publishers of crime stories via graphic novels is DC, whose original name was—not entirely by coincidence—Detective Comics.

The superhero genre has always overlapped with traditional crime stories. Batman, after all, has often been described as "the world's greatest detective." Two series deserve special mention as genuine crime stories with roots in the superhero milieu, though others could be mentioned also. *Sandman Mystery Theatre* (DC/Vertigo, 18+) features a 1990s reboot of Golden Age character the Sandman (not to be confused with Neil Gaiman's similarly named fantasy character). An amateur detective and vigilante crime fighter, mild-mannered Wesley "Sandman" Dodds pits his skills against vicious crime lords and serial killers with help from clues coming from his subconscious mind while he sleeps. The adult-themed crime noir stories are set in the 1930s and early 1940s by Matt Wagner and Steven Seagle, accompanied by moody, period drawings from Guy Davis. The original Sandman was a normal human member of the Justice Society of America, alongside actual superheroes. Unlike other JSA members, the Sandman had no powers, was armed with a unique sleeping-gas gun, and wore a green trench coat and gas mask rather than typical superhero garb.

A second superhero spin-off beginning in 2003 was *Gotham Central* (DC, 13+), a gritty police procedural exploring the daily lives of detectives in the Gotham City's police department, in a city populated by costumed superheroes and dominated by the omnipresent shadow of Batman. Batman villains such as the Joker and Poison Ivy are often involved in the storylines, and the Dark Knight himself makes a few brief appearances. Two of the main characters are detectives Crispus Allen and Renee Montoya, both featured prominently since in other roles in the DC Universe. All of the stories were written by two of the best crime writers in comics: Ed Brubaker and Greg Rucka.

Despite the natural affinity crime plots have with graphic storytelling, crime comics have seldom sold well lately. Several notable titles garnered little attention until adapted into major motion pictures: *Road to Perdition* and *A History of Violence* (both DC/Paradox Press, 18+). *Road to Perdition* (1998), written by crime novelist Max Allan Collins with art by Richard Piers Raynor, tells of 1920s mob hit man Michael O'Sullivan, who with his young son seeks retribution for the murder of his wife and other son. *A History of Violence* (1997), created by John Wagner and artist Vince Locke, introduces a small-town family man whose hidden past catches up with him. The original story differs somewhat from the movie adaptation.

Crime fiction in graphic novels often adopts conventions of crime noir films and novels. Examples include David Lapham's critically acclaimed *Stray Bullets* (self-published from El Capitan Books, 18+) and *Raymond Chandler's Marlowe: The Graphic Novel* (Ibooks, 2003, 16+), which adapts three short stories featuring iconic hard-boiled detective Phillip Marlowe. Another example is *100 Bullets* (DC/Vertigo, 18+), ongoing since 1999 from the prolific Brian Azzarello, with artist Eduardo Risso. In each story arc, the mysterious suitcase-carrying Agent Graves approaches someone with a question: If you were offered the chance to seek revenge against someone who ruined your life, with no chance of legal reprisals, would you be willing to commit murder? Graves's suitcase always contains ironclad evidence of their enemies' crimes, a handgun, and 100 "untraceable" bullets.

One of the more unusual crime stories is *Whiteout* (Oni Press, 1999, 18+), written by crime novelist Greg Rucka and with art by Steve Lieber. At a multinational research station in frozen Antarctica, federal marshal Carrie Stetko, a cranky, freckle-faced, seasoned detective, is investigating a murder. Her progress is hindered by a beautiful British secret agent seemingly bent on covering up a secret at the site. The story won a 2004 Eisner award, and a sequel followed: *Whiteout: Melt* (Oni, 2000).

Crime comics stories are not necessarily realistic. One of the best-known "over-the-top" examples is Frank Miller's *Sin City* franchise (Dark Horse, 18+), debuting in 1991. All *Sin City* stories take place in and around the fictitious Basin City, located in Washington State. The spectacularly violent and corrupt locale houses competing criminal gangs, and the "Old Town" section is actually run by prostitutes. Key characters include John Hartigan, an honest police detective framed and imprisoned; the gigantic, unstoppable anti-hero Marv; female martial arts assassin Miho; and the mysterious Dwight McCarthy, a self-appointed protector of Old Town women. Comic book legend Frank Miller created the series using a distinctive, masterful black-and-white style relying heavily on silhouette and shadow, striking imagery, and minimalist backgrounds.

Romance

Romance comics appeared after World War II, when superhero comics were on the decline, and nearly as many girls as boys read comics. In recent decades, romance comics all but disappeared, but they are making a comeback as publishers reach out to new readers. Comics with romance themes have been especially popular in manga style, but Western-style romance comics also exist.

Perhaps the best-known example of a non-manga romance comic is Alex Robinson's *Box Office Poison,* rightly described as a masterpiece, which explores the lives of a small group of New York City 20-somethings (Top Shelf, 2001, 18+). The main story follows the tribulations of Sherman Davies, a disgruntled bookstore clerk and would-be novelist who meets Dorothy Lestrade at a party. Their extended romance is made tumultuous in part by Dorothy's self-centered nature and her slovenly, disorganized lifestyle—she cannot manage money or maintain a remotely clean apartment. Sherman's roommates are college history professor Stephen Gaedel and Stephen's longtime girlfriend, cartoonist Jane Pekar. In comparison to Sherman and Dorothy, Stephen and Jane seem to enjoy a rock-solid relationship. A detailed subplot involves Sherman's best friend, Ed Velasquez, a hapless but talented comics artist trying to break into the industry. Robinson's characters are complex, believable, and subtly presented; Sherman's endless complaining and his inability to go after what he truly desires become more understandable when we learn about Sherman's tragic childhood and his ne'er-do-well father.

One of the most popular creators of romance comics today is (male) British cartoonist Andi Watson, whose work is published primarily by American companies. *Dumped* (Oni, 2002, 16+) explores the relationship between Binny, an obsessive book collector, and girlfriend Debs, who runs a vintage clothing store. *Breakfast after Noon* (Oni, 2001, 16+), set in a British industrial town, features engaged couple Rob Grafton and Louise Bright, whose future takes an unexpected turn when both lose their jobs. One of Watson's more interesting creations is *Love Fights* (Oni, 13+), an ongoing series that follows the halting romance of two ordinary people who happen to live in a world with superheroes. Jack is a comics artist who chronicles the real adventures of the heroic Flamer; Nora works for a tabloid that thrives on superhero scandals, including a juicy one involving the Flamer himself.

Oni has published a number of other romance and slice-of-life books. *Maria's Wedding* (2003, 16+), by writers Nunzio de Fillipis and Christina Weir and artist Jose Garibaldi, introduces the Pirelli family, who have gathered for Maria Pirelli's wedding. Among them are Joseph Pirelli with gay partner Matthew, family matriarch Maria (Nonna) Pirelli, outspoken but likeable cousin Frankie Pirelli, and Frankie's would-be love interest, Brenna Doyle—Maria's best friend. Other Oni titles with strong romantic themes include *Pounded* (2002, 16+) from Brian Wood and Steve Rolston, *The Everlasting* by Jamie Rich (2006, 13+), and the acclaimed *Scott Pilgrim* series (2004–to date, 13+).

As with other themes, some of the most interesting and original romance comics represent genre blends. One of the best examples is Terry Moore's extremely popular, award-winning *Strangers in Paradise* (Abstract Studios, 16+), an indescribable mixture of action, political thriller, crime, humor, slice-of-life, and romance. The main characters are Francine Peters, Katina Choovanski ("Katchoo"), David Qin, and Casey Bullocks-Femur. Talented lesbian artist Katchoo was sexually abused as a child and eventually becomes entangled with Darcy Parker, the leader of a criminal organization who uses highly trained female operatives to blackmail prominent politicians. David is Darcy's half-brother, who develops unrequited love for Katchoo. Meanwhile, former aerobics instructor Casey, ex-wife of womanizer Freddie Femur, is in love with David. The main story involves the long-standing relationship between Katchoo and her high school friend Francine. The slightly chunky Francine, who has self-esteem issues, loves Katchoo dearly, but cannot bring herself to engage in a sexual relationship with her, in part because of Francine's traditional middle-class upbringing and religious beliefs. Freddie, who once dated and humiliated Francine, is now obsessed with winning her back. The complex story often switches from present day to flashbacks, and even to future events. It is also a richly rewarding story whose fans care enormously about its unforgettable, fully realized characters.

Humor

Humor comics of every type abound, from the teen humor of Archie and friends to TV-based comics such as *The Simpsons*. Some typical varieties:

- Funny kids (Jimmy Gownley's *Amelia Rules,* Renaissance Press, 2006–present, all ages)
- Observational humor (Lynda Barry's *One! Hundred! Demons!* Sasquatch, 2002, 16+)
- Political satire (*Birth of a Nation,* written by Aaron McGruder and Reginald Hudlin, with art by the great cartoonist Kyle Baker; Crown, 2004, 16+)
- Absurdist (Judd Winick's *The Adventures of Barry Ween, Boy Genius,* Oni, 2000, 16+)
- Silly (Scott Morse's *The Magic Pickle,* Oni, 2002, all ages)
- Dark humor (Douglas Paszkiewicz's truly sick self-published collection, *Arsenic Lullaby: Year of the Fetus,* 2005, 18+)

Humor comics also incorporate cross-genre blends of every stripe, as the earlier section on horror and supernatural comics demonstrates. Slice-of-life comics with a humorous tone (what might be termed "situation comedy") are introduced in the following chapter.

Funny animal comics represent a broad subcategory that includes any story featuring anthropomorphic animals. Just as comics are not necessarily comical, "funny animal" comics are not necessarily funny. Stories may treat decidedly adult themes, with crude language, nudity, and sexual situations, such as R. Crumb's classic *Fritz the Cat* or Kate Worley and Reed Waller's *Omaha the Cat Dancer.* They may also encompass non-humor genres such as science fiction *(Tank Girl; We3; Planet of the Apes)*, fantasy *(Mouse Guard; The Rabbi's Cat;* by definition, *Fables)*, detective *(Blacksad; Hip Flask)*, historical fiction *(Usagi Yojimbo)*, and even nonfiction *(Maus)*.

Of course, many funny animal comics are still aimed at youngsters. Andy Runton's charming and wordless, award-winning *Owly* (Top Shelf, all ages) features a cute baby owl and his best friend Wormy with simple stories that provide uplifting messages for young readers. *Peanutbutter and Jeremy's Best Book Ever,* by James Kochalka (Alternative Comics, 2003, all ages), features hardworking cat Peanutbutter and troublemaking crow Jeremy.

Warner Brothers cartoon stars Bugs Bunny and Daffy Duck were longtime staples of Dell comics in the 1950s and early 1960s. Today, DC publishes *Looney Tunes* comics, and a few have been reprinted as book compilations, including *Daffy Duck: You're Despicable!* (DC, 2005, all ages).

Walt Disney's classic cartoon characters, including Mickey Mouse and Donald Duck, have been licensed to several publishers over the decades. Today, Gemstone Publishing, best known for its annual *Overstreet Comic Book Price Guide,* holds the rights to reprint Disney comics, including Carl Barks's classic Donald Duck and Scrooge McDuck stories. Gemstone has published many in slim, affordable book format, including *Carl Barks' Greatest DuckTales Stories, Donald Duck Adventures,* and *Mickey Mouse Adventures* (each all ages).

Another great funny animal series is Frank Cho's slapstick *Liberty Meadows* (16+). Set in a Maryland animal sanctuary and rehabilitation center, the outrageously misfit characters include Dean, a chain-smoking sexist pig; Ralph, a midget circus bear who is also a mad-scientist inventor; Truman, a sweetly naïve baby duck; and Leslie, a hypochondriac frog. The animals interact with an extensive cast of human characters, including Frank, the facility's hapless veterinarian, and Brandy, the gorgeous supremely capable animal psychologist. The series began as a newspaper strip but has since moved on to comic books and collections (Image Comics).

As publishers are quickly realizing the newfound interest in graphic novels of all types, the happy result is that many titles long out-of-print or never collected in book form are once again seeing the light of day, including humor titles, such as the *Archie Americana* series (all ages). Another resuscitated humor title is Frank Stack's *The New Adventures of Jesus: The Second Coming* (Fantagraphics, 2006, 18+), the complete run of this outrageous classic underground comic strip.

CONCLUSION: GENRES REDUX

Although the superhero genre is most often equated with comics, virtually every print fiction genre is represented among graphic novels to one extent or another, as we have seen. With hundreds of non-superhero titles in print, and dozens of new titles released each year, readers will truly find a wide selection to meet every possible genre and taste. In the next chapter, we turn to non-genre graphic novels.

5

American Comics: Beyond the Superhero, Part Two, General Fiction and Nonfiction

Michael R. Lavin

Not too long ago and before manga's arrival in America, everything comics-like other than superhero titles and genre fiction was lumped into the vague catchall of "alternative" comics, especially those not produced by mainstream comics publishers. Today, we find more specific descriptors—a good thing, because the medium is far too rich and diverse for such "either/or" analyses. Now the Alternative label is used mainly to describe experimental or trendsetting comics—those exploring unusual themes or employing notably different storytelling devices or artistic styles.

This chapter begins with comics that adapt works from fiction in other formats and then moves on to realistic fiction of all types, followed by nonfiction: autobiography and memoir, history and biography, current events, science, and philosophy and religion. Suggested age levels are indicated.

GRAPHIC NOVEL ADAPTATIONS

At heart, comics are about telling a great story, which makes adaptations of previous works an ideal use of the medium. Such adaptations include myths, legends, fairy tales, folklore, and classic literature.

Myths and Legends

Age-old myths from all cultures continue to capture our imagination because of their timeless relevance as well as archetypical characters and themes. Similarly, classic stories from the world's great religions carry the same power and affinity for graphic storytelling—a topic explored later in the chapter. Loosely based reconfigurations of traditional fairy tales, fables, nursery rhymes, and other folktales are discussed under the "Fantasy" category in the previous chapter.

The Age of Bronze (Image Comics, 2001–, 16+) by Eric Shanower is an extraordinary tour de force. Whether based in truth or not, Homer's *Illiad* is one of humankind's great mythic tales, with enduring messages, larger-than-life heroes, and Olympian gods. Shanower's meticulously researched artwork has garnered extensive praise from the archaeological community, and the series has already won a prestigious Eisner Award. Despite the story's complexity, every key character is fully and richly developed, and the plot is always compelling. Because of the extensive research and careful craftsmanship required, the project will take years; to date, three volumes of a projected seven have been published, with detailed maps, pronunciation guides, genealogical charts, and bibliographies.

A legend seemingly made for comics is the eighth-century Old English epic poem *Beowulf.* The basic story is likely to be familiar to readers as a result of several recent film versions. Beowulf, Swedish prince of the Geats, arrives in Denmark to aid aging King Hrothgar against the savage monster Grendel. After defeating Grendel in hand-to-hand combat and tearing off his arm, Beowulf follows the monster to its lair and kills its equally monstrous and bloodthirsty mother. Later, the mature Beowulf, now King, dies defeating a ferocious dragon. Artist Gareth Hinds's version (Candlewick, 2007, 13+) combines snippets of a stylized, 1910 translation from the original text with wordless, violent action sequences, depicting the Geat hero as a cross between a bare-chested superhero and a gigantic WWF wrestler. A more traditional comic book–style treatment of the Beowulf legend is an adaptation of the 2007 Paramount motion picture, which added new elements to the classic story in a screenplay co-written by fantasy great Neil Gaiman. This satisfying graphic novel version, also titled *Beowulf* (IDW, 2007, 18+), is written by IDW editor-in-chief Chris Ryall, with art by Gabriel Rodriguez.

One of the most remarkable comics adaptations of myth or legend is P. Craig Russell's *The Ring of the Nibelung* (Dark Horse, 2002, 16+). The two volumes retell Richard Wagner's four Ring Cycle operas, themselves based on Germanic legend. Russell has adapted much other opera and fantasy and has masterfully created lyrical text and powerful, fantastical artwork.

Erik Evensen's self-published *Gods of Asgard* (Studio E3, 2007, 10+) meticulously retells major tales from Norse mythology as a fascinating adventure story, from the creation tales to the saga of Ragnarök, the twilight of the gods. The Aesir (gods and goddesses of Asgard) are depicted with grandeur and nobility but also fraught with human characteristics and frailties, including jealousy, anger, and pride. The Xeric Foundation grant-winning work focuses on the key players—Odin, Thor, Loki, Balder, and Sif—but many other gods, frost giants, and trolls appear along the way. Evensen's research shines in well-written details and authentically rendered costumes, hairstyles, and settings, finishing with a brief but focused guide to further reading plus helpful endnotes that place the tales in context, explicating the important themes and symbology.

In contrast to Evensen's work, Marvel's version of Norse god Thor has little in common with Norse mythology. Marvel's Thor comes from Asgard, exercises control over thunder and lightning, and wields the magic hammer Mjolner, but after that, similarities end. However, *Thor: Son of Asgard* (ABDO/ Spotlight, 2007, 13+) by writer Akira Yoshida and artist Greg Tocchini is one of Marvel's few efforts to link the character more directly to his mythological roots. In this coming-of-age story, teenager Thor embarks on a quest with the brave Balder and the beautiful Sif (Thor's future wife). The always-scheming Loki is depicted here as more complex and believable than usual. The rich and exciting story emphasizes the importance of young friendships and the teenage yearning to accomplish great deeds as well as the grandeur of Asgardian society, and Tocchini's artwork is absolutely gorgeous. Though not directly based on legends, *Son of Asgard* will pique the interest of readers to explore the actual myths on their own and is appropriate for all ages.

Folktales

Related to myths and legends are the many varieties of folktales: fairy tales, nursery rhymes, fables, tall tales, and the like. A number have appeared as comics over the years. One of the primary publishers is NBM, best known for English translations of European comics. NBM fairy-tale adaptations include *The Princess and the Frog* (1996), by the late comics legend Will Eisner; the ambitious and unusual *Fairy Tales of Oscar Wilde,* from acclaimed fantasy artist P. Craig Russell; and *Fairy Tales of the Brothers Grimm* (1998), adapted by Doug Wheeler with stunning artwork by children's book illustrator David Wenzel (all of these are suitable for all ages).

Folklore and Fairy Tale Funnies (HarperCollins, 2000, 10+) targets children, but its quirkiness and artistry entertain all ages. This unique, oversize anthology was edited by Pulitzer Prize artist Art Spiegelman and his wife, *New Yorker* art editor Françoise Mouly, as first in their *Little Lit* trilogy of comics-style short stories for kids. Contributors include noted American comic artists Spiegelman, Daniel Clowes, Kaz (Kazimieras Prapuolenis), David Mazzucchelli, and late *Pogo* legend Walt Kelly; renowned Europeans Joost Swarte and Lorenzo Mattotti; and established children's illustrators Harry Bliss, William Joyce, and Barbara McClintock. Some stories are fairly straightforward but delightful adaptations of classics such as "Jack and the Beanstalk." Others ("Humpty Trouble") add an unusual twist. Little-known ethnic tales appear: Dutch, Lithuanian, Japanese, and Hasidic. The wonderful artwork covers a wide range of styles, and stories run the gamut from funny to downright weird. Selections from the entire trilogy have been collected into *Big Fat Little Lit* (Puffin, 2006, 10+).

In *The Big Book of Grimm* (DC/Paradox's Factoid Books series, 1999, 16+), Factoid veteran Jonathan Vankin retells 52 of the Grimm stories, assisted by artists with varied drawing styles appropriate to each story. Each tale is told authentically, in an attempt to undo the child-friendly sanitization that has occurred over the decades. As a result, *The Big Book of Grimm* is definitely aimed at an older audience; stories such as the grisly "Three Army Surgeons" have *Tales from the Crypt*–style surprise endings that are "grim" indeed.

The unusual, ongoing *Grimm Fairy Tales* (Zenescope Entertainment, 18+) retells classic tales using a modern situation as a frame. In every episode, a mysterious witch appears to a contemporary protagonist or couple, showing them a classic Grimm tale that relates to their current situation. Stories are written by Joe Tyler and Ralph Tedesco, with various artists. Readers may object to Zenoscope's artistic choices, considering that in an attempt to attract male comics readers, female characters are depicted on comic book covers as damsels in distress with heaving bosoms and ample cleavage. These covers appear in the graphic novel compilations as bonus pinups. Not intended for younger readers, retellings emphasize the darker, more violent, or sexual aspects of each story.

One of the most memorable and unique graphic fables is based on a true story: *Pride of Baghdad* (DC/Vertigo, 2006, 18+), from fan-favorite Brian K. Vaughan, with artwork by Nico Henrichon. During the 2003 American bombing of Baghdad, four lions escaped from their shattered zoo pen and wandered the war-ravaged city before being killed by American soldiers. Vaughan takes the viewpoint of the lions: pride leader Zill, his mates Safa and Noor, and Noor's cub Ali. The lions, so recently yearning for freedom, are now confused, hungry, and desperate. Definitely not for younger readers, *Pride of Baghdad* contains adult language and numerous disturbing episodes: bloody scenes of animals fighting, frank depictions of mating and rape, and the violent death of major characters. The point is to show the horrors of war from a nonhuman perspective. The lions like the Iraqi people may have longed for liberation, but the cost of that freedom comes at an extremely high price. Vaughan's superb writing and Henrichon's stunning art carry not only an action-filled narrative but also believable expressiveness in its animal characters.

Folktales from other countries have also been rendered as comics. Once again, NBM steps to the fore with *Songs of Our Ancestors* (10+), a three-volume series by Asian American graphic artist Patrick Atangan, who adapts stories from Japan, China, and India with gorgeous, appropriate folk-style artwork. NBM also published Will Eisner's adaptation of *Sundiata: A Legend of Africa* (2003, all ages), about a legendary king of Mali; and Rudyard Kipling's *Jungle Book,* adapted by artist P. Craig Russell (10+). A final example is *Master Man: A Tall Tale of Nigeria* (Harper Collins, 2000, all ages), a humorous story of boastful villager Shadusa that was adapted by Aaron Shepard, with lively collage art by David Wisniewski.

Classic Literature

Many of us fondly remember *Classics Illustrated* comics, some 250 issued by Gilberton Publications from 1941 through the 1960s. Notable publishers reviving the concept include Pendulum Press (as "Pendulum Classics" in the 1970s), Berkeley Publishing (27 titles 1990–1991), and Acclaim Comics (beginning in 1997). Today, the Classics Illustrated trademark has been acquired by young adult comics publisher Papercutz, which plans to republish most Berkeley titles plus new editions drawn by European artists, starting with Michel Plessix's exquisite *Wind in the Willows,* originally issued by NBM. Other Papercutz titles published to date include *Through the Looking Glass* (2008; art by Kyle Baker) and *Great Expectations* (2007; art by Rick Geary), both of which were originally published by Berkeley. (All 10+.)

Marvel had a long-running classics series in the 1970s and launched a Marvel Illustrated imprint in 2007 (10+), starting with *Treasure Island* and *Last of the Mohicans.* Marvel has been releasing these completely new full-color stories as six-issue comic book series before collecting them in both hardcover and trade paperback form. Other titles include *The Picture of Dorian Gray, The Man in the Iron Mask,* and Homer's *Illiad,* each published in 2008. All are adapted by previously retired Marvel writer/editor Roy Thomas, with outstanding artwork by a variety of relative newcomers to American comics.

Numerous other publishers have issued classic literature in comics formats. Titles range in depth and sophistication, from Peter Kuper's remarkable adaptation of Franz Kafka's *The Metamorphosis* (Crown, 2003, 16+) to ABDO Publishing's forthcoming *Graphic Classics* series for younger readers, published under the Graphic Planet imprint. Classical Comics, a new British firm, published Shakespeare's *Henry V* as a graphic novel in 2008, with at least seven more titles quickly following, including *Jane Eyre* and *Great Expectations* (13+). Each title in this series will have three editions, covering reading levels basic to advanced. Another British newcomer, Metro Media Limited, unveiled its Eye Classics series under its SelfMadeHero imprint in 2008.

Several American publishers have issued impressive series of classic literature graphically adapted. One of the most original is Eureka Productions with its *Graphic Classics* anthologies (16+); each title is devoted to a specific author or a particular genre, with both iconic examples and lesser-known works. Many focus on horror, science fiction, adventure, and humor, adapting work from Edgar Allen Poe, H. P. Lovecraft, H. G. Wells, Jack London, Arthur Conan Doyle, Bram Stoker, Robert Louis Stevenson, O. Henry, and the iconoclastic Ambrose Bierce. One of the delights of the series is to see a favorite author's works depicted in varied artistic styles, from both longtime comics artists and newer or lesser-known illustrators. Art legends such as

Gahan Wilson and Spain Rodriguez have contributed short pieces. Quality varies from story to story, as with any anthology, but overall, Eureka has created a memorable and exciting series.

Readers should not confuse Eureka's *Graphic Classics* with Barrons's series by the same name of 48-page adaptations designed for middle schoolers (10+). So far, titles include *Dracula, The Hunchback of Notre Dame,* and *Journey to the Center of the Earth.*

Lamentably brief but notable, Penguin's *Puffin Graphics* strove to provide reasonably authentic adaptations of about 150 pages for modern readers, with appendices about artists' techniques (13+). The black-and-white art and reduced page size detracted a bit from the impact, but the art and storytelling were highly engaging. Titles ranged over a variety of book types and interests: *Frankenstein* and *Dracula* through *The Red Badge of Courage, The Wizard of Oz,* and a manga-style *Macbeth.*

NBM, another American publisher, produces both American and European adaptations, including two by the late legend Will Eisner: *Moby Dick* and *The Last Knight* (Cervantes' *Don Quixote*). Eisner provides shorter and more accessible versions for younger readers of monumental works—in *The Last Knight,* by emphasizing slapstick humor and, with *Moby Dick,* by focusing on tension and climactic action (both 10+). For older readers, artist Peter Kuper tackles grim social and economic conditions in adapting Upton Sinclair's historic muckracker *The Jungle* (16+), and Italian Lorenzo Mattotti's grisly *Dr. Jekyll & Mr. Hyde* focuses on the violence and sexuality of Robert Louis Stevenson's psychological horror tale (16+).

Comics can easily accommodate radical reworking of classics, such as in Will Eisner's *Fagin the Jew* (Doubleday, 2003, 16+), which retells the story of Charles Dickens's *Oliver Twist* from pickpocket-meister Fagin's point of view. To an abbreviated version of *Oliver Twist* with a more sympathetic portrayal of Fagin, Eisner adds a lengthy and detailed backstory for the reluctant Oliver's gang leader. Throughout, Eisner fills in historical details about Jews in England and pervasive Victorian anti-Semitism.

REALISTIC FICTION

Often called "slice of life" stories, comics of this type typically involve ordinary—but often memorable—characters dealing with everyday situations in familiar settings. If they were prose novels, libraries and bookstores would categorize them as "general fiction" or "literary fiction," quiet, personal stories where character development is often more important than plotting or dramatic episodes.

Slice-of-life comics can be serious or humorous, semiautobiographical or completely fictional. Some overlap somewhat with genres such as romance, discussed in the previous chapter, and many could be assigned non-genre labels such as "family drama" or "coming of age stories." Other common themes involve friendship, love, sexuality, illness and death, work life, creativity, alienation, and self-discovery.

One subcategory focuses on controversial contemporary issues, as in *Stuck Rubber Baby* by Howard Cruse (civil rights and homosexuality, 16+; see also Appendix B-3), *Four Women* by Sam Keith (rape and its aftermath, 16+), and *Night Fisher* by R. Kikuo Johnson (recreational drug use among teens, 16+). One of the most moving and widely read is Bryan Talbot's modern classic, *The Tale of One Bad Rat* (Dark Horse, 1995, 16+). Helen Potter is a teenage runaway, living precariously on London streets after fleeing from years of her father's sexual abuse. Overwhelmed by misplaced guilt, the girl can no longer bear human touch. Her only sustaining consolations are reading (especially namesake Beatrix Potter's children's books) and her pet rat. After a series of frightening encounters in the city, Helen travels to Beatrix Potter's beloved lake country where a friendly innkeeper employs her. In a local bookstore, she finds psychology books about incest and abuse that help her to understand her situation. Finally she finds courage to confront her father and forgive herself. Amidst the peaceful countryside, Helen resumes sketching and painting, gaining contentment and confidence in her talent. Throughout, Talbot's beautiful artwork is extraordinary.

One of the most significant and critically acclaimed American comics series is *Love and Rockets* by brothers Gilbert ("Beto") and Jaime Hernandez, often dubbed "Los Bros Hernandez" (Fantagraphics, 1980s–1996, 2001–, 16+). Beto's stories, known collectively as "Palomar," are sometimes called "The Heartbreak Soup" stories and focus on townspeople in a Central American village. (See Appendix B-2 for more on Latino-themed titles.) Jaime's stories, known collectively as "Hoppers 13," are also called the "Locas" stories (*locas* is Spanish for crazy women) and star a group of American Chicano women. The best introduction to these two extended narratives is through the massive compilations *Palomar: The Heartbreak Soup Stories* (2003) and *Locas: The Maggie and Hopey Stories* (2005), which collect most of the sagas. Both brothers depict exceptionally strong and memorable female characters, with stories taking place more or less in real time. The main characters age, and individuals first seen as children eventually grow to adulthood. Both brothers also excel at exploring complex and believable personal relationships, especially among women. Otherwise each brother displays a distinctive artistic style as well as a unique storytelling voice. Both the Palomar and Hoppers 13 stories feature a great deal of melodrama and sexual tension, but each one is amazingly complex, nuanced, sensitive, and believable.

Jaime's "Hoppers 13" stories focus on characters from the fictitious California city of Huerta (Hoppers), particularly Maggie Chascarrillo and Esperanza "Hopey" Glass, who meet as teenagers in the punk music scene. The two women become lovers, though their romantic involvement and friendship wax and wane. Hopey is portrayed as lesbian, whereas Maggie is bisexual and has a number of long-term relationships with men. She is a skilled mechanic who later becomes manager of an apartment building. Although Jaime began the narrative with a science-fiction flavor involving a crashed spaceship in Africa, he soon changed to more realistic tales exploring his characters' complex personal lives.

Almost all Beto's "Palomar" stories take place in the small, rural village of Palomar. The central figure is the mysterious and statuesque Luba, who comes to town with her two small daughters and her cousin Ofelia to open a bathhouse. She eventually becomes the town's mayor and has a number of additional female children, each with a different father. Just as Jaime's first stories explored science fiction settings, Beto's had a mystical, folk-religion quality, often likened to the magical realism of novelist Gabriel Garcia Marquez. As in his brother's case, Beto eventually abandoned this approach for more straightforward realism.

Comics often combine comedy and drama into realistic stories of pathos and emotional depth. Cartoonist Lynda Barry has mastered this style of storytelling over 25 years in *Ernie Pook's Comeek,* syndicated widely in alternative weekly newspapers. The strip features a precocious, unsinkably energetic schoolgirl named Marlys Mullen and her extended family: teenage sister Maybonne; oversensitive, bullied younger brother Freddie; and cousins Arna and Arnold. The alcoholic father is long-gone, and the casually cruel and uncaring mother frequently ships the kids off to relatives. Barry's skill at conveying the magical optimism of childhood as well as its bitter disappointments and cruelties come across in stories of bludgeoning sadness, involving friendships, betrayals, first loves, sexual yearning, and public embarrassment. *My Perfect Life* (1992, 16+) follows a year in the life of older sister Maybonne: "I don't even know what's wrong because there's nothing wrong. Except my entire personality." But despite the kids' depressing circumstances, the strips are often funny, ranging from gentle nostalgia to bizarre hilarity. A constant theme is the love, support, and understanding that the three squabbling Mullen siblings provide to one another in the absence of caring adults.

By far the most wrenching of all Barry's books is *The Freddie Stories* (1999, 16+). Freddie is the most other-worldly of Barry's characters and clearly the most damaged by life. Freddie overhears a psychopathic older boy plotting to burn down the house of a Puerto Rican family and manages to prevent it. But the older boy sets fire to another house, burning an elderly woman to death, and Freddie is falsely accused. Amid the recurring horror of Freddie's experiences, Barry tones down the melodrama by focusing on the boy's quirky worldview, his love of insects and animals, and his genuine purity of heart. Although several of the Mullen compilations are out of print, Drawn & Quarterly began reprinting all five collections in 2008. D&Q has also released a new nonfiction title from Barry entitled *What It Is* (2008, 16+), which explores in a unique collage format the artist's personal approach to the creative process.

Other comics of this type based on newspaper strips include long-running classics such as *Gasoline Alley* and *The Gumps,* with their affectionate and believable view of American life. One of the best current realistic strips is Tom Batiuk's widely syndicated *Funky Winkerbean* (1972–, 13+), which follows a group of high school friends as they grow up, marry, and have families of their own. Over the years, Batiuk has tackled a number of serious topics, including teenage pregnancy, adoption, drug use, alcoholism, and—with an extended story arc—breast cancer of a major character, collected in *Lisa's Story: The Other Shoe* (Kent State University Press, 2007, 16+).

No discussion of realistic fiction would be complete without Chris Ware's acclaimed *Jimmy Corrigan: The Smartest Kid on Earth* (Pantheon, 2000, 16+), which was first serialized in Ware's groundbreaking comic series *Acme Novelty Library* (16+). Jimmy is a pudgy, hapless, and lonely middle-aged man with an unsatisfying work life, health issues, and a rocky relationship with his doting, elderly mother. The focus of this quiet, bittersweet comic is on the character's inner life. Ware is a talented and original writer/artist, whose detailed, precise drawings present intentional challenges to the reader with extremely small panels, plus a magician's trunk of artistic devices, including symbols, shifts in perspective, and visual puns to convey more subtle messages.

AUTOBIOGRAPHY/MEMOIR

Harvey Pekar pioneered the field of autobiographical comics, so it is only fitting to begin with him. Pekar was a full-time file clerk at the Veterans Administration Hospital in Cleveland, a lifelong jazz fan, and a freelance jazz critic for newspapers and magazines. In the 1970s, Pekar met the now-legendary underground cartoonist Robert Crumb, and they bonded over their mutual love of jazz. Through Crumb, Pekar quickly realized comics could convey any type of story. He began writing short pieces about his everyday life coupled with his wry, often cynical, sometimes annoying, but always honest observations. With Crumb's support, Pekar hired artists, including Crumb, to draw the stories. Pekar's groundbreaking, self-published comic book series *American Splendor* (18+) debuted in 1976 and was eventually picked up by Dark Horse in the early 1990s. Over the years, Pekar has worked with more than 50 artists, including some of the most respected names in independent comics. As his notoriety grew, much of his work was collected to encompass original work not published elsewhere as well as *American Splendor* comics. Since his 2001 retirement from the VA, Pekar has produced a number of new titles, including several not autobiographical (e.g., *Ego and Hubris* as well as *Macedonia,* which is discussed further later in this chapter).

Like *American Splendor,* most of Pekar's titles include an eclectic mix of short pieces about his daily life and interpersonal relationships, his frank and often unflattering self-analysis, brief reviews of books and music important to him, and occasional two-page biographies of significant jazz musicians. One of Pekar's standouts is *Our Cancer Year* (Four Walls Eight Windows, 1994, 18+), co-written with wife Joyce Brabner, with art by underground "commix" legend Frank Stack. The book focuses on Pekar's lymphoma, the debilitating treatment, and his eventual recovery. This is a powerful work, dealing honestly with Pekar's fears throughout the ordeal and the strain on his work and family. Another notable title is *Our Movie Year: American Splendor Stories* (Ballantine Books, 2004, 18+), focusing on the filming of the award-winning *American Splendor,* starring Paul Giamatti as Pekar. Pekar's most in-depth autobiographical work is *The Quitter* (DC Comics, 2005), with artwork by Dean Haspiel. The story focuses on Pekar's lifelong pattern of self-destructive behavior from childhood through early adulthood, especially his predilection to abandon jobs, projects, and relationships when the going gets tough.

Memoirs sometimes blur fact with fiction, as in the case of the Canadian Seth's *It's a Good Life, If You Don't Weaken* (Drawn & Quarterly, 1996, 18+; 3rd ed., 2004, real name Gregory Gallant). Seth collects work of lesser-known cartoonists of the 1940s and 1950s, and here chronicles his search for information about Kalo, supposedly an obscure Canadian cartoonist. The obsessive Seth not only scours old magazines for evidence of Kalo's work but even visits the now-dead artist's hometown and interviews family members. Readers eventually discover the in-joke: Seth invented Kalo to portray his own real-life interests. Indeed, the imaginary quest provides a wonderful means of introducing Seth himself, his compulsive behavior, and some of the things he cares about most. What makes it autobiographical work is Seth's quiet, honest depiction of his own daily life and his mild neuroses, self-doubt, and navel gazing. Along the way he explores his low-key love life, relationships with his mother and his brother Stephen, intense fascination with nostalgia, and longtime friendship with (real) fellow cartoonist Chester Brown.

Autobiography and fiction blur most profoundly in Debbie Drechsler's work. *Daddy's Girl* (Fantagraphics, 1996, 16+) is a gut-wrenching depiction of the ugly incestuous relationship between young Lily (a stand-in for the author) and her father, who repeatedly forces himself on the little girl at night, even killing Lily's beloved dog after the animal defends her. One of the most powerful stories explores the impact of the sexual assaults on Lily's younger sister Pearl, sharing the same bedroom. The wide-eyed Pearl lies terrified in the next bed, pretending to be asleep. Because Drechsler's memories of these events remain unclear, she is cautious about confirming what did and did not happen. Whether true or not, Drechsler's portrayal of childhood rape at the hands of a father is vivid, visceral, and very disturbing.

Drechsler's *Summer of Love* (Drawn & Quarterly, 2001, 16+) portrays the same family but with far different tone and subject. With parents now minor players, it is 1967 and ninth-grader Lily and her family move to a new state. Lily and sister Pearl quickly make friends, and Lily develops a crush on the older Steve, who plays in a rock band. Although he appears interested in her, she soon discovers he has a steady girlfriend. Meanwhile, Lily has several brief necking sessions with Keith, whom she does not really like. However, Pearl is attracted to girls and has been meeting a classmate for kissing trysts in the woods. The obnoxious Keith, who has already spread false rumors about Lily, discovers Pearl's secret and threatens to reveal it unless Lily "goes all the way." *Summer of Love* is a subtle and poignant look at the insecurities, hesitancy, and petty cruelty of early teenage romance and sexual yearning.

Craig Thompson's highly acclaimed *Blankets* (Top Shelf Productions, 2002, 16+) follows Thompson's first romance with Raina, a girl he meets at a winter church camp. Both the Midwestern rural families in *Blankets* hold quite conservative Christian beliefs, although Raina is more adventurous and freewheeling. For Thompson, this makes the relationship both liberating and confusing, not to mention guilt-inducing to the naive teenager. A subplot deals with Thompson's hopes for a career in art, which does not sit well with his God-fearing parents. Like so many of the very best autobiographical works, *Blankets* is richly detailed, highly personal, and achingly honest, with beautifully mood-appropriate artwork.

Family life and coming of age are keys themes in autobiographical comics. One of the most fully developed is Alison Bechdel's *Fun Home: A Family Tragicomic* (Houghton Mifflin, 2006, 18+), an exquisitely complex story focusing on Bechdel's relationship with her father. The young Alison is an imaginative, artistic child who never quite lives up to the expectations of her distant father, a high school English teacher who also runs the small town's funeral parlor in his spare time. ("Fun Home" was the children's nickname for the business.) The fastidious father cares deeply about literature—the strongest father–daughter connection—and spends years painstakingly revamping their Victorian-era home. When Alison leaves for college, her father's letters are full of advice about the novels she should read for class. At the same time, the hitherto asexual Alison discovers her true sexual orientation. Then she learns her father's lifelong secret: He is a closet homosexual attracted to teenage boys. *Fun Home* is a perfect example of what graphic novels can achieve—both artwork and narrative are individually superb at conveying the story; but taken together, the synergy is extraordinary.

Following the lead of pioneers Crumb and Pekar, many autobiographical comics take the form of warts-and-all confessions. The most embarrassingly honest cartoonist of this school is Toronto-based Joe Matt, whose confessions include *Peepshow: The Cartoon Diary of Joe Matt* (1999), *The Poor Bastard* (2003), and *Spent* (2007) (all 18+). Matt's style and comic timing are as impeccable as his subject matter is unrelenting. As portrayed in his comics, Matt is a consummate navel-gazer, a thoroughly unlikable guy who is self-absorbed, immature, cowardly, cheap, and addicted to pornography and masturbation. Although most of Matt's work focuses on his adult life, *Fair Weather* (2002, 16+) examines events from his childhood, where we see many of his most unlikable traits emerge.

Women artists have staked out their own confessional territory, including Mary Fleener, whose episodic, sometimes raunchy, observational humor appears in *Life of the Party* (Fantagraphics, 1996, 18+), and Lynda Barry's *One! Hundred!*

Demons! (Sasquatch Books, 2002, 16+), described as "auto-bifictional-ography." Unlike the Marlys Mullen stories described earlier, this collection depicts actual events from Barry's life, from her first teen job working for a pair of hippies selling jewelry and plants to the satisfaction she and her husband experienced after adopting an abused dog. A central theme is Barry's disconnected childhood as the redheaded daughter of an Irish American father and a Filipina mother.

French Canadian Julie Doucet's *My New York Diary* (Drawn & Quarterly, 2004, 16+) exhibits an uncensored, completely unembarrassed quality as the confessional comic *par excellence*; and in the recently reissued *My Most Secret Desire* (18+), she fearlessly illustrates a diverse and bizarre array of her subconscious thoughts and dreams. *Diary* depicts her experiences with newfound adult independence, studying art in Montreal and moving to New York City to pursue a career as cartoonist and illustrator. Naive from her convent schooling, she falls into a series of disastrous choices in men while struggling to improve her English, overcome her fear of her New York neighborhood, and establish herself as an artist. Doucet also drinks to excess and experiments with drugs, none of which can be good for her epilepsy. In the end, she shows her determination to succeed by fleeing from a bad-news boyfriend to start a new life with artist friends uptown. Doucet's work is suffused with matter-of-fact crudity, honest realism, and surprising charm with a distinctive style featuring exaggerated characters, visual background jokes, and erratic hand-lettered dialogue. *My New York Diary* is a small masterpiece that easily shows why Doucet is one of the most original cartoonists working today.

Health issues are a common theme in autobiographical comics, such as in Judd Winick's well-known *Pedro and Me: Friendship, Loss, and What I Learned* (Holt, 2000, 14+). Winick was a cast member on the MTV reality show *The Real World,* where his roommate was young Cuban American Pedro Zamora, who was dying of AIDS. This moving work chronicles their growing friendship, their experiences on the show, Pedro's work as an AIDS educator, and the aftermath of his death. Since its publication, *Pedro and Me* has become a fixture in high school classes of all kinds, and justifiably so. This heartfelt and meaningful classic speaks to readers of all ages.

Elizabeth Swados's *My Depression: A Picture Book* (Hyperion, 2005, 16+) deserves special mention. Not a "graphic novel" as such, this unique picture-chronicle tracks Swados's struggle with the disease, from its effects on her work and relationships to her search for a therapist and a means to living a better life. Each page consists of a single scribbled cartoon in her amateurish, but oddly effective style, with a brief, often poetic caption. This brilliant and immediate work captures the surprising range of emotions associated with depression, from leaden paralysis to anxiety, terror, and rage. Intermingled with the story are Swados's down-to-earth suggestions for coping with this debilitating illness. Swados is a remarkable renaissance woman despite her depression—an award-winning playwright, director, composer, musician, novelist, and children's book author.

In recent years, quite a few comics have dealt with cancer, including the previously mentioned *Lisa's Story* (fiction) and *Our Cancer Year* (nonfiction). Other autobiographical examples include Marisa Acocella Marchetto's *Cancer Vixen: A True Story* (Knopf, 2006, 16+) and Miriam Engelberg's *Cancer Made Me a Shallower Person: A Memoir in Comics* (Harper, 2006, 16+). Marchetto, a cartoonist for *Glamour* magazine and *The New Yorker,* survived her bout with breast cancer, but Engelberg did not—she died within a year of her book's publication. Both works depict the writers' cancer experience from diagnosis to eventual outcome with great honesty but with different approaches. *Cancer Vixen* shows unflinching clinical details of tests and treatments, combined with descriptions of Marchetto's high-profile, fashion-conscious life and her ultimate marriage to one of New York's trendiest restauranteurs. Despite the happy ending, *Cancer Vixen* is full of moments of raw emotion: fear, self-doubt, and the devastating moment when Marchetto learns she will never be able to have a child because of the treatments. In contrast, *Cancer Made Me a Shallower Person* takes an irreverent, self-deprecating, pop culture–oriented view of the ordeal. Though Engelberg's drawing style was primitive, she was a gifted cartoonist and writer. Whether laugh-out-loud hilarious or devastatingly grim and personal, her observations are always deeply affecting. A final title is the powerful *Mom's Cancer* (Abrams, 2006, 16+), which was first published a Web comic. Brian Fies employs unsparing honesty to document his mother's long, ultimately unsuccessful battle with lung cancer. The outpouring of praise and support from cancer victims and their families led to the work's republication in print.

Katherine Arnoldi's *The Amazing "True" Story of a Teenage Single Mom* (Hyperion Press, 1998, 16+) is a powerful and heartbreaking story of tragedy and triumph. Passed between family members as a child, fondled by her brother-in-law, and raped and made pregnant by a stranger as a teen, Arnoldi has the child and then couples up with a boyfriend who turns abusive. Escaping him penniless with her baby daughter, she flees out of state, finds help and kindness from strangers, makes friends, and begins a new life. She learns about financial aid and enrolls in community college, starting her on the road to independence and financial security. Throughout her ordeals, the young mother is sustained by her love for her baby and her instinct to protect her. The book ends with a list of agencies that provide assistance for abused women and runaway children.

A wide assortment of autobiographical comics focus on romantic relationships, often in a painfully revealing manner. Jeffrey Brown's pocket-sized *Clumsy: A Novel* and *Unlikely: A True Love Story* (Top Shelf, 2002, 2003, 16+) document romantic connections through brief vignettes capturing those seemingly mundane moments in a relationship that are fraught with so much meaning and importance. *Clumsy* follows Brown's long-distance alliance with girlfriend Theresa, but the couple breaks up after little more than a year, in part because of the frailty of long-distance romance and in part because of

Jeffrey's insecurities and clinginess. Brown is a trained artist, but he employs a childlike, scribbled style with badly done hand-lettering, both of which add charm as well as emphasizing the awkwardness and innocence of young love. Conveying a wonderful sweetness, simplicity, and honesty, the story has appeal for many but will resonate most powerfully with young adults. However, the cartoonish nudity and frank depiction of sexual situations may present problems for younger teens.

Coming-of-age stories focusing on first love, like the previously mentioned *Blankets,* are a common theme for autobiographical comics. An especially poignant example is Chester Brown's *I Never Liked You: A Comic Strip Narrative* (Drawn and Quarterly, 2002, 16+). This sweetly sad story recounts teenager Brown's awkwardness and confusion as he becomes romantically entangled with two girls he has known since childhood while at the same time confronting his mother's mental illness.

A cheerier example of autobiographical romance is Tom Beland's ongoing series *True Story Swear to God* (AiT/Planet Lar, Image Comics, 16+). A California newspaper columnist, Beland meets Lily at a Disneyland bus stop. She is a radio host in Puerto Rico, and the couple begins a long-distance romance. Eventually, Beland moves to Puerto Rico. Beland's simple and charming art complements his sweet, insightful, funny, and disarmingly honest writing. Like Brown's work, the comic often features memorable moments in the relationship, both large and small, from Beland cooking his first meal for Lily to meeting her family for the first time and dealing with culture clash.

OTHER TYPES OF NONFICTION

Until recently, comics treatments of nonfiction other than memoir were somewhat rare, usually commissioned for educational purposes or to commemorate an important event or anniversary. Today, nonfiction comics of all types are widely available and increasing. Children's publishers Lerner, Rosen, and Capstone have embraced nonfiction comics with tremendous enthusiasm, and more works are appearing for older audiences also. Not all are done well, however, such as the unusual *Archaeology: The Comic* (AltaMira Press, 2003, 13+), a lackluster effort written and drawn by South African archaeologist Johannes H.N. Loubser. Intended as an introductory textbook covering the basics of the discipline, information in the 168-page tome is presented via standard comics panels, with amateurish black-and-white drawings. In an effort to make the book more accessible to lay readers, Loubser narrates from the point of view of Squizee, a young girl learning about archaeology.

Comic strips featuring odd facts, people, and events (what the Library of Congress designates as "Curiosities and Wonders") enjoy a long and distinguished history. *Ripley's Believe It or Not!*, the famous single-panel cartoon created by Robert Ripley in 1918, is still syndicated today, the longest continually running newspaper comic in history. In 2003, Dark Horse issued a compilation written by W. Haden Blackman, with art by Cary Nord and others (10+). An especially popular line in this vein is the Factoid Books series (16+), published by DC Comics/Paradox throughout the 1990s. With such titles as *The Big Book of Freaks* (1996), *The Big Book of Conspiracies* (1995), *The Big Book of Weirdos* (1995), and *The Big Book of Urban Legends* (1994), this series explored peculiar phenomena thematically.

History and Biography

Biographies provide excellent material for comics. Several publishers produce entire series for younger readers, including Capstone Press's extensive *Graphic Biographies* aimed at grades 3–5 and for below-grade readers at the middle school level. A more sophisticated series from Hyperion, under the direction of James Sturm's Center for Cartoon Studies, debuted in 2007. Though intended for teens, the books are sufficiently engaging and beautiful to attract all ages. The first is Jason Lutes and Nick Bertozzi's *Houdini: The Handcuff King*. Their collaboration celebrates the power of graphic novels as a storytelling medium, focusing on a single day when the shackled Houdini leapt from Boston's Harvard Bridge into the frigid, swirling Charles River. By focusing on a specific event in Houdini's life, Lutes and Bertozzi communicate an enormous amount about Houdini's personality and methods and the times when he lived. Other titles in the series include Sturm's own *Satchel Paige: Striking Out Jim Crow,* with more on the drawing board.

Pioneer Larry Gonick's *Cartoon History* series (13+) established history as a staple of the comics medium. Gonick holds a master's in mathematics from Harvard and in the late 1970s produced a series of "cartoon history" comics for famed underground publisher Rip Off Press. When then-Doubleday editor Jackie Onassis learned of his work, a collected *The Cartoon History of the Universe* resulted from Morrow in 1982. Since then, Gonick has turned out some two dozen cartoon guides in physics, chemistry, statistics, and genetics, selling hundreds of thousands of copies in multiple languages. Though not a trained historian or artist, he researches each topic, and his artwork, though primitive, is effective. His success is due not just to visuals laced with clever, understated humor but also to his use of storytelling to make his points. The resulting titles are informative and understandable as well as funny. To date, Gonick has written three volumes of *The Cartoon History of the Universe,* covering prehistoric times through the Renaissance (various editions and publishers, 1982–2002), plus *The Cartoon History of the Modern World, Part I* (Collins, 2007) and *The Cartoon History of the United States* (HarperPerennial, 1991).

One of the first African American history comics, *Still I Rise: A Cartoon History of African Americans* (Sterling, rev. ed., 2009, 13+), begins with 1618 Jamestown and ends with the 2009 inauguration of Barack Obama as President of the United States. This ambitious work relates not only the tragedy of the African American experience but its triumphs also, most especially the unending will of its people to resist, make their voices heard, preserve and extend their culture and traditions, and above all persevere through centuries of brutality and hardship. Written by comics publisher Roland Owen Laird and daughter Taneshia Nash Laird, with art by Elihu Bey, *Still I Rise* does not always succeed in meeting this challenge in one volume. Many important people and events are covered only briefly; complicated situations remain insufficiently explained, leaving unanswered questions; and the uneven artwork often fails to provide appropriate drama. But despite these shortcomings, *Still I Rise* is an effective and important work—one that will encourage readers of all races to think and hopefully read further.

Critically acclaimed black cartoonist Kyle Baker's recent history of Nat Turner's 1831 slave rebellion is remarkable partly for its dramatic artwork and partly for the violence of the story. Baker pulls no punches depicting the horrifying brutalities of slavery and the savagery of Turner's uprising, when more than 50 whites—men, women, and children—were slaughtered. Baker chose to relate the story almost wordlessly, letting the dramatic pictures speak for themselves. The spare text comes from Turner himself, as reported by his lawyer in *The Confessions of Nat Turner.* Baker's compelling and beautifully drawn *Nat Turner* was first published in two volumes in 2006–2007 and recently republished as a single volume (Abrams, 2008, 13+).

Two African American history biographies warrant special mention. *Malcolm X: A Graphic Biography* by longtime comics editor Andrew Helfer, with art by Randy DuBurke (Hill & Wang, 2006, 16+), is a detailed, densely written work aimed at adults. Very complete for its scant size, the biography covers Malcolm X's troubled childhood, teen years as a small-time criminal, time in jail, conversion to Islam, rise to leadership in the Black Muslim movement, clash with leader Elijah Muhammed, and assassination by others in the movement. The no-holds-barred treatment includes extensive text and photorealistic art.

Sometimes described as an "interpretive biography," Canadian Ho Che Anderson's remarkable *King: A Comic Book Biography* (Fantagraphics Books, 2005, 16+) is notable for several reasons: Anderson's decision to address all aspects of the civil rights leader's life, whether flattering or not; the use of a "Greek chorus" of individuals who comment on events as they unfold; and the use of diverse artistic techniques and styles. Anderson employs both black-and-white and color art, from realistic to abstract, as well as including collages and hand-colored photographs. The result is a mature, powerful, and highly original work about a complex man and a pivotal era in American history. (See Appendix B-1 for more on African American–themed graphic novels.)

Over the years, a few nonfiction comics have addressed the history of the American West. The best come from the late Jack Jackson. Reflecting meticulous research and lovingly accurate artwork, Jackson's best-known Western titles include *Los Tejanos* (Fantagraphics, 1982), *Lost Cause* (Kitchen Sink, 1998), and *Comanche Moon* (reprinted by Reed Graphica, 2003) (all 13+).

The titles treat, respectively, the Texas Republic's Mexican hero Juan Seguin, outlaw John Wesley Hardin, and half-breed Comanche chief Quanah Parker. Unfortunately, the first two are long out of print but can be purchased from used book vendors.

George O'Connor's unusual *Journey into Mohawk Country* (First Second, 2006, 13+) recounts the 1634 travels of Dutch colonist Harmen Meyndertsz van den Bogaert in the Mohawk River Valley, west of what is now Albany. The young Bogaert volunteered to negotiate with the powerful Iroquois Confederacy to strengthen trade relations between the Dutch and the Indians. More valuable for historical than literary value, Bogaert's chronicle and O'Connor's direct excerpts unfortunately make for a rather dull narrative. In another strange choice, the artist uses a very cartoon-like style, sometimes almost humorous. The juxtaposition of this art style with the dry 17th-century text is oddly jarring. On the other hand, O'Connor clearly undertook extensive research—the Dutch and Mohawk costumes as well as the longhouses, forts, and other contemporary environs are extremely accurate. Despite its peculiar approach, *Journey into Mohawk Country* is a little-known story that will intrigue history buffs.

War/Current Events

Political events, especially those dealing with war and armed conflict, have become significant subjects for nonfiction comics. The best-known true account is Art Spiegelman's classic *Maus,* describing the experiences of Spiegelman's father Vladek in Nazi concentration camps (various publishers and editions, 16+). Spiegelman uses anthropomorphic characters to illustrate the inhuman events—mice for the Jews, cats for the Nazis, and pigs for the Poles. *Maus* also examines the long-term effects of Vladek's ordeal, including the eventual suicide of his wife (herself a concentration camp survivor) and his strained relationship with his son.

The terrorist attacks on September 11, 2001, have generated a variety of titles, including several "tribute" anthologies. Art Spiegelman's *In the Shadow of No Towers* (Pantheon, 2004, 13+) is his very personal reaction to 9/11 and the American political landscape in the months that followed, recounting Spiegelman's experiences during the attack—his home and office were both mere blocks away, and his daughter attended high school in the towers' shadow. The experience rocked Spiegelman to the core, and his account incorporating his intense antagonism toward the Bush administration will polarize most readers. Agree or not, *In the Shadow of No Towers* is a highly imaginative and engaging visual work by a comics master.

Perhaps the most significant and unusual comics work relating to 9/11 is *The 9/11 Report: A Graphic Adaptation* (Hill and Wang, 2006, 13+), based on the government's official 2004 report formally known as *The Final Report of the National Commission on Terrorist Attacks Upon the United States.* Writer Sid Jacobson and artist Ernie Colon, both retired industry veterans with decades of experience, wanted to make this important but daunting document more accessible to a general audience. Following the structure of the original report, 13 chapters cover background on Bin Laden and al Qaeda, the government's counterterrorism efforts prior to 9/11, mistakes that were made leading up to the attack, and the immediate aftermath. For the most part, Jacobson's script paraphrases the government text, although some dialogue was invented for dramatic purposes. The graphical approach actually enriches understanding of the attacks, especially the detailed timeline laying out the numerous simultaneous events. Although some commentators objected to the very idea of recasting the report into comics, the adaptation has received uniformly positive reviews as well as endorsement from Commission heads.

Readers are also beginning to see comics about the conflict in Iraq. Written for young readers, *Alia's Mission: Saving the Books of Iraq* (Knopf, 2004, all ages), by political cartoonist Mark Alan Stamaty, is a wonderfully inspiring all-age story based on a real event well known to librarians worldwide. Alia Muhammad Baker is chief librarian for the Basra Central Library. As the American invasion of Iraq looms in 2002, she worries about the library and its precious contents, much of it irreplaceable. When the government shows no interest in protecting the collection, Alia hatches a plan. With the help of friends and neighbors, she moves 30,000 volumes out of the library to safety while most of the library building is burned in the ensuing conflict. Stamaty depicts well Alia's love of knowledge and books, as well as her desperation and determination in such difficult times, conveying a "you are there" immediacy. *Alia's Mission* is an uplifting story of average people rising to the challenge of extraordinary circumstances.

Two exceptional cartoonists have produced groundbreaking comics journalism: Joe Sacco and Ted Rall. The Malta-born Sacco, who holds a degree in journalism and grew up in Australia and California, was vacationing in the Middle East in 1991 and began sketching observations in Palestine's occupied territories. He visited the Gaza Strip, refugee camps in the West Bank, and other locations in this troubled area. He also took countless reference photographs and interviewed both Palestinians and Israelis. This resulted in two 1996 graphic novels: *Palestine: A Nation Occupied* and *Palestine: In the Gaza Strip,* reprinted together in 2001 as *Palestine* (Fantagraphics, 16+).

Following his Middle East work, Sacco turned his attention to the horrific killing in the former Yugoslavia, making four 1995–1996 trips to Bosnia during the war's gradual, painful end. In *Safe Area Gorazde: The War in Eastern Bosnia, 1992–95* (Fantagraphics, 2002, 16+), Sacco reports the tragic events of an area little understood and little visited, even by journalists: the besieged, predominantly Muslim town Gorazde, designated by the United Nations as a "safe zone." In *The Fixer: A Story from Sarajevo* (2003, 16+), Sacco provides the very different viewpoint of Neven, a former paramilitary fighter now working as a "fixer," providing services such as translation to Western journalists.

The Fixer bounces through time, describing Sacco's conversations with Neven and others who know him and conveying how difficult it is to cover events in a war zone and to understand chaotic and controversial situations. Sacco has a phenomenal eye for small details that help readers understand the heart of complex situations as well as a charming, self-deprecating view of his own role as observer. Nothing like these works had ever been seen before Sacco.

In another unique journalistic voice, Ted Rall's *To Afghanistan and Back* (NBM, 2002, 16+) recounts his experiences "in-country" during the height of U.S. military operations in late 2001. Like Sacco, Rall adopts a very personal style and is a major character in the story. His mixed-format account contains prose essays, photographs, and political cartoons as well as three chapters in traditional comics. Unlike Sacco's more realistic art, Rall's goofy artistic style would be more usual for *The Simpsons,* but it is oddly effective here for this deadly subject. Another difference: unlike Sacco's indirect reporting through interviewees' voices, Rall is not shy about criticizing, with real outrage, U.S. policy as well as the mainstream media's one-sided coverage of the war. Rall's earlier *Silk Road to Ruin* (NBM, 2006, 16+) chronicles his 1997 travels through the former Soviet republics of Central Asia.

With a highly personal look at the everyday lives of the people caught up in tragic circumstances, Sacco and Rall provide a compelling alternative to traditional reporting, comparable to the best photojournalism or documentary filmmaking.

Other comics creators have followed Sacco and Rall's coverage of world conflict. In *Fax from Sarajevo* (Dark Horse Comics, 1998, 13+), comics legend Joe Kubert relates the experiences of his friend Ervin Rustemagic, whose family survived the 18-month siege of Sarajevo beginning in 1992. His powerful, full-color work is every bit as compelling as Sacco's. In the less successful *Macedonia* (Villard, 2007, 16+), Harvey Pekar and artist Ed Piskor tell the story of an American graduate student who travels to Macedonia to learn why this region of the war-torn Balkans has remained relatively peaceful despite long-standing ethnic animosities. However, the text-heavy work stints on dramatic action and character development.

Comics may work as travelogue as well as journalism. French Canadian Guy Delisle spent time in North Korea for an animation project and produced *Pyongyang: A Journey in North Korea* (Drawn & Quarterly, 2005, 13+). Despite its simple, cartoonish style, *Pyongyang* is a fascinating account providing a rare look at everyday life under Kim Jong-Il's Orwellian regime.

True Crime

In whatever media told, the grisly details of true crime hold a long-standing voyeuristic appeal. It is no surprise that graphic novels—emphasis on the graphic—are ideally suited to these stories. One of the most adroit creators is Rick Geary, whose *A Treasury of Victorian Murder* series (NBM, 13+) uses a style recalling old-time newspaper engravings. The first volume, itself titled *A Treasury of Victorian Murder,* explored three rather unremarkable cases of stabbings and poisonings, with overtones of romantic intrigue. Since this 1987 collection, Geary has produced eight more titles, including the assassinations of Presidents Lincoln and Garfield (*The Murder of Abraham Lincoln* and *The Fatal Bullet,* respectively), the fabled case of Lizzie Borden (*The Borden Tragedy*), and of course *Jack the Ripper.* Geary always provides extensive detail based on meticulous research, with biographical information on the victims as well as on perpetrators or suspects, plus maps, charts, and floor plans. The artist recently began a new series for NBM, *A Treasury of XXth Century Murder.*

Whereas Geary recounts the Jack the Ripper murders in a mere 64 pages, Alan Moore and artist Eddie Campbell devote 572 pages to their critically acclaimed version: *From Hell: Being a Melodrama in Sixteen Parts* (Top Shelf, 2004, 18+). Of the many theories about Jack the Ripper, Moore fastens on the so-called "Royal Theory" that suggests "saucy Jack" was Sir William Gull, surgeon to Queen Victoria, who became obsessed with mysticism and Masonic ritual while trying to protect the Queen's grandson from blackmail. Whether true or not, the gripping and elegantly told story is supported with extensive, accurate historical detail, although Campbell's scratchy drawing style may not appeal universally. Note that *From Hell* depicts the appalling violence of these murders in gruesome detail and includes over 40 pages of Moore's endnotes with background information about the era and the case.

Science

Although seemingly unlikely, science topics have also been given graphic novel treatment with varying success. Gonick's previously mentioned *Cartoon Guides* series has tacked genetics, environmental science, chemistry, physics, and even statistics. Two masters at popularizing science via comics are Jay Hosler, a PhD biologist and college professor, and Jim Ottaviani, a former nuclear engineer and now a science librarian at the University of Michigan. Both men self-publish through their own companies.

Hosler's charming *The Sandwalk Adventures* (Active Synapse, 2003, 13+) explains basic evolutionary biology in an imaginative and understandable manner. The premise: An aging Charles Darwin chats with a pair of sentient follicle mites living in his left eyebrow. The mites believe Darwin is God, so they ask him about the meaning of life. This clever framing device introduces Darwin's concepts of evolution and natural selection, together with biographical information about Darwin. Substantial annotations explain background and concepts in greater detail, plus a brief bibliography lists materials for further reading. Hosler is a wonderful cartoonist as well as an inventive and funny storyteller. Another Hosler book, *Clan Apis* (Active Synapse, 2000, 10+), introduces the complex life cycle, physiology, social life, and behavior of honeybees from the bee's viewpoint. Unlike such animated fare as *Bee Movie, Clan Apis* provides an extremely realistic look at bee life, from egg to adulthood and death. Hosler infuses *Clan Apis* with humor and fast-paced adventure, while interweaving facts into the story. Both works use comics to introduce sophisticated science topics in an entertaining and easy-to-understand manner.

Since 1997, Ottaviani has issued about one new title yearly through his G.T. Labs publishing firm. Intended for older teens and adults, titles focus on lives of groundbreaking scientists, famous or not. Unlike Hosler, Ottaviani does not illustrate his own work; instead, he hires talented, well-known comics artists to help him. His first two efforts were anthologies: *Two-Fisted Science* (1997, 13+) focused on notable physicists, from Isaac Newton to Albert Einstein, and *Dignifying Science* (1999, 13+) introduced a diversity of women scientists, from Marie Curie to Rosalind Franklin, whose work on DNA structure preceded that of Watson and Crick. Other Ottaviani books include *Fallout* (2001, 16+), which explores the lives of Leo Szilard and J. Robert Oppenheimer and their work on the first atomic bomb; *Suspended in Language* (2004, 16+), a biography of quantum physics pioneer Niels Bohr; and *Bone Sharps, Cowboys, and Thunder Lizards* (2005, 13+), a fascinating account of the rivalry between two 19th-century paleontologists, Othniel Marsh and Edward Cope. Ottaviani painstakingly portrays these scientists' human qualities, and his skillful dialogue and pacing often result in surprisingly compelling stories.

Philosophy and Religion

Philosophy might seem like another unusual discipline for comics, but the two can make a surprisingly effective marriage. Totem Books, an American imprint of British publisher Icon Books, has over 30 titles introducing important philosophers and philosophical topics such as *Introducing Descartes* and *Introducing Empiricism* (16+). Authored by experts, the books do not always follow the standard comics format of multiple panels per page but contain one or two illustrations per page, with dialogue balloons and several brief text paragraphs. Although providing only a cursory treatment of complex topics, the series serves as a painless and even enjoyable introduction for readers who might otherwise be intimidated. Special mention should be given to one true gem: *Introducing Kafka* (18+), written by David Zane Mairowitz and illustrated by Robert Crumb. (An edition titled *R. Crumb's Kafka* is available from ibooks.) Crumb's masterful, detailed cartoons are ideally suited to Kafka, combining absurdist humor with a sense of sadness, self-loathing, and sexual ambiguity. Icon/Totem has extended the "Introducing" series to cover psychology, science, and religion, including Christianity, Hinduism, Buddhism, and Islam. It should be mentioned that one of Totem's books, *Introducing the Holocaust* (2000, 16+), has been taken to task by reviewers for its unusual and controversial "revisionist" approach.

Fred Van Lente and artist Ryan Dunlavey take a different tack with their *Action Philosophers!* series (Evil Twin Comics, 16+). Described as "the lives and thoughts of history's A-list brain trust," the stories depict philosophical concepts with gag-style visual metaphors and irreverent, over-the-top humor ideal for neophyte adults, especially college students.

Literature and art often address or reference religion, so it should be no surprise that comics, melding words and art, address spirituality and belief. (See also Appendix B-4.) Many graphic novels tackling religion approach complex topics in a sophisticated manner, not as a watered-down "Religion Lite." Faith-based graphic novels represent a growing niche in publishing today and could easily occupy an entire chapter. Titles run the gamut of genres and approaches: science fiction (*Testament* by Douglas Rushkoff and Liam Sharpe, 18+), historical fiction (Ben Katchor's *The Jew of New York*, 16+), fantasy (*Marked,* by Steve Ross, 13+), folklore (Steve Sheinkin's *The Adventures of Rabbi Harvey*, all ages), superheroes (the *Guardian* line of comics from Urban Ministries, Inc., 13+), and of course, nonfiction (ranging from Osamu Tezuka's masterpiece *Buddha* to David Gantz's witty and informative *Jews in America: A Cartoon History*, both 13+). Religious organizations and publishers now realize that comics are a great way to reach readers of all ages.

A variety of graphic novel renditions of the Bible have been published recently, from both Christian and Jewish publishers. Most are aimed at younger readers. Examples include *The Lion Graphic Bible* (Lion, 2001), *The Picture Bible* (Cook Communication Ministries, 1998), *The Kids' Cartoon Bible* (Jewish Publication Society of America, 2002), and the *Illustrated Bible* series from publisher Thomas Nelson. Even *The Book of Mormon* is currently being adapted into comics by the talented Mike Allred, best known as the creator of the offbeat superhero Madman. The series, titled *The Golden Plates* (AAA Pop, 2004–, all ages), is published by Allred's own company. Three volumes have been issued to date.

One of the most interesting and unusual Judaism-based titles is J. T. Waldman's stunning and meticulously researched *Megillat Esther* (Jewish Publication Society of America, 2006, 16+), retelling the Old Testament's book of Esther. Another interesting reworking of Old Testament canon is fan-favorite Kyle Baker's *King David* (DC/Vertigo, 16+), which covers David's legendary battle with Goliath through his eventual rise to King of Israel. Baker pulls no punches in telling the bizarre and often gruesome tale while interjecting his distinctive brand of slapstick humor, all wrapped in vivid and beautiful full-color artwork.

In the *Eye Witness* series (Head Press Publishing, 13+), Robert James Luedke combines major events from the early books of the New Testament with a modern-day thriller reminiscent of the *Da Vinci Code*. Three volumes have been published so far: *Eye Witness: A Fictional Tale of Truth, Acts of the Spirit,* and *Rise of the Apostle*.

CONCLUSION

It is currently said that "serious" graphic novels are enjoying their own long-awaited golden age. As we have now seen, a diverse landscape of comics exists beyond the realm of superheroes. In fact, with each passing year, publishers are issuing more and more outstanding titles entirely outside even traditional genre fiction. Many librarians and teachers hope that teenage fans of superheroes and genre fiction will eventually diversify into "more serious" comics. In fact, many longtime superhero fans often do delve into a wider variety of genres, themes, and styles as their tastes broaden and mature. But by now, superhero titles have matured also, and the comics racks are filled with any number of rich, complex, and sophisticated superhero titles, from such older classics as *Watchmen* and *The Dark Knight Returns* to newer fare such as *The Authority.*

The comics landscape outside superheroes is not necessarily better than superhero stories—it is just different and more varied. Just as any creative medium contains good, bad, and in-between work, the same is true of the entire comics universe, whether superhero or not.

SUGGESTED RESOURCES

The following sources may provide some coverage of superheroes and manga but tend to devote substantial content to genre, non-genre, and alternative comic art, American and sometimes also international.

Anthologies

Anthologies can be a convenient way to get acquainted with newer and lesser-known comics creators. A number of quality series are available. All of these except for *Project: Romantic* are ongoing so far as is known. The current publisher is given unless otherwise noted.

Attitude. Vols. 1–3. New York: NBM, 2002–2006.
The Best American Comics. New York: Houghton Mifflin, 2006–2008.
Blab! Vols. 1–18. Seattle: Fantagraphics, 1986–2007.
Drawn & Quarterly Showcase. Vols. 1–5. Montreal: Drawn & Quarterly, 2003–2008.
Flight. Vols. 1–2: Berkeley, CA: Image, 2004–2005; Vol. 3: New York: Ballantine, 2006; Vol. 4–5: New York: Villard, 2007–2008.
Kramers Ergot. Vols. 1–7. Oakland, CA: Buenaventura Press, 2000–2008.
Mome. Vols. 1–14. Seattle: Fantagraphics, 2005–2009.
Project: Romantic; An Anthology Dedicated to Love and Love Stuff. 1 vol. Richmond, VA: AdHouse Books. 2006.
24 Hour Comics. Thousand Oaks, CA: About Comics, 2004–2008.

Magazines

Comic Art Magazine. Vols. 1–9. Oakland, CA: Buenaventura Press, 2002–2007.
The Comics Journal. Nos. 1–296. Seattle: Fantagraphics, 1976–2009.

Books

Gravett, Paul. *Graphic Novels: Everything You Need to Know.* New York: HarperCollins, 2005.

Kannenberg, Gene. *500 Essential Graphic Novels: The Ultimate Guide.* New York: Collins Design, 2008.

Pawuk, Michael. *Graphic Novels: A Genre Guide to Comic Books, Manga, and More.* Westport, CT: Libraries Unlimited, 2007.

Wolk, Douglas. *Reading Comics: How Graphic Novels Work and What They Mean.* Cambridge, MA: Da Capo Press, 2007.

Web Sites

Comic Book Awards Almanac. http://www.hahnlibrary.net/comics/awards/index.html

The Comics Journal (online site has additional features). http://www.tcj.com

The Comics Reporter. http://www.comicsreporter.com

GraphicNovelReporter. http://www.graphicnovelreporter.com

Lambiek Comiclopedia. http://www.lambiek.net

Sequart Research and Literacy Organization. http://www.sequart.com

6

GRAPHIC NOVELS: A GLOBAL LITERATURE

INTRODUCTION

Martha Cornog

It has been only recently in the United States that comics have come to mean serious works of substantial length for all ages. But in Japan and some other parts of the world, a tradition of serious comics developed much earlier, yielding a rich store of critically acclaimed titles. In still other countries, comics activity is expanding quickly or slowly, but expanding it is, influenced by the overarching appeal of popular American, Asian, and European titles.

Librarians would do well to consider adding graphic novels from many countries and cultures to their collections. With "globalization" a buzzword in education, science and technology, and especially consumer goods, pictured stories from other nations can lend understanding in a more immediate and entertaining fashion than news reports or even *National Geographic*. Less formally, graphic narratives created outside our nation's borders can be more cosmopolitan and sophisticated than many of our own comics, with different, even experimental approaches to plots and characters. The art spans a full range, from cartoony doodles to beautifully painted color vistas, a wider range than manga and even most American comics.

Part 1 of this chapter provides background, context, and a bit of history about creation and publishing of graphic narrative formats outside the United States. Part 2 gives suggestions and sources for helping librarians collect international work in English translation. (See Appendix B-2 for more on Latino-themed graphic novels, in English and Spanish.)

PART 1: THE GLOBAL CONTEXT OF GRAPHIC NARRATIVE

John A. Lent

Graphic Novel: Definitions

Where to start?

A graphic novel can be almost any book of visually/verbally told stories, although the term is something of a misnomer given that "graphic novels" can be long or short, fiction or nonfiction, even collections of short stories, uncompiled partial works, or magazine serials. Graphic novels embrace all genres, can be of any shape or format, and do not have to be of the "format, serious intent, and hefty weight of traditional literature" or be the "visual equivalent of 'an extended, fictional work'" (Gravett 2005, 8). Moreover, American and European interpretations of the concept have been considered to be somewhat different. In the United States, the important word has been "novel"—that is to say, the story—whereas Europeans emphasize the graphic dimension (Baetens 2001, 8).

Origins

That said, it becomes apparent that graphic novels existed long before comics critic and magazine publisher Richard Kyle coined the term in 1964 (Kaplan 2006, 14) or before cartoonist Will Eisner popularized the concept shortly after. Perhaps the Japanese were first, with the *kibyōshi* ("yellow covers"), very popular among adults in the late 18th century. The *kibyōshi* was a "smallish (5x7 inches) woodblock-printed booklet, in one to three volumes, with black-and-white interior pictures dressed up by occasionally colorful frontispieces on yellow-colored covers" (Kern 2007, "The *kibyōshi:* Japan's" 3). With hand-stitched bindings, the *kibyōshi* usually consisted of 10 to 30 pages of a sustained visual-verbal narrative, came in a number of genres, was highly topical to the times, and included elements of classical literature, parody, and satire (see Kern 2007, *"Kibyōshi: The World's First"* 2).

Other cases can be made for early appearance of graphic novels in the work of the Swiss schoolteacher, novelist, and critic Rodolphe Töpffer (1799–1846). Often thought to be the inventor of the comic strip, Töpffer called his drawings all kinds of disparaging names, but in actuality they were graphic novels. His main biographer David Kunzle used the terms "picture story" and "comic strip" to describe Töpffer's work but admitted,

> I usually refrain from the tempting new coinage *graphic novel,* which has now overtaken *comic book,* although that is exactly what Töpffer's are. What distinguishes the new graphic novel from the old comic book is length, unity of

theme, and a real moral focus; so too, Töpffer is distinguished from most of his followers in the 19th century, who typically ran their strips over a single page, double pages, or at most a few installments of a magazine. (Kunzle 2007, xi)

More recently, other examples of graphic novels existed before the format became popular in the United States. *Nobela komiks* (novel comics) in the Philippines began in the 1960s and ran in weekly, serialized versions for years. In Japan came the post–World War II "red books," many produced by Osamu Tezuka, which were soon superseded by the gigantic manga graphic novels. In China, *lianhuanhua* ("linked pictures") were published from 1918 onward (see discussion later). Appearing in large, hardcover albums after the end of the war, the Franco-Belgian *bande dessinée* constituted a type of graphic novel as did other European work, such as the Czech artist Kája Saudek's *Muriel a Andél*, (Muriel and the Angels), a mid-1960s 250-page story of a physician, a winged man from the future, and a boy who will grow up to disband all armies throughout the world (Prokůpek 2003, 323).[1]

International Graphic Novels

Delineating the contours of the term "international graphic novel" may seem simple. Obviously we include European comics and graphic novels by artists such as Pratt, Druillet, Moebius, Manara, and others imported into or reprinted in the United States in their original languages and later translated into English. We also include Japanese manga and now Korean manhwa published in English by U.S. companies such as VIZ or TOKYOPOP, as well as graphic novels with multiple creators from different countries. However, U.S.-published graphic novels may be written and/or drawn by Europeans, Latin Americans, or Asians—and sometimes by creators from still other parts of the world. The situation has become more complex recently with the Internet and globalization trends, so "you can find artists from all over the world working in American [graphic novels] as well as [graphic novels] from all over the world available in English" (Hagenauer 2007).

A few examples make the point. *Persepolis* is a graphic novel about growing up in Iran written by Iranian-born Marjane Satrapi, who now resides in Paris, and published both in Europe and in the United States. *V for Vendetta, Watchmen,* and *Lost Girls* were created by Briton Alan Moore (with David Lloyd, Dave Gibbons, and Melinda Gebbie, respectively) and are popular worldwide, particularly in the United States, where they have topped popularity and sales lists. Works by Europeans (e.g., Joost Swarte's *Modern Swarte,* Gipi's *Garage Band,* Lewis Trondheim and Fabrice Parme's *Tiny Tyrant*), by Asians (e.g., Lat's *Kampung Boy,* Tezuka's works, Byun Byung Jun's *Run, Bong-gu, Run!*), by the New Zealander Dylan Horrocks (*Hicksville*), and by other artists around the world have been put out as graphic novels by American publishers Fantagraphics, First Second, NBM, and others.

In the following sections, I attempt an overview of the development and present status of graphic novels worldwide, broken down by the continental categories of Europe, Asia, Africa, and other regions. Emphasis is on works available in English, although others are included to show the range of graphic novel development.

Europe

British comics scholar Roger Sabin wrote that there "can be little doubt that the graphic novel was in part inspired by European albums" (1996, 227). Printed in hardbound editions, these albums usually contained about 48 pages of colored strips based on one title or character. Sabin credits *Tintin* by Hergé as being instrumental early on in spearheading the development of the albums, stating *Tintin* albums were on sale in England as early as 1958. The albums were part of a system beneficial to all concerned. Stories pre-published in regular, newsstand magazines were later republished as individual stories in albums, resulting in a higher-quality product and dual royalties for the creators. The European system showed England and the United States that working in comics need not be anonymous or unglamorous and that creators could earn royalties. Moreover, European storytelling and flexible art styles offered new models and became influential (227).

After *Tintin,* France's *Asterix the Gaul* by Albert Uderzo and René Goscinny appeared in album form starting in 1961, but albums had a "spasmodic" existence in Europe throughout the 1970s. The boom came in the 1980s as the albums became intertwined with the graphic novel phenomenon. Particularly associated with European albums at that time were Titan Books, Marvel/Epic, NBM, Catalan, and Heavy Metal Publishing, which all printed books translated into English for the British and American markets. According to Sabin (1996, 221–25), albums other than those of Hergé that influenced UK and U.S. comics included the following:

- Moebius's (Jean Giraud) *The Airtight Garage,* a 1976 story about the beautiful fantasy worlds of explorer Major Grubert, as well as Moebius's saga *The Incal* and his *Arzach* collection
- Science fiction albums such as *Gods in Chaos* and *The Woman Trap* by Enki Bilal (a Yugoslav living in Paris) as well as Frenchman Philippe Druillet's *Lone Sloane,* the tale of an adventurer through time and space
- Historical drama series such as *Corto Maltese* by Italy's Hugo Pratt or *The War of the Trenches,* a description of the life of a World War I recruit done by France's Jacques Tardi

Also appearing in album format were Westerns such as *Lieutenant Blueberry* by Frenchmen Michel Charlier and Jean Giraud, various thrillers, and "eurotica," especially the work of Italians Milo Manara (*Butterscotch* and

Click!) and Guido Crepax (*Emmanuelle, The Story of O*). As Horn pointed out (2004), Crepax illustrated a number of celebrated novels of erotic literature, and his *Valentina* appeared as an album in 1968.

Many more albums-cum-graphic novels appeared subsequently, such as the following:

- The Italian Lorenzo Mattotti's *Fires,* about a navy officer's mutiny
- Other French works, such as François Boucq's *The Magician's Wife;* Philippe Dupuy and Charles Berberian's *Monsier John;* Claire Bretecher's *Where's My Baby Now?*; Frank Pé and Michel de Bom's *Broussaille* series, which originated in *Spirou* magazine in 1978 (Hill 2004); and Edmond Baudoin's *Voyage,* which started out as the 44-page *Le Premier Voyage* in 1987 and was made into a 228-page graphic novel in 1995
- Upon influence from the Continent, Irish writer Garth Ennis and artist John McCrea's 1989 *Troubled Souls,* concerning the streets of Ulster and the IRA; and Briton Alan Moore's works, usually in collaboration with others, beginning with *Watchmen* in the late 1980s and including many other titles since then

Baudoin's autobiographical works have been credited with helping shape 21st-century graphic novels (Le Duc 2004).

The artist-run L'Association has produced many French-language graphic novels since its founding in 1990 by Lewis Trondheim, J. C. Menu, Stanislas, Matt Konture, David B., and Killoffer. Trondheim was noted for *Lapinot el les Carottes de Patagonie,* a 500-page graphic novel that he began as an experiment in 1992 to teach himself to draw more effectively (Beaty 2003, 177). David B.'s masterpiece is *Epileptic,* a story in which he imagines his elder brother's epilepsy as a monster.

A new generation of Spanish publishers established publishing houses Sinsentido and Astiberri, which began to publish works of independent cartoonists and start graphic novel lines. Established at the end of the 1990s by Jesús Moreno, Sinsentido quickly brought out works "at the cutting edge of the graphical radical experience," including Ricard Castells's *Poco,* Silvestre's (Federico del Barrio) *Relaciones,* Isidro Ferrer and Grassa Toro's *Exilos,* and Grandelli and Ricci's *Anita* (Pons 2003, 146). Founded in 2001, Astiberri reprints U.S. graphic novels and those by Spanish authors, including Javier de Isusi's *Las Viajer de Juan Sin Tierra,* set in the Zapatista uprising in Chiapas, Mexico. Graphic novels are expanding as large bookstore chains such as FNAC establish graphic novel sections and as manga continues to invade Spain (MacDonald 2007). Spanish publisher Ediciones Joputa added a graphic narrative line called collection Mercat and then split off the new Edicions de Ponent to handle the line, which included *Ruinas, 24 Horas, Monólogo y Alucinación del Gigante,* and *El Pie Frito* (Pons 2003, 144–45).

Publication of graphic novels in other parts of Europe is still underdeveloped. Successful literary graphic novels have been especially sparse in the Netherlands. This has been attributed to cartoonists not deviating from paths once chosen and not willing to try new ventures (Sanders 2002, 148). The few exceptions include the following:

- Lian Ong's *Horizon,* concerning the rise and fall of a wandering people
- Hanco Kolk's *Meccano,* "modern social criticism in an experimental form"
- Guido von Driel's *De Fijnproever,* the true story of the author's "whore-hopper" friend
- Peter van Dongen's *Rampokan,* about the Indonesian struggle for independence from the Dutch in 1946

In Russia also, graphic novel–like works have been sparse, and most are translations of foreign titles such as *Maus, Asterix, Sin City, Peanuts,* and two by Hugo Pratt (Alaniz 2005, "Late/Post-Soviet" 9). Exceptions include the following:

- *She Is Anna,* an inversion of plot, characters, and motivations of Leo Tolstoy's *Anna Karenina* that was created by Zhora Litichevsky in 1997 (Alaniz 2005, "The 'Quintessentially Russian'" 117)
- Katya Metelitsa and Igor Sapozhkov's *Anna Karenina by Leo Tolstoy,* a graphic novel that sets that classic tale in a "very modern Moscow of strip joints, sushi bars, and flowing cocaine" (Alaniz 2005, "Late/Post-Soviet" 9)

Comics in any form are still under suspicion in Russia, even though the nation has been self-termed "the most literate nation in the world" (Alaniz 2005, "Late/Post-Soviet" 87). For a short while in the early 1990s, Tema Studio, one of two comics collectives, published graphic novels including Alexei Lukyanchikov's *Ekipazh* (The Crew), but by the mid-1990s, Tema had left comics for animation.

Of the rare "solo albums" in Sweden, most have been published by Galago (Strömberg 2003, 86). Titles include Max Andersson's *Pixy,* one of the few modern Swedish comics published in the United States (by Fantagraphics); Joakim Pirinen's *Socker-Conny,* about a young and uninhibited anarchist; and a number of autobiographical works mainly by Daniel Ahlgren that paint a bleak picture of a person with a "nihilistic view of life who despises most of humanity" (89–90).

Aleksandar Zograf, a Serbian graphic novelist whose *Life under Sanctions, Psychonaut,* and *Regards from Serbia* are published in English by Fantagraphics and Top Shelf, concentrates on turbulent war in former Yugoslavia. *Regards from Serbia* is a collection of Zograf's weekly strips about NATO bombings of his hometown of Pancevo, which he initially distributed via e-mail at the time of the carnage.

Asia

As indicated already, Asia has known graphic novels for centuries. Even more recent-vintage graphic novels predated the appearance of the format in most of the rest of the world. Examples include the "red comic books" that peaked in Japan in 1947–1956, normally postcard- or smaller-sized 24- to 48-page works (Isao 2001, 141); the serialized *nobela komiks* of the Philippines; the *Amar Chitra Katha* (Immortal Picture Stories) series in India; the thousands of *lianhuanhua* of China, and the best-selling renderings of the philosophies of Confucius, Laozi, and Zhuangzi by Taiwan's Tsai Chih-Chung. (See chapter 2 for much more about Japan.)

Though labeled *komiks,* the Philippine *nobelas* were a form of graphic novel in that they were serialized works of fiction featuring the same characters over long periods. Many Filipino artists wrote and drew nobelas, beginning with Francisco V. Coching, who completed 53 komiks novels over a 40-year career, beginning with *Marabini* in 1935. All but three of his stories were film successes. Other Filipino artists figured prominently among comics novels creators. Two of the most prolific were Mars Ravelo, who at any given time was writing weekly episodes of 12 different titles, and Carlos J. Caparas, who wrote 800 illustrated novels. Ravelo's most popular books were *Darna,* about a barrio girl with supernatural powers, and *Dysebel,* the story of a mermaid who fell in love with a human. The *Darna* books are being reprinted by Mango Comics in the Philippines, but so far, few nobela komiks have been translated into English (see Lent 2004, "From 1928").

The Indian *Amar Chitra Katha* series was published in English as well as in 37 other languages. Created by engineer Anant Pai when he witnessed an ignorance of Indian culture among young Indians, these 436 titles dealt with Indian history, mythology, classics, and folklore. Each book was a complete story built around an aspect of traditional Indian life. The series was popular, selling a total of 79 million copies by 1991, when publishing new titles was abandoned, and meriting many reprintings since then (see Lent 2004, "India's *Amar*"). Pai himself was an indefatigable researcher, even adding bibliographies and footnotes to stories in later editions. Despite his efforts, he was occasionally accused of committing historical inaccuracies.

The pocket-size *lianhuanhua* of China can arguably be called early graphic novels, dealing as they did with literature and current events and combining visual/verbal commentary on each page. The first lianhuanhua dealt with a Peking Opera in Shanghai and appeared in 1918, although semblances of the form existed earlier. In 1920, a lianhuanhua was devoted to literature, thus expanding the repertoire of the books. Every night during the 1920s–1930s, two new volumes—2,000 copies—of each new serial went on the market, and when 24 volumes of a serial were issued, the publishers bound them together and put them into a box for a secondary distribution. The number of lianhuan-hua publishers grew to more than 100 by the end of the 1940s, and distribution of the books expanded to Hong Kong, Indonesia, and Singapore (Shen 2001, 101–8). Thousands of lianhuanhua were published after 1949, often espousing Communist ideology in traditional storylines. One book in English resulting from lianhuanhua was *The People's Comic Book: Red Women's Detachment, Hot on the Trail, and Other Chinese Comics,* published in 1973.

Taiwan, as well, published illustrated picture books that could equate to graphic novels, many appearing in the 1960s and depicting brave heroes and diligent children being rewarded. One of the favorites was *Ershisi Xiao* (24 Tales of Filial Piety), which includes the tale of

> [a] small boy, Wang Xiang, who, on hearing that his sick stepmother would like to eat a carp in deep winter, goes to a frozen pond, takes off his coat, and tries to melt the ice with the warmth of his body. Heaven is moved by his filial piety and makes a carp jump from the pond. (Wei 2001, "Shaping" 70)

Also hailing from Taiwan was a best-selling series of graphic novels drawn by Tsai Chih-Chung, which pictorially reinterpreted the philosophies of Confucius, Laozi, and Zhuangzi. On the mid-1980s flight to Japan to sell his idea of a cartoon version of Chinese history, Tsai became engrossed in a book on Zhuangzi. So he spent his stay in Japan illustrating this book instead of selling his cartoon history. The result, *Ziran de Xiaosheng, Zhuangzi Shuo* (The Music of Nature: Zhuangzi Speaks), was published in 1986, followed by other books on Laozi in 1987 and Confucius's *Analects* in 1987–1988. Tsai's task was made difficult as he tried to present complex thoughts in simple drawings, while making didactic philosophy interesting yet accurate. By 1994, the Zhuangzi volume alone had gone through 114 Chinese reprintings as well as an English translation popular in classrooms (Wei 2001, "Redrawing" 153–54), and total sales for his works topped 30 million.

Graphic novels in the modern sense of the term (book size, one story, illustrated narrative) have become popular in many parts of Asia, particularly Japan (covered in chapter 2). In Taiwan, the Government Information Office and Chinese Comics Publishers Association have been giving Graphic Novel Awards annually since 2003 to promote the medium domestically and globally. Stipulations are that the works must be "book-length comics" of at least 120 pages and previously unpublished (Fang 2006, 5). The awards were started because book-length comics have become popular in Taiwan, in comics shops and chain bookstores as well as in traditional rental shops that stock large selections of graphic novels. Although 80 percent of the graphic novels and comics sold are manga, Taiwanese works have also been successful. Among the latter are those of Tsai Chih-Chung already discussed, as well as those of other artists:

- Chu Te-yung, whose humorous strips "Going to the Office," "Double-Sound Crackers," and "City Ladies" were compiled into a number of volumes
- "Jimmy," whose cartoon books sold well in Taiwan and China and were adapted to stage, television series, and merchandise
- Johnny Liao (Cool), whose seven books in the series about a Ching Dynasty leader, *Huang Fei Hong* (Young Master), were copyrighted in seven countries

Many of the other successful Taiwanese creators work for a half-dozen publishing companies, chief of which is Tong Li (Yang 2007; also interviews[2]).

Korean comics, known as manhwa, are increasingly being issued as graphic novels and have started to find a small market in the United States and Europe in English-language editions. In Korea, it has proved fashionable and profitable to reprint quality comics popular from the 1960s to 1990s, usually in book form, on better paper with clearer impressions, with thicker binding, and sometimes in hard cover—even encased in wooden boxes as in the case of *Thermidore*. Reprints bring easy profits, but they also fulfill adults' nostalgia for stories they read as children, issue works serialized in comics magazines but never published in book form, or complete unfinished stories and those previously censored. The best seller has been the series *Yul-Hyul-Kang-Ho* (The Ruler of the Land), created by Jeon Keuk-Jin and Yang Jae-Hyun and published by Daiwon Comics, and each of the 28 volumes sold more than 100,000 copies. The series centers on two parties called Evil and Righteous, bent on ruling Korea. Especially successful in Korea are educational graphic novels, the main one being *Meon Nara, Yiwoot Nara* (Far Countries, Near Countries), a 12-book series that has sold more than 10 million copies.

At least six companies publish English-language versions of Korean manhwa for Western markets: Ice Kunion (now assimilated into Yen Press—see next section), Netcomics, TOKYOPOP, NBM, Dark Horse, and DramaQueen. Ice Kunion is a consortium of Korean publishers that joined to bring out new titles in English; Netcomics concentrates on both print and online manhwa in English. Rather quickly, Netcomics issued 75 volumes of 25 print series plus 120 volumes of 30 series on the Web (Welsh 2007).

Southeast Asia has experienced a small explosion in graphic novel production. To compete with an onslaught of mainly manga imports, Filipino publishers in recent years began to issue high-end comic books and graphic novels on quality paper and in English. Expensively priced, they are meant for university students and young urban professionals driven by interest or childhood nostalgia for classics such as *Darna* or *Lastikman*. By the 2000s, some of the Philippine graphic novels published were *The Mythology Class,* *After Eden,* and *Trip to Tagaytay,* all by Arnold Arre; *One Night in Purgatory* and *Ang Kagila-gila las na Pakikipagsapalaran ni Zsa-Zsa Zaturnnah* (The Amazing Adventures of Zsa Zsa Zaturnnah) by Carlo Vergara; and *Siglo: Freedom* and *Siglo: Passion,* both on the Philippines' experience of freedom and published by Nautilus. (Most of these appeared in English.) One unusual twist in the Philippines is the publication of so-called *Pinoy manga* (Filipino-style manga), with the intent of appealing to the North American audience (Fondevilla 2007). As in South Korea, China, Thailand, and Singapore, the Philippine government has shown an interest in reviving *komiks,* one of its projects being the organizing of a National Komiks Congress (Maragay 2007).

With a strong push from the government, comics and animation have had a reawakening in Thailand since 2004. As I discovered while browsing Bangkok bookstores in December 2007, a considerable number of the comics appear in graphic novel format, such as the 400-page *A Day Story Comic,* subtitled "The Story of the Modern Rebel." Following are details on some of the publishers:

- Longtime comics publisher Banlue publishes graphic novels, some of old tales and television animation series.
- EQ Plus has a knowledge comics series, depicting the lives of Columbus and Joan of Arc, as well as the life of Thai King Naraesuan, missionary-to-Thailand Dr. Dan Beach Bradley, and others.
- Hesheit deals with alternative-style comics, particularly the books of Wisut Ponniwit, now residing in Japan, where he draws manga with both Tokyo and Thai settings.

In Thailand, graphic novels have been associated with both royalty and political personages. When King Bhumibol Adulyadej translated and modified the story of Mahajanaka to fit a modern society and later in 2004 decided to write about his pet dog, he did both projects as graphic novels with the famous cartoonist Chai Rachawat as his artist. His English-language *Biography of a Pet Dog, The Story of Tongdaeng* sold more than 600,000 copies within a month. Another graphic novel attempted to transform ex-President Thaksin Shinawatra from an ousted, corrupted politician into a hero who will return from London exile to resume his unfinished mission to help the poor.

In both Malaysia and Singapore, some graphic novel–like comics have thrived. Most successful in Malaysia are the nostalgic humor works of Lat (Mohamed Nor Khalid), who recounts his childhood of the 1950s and 1960s in *Kampung Boy, Town Boy,* and *Kampung Boy Yesterday and Today.* English-language versions are available from the U.S. publisher First Second. Graphic novels are also being published by Art Square Group, a relatively new firm that brings out five magazines dealing with comics, lifestyle/entertainment, and games. Singaporean publishers of graphic novels include the following:

- Comix Factory, with its annual *Mr. Kiasu* book
- TCZ Studios, primarily concerned with publishing books of artist Wee Tian Beng

- Chuang Yi Publishing, which obtains reprint rights to Japanese, Hong Kong, Taiwanese, and U.S. comics
- Asiapac Books, with its own elaborate publishing program

Since Penguin published Sarnath Banerjee's *Corridor* in 2004, about a "brilliant and banal bookseller and his bunkum customers" (Kalra 2006), other Indian publishers and authors have adopted the graphic novel format. Phantomville brought out *The Believer,* the story of an Edinburgh University anthropologist who returns to his native Kerala village to find it has changed beyond recognition. Rather quickly, the publisher announced eight other graphic novels, including *Kashmir Pending,* about "confused and easily manipulated youngsters becoming pawns in the hands of larger forces" (Singh 2007).

Virgin Comics,[3] a peculiar partnership of billionaire Richard Branson of the Virgin Group, best-selling author/guru Deepak Chopra, and Sharad Devarajan, has involved itself in graphic novel production, including the following works:

- *Virulents,* released in the United States and then England and India
- *7 Brothers*
- *Deepak Chopra Presents: India Authentic,* an Indian mythological series with each issue centering on the story of a different Indian god or goddess beginning with Ganesha, released in North America in 2007

Graphic novels play an important role in Virgin's strategy to tap into India's booming entertainment industry and to appeal to Indian youth, who make up 55 percent of the population. Virgin sees graphic novels as stepping-stones or incubators, hoping to take the stories on to animation, movies, and gaming (Badam 2007). In 2007, Virgin joined with NBC Universal to develop stories and characters originating in graphic novels and turn them into television shows for the Sci-Fi channel (Mehta 2007). Penguin has published other Indian graphic novels, including Sanjay Patel's *The Little Book of Hindu Deities* and Banerjee's second work, *The Barn Owl's Wondrous Capers,* inspired by the myth of the Wandering Jew Cartaphilus, cursed to roam the earth until Judgment Day.

Africa

Graphic novels have had three primary sources in Africa: The Storyteller Group, Sasa Sema, and Africa e Mediterraneo. Other groups such as the cartoonist-run Communicating Artists Ltd. in Kenya and the cartoonists associated with the South African zine/annual anthology *Bittercomix* are interested in the form.

Started by Neil Napper in 1988, the Storyteller Group was especially active in South Africa in the early 1990s. A group of 20 artists and writers, the studio initially was meant to preserve African literary masterpieces in comics form. With support from nongovernmental organizations, the goal changed to become a publishing house for comics used for developmental and social consciousness raising purposes. The Storyteller books were cleverly created, using varied artistic styles and literary forms, and some had huge print runs in the millions. After the mid-1990s, Napper changed the studio's role back to preserving and publishing African literature.

Sasa Sema in Nairobi was conceived by the American Lila Luce in 1994. As Luce described it,

> When I came here in 1993, I saw street children trying to read *Tintin* in English. I thought why not in Swahili. I called up Gado and other cartoonists and told them I'm this American; would you like to publish comic books? There were problems; people here were not sure I was serious. When I said I was going to do comic books, my family in the U.S. thought I was crazy. They said I was wasting my time; the cartoonists here thought so too.[4]

Between 1996 and 1999, Sasa Sema published five comics albums in Swahili, the first being *Abunuwasi* by author-illustrator Gado. In 2000, three albums in English appeared. However, no new books have been published since, as cartoonists prefer better-paying, more secure newspaper cartoon jobs.

Francophone Africa is a region from which many graphic novel artists hail, but because of economic or political reasons, a number of them now reside in Europe. In other instances, they remain in Africa and collaborate with French, Belgian, or Dutch writers/artists or draw on commission for Franco-Belgian publishers. Most cartoonists from the island of La Réunion are in the latter category, including Serge Huo-Chao-Si and Appollo (Olivier Appollodorous). Appollo created the graphic novel *La Grippe Coloniale,* written in French and Creole about returning soldiers from World War I who bring Spanish flu to the island (Lent 2005). France's Vents d'Quest publishes this book.

Following are other popular graphic novels with creators from Francophone Africa:

- Anselme Razafindrainibe's *Retour d'Afrique* (Centre du Monde Éditions,1999)
- Ivorian Gilbert Groud's *Magie Noire* (Albin Michel, 2003)
- Ivorian Faustin Titi's *Une Éternité à Tanger* (Lai Momo, 2005)
- Congolese Pat Masioni's history of genocide, *Rwanda 1994: Descente en Enfer* (Albin Michel, 2005)
- Congolese Hallain Paluku's *Missy* (Bôite à Bulles, 2006)
- Cameroonian Biyong Djehouty's *Soundjata, la Bataille de Kirina* (Menaibue, 2004)
- Marguerite Aboue's story of growing up in Côte d'Ivoire in *Aya de Yopougon* (Gallimard, 2005)

- Yvan Alagbe's *Nègres Jaunes* (Fremok, 2002) and, with Olivier Bramanti, *Qui a Connu le Feu* (Fremok, 2004)
- Man Keong Laval's *La Ballade au Bout du Monde* (Glenat, 2003)

Other graphic novels are issued by Africa e Mediterraneo in Bologna, Italy, directed by Andrea Marchesini Reggiani and Massimo Repetti. Their Africa Comics Collection series consists of about a dozen 32-page, soft-cover, black-and-white graphic novels featuring prominent cartoonists from Benin, Madagascar, Congo, the Ivory Coast, Togo, Rwanda, South Africa, the Democratic Republic of Congo, Cameroon, and Madagascar. Discussing African Francophone comics artists, cultural anthropologist Massimo Repetti said they "directly depicted an obscure world . . . the hellhole in which millions live" (2007, 523). He believed that since 2003, these authors saw graphic novels as an

> attempt to meet the need for supernational, collective communication, with a strong local tendency towards comics using the register of the everyday, autobiography, and the documentary. . . . The trend is away from an age in which comics were confined to daily papers and magazines to one founded on the centrality of the book, and the path chosen is that of the graphic novel: stories planned as complete novels. (Repetti 2007, 534)

Latin America

In Mexico, where comic books have had a very strong 70-year existence, thick "comic-novels" appeared by the 1950s, described by Mexico City comics researcher Armando Bartra (2005, 265) as presenting a

> more traditional narrative structure (introduction, climax, and outcome), unlike *pepine* comic strips with their open stories, using the suspense of a "to be continued . . ." to hook the reader. Moreover, comic-novels did not have emblematic heroes and stable characters typical of comic magazines; rather, the plot acquired preeminence over the characters. Finally, because they were published in a single issue, comic-novels did not allow making adjustments after pulsing readers' reactions—they had to be designed with a conclusive structure in advance . . .

By bringing comics to thick narrative books, Mexican artists were 40 years ahead of their counterparts in Europe.

Over the years, many comics were put in book form. Almost all of the politically oriented works of Eduardo del Río (Rius) in the 1960s and 1970s, including *Los Supermachos, Los Agachados,* and *Cuba para Principantes,* as well as others, were specially created for this format. Rius radicalized graphic narrative, playing with "devices of textbooks such as tables of contents, bibliographies, and even footnotes" to the extent that his art "overlaps the definitions of illustrated book, comic book, and something altogether new" (Rubenstein 1998, 157). More recently, Mexican strips previously published in periodicals have been compiled as books. One of these was Edgar Clément's *Operación Bolivar,* a story about "the travails of Leonidas Arkángel, a mestizo angel hunter with superpowers [who uncovers] a covert intelligence operation designed to conquer the Americas through the trade of a most potent narcotic resulting from the mass persecution and assassination of angels" (L'Hoeste 2006, 163). *Operación Bolivar* first appeared in a magazine and then was republished as two volumes in 1995 and as a single-volume graphic novel in 1999.

Reporting from his home country, Brazilian comics scholar-researcher Waldomiro Vergueiro claimed that graphic novels are not common in developing countries because of economic constraints, and almost all of those that were published were for the alternative market (2002, 159). Exceptions, however, were the graphic novels of Lourenço Mutarelli, the first being the somewhat autobiographical *Transubstanciação* (Transubstantiation) from 1991. Seen as an existentialist author, Mutarelli created heroes who reflected his own anguishes in works such as *Desgraçados* (Damned); *Euteamo, Lucimar* (I Love You, Lucimar); *A Confluência da Foquilha* (The Confluence of the Pitchfork); and *O Dobro de Cinco* (The Double of Five).

In Argentina, a number of graphic novels have been written by Carlos Trillo in association with an assortment of artists, including the album *Flopi Bach,* actually published in Barcelona, with an English-language version earlier in *Heavy Metal* magazine (L'Hoeste 2005). Carlos Sampayo and José Muñoz teamed up to create *Joe's Bar,* about a New York City bar for misfits, and *Billie Holiday,* a rich account of the great jazz singer's life.

United Kingdom

Britain's comics tradition for many years has centered on a rich menu of magazines for different ages, funny-kids to adult-edgy (Gravett and Stanbury 2006). Magazines and series for children remain popular, especially based on well-loved television programs such as *Teletubbies.* Graphic albums from the Continent helped longer works become more common, but adult-level creators found publishers for their graphic novel work mainly through small presses. Many others creators have been known for their work on Marvel or DC Comics series and titles—for example, Alan Moore, Neil Gaiman, Warren Ellis, and Garth Ennis (see part 2 of this chapter). But with the recent graphic novel boom and the success of Raymond Briggs's 1999 *Ethel & Ernest* graphic novel, mainstream UK publishers are showing interest. Random House UK's Jonathan Cape imprint more than tripled its graphic novel output over 2006–2007. Also, HarperCollins UK launched a graphic novel series, starting with adaptations of the quintessentially British Agatha Christie whodunits. Bloomsbury

(Harry Potter's UK publisher), Orion Books, and Faber & Faber are all moving into graphic novels. At the same time, several companies are focusing on adaptations of Shakespeare and classic British literature: SelfMadeHero, an imprint of Metro Media Ltd., and Classical Comics.

Canada, Australia, New Zealand, and Ireland

English-speaking Canada, Australia, and New Zealand have nourished graphic novelists whose works have left their mark on the form. Most renowned of the Canadians are Seth (Gregory Gallant), Chester Brown, and Dave Sim. Seth's most popular graphic novel has been *It's a Good Life, If You Don't Weaken,* a tale of a cartoonist similar to himself longing for the simpler life of yesteryear. His latest work is *George Sprott, 1894–1975,* about the fraudulent life of a Northern explorer. Chester Brown is best known for *Louis Riel,* a biography of Canada's founding father, which has sold more than 20,000 copies and is used in university courses. *Cerebus,* originally meant as an animal parody, is Dave Sims's masterpiece, described as equivalent to a Russian novel. British comics writer and entrepreneur Paul Gravett described *Cerebus* as a "closely examined life told without fear in 6,000 pages, serialized in 300 issues, a labor of 26 years and three months" (2005, 140).

Also related, with warts and all, are excerpts from the lives of Julie Doucet in her *My New York Diary* and Joe Matt in his *Peepshow.* Doucet's graphic novel deals with her relationship with a selfish, possessive boyfriend, and Matt focuses on his porno video obsession. (Matt is an American who lived for many years in Canada.) Among other noteworthy graphic novels by Canadians are Michel Rabagliati's *Paul Has a Summer Job,* about a summer camp counselor's experiences in 1970s Montreal; Ho Che Anderson's *King: Complete Edition,* about Martin Luther King; and Joe Ollman's *This Will All End in Tears,* a collection of five stories. The Canadian publisher Drawn & Quarterly publishes most of these creators as well as U.S. and European work.

Prominent among Australian-New Zealand graphic novels are those of Eddie Campbell of Australia and Dylan Horrocks of New Zealand, although other works exist by lesser-known cartoonists. Campbell teamed with Alan Moore to produce *To Hell,* a melodramatic rendition of the Jack the Ripper murders. Campbell also drew *Alec,* an alter ego treatment of his romances and friendships. Like Seth, Dylan Horrocks uses a cartoonist as his main character in *Hicksville.*

Ireland has an active comics community that includes the well-regarded writer Garth Ennis, who is active largely in the U.S. comics world and best known for his series *Preacher* from DC Comics. Colmán Ó Raghallaigh's *An Táin* (The Cattle Raid) recently won the 2006 Oireachtas na Gaeilge Irish Language Book of the Year for Young People. Another title attracting notice is *Mister Amperduke,* Bob Byrne's self-published, wordless graphic novel about a miniature world that falls apart when an outside menace intrudes.

Conclusion

It is not possible to know where and when the first graphic novels were published. Considering the term loosely, possible places of origin include Japan, the Philippines, Europe, and Mexico. Today, the phenomenal growth of graphic novels worldwide has extended the life span of comics, many of which were in search of an audience in an entertainment market glutted by new electronic formats. In the United States, the graphic novel advanced comics from a children's medium long dominated by superheroes and not taken very seriously to one attracting a diverse audience, made up of many genres, and increasingly recognized and respected in many circles, especially that of academia and libraries.

PART 2: A LIBRARIAN'S GUIDE TO INTERNATIONAL GRAPHIC NOVELS

Martha Cornog

The rich history of comics and graphic novels worldwide warrants the attention of librarians in the United States. These publications can expand the entertainment and information options of Americans born here as well as interest foreign-born residents. But how does one begin collecting international titles or enhance an existing collection? One major problem is identifying what is available, especially works translated into English. Few core lists and only some reviews include information about the native country of authors and artists.

To aid in selection and acquisition, I have included here some suggested international authors and titles available in translation that have received recent recognition or are considered of enduring appeal. Following, you will find sources to build more comprehensive want-lists and stay current, including Web sites for English-language publishers with strong lists of titles originating outside the United States.

Suggested International Authors and Titles to Consider

All of the following titles are in print as of 2008. Most are listed on Amazon. com (and may be available through the usual library jobbers), distributed through Diamond Comic Distributors, or available through publishers listed; a few seem to be available only through specialized country-specific Web sites or other Web-based distributors, as noted. Most have professional reviews quoted on various Web sites, have been nominated for or won awards, and/or are listed in Michael Pawuk's genre guide (2007). Others have been mentioned in comics industry sites or fan blogs. *Please note that titles are suggestions only, and librarians are urged to check further before buying.* Not all titles may be appropriate for all libraries. Some adult titles have adults-only content, including nudity and sexual situations.

Unfortunately, many of the titles mentioned by John Lent in the preceding section are not available in English or, if in English, are out of print. Some of these may be available from used-book Web sources—I recently bought an inexpensive, used copy of *The People's Comic Book,* the 1973 translation overseen by Umberto Eco, no less. With the recent explosion of graphic novel popularity, selected oldies-but-goodies are being reprinted, such as the popular British long-term strip *Modesty Blaise* and—rumored since 2006 but slow in coming—the picaresque *Corto Maltese* stories. Some new work appears only (so far) on the Web, such as a darkly amusing 28-page story from a Russian creator: Alexey Lipatov's *Stalin vs. Hitler,* http://www.comics.aha.ru/rus/stalin/2.html (English subtitles are provided). The historic and cultural references integrated into this brief Web comic make it a natural for American college students taking history or political science courses.

This list is in no way comprehensive but merely a sampling. For many more titles, check out the Web sites given in the publishers' section, following.

Franco-Belgium

Adults

David B. (real name: David Beauchard), *Epileptic,* Pantheon/Random House (18+)

Philippe Dupuy and Charles Berberian, *Get a Life,* Drawn & Quarterly (18+)
   Maybe Later, Drawn & Quarterly (18+)

Stéphane Heuet, *Remembrance of Things Past* adaptations, NBM (series, 16+)

Killoffer (real name: Patrice Killoffer, male), *Six Hundred Seventy-Six Apparitions of Killoffer,* Typocrat (18+)

Manu (Emmanuel) Larcenet, *Ordinary Victories,* ComicsLit/NBM (18+)

Jean-Jacques Sempé, *Monsieur Lambert,* Phaidon (18+)

Joann Sfar, *The Rabbi's Cat,* Pantheon/Random House (18+); *Klezmer: Tales of the Wild East,* NBM (18+)

Jean-Philipps Stassen, *Deogratias: A Tale of Rwanda,* First Second (16+)

Teen/Young Adult

Edgar P. (Pierre) Jacobs, *Blake & Mortimer: The Yellow "M"* and other titles, Cinebook (series; 10+)

Jean-David Morvan and Philippe Buchet, *Wake,* NBM (series; 16+)

Joann Sfar, *Vampire Loves,* First Second (16+)

Joann Sfar, Lewis Trondheim, et al., *Dungeon,* NBM (series; 13+)

Lewis Trondheim, *The Spiffy Adventures of McConey: Harum Scarum,* NBM (13+); *Mister i,* NBM (16+); *A.L.I.E.E.E.N.,* First Second (10+)

Children/All Ages

René Goscinny and Albert Uderzo, *Asterix,* Orion (series; all ages)
René Goscinny and Morris (real name: Maurice de Bevere), *Lucky Luke,* Cinebook
    (series; all ages)
Emmanuel Guibert and Joann Sfar, *Sardine in Outer Space,* First Second
    (series; 10+)
Hergé (George Remi), *The Adventures of Tintin,* Little, Brown (series; all ages)
Theirry Robin and Lewis Trondheim, *Li'l Santa,* NBM (all ages); *Happy Halloween
    Li'l Santa,* NBM (all ages)
Joann Sfar, *Little Vampire,* Simon & Schuster Children's Publishing (series; 10+)
Lewis Trondheim, *Mister O,* NBM (10+)
Lewis Trondheim and Fabrice Parme, *Tiny Tyrant,* First Second (8+)

Spain

Juan Diaz Canales and Juanjo Guarnido, *Blacksad,* iBooks (series; 18+)
Max (Francesc Capdevila Gisbert), *Bardín the Superrealist,* Fantagraphics (18+)
Miguelanxo Prado, *Daily Delirium,* NBM/ComicsLit (18+)

Italy

Vittorio Giardino, *No Pasaran!* ComicsLit/NBM (18+)
Gipi (real name: Gianni Pacinotti), *Notes for a War Story,* First Second (18+);
    Garage Band, First Second (13+)
Francesca Ghermandi, *The Wipeout,* Fantagraphics (18+)
Lorenzo Mattotti, *Dr. Jekyll and Mr. Hyde,* NBM (18+)
W.I.T.C.H., Volo/Hyperion (series; 10+)

Germany and Austria

Jens Harder, *Leviathan,* NBM/ComicsLit (18+)
Ralf König, *Like Rabbits,* Ediciones la Cúpula (18+) (order from www.lacupula.
    com); *Maybe . . . Maybe Not Again!* Ignite! Entertainment (18+)
Nicolas Mahler, *Lone Racer,* Top Shelf (18+); *Van Helsing's Night Off,* Top Shelf (18+)

Switzerland

Thomas Ott, *Cinema Panopticum,* Fantagraphics (18+)
Alex Baladi, *Frankenstein Now and Forever,* Typocrat (18+) (may need to order
    from www.typocrat.com; see publishers section)

Netherlands

Joost Swarte, *Modern Swarte: Joost Comics,* Fantagraphics (18+)

Scandinavia

Max Andersson and Lars Sjunneson, *Bosnian Flat Dog,* Fantagraphics (18+); *Pixy,*
    Fantagraphics (18+)

Martin Kellerman, *Rocky,* Fantagraphics (series; 18+)

Naomi Nowak, *House of Clay,* NBM, 2007 (16+)

Jason (John Arne Sæterøy), *The Left Bank Gang* and many titles from Fantagraphics (18+)

Tove Jansson, *Moomin,* Drawn & Quarterly (series; all ages)

Russia

Nikolai Maslov, *Siberia,* Soft Skull Press (16+)

Serbia

Aleksandar Zograf (real name: Sasa Rakezic), *Regards from Serbia,* Top Shelf (18+)

Malaysia

Lat (real name: Mohamed Nor Khalid), *Kampung Boy,* First Second (10+); *Town Boy,* First Second (10+)

China/Taiwan/Hong Kong (surname last)

Benjamin (real name: Zhang Bin), *Orange,* TOKYOPOP (16+)

Wang Du Lu and Andy Seto, *Crouching Tiger, Hidden Dragon,* ComicsOne and HK Comics Ltd. (series; 13+)

Wing-Shing Ma and Yimou Zhang, *Chinese Hero,* ComicsOne and DrMaster (13+)

Ru-An Wen and Andy Seto, *Four Constables,* ComicsOne and DrMaster (series; 13+)

Korea (surname last)

Byung-jun Byun, *Run, Bong-Gu, Run!* ComicsLit/NBM (16+)

Doha (real name: Doha Kang), *The Great Catsby,* Netcomics (series, 18+)

Min-woo Hyung, *Priest,* TOKYOPOP (series, 18+)

Keuk-Jin Jeon and Jae-Hyun Yang, *The Ruler of the Land,* ADV Manga (series, 16+)

Seyoung Kim, *Boy Princess,* Netcomics (series, 13+)

Myung-jin Lee, *Ragnarök,* TOKYOPOP (series, 13+)

Kara Lim, with Chi-hyong Lee (vol. 1 only) and Yun-hee Lee (other vols.), *Demon Diary,* TOKYOPOP (series, 13+)

Manhwa Novella Collection, Netcomics (series of anthologies, 16+)

Marley, *Dokebi Bride,* Netcomics (series, 13+)

Joong-ki Park, *Shaman Warrior,* Dark Horse (series, 16+)

Mi-kyung Yun, *Bride of the Water God,* Dark Horse (series, 13+)

Philippines

Arnold Arre, *The Mythology Class,* Adarna House (18+) (order from www.myBookstore.ph; this links to www.thebookfan.net, which takes a while to load; or order via araceli3@juno.com); *After Eden,* Adarna House (18+) (same ordering instructions)

Siglo: Freedom, Nautilus (anthology; 18+) (order from www.milehighcomics.com)

India

Naseer Ahmed and Saurabh Singh, *Kashmir Pending,* Phantomville (18+) (order
from www.booksatbahri.com)

Sarnath Banerjee, *Corridor,* Penguin Global (18+)

Shamik Dasgupta and Dean Ruben Hyrapiet, *Virulents,* Virgin
Comics (18+)

Saurav Mohapatra and various artists, *Deepak Chopra Presents: India Authentic,*
Virgin Comics (series, 13+)

Sanjay Patel, *The Little Book of Hindu Deities,* Plume (all ages)

Anant Pai (creator), *Amar Chitra Katha,* India Bookhouse/ACK Media (series, all
ages) (order from www.ack-media.com)

Iran

Marjane Satrapi, *The Complete Persepolis*, Pantheon (16+); *Embroideries*, Pantheon
(18+); *Chicken with Plums,* Pantheon (16+); *Monsters Are Afraid of the Moon,*
Bloomsbury (all ages)

Israel

Etgar Keret and Rutu Modan, *Dad Runs Away with the Circus,* Candlewick (all
ages)

Rutu Modan, *Exit Wounds,* Drawn & Quarterly (16+)

Central and South America

Fábio Moon and Gabriel Bá, *De:Tales: Stories from Urban Brazil,* Dark Horse
(18+); *Ursula,* AiT/Planet Lar (13+)

Carlos Trillo and Juan Bobillo, *Chocolate and French Fries,* SAF Comics (10+);
Zachary Holmes, Dark Horse (series; 16+)

Carlos Trillo and Eduardo Risso, *Chicanos* (series), IDW (18+)

JIS (José Ignacio Solorzano), *Cats Don't Exist,* Fantagraphics (18+)

Africa

Marguerite Abouet and Clement Oubrerie, *Aya* and sequel, Drawn & Quarterly
(16+)

Joe Daly, *Scrublands,* Fantagraphics (18+)

United Kingdom

The most prominent British comics luminaries are probably writers Alan
Moore and Neil Gaiman (the latter now lives in the United States), whose
work has been published primarily by U.S. companies. (Several of their
titles are discussed in chapters 4 and 5.) So, too, many other well-known
British and Irish creators in the so-called "Brit wave invasion of American
comics" are best known for long-term work on popular series for DC Comics and Marvel: Brian Bolland, Warren Ellis, Garth Ennis, Dave Gibbons,

and Grant Morrison. Some well-regarded UK creators and titles outside the DC/Marvel penumbra that are somewhat lesser known to U.S. readers include the following.

Nick Abadzis, *Laika,* First Second (13+)

Raymond Briggs, *Ethel & Ernest,* Pantheon (18+)

Ian Edginton and D'Israeli (real name: Matt Brooker), *Scarlet Traces,* Dark Horse (2 vols.; 16+)

Garen Ewing, *The Rainbow Orchid,* Egmont (forthcoming; 13+)

Judge Dredd, various creators, Rebellion (series; 18+)

Barnaby Legg, James McCarthy, and Flameboy (real name: Steve Beaumont), *Death Rap: Tupac Shakur,* Omnibus Press (16+)

Peter O'Donnell et al., *Modesty Blaise,* Titan Books (series; 16+)

Posy Simmonds, *Gemma Bovary,* Pantheon (18+); *Tamara Drew,* Mariner Books (18+)

Bryan Talbot, *The Adventures of Luther Arkwright,* Dark Horse (18+); *Alice in Sunderland,* Dark Horse (16+)

Barry Winsor-Smith, *The Freebooters,* Fantagraphics (16+)

Ireland

Bob Byrne, *Mister Amperduke,* Clamnut Comix (16+) (order from www.clamnuts.com)

Canada

Ho Che Anderson, *King: A Comics Biography of Martin Luther King, Jr.* (complete ed.), Fantagraphics (16+)

Chester Brown, *I Never Liked You,* Drawn & Quarterly (16+); *Louis Riel,* Drawn & Quarterly (13+)

Guy Delisle, *Pyongyang,* Drawn & Quarterly (13+)

Julie Doucet, *My New York Diary,* Drawn & Quarterly (16+); *My Most Secret Desire,* Drawn & Quarterly (18+)

Ann Marie Fleming, *The Magical Life of Long Tack Sam,* Penguin/Riverhead (13+)

Lynn Johnston, *For Better or For Worse,* Andrews McMeel (series, 10+)

Joe Matt, *Peepshow,* Drawn & Quarterly (18+)

Joe Ollmann, *This Will All End in Tears,* Insomniac Press (18+)

Bryan Lee O'Malley, *Scott Pilgrim,* Oni Press (series, 13+)

Michel Rabagliati, *Paul Has a Summer Job* and other "Paul" titles, Drawn & Quarterly (series, 16+)

Seth (real name: Gregory Gallant), *It's a Good Life If You Don't Weaken,* Drawn & Quarterly (16+); *Clyde Fans,* Book 1, Drawn & Quarterly (16+); *Wimbledon Green,* Drawn & Quarterly (16+)

Dave Sim, *Cerebus,* Aardvark-Vanheim (18+)

New Zealand

Murray Ball, *Footrot Flats: Gallery,* Hachette Livre New Zealand (16+)
Dylan Horrocks, *Hicksville,* Drawn & Quarterly (16+)
Roger Langridge, *Fred the Clown,* Fantagraphics (18+)

Australia

Eddie Campbell (originally from Scotland; currently living in Australia), *Alec,* Top
    Shelf (18+); *The Black Diamond Detective Agency,* First Second (16+)
Queenie Chan, *The Dreaming,* TOKYOPOP (series, 16+)
Shaun Tan, *The Arrival,* Arthur A. Levine Books (13+); *The Red Tree,* Simply
    Read Books (10+)
Ben Templesmith, *Wormwood, Gentleman Corpse,* IDW (series, 16+)

Multi-Country Anthologies

Bête Noire #1, Fantagraphics (18+)
Big Fat Little Lit, ed. Art Spiegelman and Françoise Mouly, Puffin Books (10+)
Drawn & Quarterly, Drawn & Quarterly (series of periodic anthologies and collec-
    tions; 18+; order from www.drawnandquarterly.com)
Japan as Viewed by 17 Creators, Fanfare/Potent Mon (18+)
Liquid City, Image (anthology from Southeast Asia; 18+)
The Rising Stars of Manga: United Kingdom and Ireland, TOKYOPOP (series, 13+)

Publishers Specializing in or with Strong
Lists of International Creators

For international-source graphic novels published in English, checking
publishers' Web sites can be one of the best ways to build up-to-date collections and stay current about what is coming out.

Cinebook Ltd.

http://www.cinebook.co.uk
    British publisher located in Canterbury that focuses on putting out quality
    Franco-Belgian comics in English, featuring a number for younger readers.
    Distributed in the United States by National Book Network Distribution,
    www.nbnbooks.com.

Classical Comics

http://www.classicalcomics.com
    A British publisher located in Towcester that is putting out an extensive line of
    graphic novel literary adaptations, including work of Shakespeare, Charlotte
    Brontë, and Dickens. The Shakespeare and some of the other releases are being

done in three versions: original text, plain text, and quick text to reach to readers with different needs.

DramaQueen

http://www.onedramaqueen.com

Houston-based company that publishes Japanese, Korean, and Taiwanese comics in English, mostly romance and BL (male–male romance) titles.

Drawn & Quarterly

http://www.drawnandquarterly.com

A Montreal publisher founded in 1990 to publish an anthology titled *Drawn & Quarterly* that now issues translations of European work as well as work from Canadian and U.S. creators.

DrMaster Publications Inc.

http://www.drmasterbooks.com

A Fremont, California, publisher for English-language versions of Japanese, Korean, and Chinese comics; took over most of ComicsOne's line of titles in 2003 when that company ceased operations.

Fanfare/Ponent Mon

http://www.ponentmon.com

A British/Spanish copublishing venture founded in 2003 to publish Japanese/Franco-Belgian literary comics collaborations termed "La Novelle Manga," available in English. Offices are located in Wisbech (Cambridgeshire, UK) and Tarragona (Spain).

Fantagraphics Books

http://www.fantagraphics.com

A Seattle-based publisher of the trade magazine *The Comics Journal* since 1976 that now publishes innovative and alternative comics and graphic novels from creators worldwide, in English editions.

First Second Books

http://www.firstsecondbooks.com

An imprint of Roaring Brook Press (a division of U.S.'s Holtzbrinck Publishers in New York City) that aims for high-quality, literate graphic novels for a wide age range with a lineup of worldwide talent.

Humanoids Publishing

http://www.humanoids-publishing.com

A Glendale, California, publishing house set up to put out English-language versions of European graphic novels, founded in 1998 as an American counterpart to European publisher Les Humanoïdes Associés. In 2008, Humanoids contracted with Devil's Due Publishing to release some of the extensive line of Humanoids titles through Devil's Due.

Nantier • Beall • Minoustchine (NBM)

http://www.nbmpub.com

A New York publisher founded in 1976 and among the first to bring European graphic novels to America. Incorporates the imprint ComicsLit.

Netcomics

http://www.netcomics.com

A Glendale, California, company that publishes translated Korean manhwa as well as Japanese manga and a few other titles for distribution in print and online.

SAF Comics (Strip Art Features)

http://www.safcomics.com

Located in Slovenia and handles the rights to a number of European comics titles for translation/distribution in various countries.

SelfMadeHero

http://www.selfmadehero.com

London-based imprint of British publisher Metro Media, which specializes in adapting literature into graphic novels. The Manga Shakespeare line sets the plays into different times and places, and the Eye Classics line adapts other great works such as from Poe and Kafka. The Eye Classics 2008 title *Nevermore: A Graphic Adaptation of Edgar Allan Poe's Short Stories* was published in the United States by Sterling Publishers.

Typocrat Press

http://www.typocrat.com

An independent London publisher specializing in contemporary European comics and graphic novels in high-quality English editions. However, only two titles seem to be released so far.

Yen Press

http://www.yenpress.com
>The New York–based manga and graphic novel division of Hachette Book Group USA. Releases a monthly anthology titled *Yen Plus* and looks to publish manga, manhwa, and international artists in English versions. Yen absorbed the manga and manhwa lines of ICE Kunion, a copublishing venture among several Korean publishers.

Additional Resources

More information can be gleaned about almost any comics creator or title on the Web. Wikipedia in particular can be a good place to start, although information should be considered provisional given Wikipedia's policy of allowing constant revision from anyone. The links at the end of entries can be quite useful, however. Sites for international comics awards can point to well-regarded artists and titles, although translations may not be available. Some English-language periodicals and books cover international comics broadly. Many more address specific countries, but often only in the original languages.

Web Sites

See also Web sites for publishers, listed earlier.

Lambiek Comiclopedia
>http://www.lambiek.net
>An illustrated collection of "over 10,000" short creator biographies worldwide and a good place to find out the country of origin for an unfamiliar creator. The Web site also houses a history of Dutch comics. Lambiek calls itself Europe's first comics shop, founded in 1968 in Amsterdam.

Comic Book Awards Almanac
>http://www.hahnlibrary.net/comics/awards/index.html
>An invaluable compendium of numerous U.S. and international comics awards, with winners and often nominees also. Not always up-to-date with the latest winners for any given award, but links are provided to sites with more information. Most of the European awards given at the prestigious Angoulême International Comics Festival are included under the heading Alph-Art. Do not neglect the U.S.-based Eisner and Harvey awards, which have categories for best U.S. edition of foreign material as well as international nominees in other categories. Maintained by librarian Joel Hahn.

Conversational Euro-Comics, by Bart Beaty
>Feature appearing regularly on *The Comics Reporter,* http://www.comicsreporter.com. Beaty has also written a column for *The Comics Journal* since 1997, Euro-Comics for Beginners.

ComicsResearch.org
> http://www.comicsresearch.org
> On the home page, see subject bibliography category "Countries," covering
> works about comics produced in specific countries.

Librairie Fichtre!
> http://www.fichtre.qc.ca
> A Montreal bookstore and distributor specializing in comics (*bande dessinée*),
> which sells a large stock of European and Canadian graphic novels. Most of
> the titles seem to be French-language, and Web site is French-only. (In French,
> *librairie* means "bookstore," not "library.")

Magazines

The Comics Journal

Published eight times a year by Fantagraphics. (See earlier mentions.) 1977–. Covers a wide variety of current and older U.S. comics with illustrations, some in color, predominantly reviews, previews, columns, interviews, and retrospectives, but with substantial international coverage also. "Coming Comics," a regular feature listing forthcoming titles, has an international section. A must for public and academic libraries serious about collecting comics and graphic novels for adults, U.S. or international. A good source for keeping up with what is coming out in English translation. The Web site, http://www.tcj.com, has additional features. Note: May occasionally have explicit adults-only visuals.

International Journal of Comic Art

A thick, black-and-white illustrated academic journal published semiannually since 1999 by editor John A. Lent. Beginning in 2009, a third number on bibliography will be issued yearly. A must for libraries serious about collecting international comics and graphic novels, especially in the original languages and especially academic libraries. Subscriptions are $45 for individuals, $70 for institutions. Checks should be made payable to John A. Lent/IJOCA and mailed to John A. Lent, 669 Ferne Blvd., Drexel Hill, PA 19026. The Web site is http://www.ijoca.com but may not be up-to-date.

Books

John A. Lent is editor of several scholarly area studies of comics as well as author of lengthy comics research bibliographies, included in the "Countries" resource lists on http://www.comicsresearch.org. The following works take a somewhat broader perspective.

> Beaty, Bart. *Unpopular Culture: Transforming the European Comic Book in the*
> *1990s.* Toronto: University of Toronto Press, 2007.
>> A scholarly and nuanced discussion of the evolution of comics in Europe from a for-
>> mat based on the concept of the "novel" or story to a form with the art as dominant,
>> that is, emphasizing the visual over the literary.

Scott, Randall. *European Comics in English Translation: A Descriptive Source-book.* Jefferson, NC: McFarland, 2002.

Although Scott's compendium is quite dated, many of the 543 annotated titles are still in print or are being reissued. Includes lengthy plot descriptions and brief notes about creators.

Pilcher, Tim, and Brad Brooks. *The Essential Guide to World Comics.* London: Collins & Brown, 2005.

A non-scholarly introduction to history, artists, and titles relating to graphic narrative in a wide range of countries and areas of the world, lavishly illustrated with color covers and sample pages and with bibliography and index. A gorgeous and meaty core collection title. Note: Does not cover all countries and continents.

NOTES

1. Editor's note about terminology: *Bande dessinée,* often shortened to "BD," means "drawn strip," the usual French term for the comics medium regardless of publication format. When a series of episodes that may have been published individually in a newspaper or magazine are collected into a volume for publication, the French term for that volume is "album" (*l'album*) rather than "book" or "graphic novel."

2. Cartoonists Hoong Te-Lin, Johnny Liao, Li Shen, and others, series of interviews with John A. Lent, Taipei, July 28, 2005.

3. Editor's note: As of August 2008, Virgin Comics closed its New York office. Reportedly, a corporate buy-out has happened, which will lead to a relaunch under the name Liquid Comics. See Calvin Reid, "DC Folds Minx; Virgin Becomes Liquid Comics," *Publishers Weekly,* September 25, 2008, www.publishersweekly.com/article/CA6599653.html?rssid=192.

4. Lila Luce talked about Sasa Sema's beginnings in interviews with John A. Lent, August 23–24, 2005.

REFERENCES

Alaniz, José, ed. "Late/Post-Soviet Russian Komiks: A Symposium." *International Journal of Comic Art* 7, no. 1 (Spring 2005): 3–125.

Alaniz, José. "The 'Quintessentially Russian' Komiks of Zhora Litichevsky." *International Journal of Comic Art* 7, no. 1 (Spring 2005): 110–25.

Badam, Ramola Talwar. "Virgin Comics Releases 'Virulents.'" *Washington Post,* March 27, 2007. http://www.washingtonpost.com/wp-dyn/content/article/2007/03/27/AR2007032701466.html.

Baetens, Jan. "Transatlantic Encounters of the Second Type." In *The Graphic Novel,* ed. Jan Baetens, 7–9. Leuven: Leuven University Press, 2001.

Bartra, Armando. "Dawn, Noon, and Dusk of a Tumultuous Narrative: The Evolution of Mexican Comic Art." In *Cartooning in Latin America,* ed. John A. Lent, 253–78. Cresskill, NJ: Hampton Press, 2005.

Beaty, Bart. "The Contemporary Field of European Comics: The Example of Lewis Trondheim." *International Journal of Comic Art* 5, no. 2 (Fall 2003): 168–83.

Fang, Rita. "Graphic Novels Selected for Year-End Competition." *Taiwan Aujourd'hui.* July 21, 2006. http://taiwanauj.nat.gov.tw/ct.asp?xItem=22886&CTNode=122.

Fondevilla, Herbeth L. "Contemplating the Identity of Manga in the Philippines." *International Journal of Comic Art* 9, no. 2 (Fall 2007): 441–53.

Gravett, Paul. *Graphic Novels: Everything You Need To Know.* New York: Collins Design, 2005.

Gravett, Paul, and Peter Stanbury. *Great British Comics: Celebrating a Century of Ripping Yarns and Wizard Wheezes.* London: Aurum Press, 2006.

Hagenauer, George. "Comic Art Around the World." Special issue, *CFA-APA,* no. 71 (March 2007).

Hill, Christian. "Narrative Aesthetics of Time and Space in the Comic Series, *Broussaille,* by Frank and Bom." *International Journal of Comic Art* 6, no. 1 (Spring 2004): 1–17.

Horn, Maurice. "Guido Crepax: A Memorial Tribute." *International Journal of Comic Art* 6, no. 2 (Fall 2004): 78–89.

Isao, Shimizu. "Red Comic Books: The Origin of Modern Japanese *Manga.*" In *Illustrating Asia: Comics, Humor Magazines, and Picture Books,* ed. John A. Lent, 137–50. Honolulu: University of Hawai'i Press, 2001.

Kalra, Vandana. "Pune Bibliophiles Turn a New Chapter with Graphic Novels." *Pune Newsline,* June 21, 2006. http://cities.expressindia.com/fullstory.php?newsid=189151.

Kaplan, Arie. *Masters of the Comic Book Universe Revealed.* Chicago: Chicago Review Press, 2006.

Kern, Adam, ed. "*Kibyōshi:* The World's First Comicbook?" Seven-article symposium. *International Journal of Comic Art* 9, no 1 (Spring 2007): 1–197.

Kern, Adam. "The *kibyōshi:* Japan's Eighteenth-Century Comicbook for Adults." *International Journal of Comic Art* 9, no. 1 (Spring 2007): 3–32.

Kunzle, David. *Father of the Comic Strip: Rodolphe Töpffer.* Jackson: University Press of Mississippi, 2007.

Le Duc, Dominique. "XXIst Century Graphic Novels: A Voyage with Edmond Baudoin." *International Journal of Comic Art* 6, no. 2 (Fall 2004): 238–53.

Lent, John A. "Cartooning in Réunion with Special Reference to the Work of Serge and Appollo." *International Journal of Comic Art* 7, no. 1 (Spring 2005): 462–72.

Lent, John A. "From 1928 to 1993: The First 75 Years of Philippine *Komiks.*" *Comic Book Artist,* September 2004, 74–95.

Lent, John A. "India's *Amar Chitra Katha:* 'Fictionalized' History or the Real Story?" *International Journal of Comic Art* 6, no. 1 (Spring 2004): 56–76.

L'Hoeste, Héctor D. Fernández. "Flopi Bach: A Benevolent Misogyny? *International Journal of Comic Art* 7, no. 1 (Spring 2005): 206–29.

L'Hoeste, Héctor D. Fernández. "On Angels, Drugs, and Trade: Edgar Clément's Operación Bolívar." *International Journal of Comic Art* 8, no. 2 (Fall 2006): 163–80.

MacDonald, Heidi. "Comics Have Wide Appeal in Barcelona." *PW Comics Week,* May 1, 2007. http://www.publishersweekly.com/article/CA6438253.html.

Maragay, Fel V. "Komiks Makes a Comeback." *Manila Standard,* February 26, 2007. http://www.manilastandardtoday.com/?page=felMaragay_feb26_2007.

Mehta, Stephanie. "TV's Next Hero: NBC Universal and Virgin Are Betting That Comic Books Will Inspire the New Wave of TV Shows." *Fortune,* March 2, 2007. http://money.cnn.com/2007/03/02/news/companies/pluggedin_mehta_comics.fortune/index.htm.

Pawuk, Michael. *Graphic Novels: A Genre Guide to Comic Books, Manga, and More.* Westport, CT: Libraries Unlimited, 2007.

Pons, Alvaro. "Between Avant-Garde and Commerciality: The Dichotomy of New Alternative Publishing Companies." *International Journal of Comic Art* 5, no. 2 (Fall 2003): 138–53.

Prokůpek, Tomáš. "Czech Comics." *International Journal of Comic Art* 5, no. 2 (Fall 2003): 312–38.

Repetti, Massimo. "African 'Ligne Claire': The Comics of Francophone Africa." *International Journal of Comic Art* 9, no. 1 (Spring 2007): 515–41.

Rubenstein, Anne. *Bad Language, Naked Ladies, and Other Threats to the Nation: A Political History of Comic Books in Mexico.* Durham, NC: Duke University Press, 1998.

Sabin, Roger. *Comics, Comix and Graphic Novels: A History of Comic Art.* London: Phaidon, 1996.

Sanders, Rik. "The Changing of Dutch Comics: Some Pluses and Minuses." *International Journal of Comic Art* 4, no. 2 (Fall 2002): 139–56.

Shen, Kuiyi. "*Lianhuanhua* and *Manhua*—Picture Books and Comics in Old Shanghai." In *Illustrating Asia: Comics, Humour Magazines and Picture Books,* ed. John A. Lent, 100–120. Richmond, UK: Curzon, 2001.

Singh, Jai Arjun. "The Medium Is the Message in Indian Comics." *Business Standard,* March 25, 2007. http://www.business-standard.com/search/storypage_new.php?leftnm=5&leftindx=5&subLeft=6&autono=278743.

Strömberg, Fredrik. "Swedish Comics and Comics in Sweden." *International Journal of Comic Art* 5, no. 1 (Spring 2003): 74–94.

Vergueiro, Waldomiro, and Lucimar Ribeiro Mutarelli. "Forging a Sustainable Comics Industry: A Case Study on Graphic Novels as a Viable Format for Developing Countries, Based on the Work of a Brazilian Artist." *International Journal of Comic Art* 4, no. 2 (Fall 2002):157–67.

Wei, Shu-chu. "Redrawing the Past: Modern Presentation of Ancient Chinese Philosophy in the Cartoons of Tsai Chih-Chung." In *Illustrating Asia: Comics, Humour Magazines and Picture Books,* ed. John A. Lent, 153–70. Richmond, UK: Curzon, 2001.

Wei, Shu-chu. "Shaping a Cultural Identity: The Picture Book and Cartoons in Taiwan, 1945–1980." In *Illustrating Asia: Comics, Humour Magazines and Picture Books,* ed. John A. Lent, 64–80. Richmond, UK: Curzon, 2001.

Welsh, David. "Forget Manga. Here's Manhwa." BusinessWeek.com, April 23, 2007. http://www.businessweek.com/innovate/content/apr2007/id20070423_634051.htm?chan=innovation_innovation+%2B+design_top+stories.

Yang, Kate. "'Going to the Office' Not What Chu Te-yung Does." *Taiwan Journal,* April 12, 2007, 5.

PART II

GRAPHIC NOVELS AND THE LIBRARY

7

A Place in
the Library

Francisca Goldsmith

American and British libraries have been collecting graphic novels since the format was first characterized as such in the late 1970s. In the past decade especially, U.S. library graphic novel collections have been nurtured, shaped, and promoted with increasing administrative acceptance and user awareness.

This chapter examines the current place graphic novels have in the library, reviewing practice and possibilities regarding collection development, acquisitions, cataloging and labeling, placement, circulation, and maintenance. Naturally, approaches and "best practices" are still evolving and continue to develop. (Note that graphic novel collection practices specific to academic libraries are treated in chapter 8.)

COLLECTION DEVELOPMENT

In the early years of graphic novel publishing, libraries did not generally recognize common attributes of the format. Considerable collection-development planning and procedural guidance have been evolving recently. Because early collection builders skewed toward those serving adolescents, a notable number of library and publishing institutions tended to typecast the format as of interest specifically to young adults. But the format is in no way so demographically specific, and libraries as well as publishers and review organs are now recognizing the broader claim that graphic novels can have on the general public's interest.

Selection of Titles in General

Libraries are now able to select from a wide range of graphic novel titles using standard library review resources, specialized and local resources, and vendor lists. The entry of large traditional publishers such as Macmillan and

Random House into the graphic novel arena, as well as increased popular and critical coverage of literary graphic novels, suggests that libraries can now find recent backlist titles as well as new titles available for selection.

However, many graphic novel publishers, including those specializing in manga, are not yet able to support deep backlists.[1] So library collection developers can more readily concentrate on finding new titles than on selecting retrospectively. Until the past five years, library vendors were unlikely resources for graphic novels, and so selection in many libraries developed with a reliance on resources such as Diamond,[2] built to suit commercial trade selection and acquisitions rather than for the library market. This has shaped some general selection patterns in early-adopting libraries.

Audience and Selection Considerations

With broader selection resources, including prepublication reviews for evaluating upcoming titles, some backlist availability, and published "best of" lists in such arenas as professional journals and on Web sites maintained by comics professionals and by librarians, graphic novel collection developers can now refine their selection procedures. This leads to the kind of maximum fit between local audience and local collection that is the ideal throughout any library's collection.

In libraries where more specific attention has been paid to building graphic novel collections targeted to young adults, selectors may have either omitted significant publications from the general collection because these titles were unsuitable to teens or been over-inclusive in building the young adult collection, selecting material unsuited to the age because there had been no other place to shelve these titles. These problems are most evident in early-adopting public libraries.

In fact, the graphic novel format can appeal to any age demographic (although not necessarily to every reader), and so the spread of collections throughout a general library is to be encouraged. Just as magazines for children, teens, and adults are likely to be collected, with selections considered for user relevance, the relevance of specific graphic novel selections to specific audiences should be considered.

In addition to the age factor, libraries should consider other audience realities when making graphic novel selections. If library users are exposed to works by writers or other creators of diverse ethnicities, aesthetic sophistications, political viewpoints, or genre concerns, the graphic novel selection should be no less diverse. If a preponderance of the general collection reflects local interest in African American work, or a major portion of the collection as a whole is available to Spanish-speaking readers, graphic novel selections undertaken for that audience should be sensitive to such emphasis. (See Appendices B-1 and B-2.)

The school library collection has the primary purpose of supporting the curriculum at its host institution. The school library audience includes students of a specific age range, teachers, and sometimes families. Selecting graphic novels to address the school audience is best done locally, to assure a good fit in terms of content, production quality, and accessibility.

Reviews and Other Selection Resources

New Titles

Graphic novels for a wide variety of audiences are regularly reviewed, sometimes prepublication, in such standard professional publications as *Library Journal, Booklist, School Library Journal, Publishers Weekly* (which also offers PW Comics Week on the Web and via e-newsletter), and *Kirkus.* Each of these resources is available via subscription both in print and through online access. Both *Voice of Youth Advocates* and *KLIATT* (which ceased publication in 2008) have been providing regular and substantive reviews of graphic novels as well, usually shortly after publication and most often of titles of interest to youth collection developers.

General readership newspapers and magazines, including the *New York Times,* regularly carry graphic novel reviews. Such reviews are more likely to be noticed by library users than are reviews aimed at librarians. Therefore, requests for titles in any format reviewed in these publications, including graphic novels, are more likely to be encountered by collection-development staff.

Of high importance to graphic novel collection developers are reviews and announcements in comics trade journals and comics professional Web sites, including *The Comics Journal, Diamond Bookshelf Reviews, Grovel,* and *ICv2.* Online archives of recently suspended critical resources, such as *Artbomb* (http://www.artbomb.net), *Graphic Novel Review* (http://www.graph icnovelreview.com), and the *Ninth Art* (http://www.ninthart.com), provide collection developers with background information on some older series and still active creators as well as a resource for finding reviews in the case of challenged titles.

Core Lists

Collection developers working anew with graphic novels need to refer to core lists in order to enrich new collections with earlier titles. Because many graphic novels do not stay in print for long, it is important to refer to recent core lists to build up a new collection. Such lists vary in scope by genre, recommended audience, and how frequently the list itself is updated, with titles no longer available removed and newly recognized essential holdings added. Other chapters in this book refer to specific core lists relevant to subsets of the collection.[3]

Selection Policies

Library collection policies related to graphic novels fall into two general categories. Some libraries explicitly delineate considerations for this format as unique, whereas others include the format in overall policy statements. These two basic categories seem to cut across types of libraries except, of course, those housing graphic novels archives or special collections, for which specific policies are in place.

Libraries maintain policies from which procedures flow, so typically some group of non-specialists—a library's board, a school district administrative office, and so on—must understand the whys and wherefores of policy. But it is the specialist staff that enacts the policy's hows, whos, and whats. To this end, some selection policies are complex and detailed, whereas others are broad and open-ended. Both types can address the collecting of graphic novels, but staff should understand the policy's ramifications on their ability to grow— and maintain—this type of collection. For example, purchasing replacement copies may not always be feasible when publishers often produce small runs and maintain tiny backlists. And, as noted previously, specifying one age group as the audience for the whole graphic novel collection (in a library serving multiple age groups) is a policy that raises serious issues. Indeed, the most flexible policy is one in which goals, rather than standards, are defined; such a policy allows the graphic novel collection to be maintained as best as allowed by conditions such as publishing and changing community, rather than locking the collection into a strategy that may prove unsuited to building and maintaining the best collection possible.

Public Libraries

Public library collection-development policies typically differentiate standards and practices by age and other audience characteristics as well as by format. This arises from the reality that beyond books, all formats are "newer" within public library collections, generally having been added one at a time and often only after the format became popular among patrons. Rare was the public library that collected either audio recordings or video before some substantial portion of its clientele had the interest, expertise, and equipment to use these formats.

Graphic novels are a bit different. They are books, in the broad sense— paper bound between covers, with mechanically printed contents, available in multiple copies, and requiring no apparatus beyond sufficient reading light. However, many public libraries have chosen to discuss this format as differentiated from the majority of their book collections, some even going so far as to dictate audience, repair schedules, and shelving within the collection-development policy.[4] This kind of attention hampers the general inclusion of the format within the collection. It is not that repair and shelving need to be the same as for text-format books, but these areas should be more appropriately addressed outside of collection-development policy. A less directive approach notes graphic novels as included, without prescribing detailed format-specific guidelines.[5]

School Libraries

The mission of the school library almost always gives primary importance to supporting the institution's curriculum. Therefore, school collection-development policies are likely to differ from those for public libraries because the latter generally adhere to a creed of breadth, whereas the former must be slanted to the host institution's areas of concern. Graphic novels are collected in school libraries both as direct curriculum support—as Art Spiegelman's *Maus* (1986–1997) fits into a secondary-level social sciences unit on the Holocaust—and in response to the school's interest in providing popular reading materials to encourage student reading practice.

School library collection-development policies may consider graphic novels for either or both of these purposes. Typically, school library policies are not as arbitrary as public library policies with regard to graphic novels. One exemplary school collection-development policy in which graphic novels are addressed is that of James Solomon Russell Junior High School (Lawrenceville, Virginia). This detailed policy makes reference to the state standards for school library collections and collecting. It also discusses graphic novels in terms of the collection as a whole and as suitable to the needs of this library's users (http://www.geocities.com/lisajunedenton/collection.html).

Special Collections

A number of libraries maintain special collections of graphic novels and comics. Many are in academic libraries, although some exist outside academia. Several Web sites maintain lists of such collections:

- Library of Congress, Caroline and Erwin Swann Collection of Caricature and Cartoon, "Related Collections and Sources Outside the Library of Congress," http://www.loc.gov/rr/print/coll/230_swan.html
- ComicsResearch.org, a gateway to numerous lists and bibliographies, including http://www.comicsresearch.org/academic.html#libraries
- Michigan State University Comic Art Collection, list of comics research libraries, http://www.lib.msu.edu/comics/otherlib.htm

Interested readers are referred to these institutions. Following are comments about a few types of special collections.

Prisons

Prison library collections almost always have their scope and such parameters as material types dictated by the overseeing law enforcement authority rather than by library-oriented policy makers. Collection-development policy guides for prisons generally address requirements for law materials. Often institutional policies forbid hardcover books and/or images that could be construed as provocative (sexually, behaviorally, politically). Nonetheless, prison librarians have been active in collecting graphic novels for their users, albeit without publishing collection-development policies that provide a map to such collecting.[6]

Hospitals

Hospital libraries open to patients must emulate the breadth of a small public library. The International Federation of Library Associations and Institutions has published an excellent overview of the collection policy needs of hospital libraries (http://www.ifla.org/VII/s9/nd1/iflapr-61e.pdf). The State of Washington is encouraging library staff in its psychiatric hospitals to consider including graphic novels in collections intended for patient use.[7]

ACQUISITIONS

Whereas collection-development policies provide guidance about what materials are selected and for whom, the acquisitions process addresses how materials are added to the collection. In some libraries, staff who manage selection also are engaged in acquisitions work, and in many others, one staff member selects, and another is charged with acquiring those selections. In the case of graphic novel collections, it is important that staff for both functions understand the reasons for collecting the format and the means needed to make those acquisitions.

Purchasing

The most common way for adding materials to the library's collection is through purchase. Although this may seem obvious for most types of materials, it is important to recognize that graphic novels may not be available from the library's usual purchasing outlets. In some libraries, graphic novels may be added to the collection only after the material is fully previewed by the selector(s). Although libraries with this process in place may be able to work with local comics shop staff, for other libraries this may mean that the selections are brought into the library already purchased, rather than as part of the ordinary acquisitions flow. This is an expensive and inefficient acquisitions method, given that it can leave the library in possession of materials they deem unsuitable to add to the collection but have already purchased for it. Preferably, staff entrusted to select graphic novels will have the latitude to use reviews and their professional knowledge to make selections for purchase and then move those purchases into the acquisition stream as would happen with other material types.

Moreover, some libraries also restrict their graphic novel collection to donated materials. This is discussed in some detail in a subsequent section.

Anytime a collection is built through acquisitions avenues that deviate from the library's customary path, the collection is set aside by that institution as "special." This kind of valuation may be positive or negative, but it should be recognized as something other than the norm.

Vendors

Two general types of vendors provide graphic novels to library collections: general library book vendors and specialized comics vendors. Many libraries use both types in order to build and maintain graphic novel collections.

Baker & Taylor, Book Wholesalers Inc., Brodart, and Ingram all offer robust purchasing services to all kinds of libraries, including materials from diverse publishers, some backlist offerings, online ordering and payment tools, and customized preprocessing of purchased materials. Each includes graphic novels among their offerings. Many libraries order their graphic novels directly through the same one or two of these channels through which they purchase adult fiction and nonfiction, children's fiction and nonfiction, and reference materials.

Diamond is the nation's largest distributor of comics to the trade. Some libraries utilize Diamond's services as a quasi-jobber. Because libraries rarely buy in the bulk Diamond requires, these libraries use its resources indirectly, choosing titles from its list of new and forthcoming publications and purchasing from a comics shop or online. Libraries in communities where local comics shops and bookstores stock robust graphic novel collections may purchase off the shelf at these businesses. Although discount rates will be relatively poor in such settings, the ability both to preview the material and to take patron-shoppers and new-to-comics staffers on an inspiring field trip can balance the investment.

Purchasing Cycles

As may be the case with any collection treated outside the normal purchasing methods of the library, some institutions buy graphic novels infrequently, leading to a glut or starve flow of materials into the collection. Some libraries do incorporate their graphic novel purchasing as a normal part of their acquisitions stream, so that new or replacement materials are purchased as frequently as are other new or replacement texts. School situations, where fewer staff are available to do both technical and public service jobs, are highly likely to make do with one or two buys of graphic novels a year—but this may match what they are able to achieve for other acquisitions as well! In any library situation where the community is seeking a regularly refreshed collection, it is important to add new materials on a regular and as frequent as possible basis. It is frustrating to users to have months or even a year elapse before new acquisitions appear. Frustration readily leads to loss of respect for the collection and the collection's institution. Far better to provide a steady, if smaller, flow of truly new graphic novels to your users to keep them returning to the collection to seek new options for reading.

Donations

Libraries that may be only experimenting with graphic novels are prone to rely on donations rather than purchases. Although this may save staff selection time and money for new materials, donations rarely provide the balance that a well-selected collection can. Spending processing resources on materials that come to the collection already used or because they were not saleable is often no savings. This means that sometimes donations are never completely processed but simply housed as a browsing collection that may ebb and flow as readers remove and add to it.

Although this has dissatisfying long-term results, watching the ebb and flow of donations may help libraries new to graphic novels better understand what graphic novel readers want and who those readers might be.

BIBLIOGRAPHIC ACCESS

The role of any library is to organize information for prospective users (including staff). Browsing collections that are accessible through no means other than physical scan of titles fails to provide valuable details to prospective users: What is the collection's scope? How are its parts related to its whole? How are the parts related to each other? How is any of it related to the specific reader's interest?

Cataloging

Classification and descriptive cataloging arrange a library collection systematically. Classification places materials devoted to similar subjects in close proximity, and descriptive cataloging allows those who approach the collection through its index—currently most likely to be a Web-based catalog—to identify specific titles that may share such desirable traits as author, artist, subject theme, size, sub-collection, and/or immediate availability.

The cataloging of graphic novels has both practical and theoretical histories that do not always converge. The fact that the graphic novel is a format has led many local catalogers and the Library of Congress to place graphic novels—regardless of subject matter—together in a format-specific category. So whether graphic novels in the collection cover mystery, health science, military history, or science fiction, they may be brought together under a classification number as singular as 741.59.[8]

Libraries with substantial graphic novel collections tend to classify them in one of three ways:

1. According to the Dewey scheme noted above, with greater or less refinement of the decimal to indicate creator nationality or genre

2. By separating fiction from nonfiction and placing nonfiction within the subject classification appropriate to the title, such as European History or AIDS Education, and fiction either as a sub-collection of its own or similarly interspersed within the general fiction collection, which may be arranged simply by author rather than call number
3. By placing all graphic novels into a collection outside the library's overall classification system, often assigning a descriptive classification such as "GN" or "Graphic Novel" to each title

Across the past decade, some early-adopting libraries as well as the Library of Congress have made concerted efforts to identify a classification niche for graphic novel materials that both normalizes their content and identifies their format specificity.[9]

Some academic libraries with graphic novel collections may classify them as browsing collections, with minimal cataloging and perhaps using either truncated class numbers or only the name of the browsing collection. Other academic libraries may treat the collection as an archive and build a classification system specific to the collection's research purposes.

School libraries tend to classify graphic novels in much the same way as public libraries: in some schools, the collection may be small and relatively unanalyzed, and in others, topical graphic novels are classified with the most general Dewey number for comics (741.5) or for the specific subject of the work (such as 362 for AIDS Education).

Tracing Creators

Beyond classification, library cataloging should provide users with information that can enhance the description of each item or provide additional access points. With graphic novels, providing catalog tracings for all creators allows inquirers to find not only works by the same authors but also those by the same illustrators, pencillers, letterers, and/or story creators. Although many graphic novels may be the work of a single person or writer/artist duo, others share, as with comic books, the input of a creative team. Cataloging such team-built work may involve tracings for those who contributed the storyboard, artwork, layout, and other aspects of technical details that create the whole.

Fictional Characters

Like much fiction in other formats, graphic novels sometimes represent series in which the same characters appear in various storylines from multiple authors. Tracing fictional characters in such stories further enhances library users' access to similar books. For instance, both the Star Wars universe's Nomi Sunrider (Veitch et al. 1994) and the Batman stories (e.g., Loeb,

2001; Miller and Mazzucchelli, 1988) can be found by tracing the names of these characters through the catalog to diverse titles.

OCLC Records

As graphic novel collections have become more accepted and supported in libraries, catalog records in the OCLC database have become more numerous. Ten years ago, librarians working with graphic novel collections had to create original cataloging for many new graphic novel acquisitions. Now with more libraries supporting such efforts, OCLC records for graphic novels are more likely to be found within the WorldCat database. For smaller libraries, libraries with few catalogers, and vendors developing graphic novel collections for sale with full cataloging available to purchasers, this trend means that suitable records can be found readily online rather than having to await local efforts.

Local Subject Headings

The development of canonical subject headings at the national level is a slow and deliberate process. Local graphic novel collections may profit from added access points that are accepted locally and that address local interests instead of only those published for a national audience. Manga, or Japanese comics, are extremely popular in many public and school libraries. Although the term "manga," which suggests a specific aesthetic as well as potentially indicating storylines, has yet to become an authorized Library of Congress subject heading, many local collections are or should be adopting the term as a local subject heading.

Materials Labeling

Typically, items held in library collections are processed to include some amount of labeling, which may include some or all of the following:

- Spine markings providing call number and/or sub-collection
- Property stamps: along the closed edges of the pages, on predetermined pages within, or both
- Half-labels that indicate such identifying elements as call number, title, and owning location, all in one predetermined area on an inside cover or flyleaf
- Book pockets or date-due slips

Because of the visual nature of graphic novels, any of these possible labels can intrude on content. At the same time, such labels are affixed to library items for valid reasons, such as identifying the owning institution and allowing for ready shelving in the appropriate location.

In addition to labels affixed by the owning library, graphic novels are now being labeled with age recommendations by some of the major comics publishers. Unlike the small suggested age ranges affixed to the inside flap of many juvenile novel dust jackets, age labeling from TOKYOPOP and some other houses is large and permanently affixed, usually on the back cover of the volume. In addition, some titles are marked "Parental Advisory." Library users may not be able to distinguish between this publisher suggestion and the library's collection policy, if any, related to readers' ages.

Labels as Finding Aids

Without labels of any sort, it becomes difficult and perhaps impossible to maintain shelving order or locate a specific item. Labels serving as finding aids provide quick visual access to the item's address within the collection and ownership by the particular institution. However, labels should be limited to the role of finding aid. Graphic novels should not suffer editorial labeling *from the library* such as "parental advisory" or proscriptive age limitations for borrowers. Such labeling runs counter to the tenets of intellectual freedom supported by American Library Association's Bill of Rights. The library may place graphic novels in collections intended for specific age groups and label them "TEEN," for example, but should not itself label an item by age-range as warranting possible censorship. Because some publishers imprint graphic novel covers with such terms as "parental advisory" or specified ages for readership (e.g., "16+"), some library staff falsely believe that the library is obligated to abide by these suggestions. But there is no force of law behind these suggestions. Communities and community standards differ, and the advice must be balanced by library staff members with their own local knowledge of the community.

Scarce Real Estate

Because graphic novel covers and/or interiors may be fully designed, the book's real estate for supporting affixed labels may be limited. Staff processors need to be sensitive both to the visual integrity on which labels may intrude and to staff and library users who look for such labels in specific locations. Although it is aesthetically unfair to cover an integral image, it is also unfair to place a regulation label—for instance, one that normally appears wrapped around the book's spine, one-quarter inch from the bottom—in an alternative location not readily noticeable.

By reviewing possible labeling issues a graphic novel collection might raise, processing staff may identify the best local alternative label locations or means.

COLLECTION PLACEMENT

Where any collection is housed in the library informs both staff and patrons as to its intended audience, its worth to the larger collection and the library as a whole, and how the library views its users.

Suitable Space

Who is the intended audience—or audiences—for the library's graphic novels? The answer must guide the collection's placement in any facility that holds more than a single type of book collection. Placing graphic novels intended for both adults and teens in an area set aside for teens invites adults into that space. Placing all graphic novels into a single area forces children, teens, and adults to browse materials that may not be suitable for them; this also sends the message that graphic novels are interchangeable age-wise, a statement libraries rarely make with other print materials. (See chapter 10, on censorship issues.)

Because browsing is a regular event in graphic novel collections, the space chosen for them should be well lit and include clear instructions—either with signage or location of furniture—for putting aside materials withdrawn from the shelf but then no longer wanted by the browser.

Placing the graphic novel collection near a staffed service point may be a precaution taken in libraries that fear unusual levels of theft or mutilation. Such placement may also indicate to users that staff is conversant with the collection and ready to provide guidance about the format. If that fits your library's circumstances, then such placement can boost readers' advisory work with graphic novels—which in turn may boost graphic novel circulation.

Shelving

Like other print books, graphic novels come in a wide range of sizes. Many are no more extremely proportioned than are children's nonfiction, some near folio-sized and many others shaped like the trade paperbacks that they may be. As graphic novel collections in libraries have gained popularity and provided some financial incentive to publishers, more titles are becoming available in well-bound editions especially suitable for library shelves.

Many graphic novels, however, are both large in page size and thin in number of pages. Such dimensions require prospective readers who are faced with spine-out shelving to pull possibilities from the shelf just to get a clear reading of the actual titles, let alone decide whether the books appear of interest. To guard against whole shelves dumping due to removal of strategic keystone books from the line, special shelving may be warranted. Metal shelves with moveable slats (built for paperback or DVD shelving) work well with such slippery contents. Slanted shelving and a slat wall with ledges or baskets for face-out shelving also provide steadier housing for graphic novels.

Some libraries place all or parts of their graphic novel collections on book trucks, spine up. This may invite browsers while keeping materials in relatively good order. However, as a permanent solution to shelving, this suggests that the library has not found a real "home" for the collection.

Displays

Graphic novel displays belong both within a library and during programs relating to such materials. Passive displays—in cases, along walls, and so forth—are enhanced by showing interior pages of graphic novels as well as their covers. Select page spreads that are relatively large-paneled and on which the action can be interpreted without necessary reference to the whole plot. When the display is in a truly public place, page spreads should be chosen with a sensitive eye toward passersby who may be too young or too old to view some images with comfort.

Graphic novels selected for display during a library program may be temporarily housed on a book truck within the program area or set upright on a nearby table. Those attending the program may want to handle these materials, so staff should make sure that whatever bibliographic control is needed at the program site is in place. Occasion-specific displays of graphic novels need not be limited to programs specifically about the format but can also be included where the subject matter of selected titles offers alternatives to the narrative text or film content at the heart of the program.

CIRCULATION ISSUES

Except in archival settings, graphic novels are most likely to be among a library's circulating collections rather than held for in-house use only. However, although hardcover editions are increasingly available within the format, many graphic novels are likely to be more delicate than books from university presses or large trade publishing houses.

In addition to physical issues relating to circulation, policy concerns as well need to be identified and possibly addressed by circulation procedures. Some public libraries do not allow children under a certain age to borrow VHS or DVD materials. With a format as visual as graphic novels, will that policy attach to it as well?

As discussed previously under "Materials Labeling," some graphic novel publishers are affixing age recommendations permanently to the covers of their publications. How will the library discuss this apparent prescription with concerned borrowers? That question must be considered before such discussions happen. Staff need to be informed that such advisories are affixed by publishers to aid booksellers engaged in direct consumer selling, rather than as an enforceable caveat for libraries. The best preparation for this discussion with a concerned user is staff familiarity with both the collection and the community it serves, but this ideal is not always in place at the point where the complaint and the recipient staff come together. The library should, however, be sure to have a consistent, community-oriented policy about how complaints are received as well as how materials are selected, and all staff should be both familiar with these policies and knowledgeable about how to access them for inquiring community members.

Security System Requirements

Like materials labels, various security systems require affixing matter to each item in the collection. Magnetic-based security systems often rely on small strips that are attached between pages of books. The strips are narrow, but placement may intrude on the gutter space or even cross-spread artwork if not placed with sensitivity to the integrity of each item.

Another, increasingly popular means of securing the collection is through the application of radio frequency identification (RFID) tags. Although the hot spot of the tag is itself generally no larger than the top surface of a pencil eraser, the patch that is affixed to the material also includes an antenna, thereby making the entire piece about an inch and a half square. In order to preserve the working order of the tag, it is generally located on the front or back interior cover, rather than being affixed to the outside where it would be rubbed by neighboring books. For most graphic novels, this kind of placement causes little chance of intruding on content.

Although theft will be discussed in more detail later in the chapter, it should be noted here that one of the positive aspects of RFID security systems is the technology's ability to communicate which specific item was taken through the security gates without being properly checked out. Other mechanical security devices alert the library to the fact that something is being removed, but RFID also provides—usually through the barcode encoded in the chip and attached to the catalog record—information about what exactly has walked away.

Smaller school and even public libraries may rely on no mechanical security system but ask that staff do a visual check of book bags or other means through which library visitors may carry away materials. This system is no more or less effective in securing graphic novels against theft than it is in keeping other materials safe.

Remote Return Mechanisms

Libraries receive returned materials through a variety of mechanical return paths. Borrowers may place materials through a small slot in a desk, and the material then passes into a bin immediately below. Or they may push the material through a flap and into a weatherproof box located outside the library building (and thus useable outside the library's scheduled hours). Both RFID and non-RFID return systems are in use that allow borrowers to go beyond simply returning items and actually check in what they have borrowed. Such equipment generally requires that materials be pushed through a mechanical door, scanned, and then dropped into a bin that may be on a conveyor belt.

All these options create some amount of wear and tear on materials. High-circulating, typically glue-bound and soft-cover graphic novels are not the best candidates for dropping, spending time in a possibly damp environment, placed beneath a mounting stack of heavier returns, or falling from a distance through which their covers may become open before they land. The best mechanical return options for graphic novel collections are those that allow the least amount of free fall between entry and landing and that do not become filled with heavier materials. Alternatively, frequent clearing of mechanical returns and regular checking on condition of returns may increase the life expectancy of fragile graphic novels.

Theft and Mutilation

The topic of theft is frequently raised by library staff working with graphic novel collections in public libraries. The electronic discussion list Graphic Novels in Libraries, which serves as a forum for librarians involved with comics in the collection, regularly features threads in which the matter is discussed. Complaints are common about the unhappy effect of theft on both budget and morale, and sympathy is voiced for staff fielding a current situation of "disappearing" materials.[10]

Considering theft rates for graphic novels without examining theft rates of other focused interest collections can, of course, exaggerate the impact. Because graphic novel collections tend to be smaller than, say, a public library's genre paperback collection or its DVD collection, theft of relatively few items does create a larger apparent hole. As discussed in "Security System Requirements," the vulnerability of the graphic novel collection can be checked to some degree by choices made in terms of stripping, tagging, or otherwise controlling "walk out" access.

Theft—Or Intellectual Freedom Issue?

In some cases, library staff plagued by disappearing graphic novels need to consider whether the items are being stolen by library users who, for whatever reason, do not use the traditional borrowing mechanism (reasons should be investigated) or whether the disappearances are due to someone making an anonymous challenge to specific titles in the collection or even to the format as a whole. It is not useful or accurate to assume that "graphic novel enthusiasts (at least in my community) are also thieves." There is an equally good chance that thefts can be attributed to someone who hopes to prevent others from seeing the materials. (This could even be a library staff member who has strong feelings about certain items or images and hesitates to express them directly.)

So to decide how to prevent stealing, staff must investigate the nature of the thefts. Is it possible to pinpoint the times of day that the thefts occur? Are the thefts in large batches or in small but ongoing pilferings? Is it possible to monitor the collection more carefully, especially if there are suspicions about the thieves' identity, in order to check out suspicions? Investigate the actual events rather than become either blind to them or cynical about library users.

Theft of Ideas: Copyright

Mutilations of graphic novels, currently most especially manga, may be toward the end of using images as decorative elements for one's own personal effects. A student may so admire a particular manga character that she snips a page where he is featured and then affixes his picture to her binder. This of course is also theft, but beyond mutilation of the library material, the perpetrator is also misusing copyright-protected material by placing it outside its context and treating it as something else—binder cover rather than a page in a narrative.

Especially among middle school children, whose moral reasoning is still developing, such mutilations may not be hidden from library staff because perpetrators are not clearly aware of their crime being perceived as such. Question the evidence directly in cases where mutilation is a fact and where collection users are sporting its outcome.

The censor, too, can work through mutilation rather than all-out theft of an entire work. Again, monitoring the use of the collection may be the arduous but necessary method needed to identify the culprit(s).

Education Toward Maintaining the Collection

Whether thefts and mutilations are due to fans or would-be censors, library users (and staff, if necessary) need to be educated about the consequences. In the case of fan theft, library staff should make every effort to identify the culprit(s) and stress that a crime has been committed. What are the penalties for theft in your library? Revoking library access? A call to police? In addition, the staff needs to alert other users of the collection to the fact that resources are limited and that the collection's compromised status cannot be ignored.

In the case of censors, the same criminal injunctions can be invoked. But it is also a warning call to the library that the users may, in general, not understand how to challenge library materials that they do not accept.

Collection Budgets and Dealing with Theft or Mutilation

Collections that are heavily pillaged cannot be restored without stressing the library's materials budget. Be sure to let library users know why the collection has been diminished and the fact that it cannot be rebuilt without cost that may diminish other collections, or that it cannot be rebuilt without compromising purchase of new materials. Be direct, explicit, and informative. This is not the time to cast blame on people who are simply suspects or the time to gossip about anyone actually found guilty of theft or mutilation. Education is preventive against future episodes, not revenge for past ones.

How the library incorporates loss through theft and mutilation into its materials budgeting is a larger issue than the effect of bad behavior on the graphic novels collection. If theft and mutilation are issues only for this particular collection, then any replacement funds set aside to address wear and tear must be shared with replacing materials stolen and purposely damaged. This will have a clear and visible impact on the state of the collection, an object lesson that should be made clear to users. Some libraries have posted signs to alert users to theft/mutilation situations and consequences.

Interlibrary Loan

Because the graphic novel format is that of the bound book, the medium is rarely excluded from interlibrary loan rules in the way that audiovisual media frequently may be. However, depending on local cataloging custom, it may be difficult to determine the specific volume number of a series graphic novel that is wanted or that is available for interlibrary loan. The interlibrary loan system supported by use of OCLC WorldCat depends on owning libraries to keep their bibliographic item records up-to-date, an issue that may be problematic for libraries where graphic novels receive little cataloging treatment at both the acquisitions and deaccessioning ends of the library's holding term.

PRESERVATION AND COLLECTION MAINTENANCE

During the first two decades of graphic novel publishing, almost all titles were available to consumers—including libraries—in paperbound format only. Popular circulating collections, especially in public and school libraries, presented staff with dramatic burdens in terms of damaged materials: poorly glued bindings, lightweight covers, lost pages, and both gutters and paper quality inadequate to rebinding efforts.

Some library vendors began to offer pre-bound editions, using the original paper covers laminated to board. While providing a sturdier case for the book, these covers often intruded on page gutters and made it difficult for readers to lay the open book flat.

More recently, publishers have begun to recognize the wisdom of providing "library editions" with traditional, stitched-spine hard covers. Although the majority of popular titles continue to be available only in paperbound editions, binding glue has improved, and libraries are learning to take prophylactic steps to preserve their graphic novels.

Offsetting Wear and Tear

At the 2002 "Getting Graphic @ Your Library" pre-conference during ALA's annual meeting, a room full of 60 graphic novel librarians discussed and traded methods of coping with wear and tear on their collections. Among the simplest methods was that of spine-taping paperbound items before initial circulation. Other methods included saddle-stapling paperbound graphic novels before or after spine glue loosened; building up paper covers with lightweight cardboard laminated to the original paper cover; and even punching holes in the spine edge and inserting binder rings.

Libraries with more generous collection budgets worked to offset the wear and tear on new volumes in highly popular series by purchasing multiple copies at the outset and spreading the initial flurry of circulation among several copies.

Recognizing and repairing damage as soon as possible extends the life of any book, including graphic novels. Continuing to circulate material that has been compromised by wear and tear, without addressing the material's need for rejuvenation, will only lead to more damage—and less likelihood that the damage can be repaired readily or inexpensively.

Weeding

Weeding graphic novel collections or individual graphic novels is an ordinary aspect of collection maintenance. Although ongoing demand may drive more worn graphic novels toward repair rather than replacement queues, the reasons for removing graphic novel material from the collection are the same as for other books and media formats.

Condition

Irreparable condition is the leading cause for weeding any particular graphic novel from the collection. When any item defies repair and is dirty, has missing pages, or is otherwise compromised in integrity, it is no longer suitable for circulation.

Datedness

There are graphic novels that may present challenges to current information, but more likely, datedness may arise from changes in mores. This certainly does not mean that weeding should occur whenever the librarian notes material that was published in another time period or that reflects acceptable standards of another time period. However, the librarian should take into consideration the collection's audience and whether the dated nature of a specific title can be handled well. Examples could include reprint volumes of some mid-20th-century comics with women depicted in an extreme "pin-up" style, which are perceived differently by many in our postfeminist culture than they were by readers of the period, and some *Tintin* titles as they were originally published, with native peoples of Africa and Asia depicted with colonial stereotypes of physical and character features.

Out of Scope

Like datedness, a title can be judged as worthy of weeding for its failure to be within the scope of the collection only when there are clear parameters of what that scope is. Dislike based on specific content or aesthetic is not the same as judging it out of scope. However, finding material more suitable to children in an adult collection may well call for the decision that that material is out of scope. Here, it may be simply transferred to the children's collection. On other occasions, the judgment that a work is out of scope is likely to lead to its removal from the collection as a whole. An example might be a Chinese-language title published in Taiwan. In a collection that contains no other Chinese materials and whose audience is not literate in Chinese, this book may be viewed as falling outside the scope of the collection.

Redundancy

In the few libraries that are able to buy multiple copies of new titles, the first rush of popularity may fade before those extra copies are lost, damaged, or otherwise missing in action. Weeding redundant copies of graphic novels is a luxury few libraries have yet to enjoy but is necessary where space is limited and duplicates and triplicates are underused.

THE FUTURE OF GRAPHIC NOVELS IN LIBRARIES

Given the continued interest in graphic novels from comics fans, mainstream and comics publishers, and comics creators with publishing aspirations, graphic novel publishing shows no sign of abating. In addition, new findings about literacy have greatly increased the interest of the educator establishment in offering the format widely for multiple purposes. (For example, see

Stephen Krashen's 2004 book.) So in the long term, inclusion of this format in library collections is likely to grow rather than shrink. Fortunately, the average graphic novel package—the traditional paper book form—requires little re-gearing by libraries. Technical concerns, including cataloging, security measures, and policy, are always works in progress in the modern library setting; graphic novels present a situation that differs very little from other book types in these matters.

Certainly as long as libraries collect and provide access to print materials, and as long as readers enjoy the format, graphic novels deserve a solid and even exemplary place in library collections.

NOTES

1. As used here, "manga" refers both to Japanese comics and to domestic graphic novels designed using Japanese comics sensibilities. Manga continues to enjoy considerable popularity among children and teens, not only in Japan and the United States but in other cultures also.

2. Diamond Comics Distributors is the giant of the U.S. sequential art distribution network. Comics distribution works differently from most book distribution, especially concerning returns. Because Diamond does not accept returns of unsold product from local vendors, vendors tend to purchase conservatively, making it difficult for agencies such as libraries to obtain backlist titles. Diamond publishes a periodical, *Previews,* which features new and upcoming titles, and most of its customer base utilizes this as their primary selection tool.

3. See in the chapter references the recent book-length resources by Gorman (2008), Pawuk (2007), and Serchay (2008, forthcoming), useful for building core lists generally.

4. See, for example, the Campbell County, Wyoming, Public Library System's policy at http://ccpls.org/coldev/html/YA/xv-gn.html.

5. Examples of this approach can be found at these libraries: Tempe Public Library in Arizona, http://www.tempe.gov/LIBRARY/admin/policies/colldev.htm; Monterey Public Library in California, http://www.monterey.org/library/cdp/cdp11.html; and Newark Public Library in New Jersey, http://www.npl.org/Pages/AboutLibrary/colldevpol06.html.

6. For an overview of prison library collection interests, see "What Do Prisoners Read? Prison Libraries and Collection Development," (http://www.ala.org/ala/aboutala/offices/olos/incarcerated-exoffenders/btw03.cfm). Sue Wilkinson's discussion of prisoner literacy and the role of the prison library, in "HMP Birmingham: Reader Development" (http://www.openingthebook.com/uploads/newbout/mainsite/downloads/strategies/HMP%20BIRMINGHAM%20RD%20STRATEGY.doc), addresses the place of graphic novels in the prison library and in library programming.

7. Washington Library Association Children and Young Adult Services Interest Group, untitled article, *CAYAS Newsletter,* May 11, 2007, unpaged.

8. See "New and Changed Entries to the Full and Abridged Editions of the Dewey Decimal Classification System," February 2006, at http://www.oclc.org/dewey/updates/new/.

9. See the online catalogs for the Hennepin County Library in Minnesota (https://catalog.hclib.org/ipac20/ipac.jsp?profile=elibrary), MARINet in California (http://199.88.71.7/), and the Boston Public Library in Massachusetts (http://catalog.mbln.org/ipac20/ipac.jsp?

profile=bpl1#focus) for typical approaches by public libraries to classifying graphic novels.

10. For example, http://lists.topica.com/lists/GNLIB-L/read/message.html?mid=913 873266&sort=d&start=21475 presents such a discussion from July 2007.

REFERENCES

Gorman, Michele. *Getting Graphic! Comics for Kids,* Columbus, OH: Linworth, 2008.

Krashen, Stephen D. *The Power of Reading: Insights from the Research.* 2nd ed. Westport, CT: Libraries Unlimited, 2004.

Loeb, Jeph. *Batman: Dark Victory,* New York: DC Comics, 2001.

Miller, Frank, and David Mazzucchelli. *Batman: Year One.* New York: DC Comics, 1988.

Pawuk, Michael. *Graphic Novels: A Genre Guide to Comic Books, Manga, and More.* Westport, CT: Libraries Unlimited, 2007.

Serchay, David. *The Librarian's Guide to Graphic Novels for Adults.* New York: Neal-Schuman, forthcoming.

Serchay, David. *The Librarian's Guide to Graphic Novels for Children and Tweens.* New York: Neal-Schuman, 2008.

Spiegelman, Art. *Maus: A Survivor's Tale,* New York: Pantheon, 1986–1997.

Veitch, Tom, Chris Gossette, Janine Johnston, and David Roach. *Star Wars: Tales of the Jedi: Knights of the Old Republic.* Milwaukie, OR: Dark Horse, 1994.

8

COMICS AND GRAPHIC NOVELS IN THE ACADEMIC LIBRARY COLLECTION

Lorena O'English

COMICS AND HIGHER LEARNING: AN INTRODUCTION

A 1991 review of Randall Scott's *Comics Librarianship* gently chided the author for spending too much space justifying the value of a comics collection.[1] Nevertheless, even as the universe of comic books and strips has expanded to include book-length graphic novels and trade paperbacks, academic librarians and others still find themselves needing to articulate the value of collecting the medium.[2] Given that multiple academic departments have fully adopted the study of graphic novels and other sequential art formats, librarians will hopefully find that additional justification is no longer necessary, and time and resources can now be focused on treating graphic novels just like other publications.

This chapter explores the scholarly infrastructure of comics studies that has built up over time and the increased attention paid by other academic disciplines to sequential art and narrative, as well as issues of more immediate concern to academic librarians who desire to move from a handful of graphic novels in the catalog to a sustained collection used for both scholarship and recreational reading. The terms "graphic novel" and "comics" are used interchangeably and include trade paperbacks and comic book compilations. Although some graphic novels such as Marjane Satrapi's *Persepolis* titles are created and published from the beginning as complete narrative works (sometimes called original graphic novels, or OGNs), many others originally appeared as periodical comics in a series format over time. These may constitute limited series, such as most of Alan Moore's works and Art Spiegelman's *Maus*. Also, trade paperbacks may collect one or more story arcs from a long running series, such as Jaime and Gilbert Hernandez's *Love and Rockets,* or from superhero, horror, Western, or other genre series from companies such as Marvel Comics or DC Comics.

Of course, not all graphic narratives are fiction; increasingly, the term "graphic novels" is used to include graphic nonfiction such as autobiography, reportage, and historical work. (The term "graphic narrative" is gaining ground as an alternative.) Works such as Daniel H. Pink's *The Adventures of Johnny Bunko: The Last Career Guide You'll Ever Need* and *American Widow,* Alissa Torres and Sungyoon Choi's wrenching graphic memoir of losing a husband in the September 11, 2001, destruction of New York City's World Trade Center, are good examples of such works.

GRAPHIC NOVELS IN THE ACADEMIC SETTING

Graphic novels and other forms of comics fit into academic learning in a variety of ways: as a subject of study in themselves, to support the curriculum across subject boundaries (including foreign language study), on a "how-to" basis for personal and professional development, and for leisure reading.

Comics as the Subject of Scholarly Study and Analysis

Comics in the Classroom

In 1990, Randall Scott predicted that courses covering comics themes might increase, following expansion of coverage by academic libraries:

> It is suddenly much easier to provide reasonable support for high school and the undergraduate college level study of comics. Whether this will lead to an increase in such studies is hard to say, but the possibility seems reasonable. There are more academic library comic collections than there are college courses taught on comics for sure. Libraries seem to be leading the way in introducing comics to academia right now. It is a good time to be a comics librarian.[3]

Scott's prediction came true, and the past few years in particular have seen an increase in courses using graphic novels or studying them. For example, an honors course at Portland State University explores Art Spiegelman's *Maus* and Chris Ware's *Jimmy Corrigan: The Smartest Kid on Earth.* Such courses may turn up in English, comparative literature, and interdisciplinary studies departments as well as others. (For a sampling among numerous university offerings, see Appendix A to this chapter.)

The Environment of Comics Scholarship

More broadly, the study of comics as such has firmly wedged itself into the folkways of academia, establishing structures that go along with academic interest and attaching itself to traditional and interdisciplinary areas. A variety of publications have appeared from scholarly presses; notably, the University Press of Mississippi's Studies in Popular Culture series includes a number of critically acclaimed scholarly titles examining comics, their creators, and their subcultures. *Image & Narrative* (http://www.imageandnarrative.be), *ImageTexT* (http://www.english.ufl.edu/imagetext), and *Word & Image* (http://www.tandf. co.uk/journals/titles/02666286.asp) are all online peer-reviewed journals focusing on sequential art and visual narrative. The *International Journal of Comic Art,* edited by noted comics scholar John Lent, publishes peer-reviewed interdisciplinary articles on all aspects of comic art and text from both a U.S. and an international perspective, and *Mechademia: An Annual Forum for Anime, Manga, and Fan Arts* focuses on Japanese materials and influences (http://www. mechademia.org). Two new journals in the field have recently emerged: *European Comic Art* (http://www.eurocomicart.org), started in 2008 as "the first English-language scholarly publication devoted to the study of European-language graphic novels, comic strips, comic books and caricature," and *SIGNs—Studies in Graphic Narratives* (http://www.graphic-narratives.org). Peer-reviewed journals in other disciplines occasionally include articles or even special issues devoted to research related to graphic novels or publish reviews of graphic novels relevant to their interests.[4] Along with this, the field is slowly establishing citation styles and debating issues of publication rights and permissions and how illustrations and text should be used in scholarly writing.[5]

ELECTRONIC MAILING LISTS

These scholarly oriented lists provide opportunities for extensive, in-depth discussion of comics-related themes from a broad range of disciplinary perspectives, as well as announcements about new works and calls for publication and conference proposals.

Comixschl-list (Comix Scholars Discussion List), http://www.eng lish.ufl.edu/comics/scholars/

AMRC-L (Anime and Manga Research Circle), http://www.cjas. org/~leng/amrc.htm

BDFIL (Bande Dessinée Discussion List), http://www.shef.ac.uk/ ibds/bdfil.htm (site in English)

A number of conferences and conference tracks provide opportunities for scholars to present their research. (See text box.) The subfield of medieval comics has its own organization, the Medieval Comics Project, and in recent years there has been a comics panel or workshop at each meeting of the International Congress on Medieval Studies in Kalamazoo, Michigan.[6] Conferences in almost any discipline may have papers or panels relating to graphic novels; an example is the 2008 American Philological Association conference, which included a panel on Classics and Comics.[7] Even the virtual world Second Life is venturing into this territory: 2008 saw Met@Morph, a Web comic–oriented conference featuring "an international roster of web comics creators, Second Life comics creators, scholars, teachers, students, and designers."[8]

SIGNIFICANT CONFERENCES

International Comic Arts Forum (http://www.internationalcomi cartsforum.org)

International Conference on Narrative (Society for the Study of Narrative Literature, http://narrative.georgetown.edu)

Popular Culture Association annual conference: Comic Arts and Comics Area track (http://www.comicsresearch.org/CAC/index.html)

International Bande Dessinée Society Conference, biennial (http://www.shef.ac.uk/ibds)

International Conference on Asian Comics, Animation, and Gaming, sponsored in 2006 by the York Centre for Asian Research (http://www.yorku.ca/ycar/ACAG%202006/index.html)

Related professional associations include the National Association of Comic Arts Educators, the Comic Art Working Group of the International Association for Mass Communication Research, and the both academic and enthusiast Sequart Research & Literary Organization. The distinctions among scholar, practitioner, and enthusiast/fan are perhaps a little grayer than in other academic disciplines, and all three may mingle in virtual and physical discussions. Each year, the fannish (and increasingly Hollywood-oriented) San Diego Comic-Con is paralleled by the more academically oriented Comic Art Conference.[9]

Many academic programs relate to comics studies, although one must distinguish between programs providing professional training in comic art (mainly art departments or schools, or specialized programs such as the Center for Cartoon Studies or the Joe Kubert School of Comic and Graphic Art) and those concentrating on the scholarly study of works in comics format by offering specific courses or even advanced degrees (notably, the University of Florida's advanced degree in Comics and Visual Rhetoric).

Comics as a Resource for Academic Study

The field of literature is a natural place to look for scholarly interest in comics and graphic novels. Indeed, the past few years have seen an explosion of articles throughout a wide range of journals, offering scholarly analysis and exploring linkages between literary fiction and comics work.[10] The entire Winter 2006 issue of *Modern Fiction Studies*—12 articles—was devoted to graphic narrative, including an exploration of political themes in Marjane Satrapi's *Persepolis* and Art Spiegelman's *In the Shadow of No Towers,* an analysis of several writers using Walter Benjamin's historical materialist criticism, two different examinations of Chris Ware's works, an interview with writer/artist Alison Bechdel, and an assessment of a graphic novel focusing on African American women's history: *Icon: A Hero's Welcome.* The March/April 2007 issue of *World Literature Today* offered several critical articles on graphic novels and their placement in literature as well as brief articles on major creators, including Lynda Barry and Joe Sacco, and the Fall 2007 issue of *MELUS,* the journal of the Society for the Study of the Multi-Ethnic Literature of the United States, was devoted to articles on the representation of race and ethnicity in comics and graphic novels.[11] A recent interview with Peter Gutierrez of the National Council of Teachers of English highlights the multiple literacies communicated through graphic storytelling. The interview appeared in *Diamond Bookshelf,* an online newsletter for librarians and other educators from Diamond Comic Distributors.[12]

However, the study of comics extends beyond literature departments to many fields, including art, history, communication, linguistics, business, and sociology. In addition to being its own subject of scholarship, comics are also used as one more form of delivering information in the study and teaching of other subjects, including history, political science, and popular culture. Although not intended as a textbook, physics professor James Kakalios's *The Physics of Superheroes* may be used to show how scientific principles can be referenced in proving or disproving comics phenomena, and *Caped Crusaders 101: Composition through Comic Books* includes chapters on race, political affairs, corporate responsibility, gender, and more, providing questions for "thinking, debating, writing" that can be used in college-level classes.[13]

Graphic novels have considerable value as teaching and learning tools in K–12 schooling and are increasingly being studied in teacher education.[14] *Building Literacy Connections with Graphic Novels: Page by Page, Panel by Panel* offers examples of how these works can enhance classroom study in both high school and college, including pairing graphic novels with thematically similar titles to showcase mood and tone (for example, comparing Hawthorne's *The Scarlet Letter* with Spiegelman's *In the Shadow of No Towers*).[15] Another valuable resource is the National Association of Comics Art Educators (NACAE), which has a cornucopia of ideas on its Web site, including syllabi, lesson plans, and activities (http://www.teachingcomics.org).

To support academic study of graphic novels, academic libraries should be acquiring not just critical works but also works about the history, sociocultural impact, and economics of the industry itself. Although the more industry-specific works may not be published by scholarly presses and may be of interest to comics fans as well as academics, these titles provide useful primary source material and other perspectives. The tagline of TwoMorrows Publishing (http://www.twomorrows.com) is "Celebrating the art and history of comics"; and publications such as the Modern Masters, Comic Introspective, and Companion series and *Alter Ego* magazine (edited by noted comics creator and editor Roy Thomas) provide histories, interviews, art, and more for both fans and scholars. A growing bio-biographical literature examines comics creators, including Dooley and Heller's *The Education of a Comics Artist: Visual Narrative in Cartoons, Graphic Novels, and Beyond* as well as larger studies such as Canadian archivist John Bell's *Invaders from the North: How Canada Conquered the Comic Book Universe*.[16]

Matthew J. Pustz's *Comic Book Culture* and Bradford W. Wright's *Comic Book Nation* provide scholarly treatment of fan culture sociology and the cultural and historical impact of the medium in the United States.[17] Titles such as *Comics Above Ground: How Sequential Art Affects Mainstream Media* and Rabbi Simcha Weinstein's *Up, Up, and Oy Vey!: How Jewish History, Culture, and Values Shaped the Comic Book Superhero* provide additional context for the origins and larger implications of the comics medium.[18]

The business side of comics is also of interest. Besides *Comic Book Nation,* foreign affairs and business journalist Dan Raviv's *Comic Wars: How Two Tycoons Battled over the Marvel Comics Empire—and Both Lost* is an entertaining look at an iconic comics company and a good reminder that comics and graphic novels are not just literary, cultural, and historical artifacts but also a multimillion dollar industry worthy of study in itself. (Comic book sales researcher John Jackson Miller reported that the estimated U.S. market for the industry was $475–550 million in 2006, not including sales of manga.)[19] Indeed, management lessons have been drawn from examples of innovation and teamwork within the comic book industry.[20]

Finally, in addition to superhero comics and other works from established companies such as DC and Marvel, there has been significant academic interest in alternative comics, ranging from the underground "comix" of the 1960s and 1970s to the autobiographical and experimental titles that began in the 1980s and remain popular today. In *Alternative Comics: An Emerging Literature,* Charles Hatfield writes,

> Crucial to this new movement were the rejection of mainstream formulas; the exploration of (to comics) new genres, as well as the revival, at times ironic recasting, of genres long neglected; a diversification of graphic style; a budding internationalism, as cartoonists learned from other cultures and other traditions; and especially, the exploration of searchingly personal and at times boldly political themes. What's more, alternative comics invited a new formalism, that is, an intensive reexamining of the formal tensions inherent in comics.[21]

Hatfield includes a chapter on irony and self-documentation in autobiographical works and makes a strong case for accepting comics, comix, and graphic novels as literature.

Comics in Foreign Languages
(and as Resources for ESL)

Comics and graphic novels are not uniquely American, of course, and in fact are more popular and socially salient in many other cultures. Foreign-language comics offer very useful tools for students learning these languages, especially given that students can use panel art to provide context for the text. Such comics also provide windows into other cultures, showing different perspectives and manifestations of history, gender relations, social standards, business practices, and more. Students can use them to improve reading comprehension as well as for speaking and translation practice. Even original or translated English-language comics can provide insights into foreign culture, history, and language; examples include Japanese manga from TOKYOPOP and other publishers; works published by Roaring Book Press's comics imprint First Second, including *Kampung Boy* (Malaysia) and *Klezmer* (prewar Eastern Europe); and the autobiographical *Persepolis* and its sequels (Iran). Not all of these ventures may have long-term success, however; Virgin Comics, a joint British-Indian comics publisher since 2006, shut down its New York Office in the fall of 2008.[22]

In 1977, James W. Brown discussed the use of comics in Europe, especially France, to teach foreign languages and noted sadly about the United States,

> Despite their prevalence in textbooks using an audio-visual approach, despite their pervasiveness as a modern form of communication, despite their appeal to students of all ages and at all levels of instruction, comics have been relatively ignored by North American scholars of foreign language pedagogy.[23]

His review is still relevant and useful, but 30 years later, the medium is increasingly used in the United States as a tool for foreign language acquisition, for example, in preparation for the Business French exam, *Certificat pratique de français commercial et économique.*[24]

The world of international foreign language comics is indeed large, although distribution difficulties have limited availability in the United States. New partnerships are being established, however, and foreign comics are increasingly available. (See chapter 6.) European-language *bandes dessinées* (BD) such as the *Tintin* series, the *Astérix* books, or the Corto Maltese series, along with more modern works, are being joined by non-Western works, especially from Asia. *The 99* is a monthly comic based on Middle Eastern culture and history and is available in both English and Arabic from Teshkeel Comics.[25] Works available in two languages, including translations of English-language originals such as the Italian translation of Alan Moore's *V for Vendetta,* can be very useful for the language learner.[26] Increasingly available Web comics present additional opportunities for discovering and accessing foreign-language comic strips.[27]

For many students, the foreign language they are studying is English as a second language (ESL), whether in the United States or in their home countries, and English-language comics can be extremely valuable. Stephen Cary's *Going Graphic: Comics at Work in the Multilingual Classroom* provides ESL instructors with 25 exercises that can be used at multiple levels of English proficiency and also for non-English language instruction.[28]

Creating Comics for Fun, Publicity, and Careers

Many who read science fiction feel an urge to write it themselves, and perhaps the same is true for comics readers. Librarians, art departments, and others may want to host comics writing and drawing contests, including programs such as a 24-Hour Comics Day challenge, an event where participants create a 24-page comic in one 24-hour period;[29] assign graphic novel creation projects; or use comic art and narrative to promote library events, collections, and more. Some people may be naturally talented in creating visual art or constructing narrative, but for others there are resources available to fall back on, including opportunities within their own institutions such as students, staff, and faculty in art and composition departments. An excellent example of this is the graphic novel *Shake Girl*, created and published through the Stanford Graphic Novel Project. Not only is this an exercise in creativity; the story also draws attention to Cambodia and the use of acid attacks as a form of violence against women.[30] Computer software is also available to make it easier to create short or longer-length works using photographs or other preexisting images. (See text box.)

COMICS-CREATING SOFTWARE
AND WEB APPLICATIONS

Comic Book Creator and TOKYOPOP Manga Creator (Planetwide Media), http://www.mycomicbookcreator.com
Comic Life, http://plasq.com/products/
Comeeko (free), http://www.comeeko.com/
ToonDoo (free), http://www.toondoo.com
QuickToons (free), http://www.quicktoons.com/
Comiqs (free), http://comiqs.com
Pixton (free), http://www.pixton.com
Other free resources can be found at http://www.shambles.net/pages/school/cartoons/.

An academic graphic novel collection should include not just the works themselves along with critical titles, but also resources about the industry and some practical "how to" items. These may be of interest to researchers in fields such as business or comics studies in addition to students and others who are considering the field as a professional opportunity.

RESOURCES FOR POTENTIAL CREATORS

Drawing Only

> *How to Draw and Sell Digital Cartoons* by Leo Hartas (Barron's, 2004)
> *How to Draw Art for Comic Books: Lessons from the Masters* by James Van Hise (Pioneer Books, 1989)
> *Manga University* (http://www.howtodrawmanga.com)
> *Wally Wood's 22 Panels That Always Work: Unlimited Edition* (http://joeljohnson.com/archives/2006/08/wally_woods_22.html)

Writing and Storytelling Only

> *99 Ways to Tell a Story: Exercises in Style* by Matt Madden (Penguin/Chamberlain Bros., 2005)
> *DC Comics Guide to Writing Comics* by Dennis "Denny" O'Neil (Watson-Guptill, 2001)
> *Graphic Storytelling* by Will Eisner (Poorhouse Press, 1996)
> *Writing for Comics with Peter David* by Peter David (Impact Books, 2006)

Drawing, Writing, and Storytelling

> *The Complete Idiot's Guide to Creating a Graphic Novel* by Nat Gertler and Steve Lieber (Alpha Books, 2004)
> *Drawing Words and Writing Pictures: Making Comics from Manga to Graphic Novels* by Jessica Abel and Matt Madden (First Second, 2008)
> *Making Comics: Storytelling Secrets of Comics, Manga, and Graphic Novels* by Scott McCloud (Harper, 2006)
> *Writing and Illustrating the Graphic Novel: Everything You Need to Know to Create Great Graphic Works* by Mike Chinn (Barron's, 2004)

Comics as Leisure Resources

Library patrons like comics. In 2007, librarians at Eastern Illinois University reported that graphic novels purchased for coursework had become popular with students as leisure reading.[31] Although no formal study of graphic novel reading on campus has been conducted at Washington State University, librarian experience and circulation statistics indicate that graphic novels have a relatively high rate of use. Public libraries report a similar pattern: a survey of adult graphic novel readers at the Octogone Public Library in Montreal found that "the adult sequential art collection represents about 5 percent of the overall adult collection, but as a component of our circulation, it accounts for 13 percent of the adult and 11 percent of the overall (adult and children) borrowing."[32]

Leisure reading has been shown to relate to non-leisure achievement. A 1999 study found a "weak but statistically significant correlation . . . between cumulative grade-point average and time spent reading for pleasure during vacations."[33] The 2007 National Endowment for the Arts report, *To Read or Not to Read: A Question of National Consequence,* noted a number of studies that showed positive correlations between reading for pleasure and achievement, including higher literacy and math test scores.[34] Education professor and theorist Stephen Krashen noted that when less-literate adults (and children) read recreationally, "good things will happen," including the increased ability to both understand academic writing and write academically and professionally.[35] Krashen strongly supports the value of reading comics for pleasure; although his work is aimed at K–12 educators, it is worth examining for research and anecdotes highlighting the overall value of reading comics. Graphic novels have also proven to be of value to college-age reluctant readers.[36]

Recent studies have indicated that the general American population, including college students, spends less time reading for pleasure than in the past, although such studies generally have a limited definition of reading.[37] In this environment, the value of providing access to recreational reading resources, including graphic novels, must be considered in the context of the responsibility of academic libraries to serve the recreational as well as scholastic needs of all their patrons.[38] In recent years, more academic libraries are allocating all-too-limited resources toward encouraging pleasure reading by promoting books (including varying levels of readers' advisory services) and through providing browsing collections.[39]

Student response to browsing collection projects at the University of North Carolina Libraries and other academic libraries indicate that students appreciate the accessibility of fiction that is shelved together.[40] This has implications for a graphic novel collection: if the collection is not all shelved in the same physical place (usually the PN6700s), the graphic novel titles need to have excellent bibliographic access via consistent subject and/or form headings.

ISSUES UNIQUE TO ACADEMIC
LIBRARY COLLECTIONS
Collection-Development Policies

Although academic librarians are generally spared the challenges to their graphic novels that regularly confront public and school librarians, it is still a good idea to include graphic novels in official collection-development policies, thus treating them like other parts of the collection. However, many academic libraries do not have a graphic novel policy, either explicitly as its own separate statement or implicitly, as part of other subject area statements.

Given the importance of material donations to many academic graphic novel collections, librarians may find that a clear policy dealing with acceptance of donated comics is also helpful.

Libraries that do have explicit or implicit collection-development policies for graphic novels usually have substantial and long-established research collections or comic art archives, often as part of special collections. The Columbia University Libraries policy is an exception, with a specific collection-development statement for graphic novels that notes their relevance to literature, art, film, and cultural history. The policy includes language regarding formats, dates, languages, and place of publication and serves as an excellent model for other academic libraries.[41] Other resources to consider in drawing up a graphic novel collection-development policy include Steve Miller's *Developing and Promoting Graphic Novel Collections* and Francisca Goldsmith's *Graphic Novels Now: Building, Managing, and Marketing a Dynamic Collection.*[42] Although not specifically intended for academic libraries, both books are also excellent resources for issues beyond collection development.

Collection-development statements are not usually updated very often, but as academic library graphic novel collections become more extensive, policies are sure to follow. As a side note, it is interesting to speculate on what effect consortia/union catalogs such as the Pacific Northwest's Orbis-Cascade Alliance's Summit Union Catalog and Ohio's OhioLink might have on the actual impact and meaning of those collection-development policies, as individual campus library holdings merge into large regional union catalogs. If patrons can generally get what they want from another library through a system that minimizes individual library branding, does it really matter that their own library's graphic novel (or other) policies might be more restrictive?

An interesting perspective on collection development comes from a recent MLS thesis. Jessica Zellers employed a feminist lens and content analysis technique to evaluate a sample of graphic novels. Her work focused on images of sex and violence, and she proposed that graphic novel collection-development policies that focus on criteria such as awards versus content end up privileging sex and violence and lead to collections more likely to be of interest to men. She suggested, "A collection development policy that does not specifically address the content of graphic novels will likely develop a disproportionate number of titles geared toward masculine readers. A collection that adequately represents feminist and feminine graphic novels cannot be achieved without a deliberate awareness in the collection development policy."[43] Of course, this same argument can be applied to issues of race and class as well as gender.

Selection and Acquisition

An academic library just building a graphic novel collection or looking to fill in holes may want to start with some of the recent readers' advisory/genre guides. Paul Gravett's *Graphic Novels: Everything You Need to Know* and

Michael Pawuk's *Graphic Novels: A Genre Guide to Comic Books, Manga, and More* are two good examples,[44] but there are a number of others.

Continuing the collection will take a little more effort, including monitoring both librarian and popularly oriented sources: reviews in library publications, award winner lists, comics publisher and distributor catalogs and other publications (such as those available at conferences and on the Web from BWI and Diamond Distributors), and not least, the local comics shop if one is accessible. Stakeholder recommendations should be actively encouraged, especially requests to purchase certain titles to support teaching and scholarly work on campus.

SOME STARTING POINTS FOR REVIEWS
AND RECOMMENDATIONS

Library Publications That Include Graphic Novel Reviews

> *Booklist*
> *Choice*
> *Library Journal*
> *School Library Journal* (for curriculum collections)

Industry and Popular Culture Sources

> *The Comics Journal*
> *Entertainment Weekly*
> *ICv2 Insider's Guide* (see http://www.icv2.com)
> *Otaku USA* (http://www.otakuusamagazine.com)
> *Publishers Weekly*
> *Wizard Magazine*

Award Lists

> *Publishers Weekly* Annual Best Books of the Year—Graphic Novels
> The Eisner Awards (http://www.comic-con.org/cci/cci_eisners faq. shtml)
> The Harvey Awards (http://www.harveyawards.org)
> A good meta-list of awards and recipients is available at the *Comic Book Awards Almanac* (http://www.hahnlibrary.net/comics/awards/index.html)

Online Review Sources

> Seemingly hundreds of blogs and aficionado sites review graphic novels and comics. One from an academic librarian is *Yet Another Comics Blog,* from University of Michigan librarian Dave Carter (http://yetanothercomicsblog.blogspot.com).

Graphic novel acquisitions has certainly changed since Randall Scott called collecting comics "grasping at straws" in 1990, but it is still difficult. As he noted then,

> Routines and policies can be set up to catch the bare bones of a good collection, namely the outstandingly creative publications and the products of research, but comics as a mass medium are an enormous field of study. No budget can cover it all.[45]

Graphic novels and trade paperbacks were not as common in 1990, nor were the vast online bookstores of today. Although academic library vendors such as Blackwell Book Services and YBP Library Services generally do not provide much in the way of graphic novel coverage, Amazon and other online sources (including international stores for foreign-language titles), special orders at your local comics shop or bookstore, ordering direct from publishers and distributors via print or online catalogs, and using library vendors make acquisitions much easier than in the past.

Cataloging and Shelving Issues

Searching for Graphic Novels in Library Catalogs

Ideally, cataloging records represent items library users want and provide access points that allow users to locate them in a library catalog. In the case of graphic novels, the format as well as the content often drives interest and search strategy, similarly to how users might browse for an audiobook or feature film without having a particular title in mind. However, graphic novels often fall under a patchwork quilt of subject headings and—when used—genre and form headings. As a result, users often cannot make a comprehensive search of all works in this format because of a lack of understanding about how graphic novels are cataloged, a situation compounded by cataloging inconsistencies.

Library of Congress Subject Headings (LCSH)

The LCSH heading "Comic books, strips, etc." has existed for many more years than the "graphic novel" subject heading or form heading, and along with graphic novels it includes many works that are explicitly not graphic narratives, such as *Garfield* compilations and other newspaper strip collections. The heading can be subdivided by geographic location, subject, and author, providing extensive information about the topical nature of the work. More recently published titles may have a graphic novel subject heading in addition to or instead of the "Comic books" header; graphic novels may also have other MARC 6xx field subject headings indicating subject, creators, or other descriptive information. In some cases, they may also have form headings, leading to the confusing instance of having two "graphic novel" headings: a subject heading and a form heading. If a graphic novel has not been cataloged as such in either subject or form fields, a user who does a basic keyword search for "graphic novel*" will not necessarily find it and thus will have unknowingly run an incomplete search.

Form Headings

Given the unique and diverse character of graphic novel content, authorship, and publishing, bibliographical records may require additional or specialized data that permit users to identify graphic novels from among other kinds of library materials. In addition, public services librarians may want to produce a list of graphic novels titles for patrons specifically interested in this format, as well as for collection promotion and development. Besides Library of Congress headings, also including the form heading "Graphic novels" in cataloging records can serve as a bibliographic "stamp" aiding both users and librarians.

Typically recorded in the 655 field of the MARC record, form and genre headings describe material types and formats. Depending on the library catalog, this field may or may not be indexed for searching. Although including this heading in records residing in catalogs that do not index the 655 field does not necessarily ease the search for graphic novels, it does provide additional context for the item described. Likewise, should an owning institution decide to expand the index of searchable fields, the data will be available. Alternatively, catalogers might consider inputting the "Graphic novels" form heading in another, indexed field, such as the 690, that features locally devised information such as topical and subject headings.

Assigning form headings is traditionally a cataloger's prerogative. Unfortunately, including form and genre headings in MARC records is a fairly recent practice, and cataloging departments have not always used them consistently. Public services librarians who select graphic novels for collections and wish to highlight these titles for patrons may be frustrated by inconsistent descriptions in the catalog, especially in regard to the assignment of form headings for quick identification of these increasingly sought-after materials. In addition, catalogers and reference librarians may have differing perceptions about what qualifies as a graphic novel in the first place. An item may be a clear example of a graphic novel to the librarian who selected it for the collection, whereas the cataloger may interpret the title in hand as an illustrated adaptation of a literary work, as a comic book, or as work of fine art, options that affect how the item will be described.

Catalogers and public services librarians can collaborate in providing more consistency to graphic novel cataloging and increasing accessibility through the catalog. Selectors, for example, could specify which titles they would like cataloged with the "Graphic novels" heading in the form field by either annotating the order form or attaching an appropriately marked flag or slip to the order form for inclusion in the item upon its arrival in the cataloging department. Alternatively, acquisitions staff could add text to order records according to input from selectors, notifying catalogers that the item requires the appropriate form/genre heading. Whatever solution public services and cataloging personnel agree on, more effective description and control of graphic novels will result when all players meet on common ground.[46]

Locating Graphic Novels

Much of the literature dealing with where to shelve comics and graphic novels is intended for public and school libraries,[47] but there is discussion in the academic library literature as well.[48] Should graphic novels be placed in a distinct browsing collection, if available; classed in the LC PN6700 section under "Comic books, strips, etc." with appropriate geographic location, subject, and author subdivisions; or classified and shelved according to their specific subject, nation of origin, and so on, with critical works collocated with them just as traditional novels are shelved with their critical works? Or should it be a combination? Are there some works that should be shelved in closed or remote storage, in order to ensure that they remain in the collection?[49] The answer depends on the specific needs of each academic library, but funding and workflow issues may end up deciding the issue, and extensive retrospective conversion projects are often not possible in today's climate of decreasing budgets and staffing levels.

This is not just an academic library issue or even a library issue: some bookstores are starting to interfile graphic novels into subject shelves to increase sales.[50] At Washington State University, the decision was made in 2007 to class graphic nonfiction in the appropriate subject classification (for example, *A Dangerous Woman: The Graphic Biography of Emma Goldman* is located in the HX section along with other works about socialism, communism, and anarchism) and to class most graphic fiction in the PN6700s. However, some works by particularly well-known creators that have been the subject of extensive critical analysis are classed elsewhere in the Ps, in the appropriate literary location assigned to them by LC.

These issues of selection and cataloging cross subject areas and library departments. Libraries may want to consider holding a graphic novel summit to make sure that all internal library stakeholders are communicating. This could be an opportunity to discuss issues such as selection (who, what, and how), cataloging and bibliographic control (i.e., consistent subject headings and the use of form and genre headings), shelving (format versus content, fiction versus nonfiction), and opportunities for promotion to the academic community. If the library does not have an official collection-development policy, this would be an opportune time to draft one, indeed, a good time to formalize the end results of the discussion and create a synchronized set of graphic novel policies in general.

Publicity and Marketing

Academic libraries may believe that their collections speak for themselves, but in reality libraries must continually promote their collections, including their graphic novels.

A number of techniques have been suggested for marketing graphic novels to academic faculty, including creating exhibits, highlighting the collection when contacting department liaisons, working with campus media outlets, and, where appropriate, doing extensive outreach to pre-service education programs. Tactics useful for marketing directly to students include featuring graphic novels in standard communications, showcasing graphic novels that appeal to women, pushing foreign-language graphic novels as tools for language skills and cultural awareness, doing book talks, creating collaborative spaces for discussion, encouraging students to create their own graphic novels, and sponsoring graphic novel creation contests.[51]

Providing resources for comics study also promotes the collection. Besides the primary works themselves, librarians can provide subject guides such as those created by the Columbia University Libraries and other academic libraries.[52] In addition, librarians who familiarize themselves with Scott's 230 topics for comics-related student research may be able to suggest engaging paper topics for students who cannot decide what to write about.[53]

Marketing and outreach go hand in hand, and academic librarians should be looking for opportunities to participate in campus events such as brownbag get-togethers, lecture series, and poster sessions. Outside collaborations offer additional opportunities, such as partnering with campus art museums to create exhibits featuring sequential art or with visiting author programs that bring comics creators and theorists to start a campus dialogue about the engaging, provocative, and controversial issues surrounding comics content.

Staffing

In *Comics Librarianship,* Scott notes, "Once a comics collection has been established, whoever is in charge becomes a *de facto* expert."[54] He was talking about a formal comic book collection, but in most academic libraries today, graphic novels are more likely to be integrated into the general collection rather than constituting a special collection managed by a "comics librarian." Maintaining a graphic novel collection is most likely to be one small part of one or more librarians' work, and likely a labor of love and affinity rather than part of a formal job description. But who in fact should manage the collection, and should it be considered a separate collection at all? As graphic novels increasingly move out of the purely literary sphere and cover subjects throughout the LC classification, the case can be made that all selectors may potentially purchase graphic novels when particular titles fall within their discipline. Either way, specific selectors may find that other librarians will request that particular items be purchased. Although subject specialists might find it natural to add graphic novels to the general collection, this does not necessarily give them expertise in larger issues of graphic novel scholarship and importance. Fewer librarians and increased responsibilities make it more likely that someone will end up taking on the unofficial role of the "person who knows stuff about comics and graphic novels." Anyone in that position should immediately read Scott's *Comics Librarianship* along with the Miller and Goldsmith books previously mentioned! (See note 42.)

That said, the increasing importance of graphic novels in higher education and society as a whole suggests that academic libraries wanting to make graphic novels a meaningful part of their collections should encourage development of selector expertise. This can be done by supporting attendance at scholarly and popular comics conventions (such as the monumental San Diego Comic-Con) in the same way as other library or disciplinary conferences; purchasing comics-related monographs and subscriptions to publications relevant to the topic, including popular or trade magazines such as *Wizard Magazine* or *The Comics Journal* as well as scholarly journals; and giving annual review, promotion, and tenure credit for comics-related activity and scholarship.[55] Although many libraries and librarians rely on catalogs and materials provided by comics publishers and distributors to learn about particular titles, the development of in-house expertise can provide added value in selection decisions, outreach, and subject knowledge.

Academic collection development is not just a library-driven activity, of course; it largely reflects the teaching and research needs of the larger campus community. Students and teaching faculty who use comics and graphic novels in their classes and research are strong stakeholders in the development of a graphic novel collection, and their recommendations and expertise should be requested, welcomed, and implemented when appropriate.

Funding Issues

Although graphic novels are relatively inexpensive individually, the cost still adds up, especially when processing, mending, and replacement are factored in, or if a library attempts to decrease potential theft and increase durability by library-binding their copies. In an era of decreasing budgets, even spending $500 per year may require consideration.

Although for at least one academic library, graphic novels (housed in Special Collections) have been acquired through financial gifts and material donations, with no state funds being used, the scholarly value of graphic novels is generally uncontested these days, and most academic libraries purchase them out of general funds, even if financial gifts and material donations are also very important.[56] The graphic novel circulating collection at the University of Washington was started through an initial grant from the Friends of the Libraries in 2005, and the Western Illinois University Libraries received a collection grant in 2006 as well, whereas graphic novels are a category on the University of Oregon's collections wish list, targeted toward alumni and library supporters.[57] Even large comics and graphic novel special collections such as the Cartoon Research Library at Ohio State University continue to depend on donated materials.[58]

How a graphic novel collection is funded is partially tied to how the collection is perceived in a particular academic library—and how it is perceived and supported by its campus community. Funding limitations combined with a lack of academic department interest and support have limited the continuation of a graphic novel collection at the University of Memphis, for example.[59] (See case study later in this chapter.) Are graphic novels bought by one person (a graphic novel subject specialist, or more likely the literature librarian), or are they bought by virtue of their content rather than their format? *Maus* might be purchased by the history bibliographer, for example, and Aaron McGruder and Reginald Huldin's social and political satire *Birth of a Nation* might be bought by the political science librarian. Should there be a separate fund code for graphic novels, or should they be bought under general collection development? In a multi-library system, what is the potential impact on users if they are located at different libraries based on the fund code used for purchase? It is clear that graphic novels share some of the same characteristics and issues as DVDs and other audiovisual formats in terms of collection-development policies and cataloging issues.

CASE STUDIES

Washington State University

The Washington State University Libraries have a long tradition of collecting sequential art publications, with a focus on alternative and underground comics (or comix) of the 1960s and 1970s via the Comix Collection, the Lynn R. Hanson Comix Collection, and the Paul Brians Comics Collection housed in the Manuscripts, Archives and Special Collections unit (MASC).[60] A circulating graphic novel collection was until recent years quite limited, but in 2004 the collection was significantly expanded via a successful proposal to use a portion of a regularly given collections gift. Unfortunately, the donors disapproved of some of the titles purchased, an issue that other librarians who purchase graphic novels from gifts other than permanent endowments might want to keep in mind. The new acquisitions were very popular, however, and the collection has been enhanced since then through normal collections fund-code allotment purchases, especially since the hiring of a foreign languages and cultures librarian who purchases non-English-language graphic novels for language courses. That librarian reported that they have been popular with graduate students, who indicated a need for materials that combine visuals and text to help them as they work to scaffold their foreign language study within frameworks that make sense to them.[61]

As with many other academic libraries, numerous issues have had to be worked out or are still being worked out. Graphic novels are purchased by multiple subject specialists, including those focusing on literature, foreign languages, and education (for the juvenile fiction and curriculum collection). There was some inconsistency both in how items were classed and shelved under the LC system and in terms of what subject headings and genre/form headings were assigned. To provide greater bibliographic control and consistency, a number of stakeholders met in a mini-summit and worked out a policy to follow. The policy followed procedures discussed in library-related electronic message lists, and included provisions to ensure the following:

- Graphic nonfiction will be classed by discipline.
- Graphic novels by certain notable creators such as Neil Gaiman will be classified according to the assigned LC classification.
- Other graphic novels will continue to be shelved in the PN6700 call number range (traditionally associated with "Comic strips, comic books, etc." and able to be subdivided by geography, etc.).
- LCSH headings will be assigned for topical content in the MARC 650 field and will also include the "Comic books" subheading, e.g.:
  - 650_0 Runaway teenagers $v Comic books, strips, etc.
  - 650_0 Spider-Man (Fictitious character) $v Comic books, strips, etc.
- The form heading "Graphic novels" will be included for all identified graphic novels (including trade paperback collections) in both the MARC 655 field and the local information 690 field, in order to provide current and future search capabilities.
- Added entries will be included as necessary to include all applicable creators, including artists and translators.[62]

This policy does not include any of the counterculture comics housed in MASC, and the classification aspects do not apply to graphic novels housed in the juvenile fiction and curriculum collection. In addition to correcting the occasional identified cataloging error, some provisions for retrospective conversion were made, allowing for workflow and staffing considerations. The collection will be reviewed, and all graphic nonfiction works classed in PN6700 will be moved to their disciplinary areas. Also, all items with the

"Comic books, strips, etc." subject heading will be evaluated to see if they need a graphic novel form heading added. This will enable patrons to find a complete list of graphic novel holdings by doing a search for "graphic novels" or "graphic novel*." Easy genre searching waits on a reindexing of the catalog, which is planned for the near future. This policy follows similar decisions to classify audiobooks and feature films with a common subject heading so that they could be searched as a format.

University Of Memphis

Case Study by Christopher Matz

In 2002, the Department of English faculty chair contacted the library about upgrading resources to attract PhD-level research into comics as literature. At the university, only two courses examine comics as serious literature, both through the Department of English. Each balances theory with analysis of significant works and creators, all toward presenting comics as a subject for study in secondary school and college. As of 2007, no other departments have requested comics for the library.

Before 2002, comics-related library holdings reflected a variety of academic studies of the medium along with several of the standard primary works used for the graphic novel classes—or more precisely, the library catalog reflected those holdings. After several surveys of the stacks, many of the titles were declared lost, requiring replacements. Other books needed repair, and some were damaged beyond practical use. That due diligence produced the initial list of purchases along with requested core titles for the English classes. Titles already in the collection—including original works by Lynda Barry and Chris Ware along with academic studies by Ron Goulart and Trina Robbins—were re-shelved in reserve, creating a greatly expanded reading list for the English classes most apt to use them (but not restricted to their use).

Unfortunately, budgetary restrictions left the English department and the library with more enthusiasm than financial wherewithal to proceed. However, the Friends of the Library stepped up with a six-month stipend to replace the missing and damaged holdings and add brand-new important titles. This put the collection on the map, and although comics have not achieved that growth since the initial year, there has been a modest flow of requests from English faculty and graduate students as that department begins to tap the medium's scholarly potential. Most growth in the last several years has come through gifts. The monograph budget squeeze means that on the rare occasions when discretionary money is available, English and other departments that participated in the library's comics project have stated their preferences for volumes other than comics, disappointing but understandable.

The purpose of this segment of the overall collection is to support the two English classes by reserving selected titles during fall and spring semesters. At other times during the year, titles containing primary work by creators are held in permanent reserve while titles devoted to study of the medium are returning to the general circulating collection. The "permanent reserve" strategy should be rethought (see further discussion later in the case study).

Primary emphasis is on U.S. contemporary materials, though attention is given to historically significant works since 1900. The collection has been built with comparatively inexpensive reprint materials to stretch out the limited funds. Materials from other parts of the world and in other languages will be accepted if donated. Only monographs in the form of collected reprints (trade paperbacks) and original work (graphic novels) are collected, as well as studies of art and the medium. Due to budget cutbacks, no subscriptions to comics-related periodicals are purchased, although *The Comics Journal* has been requested. No access is available to any comics-specific databases.

As publicity, the Friends of the Library hosted an exhibit that was covered by local media in a positive way that helped reorient default biases against comics in academic libraries.[63] The Department of English aided that effort, inviting comics creators to its annual River City Writing Series for presentations and readings. Library staff showed resistance initially, but in general, the technical services staff is now confident to order, catalog, and shelve comics. It was a difficult sales job that turned into a teachable moment, making technical services, public services, and faculty a little more sensitive to each other's circumstances.

Some things should have been done differently. Comics should not have been put on permanent reserve at all. Faculty members had wanted control over "their" materials, and also, permanent reserve was thought to protect these titles from damage and theft. But the rate of missing books among comics and related materials is nearly three times higher than a typical library book, and most of the missing were originally shelved in permanent reserve. Rather than protect these materials, permanent reserve put a target on them, maybe confounded by effective publicity. Perhaps worst of all, permanent reserve created a perception that comics should stand apart from the primary collection. Nothing could be further from our intentions; solving that misconception has become a priority.

A significant misstep was underestimating the supernova of interest in manga and other Asian-style comics and cartoons. If there are manga readers among the library's constituents, they have been silent and, indeed, must be getting their reading needs met elsewhere. The international languages department has had only a polite acquaintance with the library so far; that must be immediately improved.

CONCLUSION

Inclusion of graphic novels and other comics publications in academic library collections cuts across disciplinary lines and across traditional boundaries of technical services and public services. As noted, a summit of stakeholders to make decisions about cataloging, classification, and collection development can save a lot of retrospective conversion later on and make the whole experience of searching for graphic novels and related resources easier on library patrons and staff.

The use of graphic novels and comic books in academia and society at large is not likely to diminish in the near future. In 1995, George Dardess saw the coming visual revolution, noting,

> We see more and more evidence that visual learning, stimulated by developments in computer and communications technology, will play a dominant role in people's understanding of themselves and of their own and each other's cultures. Such an emphasis is likely not merely to challenge the centuries-old prejudice against the sequential art narrative, but to overwhelm it.[64]

Academic libraries must continue to support this medium, adapting to changes within and without as "comic books" have morphed into graphic novels and trade paperback collections. Questions about local issues such as collection development, cataloging, and classification go along with larger questions about the economics of the traditional comics industry, the future impact of Web comics, and issues of sustainability: issues not only of the potential future, but also of guaranteed academic study.

RESOURCES

In addition to the books, Web sites, and other resources mentioned in this chapter for the academic use of graphic novels, there are a number of other resources of interest to academic librarians, starting with noted comics scholar John Lent's "Comic Books and Comic Strips: A Bibliography of the Scholarly Literature," published as a bibliographic essay in *Choice*,[65] and Leslie Bussert's 2005 resource essay published in *College & Research Library News,* which includes an excellent overview of review resources.[66]

Other useful sources follow. All Web pages were verified on May 20, 2008.

Comic Adventures in Academia. An online blog/column written by Columbia University librarian Karen Green covering issues of interest to librarians.[67] (ComiXology provides reviews and other information about comics, with an interactive Web 2.0 sensibility.) http://www.comixology.com/columns/comic_adventures_in_academia/.

The Comics Chronicles. This is a great resource for industry information and comics sales data. http://www.comichron.com.

Comics Research Bibliography. An "international bibliography of comic books, comic strips, animation, caricature, cartoons, bandes dessinees, and related topics." http://www.rpi.edu/~bulloj/comxbib.html.

ComicsResearch.org. This site includes a number of annotated bibliographies covering multiple aspects of comics, including genres, interview compilations, and country- or region-specific works, along with links to academic resources and more. http://www.comicsresearch.org.

GNLIB: Graphic Novels in Libraries. This mailing list has a high percentage of public and school librarians and is an excellent way to keep up with new titles and contemporary issues. http://groups.yahoo.com/group/GNLIB-L/.

ICv2. This organization publishes the *ICv2 Insider's Guide* covering graphic novels and manga and maintains a Web site of news and sales data. http://www.icv2.com.

Online Bibliography of Anime and Manga Research. "Lists materials within three broad categories: academic writings, fan-written non-academic works, and newsmedia articles." http://www.corneredangel.com/amwess/.

PW Comics Week. An e-mail newsletter that is also Web-accessible, from *Publishers Weekly.* http://www.publishersweekly.com; at top of page, click on "Newsletters."

NOTES*

1. Terry L. Shoptaugh, "Review of Comics Librarianship: A Handbook," *Journal of Academic Librarianship* 17, no. 4 (1991): 237.

2. Chris Matz, "Collecting Comic Books for an Academic Library," *Collection Building,* 23, no. 2 (2004): 96–99. See also Jody Callahan, "Comics: Nothing to Laugh At," *Memphis Commercial-Appeal,* May 23, 2006, B-1.

3. Randall W. Scott, *Comics Librarianship: A Handbook* (New York: McFarland, 1990), 24.

4. See, for example, Bill E. Peterson and Emily D. Gerstein, "Fighting and Flying: Archrival Analysis of Threat, Authoritarianism, and the North American Comic Book," *Political Psychology* 26, no. 6 (2005): 887–903; the review of two graphic novels in Ted Rall, "Drawing Behind the Lines," *Foreign Affairs* 142 (2004): 72–75; and the special issue "Periodical Comics and Cartoons" of *American Periodicals: A Journal of History, Criticism, and Bibliography* 17, no. 2 (2007).

5. Allen Ellis, "Comic Art in Scholarly Writing: A Citation Guide," Comic Art and Comics Area, Popular Culture Association. http://www.comicsresearch.org/CAC/cite.html; Gene Kannenberg Jr., Seetha A. Srinivasan, and Joseph Witek, "Illustrations or Quotations? Permission & Rights for Publishing Comics Scholarship," Based on a Roundtable Discussion at the Comic Art & Comics Section of the 2000 Popular Culture Association/American Culture Association Annual Meeting, April 22, 2000, http://gator.dt.uh.edu/~kannenbg/per missions.html.

*All Web pages accessed September 10, 2008.

6. Medieval Comics Project, http://medievalcomicsproject.org/; "CFP: Comics Get Medieval at Kalamazoo (9/1/07; Kalamazoo 5/8–11/08)," http://www.h-net.org/announce/show.cgi?ID=157532.

7. See librarian Karen Green's account of the conference in her "Comic Adventures in Academia" column: Karen Green, "Conventional Comics, or Conference Calling," *comiXology: Comic Adventures in Academia,* February 1, 2008, http://www.comixology.com/articles/21/Conventional-Comics-or-Conference-Calling.

8. Beth Davies-Stofka, "You're Invited: Met@Morph in Second Life," *Comic Book Bin: Comic News,* September 30, 2008, http://www.comicbookbin.com/SecondLife001.html.

9. National Association of Comics Art Educators (NACAE), http://www.teachingcomics.org/; Comic Art Working Group of the International Association for Mass Communication Research, http://www.iamcr.org/content/blogcategory/44/132/; Sequart Research & Literary Organization, http://sequart.org/; Comic Arts Conference, http://fac.hsu.edu/duncanr/cac_page.htm.

10. See Lorena O'English, J. Gregory Matthews, and Elizabeth Blakesley Lindsay, "Graphic Novels in Academic Libraries: From Maus to Manga and Beyond," *Journal of Academic Librarianship* 32, no. 2 (2006): 174.

11. Some of these resources were identified by my colleague, Elizabeth Blakesley Lindsay. Personal communications, Elizabeth Blakesley Lindsay, July 2007.

12. "Graphic Storytelling and the New Literacies: An Interview with NCTE Educator Peter Gutierrez," *Diamond Bookshelf,* http://diamondbookshelf.com/public/default.asp?t=1&m=3&c=40&s=325&ai=74165.

13. James Kakalios, *The Physics of Superheroes* (London: Duckworth, 2006); Jeffrey Kahan and Stanley Stewart, *Caped Crusaders 101: Composition through Comic Books* (Jefferson, NC: McFarland, 2006).

14. See O'English et al., "Graphic Novels in Academic Libraries," 179; and Mary Jane Haney, "Graphic Novels: A Sure Bet for Your Library," *Collection Building* 26, no. 3 (2007): 72–76.

15. Douglas Fisher and Nancy Frey, "Altering English: Re-Examining the Whole Class Novel and Making Room for Graphic Novels and More," in *Building Literacy Connections with Graphic Novels: Page by Page, Panel by Panel,* ed. James Bucky Carter (Urbana, IL: National Council of Teachers of English, 2007), 31–33.

16. Michael Dooley and Steven Heller, eds., *The Education of a Comics Artist: Visual Narrative in Cartoons, Graphic Novels, and Beyond.* (New York: Allworth Press; School of Visual Arts, 2005); John Bell, *Invaders from the North: How Canada Conquered the Comic Book Universe* (Toronto: Dundurn, 2006).

17. Matthew Pustz, *Comic Book Culture: Fanboys and True Believers* (Jackson: University Press of Mississippi, 1999); Bradford W. Wright, *Comic Book Nation: The Transformation of Youth Culture in America* (Baltimore, MD: Johns Hopkins University Press, 2001).

18. Durwin S. Talon, *Comics Above Ground: How Sequential Art Affects Mainstream Media* (Raleigh, NC: TwoMorrows Pub., 2004); Simcha Weinstein, *Up, Up, and Oy Vey: How Jewish History, Culture, and Values Shaped the Comic Book Superhero* (Baltimore, MD: Leviathan Press, 2006). On a related note, the American Library Association's reading and discussion series, *Let's Talk About It: Jewish Literature—Identity and Imagination,* included the theme "Modern Marvels: Jewish Adventures in the Graphic Novel" for 2008–2009 programming.

19. Dan Raviv, *Comic Wars: How Two Tycoons Battled over the Marvel Comics Empire—and Both Lost* (New York: Broadway Books, 2002); John Jackson Miller, "Final

North American Comics Market Estimates for 2006," http://www.cbgxtra.com/Default. aspx?tabid=1528.

20. Alva Taylor and Henrich R. Greve, "Superman or the Fantastic Four? Knowledge Combination and Experience in Innovative Teams," *Academy of Management Journal* 49, no. 4 (August 2006): 723–40.

21. Charles Hatfield, *Alternative Comics: An Emerging Literature* (Jackson: University Press of Mississippi, 2005), x. Note: I am grateful to Elizabeth Blakesley Lindsay for a portion of this analysis.

22. Calvin Reid, "Virgin Comics Shut Down," *Publishers Weekly,* August 26, 2008, http://www.publishersweekly.com/article/CA6590174.html.

23. James W. Brown, "Comics in the Foreign Language Classroom: Pedagogical Perspectives," *Foreign Language Annuals* 10, no. 1 (February 1977): 18–25.

24. Edward Ousselin, "Integrating Elements of the Communicative Approach into the Preparation for the Paris Chamber of Commerce Certificat Exam," *Global Business Languages* Vol. 1, *Pedagogy in Languages for Specific Purposes* (1996), 3–5, http://www.cla. purdue.edu/fll/GBL/BackIssue/VOL1/Ousselin.pdf.

25. Teshkeel Comics, http://www.teshkeel.com. See also Megan A. Wong, "A Comic about Truth, Justice, and the Islamic Way: Muslim Superheroes Populate a New Comic Book Designed to Entertain—and Serve a Serious Purpose," *Christian Science Monitor,* April 25, 2007, http://www.csmonitor.com/2007/0425/p13s01-algn.html; and Piney Kesting, "The Next Generation of Superheroes," *Saudi Aramco World,* January/February 2007, http://www.saudiaramcoworld.com/issue/200701/the.next.generation.of.superheroes.htm.

26. Alan Moore and David Lloyd, *V per Vendetta,* trans. Leonardo Rizzi (Milan: Rizzoli, 2006).

27. See, for example, *Comixpedia: Web Comics by Nationality,* http://www.comixpedia. org/index.php?title=Category:Webcomics_by_nationality.

28. Stephen Cary, *Going Graphic: Comics at Work in the Multilingual Classroom* (Portsmouth, NH: Heinemann, 2004).

29. *24 Hour Comics,* http://www.24hourcomics.com/. Note that this is an example of "Oubapo," or constraint-based comics; see the Web site *Oubapo-America* (http://www. tomhart.net/oubapo/) for more information about these challenging exercises in creativity.

30. The Stanford Graphic Novel Project, "Shake Girl, the Graphic Novel: About," 2008, http://www.stanford.edu/group/cwstudents/shakegirl/about.html.

31. Julie Elliot, "Academic Libraries and Extracurricular Reading Promotion," *Reference & User Services Quarterly* 46, no. 3 (May 2007): 38.

32. Oliver Charbonneau, "Adult Graphic Novel Readers: A Survey in a Montreal Library," *Young Adult Library Services* 3, no. 4 (Summer 2005): 39.

33. Jude D. Gallik, "Do They Read for Pleasure? Recreational Reading Habits of College Students," *Journal of Adolescent & Adult Literacy* 42, no. 6 (March 1999): 484.

34. National Endowment for the Arts, *To Read or Not to Read: A Question of National Consequence,* Research Report #47, November 2007, 68–74, http://www.nea.gov/research/ ToRead.pdf.

35. Stephen D. Krashen, *The Power of Reading: Insights from the Research,* 2nd ed. (Westport, CT: Libraries Unlimited, 2004), x, 91–110.

36. Rocco Versaci, "Graphic Novels: Books That Matter," in *RHI: Reaching Reluctant Readers,* http://www.randomhouse.com/highschool/RHI_magazine/pdf/versaci.pdf. Note: Versaci has recently published a new work, *This Book Contains Graphic Language: Comics as Literature* (New York: Continuum, 2007).

37. The 2007 National Freshman Attitudes Report indicated that freshmen women enjoy reading more than male students, but still only about one-half of the students surveyed received personal satisfaction from reading. Noel-Levitz, *Second Annual National Freshman Attitudes Report,* Coralville, IA: Noel-Levitz, 2007, 4, http://www.noellevitz.com/NR/rdonlyres/3934DA20-2C31-4336-962B-A1D1E7731D8B/0/07FRESHMANATTITUDES_report.pdf. Other studies of the decline in reading include the 2004 National Endowment for the Arts report *Reading at Risk* (http://www.nea.gov/pub/ReadingAtRisk.pdf) and its 2007 report *To Read or Not to Read: A Question of National Consequence* (see note 34, above).

38. O'English et al., "Graphic Novels in Academic Libraries," 175.

39. Bette Rathe and Lisa Blankenship, "Recreational Reading Collections in Academic Libraries," *Collection Management* 30, no. 2 (2005): 73–85.

40. Rathe and Blankenship, "Recreational Reading Collections," 80; and Elliot, "Academic Libraries and Extracurricular Reading Promotion," 38.

41. Columbia University Libraries Collection Development, "Graphic Novels," http://www.columbia.edu/cu/lweb/services/colldev/graphic_novels.html. Note: Columbia University's graphic novel selector Karen Green writes a monthly column, *Comic Adventures in Academia,* on the comics Web site *comiXology* (http://www.comixology.com), specifically about academic library graphic novel librarianship.

42. Steve Miller, *Developing and Promoting Graphic Novel Collections* (New York: Neal-Schuman, 2005); Francisca Goldsmith, *Graphic Novels Now: Building, Managing, and Marketing a Dynamic Collection* (Chicago: American Library Association, 2005).

43. Jessica H. Zellers, "Naked Ladies and Macho Men: A Feminist Content Analysis of a Burgeoning Graphic Novels Collection," Master's thesis, University of North Carolina, 2005, 4, http://hdl.handle.net/1901/140.

44. Paul Gravett, *Graphic Novels: Everything You Need to Know* (New York: Collins Design, 2005); Michael Pawuk, *Graphic Novels: A Genre Guide to Comic Books, Manga, and More* (Westport, CT: Libraries Unlimited, 2007).

45. Scott, *Comics Librarianship,* 39.

46. Much of this section came from conversations with and the work of J. Gregory Matthews, and I am indebted to Greg for his expertise. J. Gregory Matthews, personal communications, July 2007.

47. See, for example, the section "Where to Shelve Graphic Novels" in a collaborative pamphlet published by the National Coalition against Censorship, the American Library Association, and the Comic Book Legal Defense Fund, *Graphic Novels: Suggestions for Librarians,* http://www.ala.org/ala/oif/ifissues/graphicnovels_1.pdf; as well as Miller, *Developing and Promoting Graphic Novel Collections,* 50–54; and Goldsmith, *Graphic Novels Now,* 52–59.

48. A more extensive discussion of academic library classification issues can be found in O'English et al., "Graphic Novels in Academic Libraries," 175–78.

49. Academic librarian and comics columnist Karen Green comments on some of the issues related to this: Karen Green, "Naughty Bits," *comiXology: Comic Adventures in Academia,* January 4, 2008, http://www.comixology.com/articles/15/Naughty-Bits.

50. Kathy Matheson, "That's PROFESSOR Wonder Woman to You," *ASAP,* May 9, 2007, http://asap.ap.org/stories/570688.s.

51. O'English et al., "Graphic Novels in Academic Libraries," 178–80.

52. Columbia University Libraries Subject Guides, "Welcome to Columbia University's Graphic Novels Page," http://www.columbia.edu/cu/lweb/eguides/graphic_novels/index.html. See also Yale University Libraries, "Comic Books, Comic Strips and Graphic Novels," at http://www.library.yale.edu/humanities/media/comics.html; and the University of North

Carolina's "The Graphic Novel: A Sloane Art Library Brief Guide," at http://www.lib.unc.edu/art/graphicnovels.html.

53. Scott, *Comics Librarianship,* 125–29.

54. Scott, *Comics Librarianship,* 103.

55. Librarians are increasingly attending comics conventions, as evidenced in Ann Kim and Michael Rogers, "Librarians Out Front at Comic Con," *Library Journal,* April 1, 2007, 15; Some librarians are involved in comics scholarship in a less academic way. An example is Washington State University librarian Mark O'English, who was a writer and researcher for the Marvel Handbook series; see the Comic Book Database, "Mark O'English," http://www.comicbookdb.com/creator.php?ID=4246.

56. "Special Collections at the University of Wisconsin-Madison—Collection Development Policy: Comic Books," http://www.uwm.edu/Library/special/colldevpol.html.

57. "Graphic Novels Collection Purchase for Odegaard Undergraduate Library," *Friends of the University of Washington Libraries,* Autumn 2005, 4, http://www.lib.washington.edu/support/pdf/Friends 2005 SummerAutumn.pdf. In 2007, the University of Washington Friends also funded an African graphic novel collection to support scholarly work; see http://www.lib.washington.edu/support/pdf/Friends_2007_SummerAutumn.pdf; Darcie Shinberger, "University Libraries Receives Collections Grants," August 8, 2006, http://wiu.edu/newsrelease.sphp?release_id=4647; UO Libraries, "Collections Wish List," http://libweb.uoregon.edu/colldev/cdpolicies/collections.html.

58. University Libraries Cartoon Research Library, "Support Us," http://cartoons.osu.edu/?q=content/support us.

59. Chris Matz, "Collecting Comic Books at the University of Memphis: An Ending?" Paper presented at the 26th Charleston Conference, Charleston, SC, November 9, 2006, http://eprints.rclis.org/archive/00008803/01/Matz_Collecting.pdf.

60. For information about the content of those collections, see Steve Willis, *Folkomix: A Catalog of Underground, Newave, and Small Press Comix in the Washington State University Rare Books Collection* (Pullman, WA: Morty Dog: 1985), along with its two supplements; and "Paul Brians Comics Collection, 1950–2004," http://www.wsulibs.wsu.edu/Holland/MASC/finders/cg710.htm.

61. Gabriella Reznowski, personal interview, December 18, 2007.

62. Cataloging Department, Washington State University Libraries, "Cataloging Graphic Novels at WSU Libraries," created December 19, 2007; and Lihong Zhu, e mail message to author, December 20, 2007.

63. Jody Callahan, "Comics: Nothing to Laugh At," *Memphis Commercial-Appeal,* May 23, 2003, sec B.

64. George Dardess, "Bringing Comic Books to Class," *College English* 57, no. 2 (February 1995), 217.

65. John A. Lent, "Comic Books and Comic Strips: A Bibliography of the Scholarly Literature," *Choice* 44, no. 11 (July 2007): 1855–67.

66. Leslie Bussert, "Comic Books and Graphic Novels: Digital Resources for an Evolving Form of Art and Literature," *C&RL News* 66, no. 2 (February 2005): 103–6, 113.

67. See interview with Karen Green: Laura Hudson, "Comics Go to the Ivy League," *Publishers Weekly,* October 25, 2008, http://www.publishersweekly.com/article/CA6608665.html?nid=2789.

Appendix A

SELECTED RECENT COLLEGE COURSES THAT COVER OR INCLUDE GRAPHIC NARRATIVES*

Henderson State University

Dr. Travis Langley, PSY 4003/5003 01: Comics & Psychology (Spring, 2008), http://fac.hsu.edu/langlet/comics_psy/comics_info2008.html

Kansas State University

Philip Nel, English 830: Image, Text, Ideology: Picturebooks and Illustrated Texts, http://www.k-state.edu/english/nelp/childlit/830.html

University of Massachusetts

Comparative Literature Department, 393B Comic Art in North America and 393C International Graphic Novel, http://www.umass.edu/complit/courses_cat_undrgrad.shtml

University of Michigan

Eric Rabkin, English 417/549: Graphic Narrative (Winter 06), http://www-per sonal.umich.edu/~esrabkin/417GNw06.htm

DePaul University

Ken Bill, Graphic Novels/Graphic Literature, Interdisciplinary Studies Program /American Studies, http://web.english.ufl.edu/comics/teaching/kbill.shtml

Georgia Southern University

Michael Pemberton, Writing 3030A: The Comic Book in American Culture, http://class.georgiasouthern.edu/writ3030/syllabus.htm

Stanford University

Andrea A. Lunsford, English 87Q: The Graphic Novel: Literature Lite? http://www.stanford.edu/~lunsfor1/Comics05.doc

University of North Texas

Shaun Treat, Communication Studies: Mythic Rhetoric of the American Superhero, http://www.unt.edu/newuntfeatures/superhero.htm

*All Web pages accessed September 10, 2008. A number of these courses were identified by my colleague, Elizabeth Blakesley Lindsay.

9

JAPANESE ANIME

Gilles Poitras

Librarians are becoming increasingly aware of anime as well as manga through news programs, business magazines, library professional literature, and that most important source of information, patron requests. How do how anime and manga relate to each other, and how can librarians add anime to their collections? This chapter is designed to answer these questions. I will also describe how anime and manga are different from American cartoons and why they have appealed to groups not reached by our own comics and animation entertainment industries.

Anime and manga have become successful in the West partly because the public finds the types of stories they tell appealing. By "the public," I mean the public that has discovered them, given that for many people, anime and manga are just not something they know much about and may think of simply as cartoons made in Japan. However, for those who have spent the time to take a serious look, discovering this vast range of tales and the ways they are told visually can be a very pleasurable experience.

BEFORE WE GO ANY FURTHER: SOME DEFINITIONS

What Is Anime?

In common non-Japanese usage, *anime* is simply animation made in Japan, by Japanese, and for a Japanese audience. In Japan, the word means any animation made anywhere in the world. Commercial Japanese anime dates back to theatrical shorts in 1917. Modern anime is commonly held to date from the 1960s, with the work of Osamu Tezuka, best known in the United States for *Astro Boy, Tetsuwan Atom* in Japanese. (See Schodt 2007 for an excellent study of Tezuka and his Atom/Astro character.) Anime is released in three ways in Japan. Theatrical feature films and television shows are familiar forms, as they are here. In addition, a significant percentage of anime goes straight to video; Japanese refer to this with the English phrase "original video animation," OVA for short. Some non-Japanese write this as OAV.

The anime market is a significant one in Japan, with 2006 sales estimated by Japan's Media Development Research Institute at 241.5 billion yen, about $2.0 billion U.S. ("Japanese Anime Market" 2007). On the American side, the most readily available statistic is the number of yearly DVD new releases (Anime on DVD Anime Checklist), averaging 700–800 for the last several years—substantial but with gross sales of new plus backlist titles more likely in the millions than billions.

Although anime is sometimes erroneously referred to as a "genre," anime is in reality a medium that includes any genre that can be found in cinema or literature. For this reason, the evaluation of anime titles for a library collection should be done with all the care that goes into evaluating movies or novels, even more so given that it is often hard to get good reviews of anime to aid with selection. For a general overview of anime as a medium, see my own *Anime Essentials* (2001). Other valuable background books that would interest anime fans include my own *The Anime Companion* and its sequel (1999, 2005) plus two by Patrick Drazen (2002) and Susan Napier (2000). Hayao Miyazaki, Mamoru Oshii, and Satoshi Kon are well known as three of the great anime directors, so the books about them by Helen McCarthy (1999), Andrew Osmond (2008), and Brian Ruh (2004) are sure to be popular. My own Web site has a large section devoted to "The Librarian's Guide to Manga and Anime," http://www.koyagi.com/Libguide.html, which addresses many of the topics in this chapter and is updated regularly. (See specific sublinks later in the chapter.)

What Is Manga?

Manga is a Japanese word that can be roughly translated as "comic books," graphic novels, or sequential art. In reality, manga is far more complex than such materials in the West. Originating in political cartoons and strips in the late 19th century and then expanding to magazines aimed at children in the 1930s, manga has evolved over decades to a more varied and complex medium for telling stories. Manga can include almost every genre imaginable, from funny stories to serious literature. Looking at some books about manga, such as Frederik Schodt's *Manga! Manga!* (1986) and *Dreamland Japan* (1996) and Paul Gravett's *Manga: Sixty Years of Japanese Comics* (2004), will probably be the best way to understand this unique form of publishing. See chapter 2 for much more information about manga as a medium, plus guidelines and resources for adding titles to library collections.

CHARACTERISTICS OF ANIME AND MANGA

The Relationship between Anime and Manga

Most anime series have been based on manga for the simple reason that a popular manga is quite likely to be a popular anime. Also, a popular anime may spin off a manga. This may occur with an artist adapting the anime plot, or the result may be a bound book composed of still frames extracted from the anime with dialogue and sound effects stripped in. This may be referred to as "cinemanga," "anime manga," or "animanga." Some of Hayao Miyazaki's well-known anime films, such as *Spirited Away,* have cinemanga equivalents.

In Japan, the manga industry is larger and has wider market penetration than anime. Manga actually has high respect among adults: even politicians will include "reading manga" in lists of their leisure activities.[1] Given the huge number of manga written in Japan, there is a rich field of titles for harvesting stories. For libraries, the connection between manga and anime means that it may be a good idea to coordinate purchases between book and video librarians for series available in both formats. A list of titles in both formats is available at http://www.koyagi.com/AM.html; and for specific titles, such information can be verified in the "encyclopedia" section of Anime News Network, http://www.animenewsnetwork.com.

Coordination should also include related live-action movies, novels, soundtracks, and books about specific anime and manga series. However, be aware that at times manga versions of a story may be aimed at an older audience than the anime. For example, the *GTO* anime episodes are pretty much safe for teens and up, but the manga is very adult. Moreover, style and quality may differ markedly among formats. For example, the *Samurai Champloo* manga, released after the television series, is a more-or-less typical martial arts action manga. However, the anime is artistically elegant, and the plotting is much subtler and has broader appeal.

How Is Anime Different from U.S. Cartoons?

Superhero and alternative comics have historically dominated the market for comic books and graphic novels produced in English.[2] As for American animated cartoons, plots have been targeted to children and young people for decades, ranging from the classic Disneys such as *Snow White* to more modern DreamWorks stories such as *Shrek.* But Japanese anime and manga encompass a much wider range of audience ages, genres, and content, and anime can range from the wildly comic *Sgt. Frog* to the darkly symbolic *Ergo Proxy.* Much anime is decidedly adult.

Once I asked my young nephews what they liked about anime compared to American animation. They told me that a major difference is that anime has a story—they meant an overall story—and you can never be sure what the ending will be. It is not unusual for a major character in an anime or manga to die, lose the one they love to another, or fail at what they are trying to do. Even in works aimed at small children, these things happen. For Americans used to stories with consistently happy endings, this is a little hard to handle. Another thing my nephews liked was that the characters are more complex. Villains can be understandable and even change their ways, and heroes can show bad traits and even commit horrid acts. Of course, my youngest nephew also said he liked "cool robots." The same things draw young people and adults to anime and manga today.

In Japan, and to a lesser degree in the United States, manga are usually published as serialized stories in magazines; successful stories are later collected into books. Stories are usually single works ranging from one volume up to thousands of pages over a series of volumes. The result can be a multivolume series for one long story, as is the case with Rumiko Takahashi's romantic comedy *Maison Ikkoku,* Tohru Fujisawa's *GTO,* and Takehiko Inoue's *Vagabond,* a retelling of the story of the famous swordsman Miyamoto Musashi. This is unlike much American serialized comics, whether print or animated, that may have an "ending" only for a particular episode or plot arc. When a manga is adapted into an anime or when an original anime story is written, it also is usually a single story told over a series of episodes. Anime television series are commonly 13 or 26 episodes long, and occasionally they go for 52 episodes or more. For librarians, this means you may have to commit to getting an entire series in anime as well as for manga.

Broad Categories of Anime and Manga

In Japan, anime as well as manga are created for several broad consumer segments. The two terms most commonly used by English speakers are *shōnen* and *shōjo,* broadly translated as "boys" and "girls." *Shōnen* usually refers to boys from grade school to the late teens. Then there is *seinen,* a term less used in English, referring to men in their late teens through twenties, and works produced for this older group are very different from those for the younger crowd.[3] *Shōjo* is usually used to refer to girls in a broad sense by English speakers. In Japan, the term is usually used for girls from grade school to their teens. Shōnen titles tend to be more action-oriented, often incorporating traditional values of duty and honor, whereas shōjo deals more with the emotional, and occasionally sexual, aspects of relationships. The categories are not mutually excusive. For example, the shōjo anime *Here Is Greenwood,* about the experiences of a young man in a high school boys' dorm, has been very popular with boys as well as the intended audience of girls. On the other side, shōnen titles such as *Chobits* can deal with relationships and have wide readership crossing genders.

A related term, also not used much outside Japan, is *josei,* used for women from teens through mid-thirties. Yet another term is *redikomi,* a contraction of "ladies comics"—these are often sexually explicit. A popular subset of josei manga and redikomi is known in the West as *yaoi.* In Japan, this genre has also been called *tanbi-kei, shōnen-ai,* boys' love, or BL. Yaoi features male–male love stories, created by women for women readers. Such tales can range from platonic to pornographic depending on writer and target audience.[4] Some well-known anime titles include the very sexually explicit *My Sexual Harassment,* the subtle supernatural action drama *Mirage of Blaze,* and the romantic comedy *Gravitation.*

Emotional Content in Anime and Manga

One of the reasons anime and manga have captured so much attention is because the feelings of the characters play a significant role in the tales. I find this to be a traditional element in these stories because emotions have played a strong role in Japanese literature from the earliest poems to the present day. This can result in some intense moments in comedic works as well as moments in serious works that require comedy to break the tension. Some Americans have trouble with this, with what I call the "Shakespearean quality" of anime and manga stories. It is common in a serious anime for comedic moments to occur, or tragic moments in normally humorous anime. For most people, recalling the similar use of humor and seriousness in the works of Shakespeare makes this mix more understandable.

WHAT ABOUT PROBLEMATIC CONTENT?

What Age Is This Appropriate For?

Anime, like manga, are not just for children or even teens. Historically, the market for anime videos in English was mainly college students and adults until about 1995, when teens began joining the existing fan culture. It was not until the 21st century that significant numbers of American preteens began to discover anime as well as manga, mainly as a result of the growing presence of anime on television. This has to be kept in mind when building a collection, given that the number of translated titles for older teens and adults is increasing. So librarians should consider purchasing anime specifically for teens and adults as well as for children. Children enjoy many titles aimed at an older audience just as children enjoy reading many novels or watching movies intended for adults, so on that basis alone, one should not limit purchases to very young age groups. In fact, the majority of titles available in English are aimed at teens. Few are aimed at small children, though many are "kid safe."

However, a great many anime are created for adults and contain very adult content. Classic and highly praised titles such as *Ghost in the Shell, GTO,* and *Genshiken* have some nudity or sexual language and should not be shelved with fare for younger patrons. The manga equivalents are also available and have more adult content. In addition, there are critically acclaimed anime such as *Perfect Blue,* the *Patlabor* movies, *Samurai X: Trust and Betrayal,* and *Grave of the Fireflies* that appeal to sophisticated film viewers and could bore many children. Therefore, it is *imperative* that libraries shelve such anime separately with the adult collection, not near children's or teen sections. To bundle all anime together as "kiddy cartoons" is inviting challenges and disastrous publicity from angry parents. On the other hand, buying only sub-adult fare limits the richness of collections and neglects grown-up fans. Buying mature titles means you can appeal to a whole new audience.

Reviews will be a useful source of information about where to class and shelve a particular title (see discussion later in this chapter). Another good resource is GNLIB, the Graphic Novels in Libraries e-mail list, where you can ask questions and get replies from highly experienced librarians. Information on how to subscribe is at http://groups.yahoo.com/group/GNLIB-L/. Although not all anime disc cases will include age ratings, many show ratings based on systems developed by the distributors. The majority of distributors have created their own ratings, given that MPAA ratings are too costly for small companies to use. One will find ratings such as 17+ or 13 up and, for sexually explicit titles, phrases such as "Absolutely Not for Children" on the front cover.

Please note in regard to children's collections that one must consider that in Japan the definitions of children's and adults' entertainment are more ambiguous than in the United States. For example, some types of light sexual humor, often at the expense of adult dignity, are found in some works designed for school-age children. A good example is the popular *Ranma 1/2* from the manga by Rumiko Takahashi, author of *InuYasha* and *Maison Ikkoku.* Among its slapstick humor and general silliness, *Ranma 1/2* pokes fun at adult lechery, infantile behavior, and general stupidity. Although this has been considered family viewing in Japan, libraries in conservative areas may want to consider shelving such materials in teen collections.

Violence

Until recently, many of the anime and manga translated into English were of an action-oriented nature, science fiction and fantasy being the two genres most represented. These are usually no more violent than what can be seen in American comics, on television, or in movie theaters. But there are cases where violence can be carried to an extreme. Simply checking the notes on a video box or flipping through a manga will often provide a clue about this. However, be aware that some U.S. anime companies have exaggerated the violence or sexual content in their promotions to encourage sales, and the content may actually be milder than implied. Input from other librarians familiar with the titles can be extremely useful here.

Nudity

Slight nudity is not unusual in some anime and manga, even in titles for children. This is a result of a different culture's views about naked bodies. Often, nudity is used for comic effect, and the characters involved may be highly embarrassed. Or a character may simply be taking a bath, as in the delightful children's classic anime *My Neighbor Totoro,* when the father and his daughters take a bath together, a normal parent–child emotional bonding activity in Japan. Sometimes nudity or partial nudity may be used simply to sell the product, much like American entertainment. Anime shown on U.S. television will have nudity edited out or covered up by digital editing. The video release of the same title will usually not have the edits unless it is specifically marketed as the television version.

Sexual Content

Given that some anime is released in the straight-to-video OVA format for specific market niches, it should not be too surprising that erotic and pornographic anime exist. This is also common for manga, which has even more specialized markets. However, sexually explicit anime are usually easy to avoid because they are marketed as such in specific product lines. It is possible to easily create a huge collection of anime without any explicit sexual content.

In most anime series, sexual content—if it exists at all—is hinted at rather than shown. One example is Akemi Roppongi in the *Maison Ikkoku* anime calling a neighbor to come and pay her bill at a love hotel because the guy she was with left without paying. Other examples may include a scene with cleavage, innuendo, panty shots, or hints of something having happened off camera. Then there are series with different target ages for different media. For example, with the highly popular *Revolutionary Girl Utena,* the five-volume manga has no sexual content and is aimed at schoolgirls; the television series, with implied incest and off-screen sex, at teens; and the movie, with more overt lesbian themes and some nudity, at young women. (An additional stand-alone manga volume titled *Revolutionary Girl Utena: The Adolescence of Utena* is based on the movie plot and has a similar audience.)

But note that many anime do include sexual joking. Librarians concerned about *any* references to sexual themes or nudity, direct or in hints, must view all new materials. An additional concern: Sometimes sexual content escalates through the episodes as the main characters finally commit to each other. A later episode of *Maison Ikokku* has Mitaka tell Kyoko that he has reserved a room in the hotel where they are dining and will continue to do so until she says yes. Some titles, particularly titles aimed at teen girls, may have a single sexual event in an entire series that is otherwise largely free of sexual content, such as when main female characters apparently lose their virginity off camera, as, for example, in *His and Her Circumstances* and the *Revolutionary Girl Utena* TV series. Again, these occurrences are late in the series.

Smoking and Drinking

Because animation in Japan is not considered to be just a medium for children's stories, it is not surprising to find scenes where characters smoke and drink. One will even find occasional cases where delinquent teens may light up a cigarette or have a drink. However, such behavior in manga and anime is the exception and usually has a place in the story. Alcohol and tobacco are almost always consumed by adults and in a proper adult context.

COLLECTION-DEVELOPMENT CONSIDERATIONS

Identifying Key Titles to Consider

Patrons will often be requesting recent titles such as anime seen on television or anime equivalents to manga available at the local chain bookstore. This is, of course, very similar to the requests we get for novels and movies. When building a collection, however, it is important to look not only at current releases and demands of your patrons but also at older releases that may be worth acquiring to build up a core collection. Therefore, lists of recommended titles may be of help for retrospective purchases and for adding old and new classics. See a list of recommended titles with indexes by length and creator at http://www.koyagi.com/recommended.html. Specialty Web sites devoted to major anime studios can also be useful. One such Web site is devoted to the work of Studio Ghibli, home of popular directors Hayao Miyazaki and Isao Takahata, and includes worldwide information about published books and video releases as well as anime titles. (See http://www. nausicaa.net.)

Key Titles for a Core Collection

For Kids:
  My Neighbor Totoro
  Castle in the Sky
  Kamichu!
For Teens:
  Tokyo Godfathers
  Gunbuster and *Gunbuster 2*
  Macross
For Adults:
  Maison Ikkoku
  Ghost in the Shell (movies, plus TV series subtitled *Stand-Alone Complex* or *S.A.C.*)
  Millennium Actress

Finding Reviews

Locating adequate reviews of anime can be difficult at times. Manga are reviewed regularly in sources such as *Publishers Weekly, School Library Journal, Voice of Youth Advocates* (*VOYA*), *Booklist, Kirkus Reviews,* and *Library Journal.*[5] *Video Librarian* covers anime regularly but only 5 to 10 titles per issue. Much more helpful are specialized sources, especially anime-heavy magazines such as *Protoculture Addicts* and the new *Otaku USA.* Online resources include Anime on DVD, Anime News Network (which has useful graphs of viewer rankings), Anime Jump, and—for their well-done in-house age ratings—The Right Stuf online retailer. In addition, Sequential Tart, a site with a female focus, covers both anime and manga.

Over two dozen U.S. companies distribute anime as a major product line, some of the largest being A.D. Vision (ADV), Bandai Entertainment, FUNimation, and Media Blasters. For a full list with links, see http://www.koyagi.com/release.html. The company Web sites are good places to check for dates, availability, citation information, and other details as well as brief descriptions of titles.

Anime: Finding Reviews

Anime Jump: http://www.animejump.com
Anime News Network: http://www.animenewsnetwork.com
Anime on DVD Reviews: http://www.mania.com/reviews_by_ title.html
The Right Stuf: http://www.rightstuf.com
Sequential Tart: http://www.sequentialtart.com

How to Buy Anime

Buying anime can be relatively easy these days, and your regular video sources may be sufficient. However, some titles may prove difficult and may be available only through local anime and manga specialty shops or online retailers. The stores will usually not be familiar with working with libraries and may require some sort of prepayment such as via a credit card. However, many of the online shops may have sales or discounts that can save libraries money. To find local stores, ask young anime enthusiast patrons. You can also check the online Comic Book Locator Service (see http://csls.diamondcomics.com) and call the store nearest you to ask if they carry anime. If not, they will probably be happy to refer you.

Online Anime Vendors

http://www.animecastle.com
http://www.animenation.com
http://www.rightstuf.com

Some libraries with specialized collections may want to order direct from Japan. In these cases, it is often best to order from a Japanese retailer or a retailer specializing in imports because regular U.S. distributors often impose excessive price hikes. For videos and books, the Kinokuniya stores in the United States as well as many shops in California and Hawaii Japantowns can obtain goods, as can some anime specialty shops that stock large quantities of Japanese works imported directly. It is helpful if you have the ISBN or product number available. Be aware that DVD discs will almost always be region 2 and will not have subtitles or English tracks.[6] There are exceptions, such as the Ghibli anime and documentary titles. Although they are region 2 discs, they are subtitled in English, and most of their anime titles are already available in the United States. Do be careful to not buy pirated goods—see later discussion of this issue.

Tips for Collection Development and Cataloging

1. Subscribe to GNLIB, the Graphic Novels in Libraries e-mail list, noted earlier in the chapter. This is a great place to ask questions and participate in librarian discussions about anime as well as manga and other graphic novels.

2. Be aware that English releases of manga and anime series may have different titles, such as *Kare Kano* (manga) and *His and Her Circumstances* (anime) or *Onegai Teacher* (manga) and *Please Teacher* (anime). Including alternative titles in your catalog may be a good idea. Also remember that one version may have more mature content than another. For example, the movie *Blood: The Last Vampire* has no sex or nudity; the *Blood the Last Vampire* 2002 manga is very adult; the novel *Blood the Last Vampire: Night of the Beasts* is very intellectual; the television series *Blood+* has one instance of off-screen sex; and the *Blood+* manga is quite violent at times.

3. Do not collect for just one age group—there are many wonderful titles for children, teens, and adults. Focusing too much on one age group will limit the collection just as it would for other areas of the library. A common problem is spending too much time and resources on kids and teen collections while ignoring adults.

4. Shelving should be divided up as it would be for other material, usually separate sections for children, teens, and adults. It may be tempting with a small collection to place all the anime in a single section. However, given the diversity of genres and age-appropriate content, such an approach could be problematic. (See earlier caveats.) In any case, given the anime's continuing popularity, single sections fill up quickly.

5. You may want to include headings in catalog entries that will allow patrons to search easily for a list of all your anime. This will help them identify titles they have not seen yet.

6. Because anime series are almost always a serialization of a single story, videos should be obtained in sequence. Remember that for long series you may have to commit resources to continue buying new releases.
7. For series, be sure volume numbers are on labels so that patrons know the sequence. Not all series have volume numbers clearly printed on them.

Redubbed versus Subtitled Versions of Anime

One old controversy in fandom is over the preference between viewing subtitled anime versus anime redubbed into English. Today this is less of a consideration, given that most videodiscs include both a redub and a subtitled track. Be aware that some series are issued as a redubbed version highly edited for television broadcast as well as an uncut subtitled version sold separately, sometimes with different titles. An example of this is the highly edited *Cardcaptors* (redubbed only) and the unedited *Cardcaptor Sakura* (subtitled only), which are the same show. In some cases, a title exists only in a redubbed or subtitled version but not both versions on one video. It is a good idea to consider relying on a redubbed version when the audience will be younger children. However, I have seen grade school children who were already fans do quite well at keeping up with subtitled anime.

Pirated Anime and Manga Goods

Anime and manga enjoy wide popularity outside of Japan. This has resulted in a certain amount of shoddy pirated goods on the market, especially important to remember if you are planning a display or are creating a collection of anime soundtracks. Commonly, one sees cheaply made posters, music CDs on the Son May (SM) label, and region-free videodiscs. These materials should be avoided in obtaining materials for your collection. Any goods made in Japan or released by U.S. companies are likely to be legitimate. However, some pirates release their discs with Japanese text on the boxes. A major clue with discs is that many pirated goods include Chinese subtitles and are region free. (See the Pirate Anime FAQ Web site, http://www.otakunews.com/piratefaq.php.) Pirated anime can be much cheaper than legitimately produced goods and therefore tempting. However, libraries should stick with American companies that issue licensed products even though these may be more expensive to buy and replace.

ANIME: FANS, PROGRAMS, AND YOUR COMMUNITY

Reach out to patrons who are anime fans. They can tell you what they are interested in and how to attract other fans to the library, help identify new hot titles and missing classics, help find experts to give talks, and assist with programs such as anime clubs, anime trivia contests, and cosplay contests. Other community resources include staff at local anime retailers and rental outlets, who can share information about what series are popular in the community. Keep in mind that although the largest group of fans may be young people, anime lovers can be of any age.

Anime Clubs

The growing popularity of manga and anime has resulted in a large number of clubs, usually on college and university campuses and at high schools. Clubs often do more than just watch anime. Many clubs produce newsletters, have member-lending libraries for videos and occasionally books, and organize special events.

If there is already an anime club in your area, they may be willing to meet with librarians to discuss recommended titles and even screen commercially available anime to help with selection. Such club contact can easily become an ongoing relationship, providing your library with knowledgeable volunteer consultants and mutual publicity. To locate a local club, check out the Web site for Otakon, the annual Baltimore conference for anime, manga, and j-pop fans, which has a list of clubs in geographical order at http://www.otakon. com/community_clubs.asp.

You can also start an anime club at your library or partner with a local club by providing space. Either way, please note that most DVDs are not licensed for public performance. If your library or the anime club does not obtain a license, showing anime to groups at the library is unlawful, and your library could be implicated. So you should be sure to get the appropriate permissions in the library's name from the U.S. distributor. Some independent anime companies have programs for clubs and will provide videos and free items. Many libraries already have a public performance license that covers anime distributed by major studios such as Go Fish, a subsidiary of DreamWorks, and Buena Vista, the distributor of Studio Ghibli anime. Two major companies that handle such licensing are Movie Licensing USA (www.movlic.com/ library/library.html) and Motion Picture Licensing Corporation (www.mplc. com). For contact information for many of the U.S companies, see http:// www.koyagi.com/showpermissions.html. Be aware that clubs may show fan-subtitled releases of anime not commercially available outside of Japan. If you let a club use your space for events, it should be clear that they are responsible for their activities.

Anime Conventions

Chances are good there is an anime or anime/manga convention in your region. Attending a convention for a day or more is a good way to talk to dealers, distributors, representatives of U.S. production companies, and local fans who do not necessarily use the library (yet). You will get an idea of the variety of material out there and what fans are interested in. Also, it may be possible to piggyback onto conference programming and arrange for a guest of honor or anime notable to speak at the library. See AnimeCons.com for a list of conventions and their Web sites (http://www.animecons.com/).

Fan Activities and Collection Development

Your anime-savvy patrons are likely to be interested and involved in fan activities that will fuel a demand for books not directly related to anime and manga. In many cases, a library will have books on these topics already. Library programs can be built around any and all of these areas with fan creations, speakers, and contests. Displays can also highlight these themes.

Cosplay

Cosplay, from costume play, means dressing up like a favorite character. This activity can lead to an increased demand for books on not only costuming but also basic sewing. For photo books of cosplayers showing off their work and guides on how to do cosplay costumes, see Hidetoshi Shimazaki and Jennifer Cahill's *Cosplay Girls* titles (2003, 2007), Jan Kurotaki's *Everybody Cosplay* (2007), and Gerry Poulos's *Cosplay* (2006). For information on some actual fashion trends, see Patrick Macias's *Japanese Schoolgirl Inferno* (2007).

Animation

Some patrons may be interested in reading about animation techniques—not only the latest computerized methods but also older hand-done animation, which after all is the foundation for much of computer animation. (See Culhane 1988; Laybourne 1998; Williams 2002; and—specifically on anime—Yoyogi and A.I.C. 2003.)

Drawing Anime and Manga Characters

Fans may want to improve their ability to draw, so good books on drawing and color techniques are useful. Be careful with "how to draw manga" books written by non-Japanese. Some are excellent, but most are cheaply done to capitalize on the popularity of manga with children. There are many good books in translation from Japanese authors on drawing techniques aimed at aspiring manga artists. Graphic-sha in Tokyo puts out three series with numerous volumes each: How to Draw Anime & Game Characters, How to Draw

Manga, and More How to Draw Manga. Watson-Guptill has four series, all books with Japanese authors: Let's Draw Manga, Manga University, Manga Pose Resource Book, and Tezuka School of Animation. For a full list, see http://www.koyagi.com/recDrawingBooks.html. Librarians should note that many of these books are aimed at serious illustrators and may include drawings of people who are nude or scantily dressed.

Writing Original Stories

Fan fiction or "fan fic" is also popular, writing stories with characters from favorite series. These stories are distributed among fans. Not only anime fans do this; such hobby fiction has been in existence for decades, particularly for well-known series such as *Star Trek* and the Edgar Rice Burroughs stories. Good books on story writing are helpful here.

Japanese Culture and History

Some patrons will develop an interest in Japan, so librarians may wish to add more books on Japan to their collection. This is a particularly tricky area—frankly, many such books do not tell you much about day-to-day life and culture, the areas anime and manga fans are likely to find most interesting. I maintain a list of books I personally find useful for understanding the cultural content of anime and manga at http://www.koyagi.com/ACPages/bibliography.html. This bibliography may be useful in building a collection of secondary materials. See also http://www.koyagi.com/links.html, which provides useful links to online resources relating to Japanese culture.

Japanese Language

Some patrons will want to learn the language, so good books plus instructional CDs and DVDs on conversational Japanese are called for here.[7] Two books directly related to manga are *Mangajin's Basic Japanese through Comics* (1993) and Lammers (2005). See also the multivolume Japanese for Busy People series from the Association for Japanese-Language Teaching (1994–).

WHAT SHALL THE FUTURE BRING?

What of the future? After all, in 5 to 10 years things may be different from what I describe. As I write this in summer 2009, the anime industry has been somewhat flat for a few years in the number of new titles, and even manga, which maintains a good pace, is leveling off. The fan base for both seems to be increasing when one looks at the growing number attending conventions. In any case, I feel that anime will be part of popular entertainment for some time.

When anime and manga were first released in the United States, the majority were aimed at older consumers, college age and up. Today, kids and teens are very visibly interested in these products, and their consumption has been growing significantly for over a decade. However, I urge librarians to develop collections not only for kids and teens but also for adults. After all, the teen fans of *Sailor Moon* in the mid-1990s are now grown, and today's kids and teens are growing up. Moreover, material for the adult market will be significant in expanding the variety of genres and will continue to grow. If libraries do not develop collections for all ages, they will be limiting the potential of their collections both in richness and in appeal to patron interests.

NOTES

1. Editor's note: After being selected in 2008 as Prime Minister of Japan, Tarō Asō complained about not having enough time to read manga in his new job and quipped that he was apparently more well known in Japan for being a manga geek than a prime minister. See "Japanese Prime Minister Needs More Manga Time," *ICv2*, October 30, 2008, http://www.icv2.com; and "Manga Fan Prime Minister Asō Opens Tokyo Film Fest," Anime News Network, October 21, 2008, http://www.animenewsnetwork.com/news/2008-10-21/manga fan prime minister aso opens tokyo film fest.

2. "Alternative comics" are sometimes referred to as art comics, independent or "indie" comics, and other terms. These expressions refer to American comics that do not fall into the conventional action and superhero genres of the last 40 years. Well-known examples include *Ghost World* by Daniel Clowes and *Maus* by Art Spiegelman. With the recent U.S. rise of graphic novels as a medium, the term "alternative" is falling out of use. Informally, "indie" is sometimes used for titles produced by American publishers other than DC Comics and Marvel.

3. There is also an interesting market in romance stories for boys dealing with the hopes, fears, and anxieties they have concerning relationships. One of the best authors in this genre is Masakazu Katsura, who wrote the manga equivalents of *Video Girl Ai*, and *DNA²*. Other examples include *Kimagure Orange Road*, and *Chobits*.

4. The Japanese use *yaoi* to refer only to fan-produced comics, usually parodies of commercial products, and use the other terms for commercial products.

5. Editor's note: See the collection-development article on anime: Robin Brenner, "Anime's Brave New World," *Library Journal*, July 2007, 46–49.

6. The world is divided up into nine DVD regions. For example, region 1 is the United States and Canada, and region 2 is Europe, Arabia, Turkey, South Africa, and Japan. A disc made for a particular region can be viewed only using a player made for discs from that region. The newer Blu-ray format discs operate under a different region code system, with the U.S. and Japan in the same region. But these discs require special players. Some people obtain region-free players so that they can watch films from other regions.

7. The Japan Foundation's worldwide survey of Japanese language classes for 2003 reported in the United States a figure of 42,018 students for higher education and 140,200 for all schools (Japan Foundation, "Outline of the Results of the '2003 Overseas Japanese-Language Education Organization Survey,'" http://www.jfbkk.or.th/jl/outline_2003_survey.pdf. Accessed September 12, 2006).

REFERENCES

Association for Japanese-Language Teaching. *Japanese for Busy People.* New York: Kodansha, 1994–.

Culhane, Shamus. *Animation Script to Screen.* New York: St. Martin's Press, 1988.

Drazen, Patrick. *Anime Explosion! The What? Why? And Wow! Of Japanese Animation.* Berkeley, CA: Stone Bridge Press, 2002.

Gravett, Paul. *Manga: Sixty Years of Japanese Comics.* New York: Harper Design International, 2004.

"Japanese Anime Market Grew to 242 Billion Yen in 2006." Anime News Network, August 2, 2007, http://www.animenewsnetwork.com/news/2007-08-02.

Kurotaki, Jan. *Everybody Cosplay.* Houston: ADV Manga, 2007.

Lammers, Wayne P. *Japanese the Manga Way.* Berkeley, CA: Stone Bridge Press, 2005.

Laybourne, Kit. *The Animation Book.* New York: Three Rivers Press, 1998.

Macias, Patrick. *Japanese Schoolgirl Inferno.* San Francisco: Chronicle Books, 2007.

Mangajin's Basic Japanese through Comics. Atlanta: Mangajin, 1993.

McCarthy, Helen. *Hayao Miyazaki: Master of Japanese Animation.* Berkeley, CA: Stone Bridge Press, 1999.

Napier, Susan J. *Anime: From Akira to Princess Mononoke.* New York: Palgrave Macmillan, 2000.

Osmond, Andrew. *Satoshi Kon: The Illusionist.* Berkeley, CA: Stone Bridge Press, 2008.

Poitras, Gilles. *The Anime Companion: What's Japanese in Japanese Animation?* Berkeley, CA: Stone Bridge Press, 1999.

Poitras, Gilles. *The Anime Companion 2: More . . . What's Japanese in Japanese Animation?* Berkeley, CA: Stone Bridge Press, 2005.

Poitras, Gilles. *Anime Essentials: Everything a Fan Needs to Know.* Berkeley, CA: Stone Bridge Press, 2001.

Poulos, Gerry. *Cosplay: Catgirls and Other Critters.* Berkeley, CA: Stone Bridge Press, 2006.

Ruh, Brian. *Stray Dog of Anime: The Films of Mamoru Oshii.* New York: Palgrave Macmillan, 2004.

Schodt, Frederik L. *The Astro Boy Essays.* Berkeley, CA: Stone Bridge Press, 2007.

Schodt, Frederik L. *Dreamland Japan: Writings on Modern Manga.* Berkeley, CA: Stone Bridge Press, 1996.

Schodt, Frederik L. *Manga! Manga!* Tokyo: Kodansha International, 1986.

Shimazaki, Hidetoshi, and Jennifer Cahill. *Cosplay Girls: Japan's Live Animation Heroines.* Tokyo: DH Publishing, 2003.

Shimazaki, Hidetoshi, and Jennifer Cahill. *Cosplay Girls 2: Japan's Live Animation Heroines.* Tokyo: DH Publishing, 2007.

Williams, Richard, *The Animator's Survival Kit.* London: Faber & Faber, 2002.

Yoyogi Animation Gakuin and A.I.C, *How to Draw Manga: Making Anime.* Tokyo: Graphic-Sha, 2003.

WEB SITE REFERENCES

Anime Castle. http://www.animecastle.com.

Anime on DVD Anime Checklist. http://www.mania.com/yearlychecklist.php.

AnimeNation. http://www.animenation.com.

Beveridge, Chris, webmaster. "Anime on DVD Reviews." http://www.mania.com/reviews_ by_title.html.

DeLorme, Daniel. "Encyclopedia." Anime News Network. http://www.animenewsnetwork. com/encyclopedia/.

Diamond Comic Distributors, Inc. Comic Book Locator Service. http://csls.diamondcom ics.com.

Macdonald, Christopher, ed. Anime News Network. http://www.animenewsnetwork.com.

Miller, Steve, Web master. GNLIB: Graphic Novels in Libraries. http://groups.yahoo.com/ group/GNLIB-L/.

Motion Picture Licensing Corporation. http://www.mplc.com.

Otakorp, Inc. "Community: Clubs." Otakon 2007. http://www.otakon.com/community_ clubs.asp.

The Pirate Anime FAQ. http://www.otakunews.com/piratefaq.php.

Poitras, Gilles. "Books on Drawing Techniques." Gilles' Service to Fans Page. http://www. koyagi.com/recDrawingBooks.html.

Poitras, Gilles. "Japanese Cultural Reference Links." Gilles' Service to Fans Page. http:// www.koyagi.com/links.

Poitras, Gilles. "Japan Research—Secondary Sources." Gilles' Service to Fans Page. http:// www.koyagi.com/ACPages/bibliography.html.

Poitras, Gilles. "The Librarian's Guide to Manga and Anime." Gilles' Service to Fans Page. http://www.koyagi.com/Libguide.html.

Poitras, Gilles. "Obtaining Permission for Public Anime Showings." Gilles' Service to Fans Page. http://www.koyagi.com/showpermissions.html.

Poitras, Gilles. "Official USA Anime, Japanese Cinema & Manga Release Date Information Sources." Gilles' Service to Fans Page. http://www.koyagi.com/release.html.

Poitras, Gilles. "Recommended Anime, Manga and Books." Gilles' Service to Fans Page. http://www.koyagi.com/recommended.html.

Poitras, Gilles. "Titles Available in More Than One Format in the U.S." Gilles' Service to Fans Page. http://www.koyagi.com/AM.html.

The Right Stuf International Inc. http://www.rightstuf.com.

Sequential Tart. "The Report Card." http://www.sequentialtart.com/reports.php.

Swank Motion Pictures. "Public Libraries." Movie Licensing USA. http://www.movlic. com/library/library.html.

Team Ghiblink. Nausicaa.net. http://www.nausicaa.net.

Toole, Mike, ed. Anime Jump! http://www.animejump.com.

All URLs were verified August 12, 2008.

10

CENSORSHIP OF GRAPHIC NOVELS IN LIBRARIES

Martha Cornog and Erin Byrne[1]

A PICTURE IS WORTH A THOUSAND WORDS

The censors and the "politically correct" tend to pick on the comic industry because they regard comics as products for kids and thus view adult/mature comics as inappropriate, or even illegal.

(CBLDF 2006–2007)

I don't care what type of evidence or what type of testimony is out there, use your rationality, use your common sense. Comic books . . . are for kids.
Prosecutor in Texas v. Castillo, *2000, quoted in McWilliams 2006*

Comics have been theoretically protected by the First Amendment ever since *Winters v. New York* in 1948. At that time, the New York Court of Appeals threw out a New York statute aimed at prohibiting comics and publications focusing on crime and horror because the statute was overly vague and in violation of the First Amendment (First Amendment Center n.d.). But theory has been overridden for decades by emotion and bad logic. In his book *Seduction of the Innocent,* Dr. Fredric Wertham concluded that reading comic books caused juvenile delinquency and that the images themselves—both the obvious ones and the ones he claimed were hidden—were suggestive and harmful to young readers (Wertham 2004/1953). A psychiatrist, Wertham believed that comic book violence begat societal violence. His 1954 testimony at a special Senate Subcommittee to Investigate Juvenile Delinquency helped usher in the Comics Code Authority (CCA), a self-regulatory ratings code for the entire industry developed by a trade association of comics magazine publishers. No one thought to propose a more focused approach: to change the comics distribution system so that edgier content could be limited to adults-only. At that time, comics were sold at newsstands open to all, and anyone old enough to gather a few coins together could buy anything they wanted.

Wertham was not the only heavy-hitter critic of comics—then-FBI Director J. Edgar Hoover commented on the subject also—but Wertham's vitriolic slash-and-burn from the seemingly scientific perspective of psychiatry had a catalytic effect and perhaps the strongest impact, despite flawed logic (Hadju 2008; Lent 1999). In associating juvenile criminals with the comics they purportedly read, he and many others failed to account for the magnitudes-larger groups of Americans who read comics but remained law-abiding. No simple foe of liberty, Wertham strongly supported "Negro" rights and strove to correct racial inequality in mental health care (Hajdu 2008, 100). Ironically, decades later, Wertham would have something of an about-face, admitting that comic book readers often grow up to be normal, well-adjusted adults (McWilliams 2006). He would even write *The World of Fanzines,* praising the "sincere and spontaneous" community spirit of comics-fan amateur subcultures (Wertham 1973).

The CCA imposed limitations on all comics plots relating to crime, violence, horror, sex, marriage, and nudity and banned derogatory portrayals of authority figures. Conflict between good and evil was acceptable only if the good side always won (Lavin 2002). The code is in limited use today, partly because of the success of the so-called underground comix of the 1960s and the subsequent shift in comics distribution from newsstands to independent stores—where access by young people can be better controlled. In any event, the CCA was never applied to graphic novels, unknown as such at the time. Nonetheless, Wertham's legacy resurfaces whenever lawmakers and review groups in any context neglect to apply First Amendment principles to graphic narrative at a level equal to all-text materials.

Comics creators and retailers have taken the brunt of censorship efforts in the last several decades—only in very recent years have libraries stocked enough graphic narrative to provoke challenges. And it was the creators and retailers who first organized to fight back. To preserve First Amendment rights for members of the comics community and to fight censorship, publisher Denis Kitchen founded the Comic Book Legal Defense Fund (CBLDF, http://www.cbldf.org), officially incorporated as a nonprofit charitable organization in 1990. In practice, the organization has helped over a dozen comic book retailers and comics professionals fend off censorship attempts, some successfully, some not, raising over $200,000 over the past five years to defend against suits brought for charges on grounds including obscenity and defamation. The CBLDF's guiding principle is that comics should be accorded the same constitutional rights as literature, film, or any other form of expression.

Now as more graphic novels appear in library collections, so are more censorship efforts and challenges directed at libraries. Recently, the CBLDF joined together with the National Coalition Against Censorship (NCAC) and the American Library Association's Office for Intellectual Freedom (OIF) to draft "Graphic Novels: Suggestions for Librarians," a useful introduction to issues associated with graphic novels in libraries, including censorship.[2] We recall the cliché, "a picture is worth a thousand words." Indeed so, and it is just this quality that may evoke a *thousand challenges* to prevent others, particularly young people, from seeing them. Pictures are different from words, and in some ways, objections to graphic narratives may show different patterns from objections directed toward textual materials. In this chapter, we examine these differences, review strategies for preventing challenges, discuss how to deal with challenges that do occur, and present case studies. Finally, we will suggest how censorship efforts can have educational and creative outcomes, even when items are removed.

THE WAY IT IS: GRAPHIC NOVELS AND CHALLENGES

What's Different about Graphic Novels?

Librarians are certainly used to the notion of censorship—Banned Books Week has been a tradition in the profession since 1982, and ALA's classic *Intellectual Freedom Manual* is in its seventh edition. Numerous resources and several organizations are available to help librarians when patrons challenge such controversial stand-bys as the Harry Potter series, *And Tango Makes Three, Forever,* and the perennial *The Adventures of Huckleberry Finn.* So what's different about graphic novel challenges?

First, the matter of likelihood. In many libraries, people may be *less* likely to notice and challenge graphic novels as compared to books—in some areas, the format seems be under the social radar for several reasons. Children and teens may consider them "their own thing" and hide titles from parents. Or the parents themselves may simply ignore graphic novels, automatically considering them "kid stuff," trivial, or akin to the newspaper strips and comics they themselves are used to, such as *Peanuts, Cathy,* or *Superman.* And in the case of manga, even when parents are aware that their children are fans, black-and-white does much to mitigate content. In black-and-white, blood is just not as viscerally gripping as the red stuff, nor is flesh so sensuous as when pink or tawny. It is also likely that many conservative parents keep their children away from *all* comics formats because of assumptions about fantasy/supernatural content, so the issue may be less likely to even come up for these families. Whatever the reason, increased media coverage may pull comics back into the radar and increase public attention in the near future.

However, once someone has engaged with a graphic novel and actually taken time to look carefully at the content, they may be *more* likely to have a negative reaction to "questionable" material, and a stronger reaction than with similar content in all-text books. A picture is simply more in your face: immediately accessible—indeed, unavoidable—to the eye and mind than written sentences, and there can be much less fuzziness or poetics about what is intended. The result is a kind of double standard for visual versus written media.

> "Some people find graphical depictions of things more offensive than text," said Carrie Gardner, a spokeswoman for the ALA's Committee on Intellectual Freedom and a professor at Catholic University in Washington DC. Gardner said the disputes concerning graphic novels are similar to what happened when libraries began carrying videotapes and providing access to the Internet. (Associated Press 2006)

Thus for graphic content, it can be harder to explain the concept of "context." In our modern world, pictures are taken out of context even more than quotations—just look at newspaper and tabloid photos. Opening *Fun Home* to the panel showing lesbian oral sex has proven quite disturbing to some people, never mind Alison Bechdel's artful and sympathetic story embedding the image. Another reason for a stronger reaction can be (again) the old saws that "comics are for kids," and "comics are trivial." Readers with no prior exposure or expectations relating to graphic narrative with serious content may be thrown completely. They may be quite accepting of prose memoirs describing sexual episodes, which of course would be shelved with the adult books. But a graphic novel memoir created for adults is for them a chimera.

A second way in which challenges of graphic novels may be different: there may be more objections, if not actual challenges, from *other library staff* than happens with all-text material. Here, the objection may be either to a particular title or to the format itself. As happened with films and DVDs years ago, library staff not familiar with graphic novels, especially recently, may question whether the format "belongs in the library." Complaints may be made that comics are trivial, trash, violent, and obscene, and they may distract young people away from reading "real" books. The "graphic" in "graphic novel" may automatically conjure up the "graphic = sex" equation. An additional problem specific to staff objections is that apparently few libraries have traditions or procedures for handling them in an organized and fair manner.

A third difference in censorship of books versus graphic novels: we still have little data about the latter. The OIF has kept statistics since at least 1990 on library censorship–related incidents reported to them. But because graphic novels are relatively new to libraries, these statistics apply mostly to books. The OIF has analyzed data by reason, initiator, and several other variables but unfortunately not by format, so the data on graphic novels as such have not been available for analysis. As for the CBLDF, their historical focus has been retailers and creators. So no group has been keeping focused track of library incidents relating to graphic novels specifically. Only in 2006 did the two organizations join with the NCAC to address the problems we are considering here. Hopefully, more information will be collected in the future.

However, we do have some very preliminary data about challenges to graphic novels as compared with challenges to text-only books, and some differences seem evident.

Patterns of Complaints and Challenges

What actual data do we have about censorship of graphic novels in libraries? The OIF did a survey of public libraries in 2005, and 185 responded.[3] A total of 97 percent (n = 179) included graphic novels in their collections. Of these, 19 percent (35) reported one or more problems or challenges. Problems included poor binding, theft, and difficulty finding reviews—all sometimes used as excuses by reluctant staff for not buying graphic novels. As for challenges, these 35 libraries reported a total of 149: 75 challenges or objections from patrons or the community and 74 incidents involving some type of objection from library staff or administration. Unfortunately, information about outcomes of these challenges and incidents is not available, nor are any other data that might suggest commonalities among the 35 libraries—such as by geographic location or size.

A 2006 Associated Press article reported that ALA's Office for Intellectual Freedom recorded at least 14 challenges relating to graphic novels in U.S. libraries over the preceding two to three years. (These were reported to the OIF independently of the just-mentioned survey.) But the records do not include information about the outcome of many of these challenges either. Also, there are no data yet about the frequency of graphic novel challenges compared to frequencies for books and other media.

One of the chapter coauthors compiled data about library censorship cases from personal e-mail and clipping files and followed up with Web searches and questions to some of the librarians. The following analysis is based on only 40 cases and is certainly not authoritative, but it may be taken as indicative of some of the current patterns. However, full information could not be obtained about all of these cases. (In most challenges involving more than one title, each title was tallied as a separate case.)

Initiators of Challenges

In the majority of the cases (25, or 62.5%), a parent or grandparent brought the challenge or raised the objection. Of the others, 2 were adult patrons not acting in the parental role (5.0%), 1 was a high school student (2.5%), 2 were local organizations (5.0%), and 4 were other library staff (10.0%). In 6 cases, information was not available about the source of the challenge (15.0%). For comparison, OIF's general censorship database of over 3,000 cases from 2000–2005 shows 60.4% initiated by a parent or guardian and 7.0% from other library staff (OIF). (These would be nearly all text-format books, but a small number of graphic novels would also be included.)

Reasons

Why are graphic novels challenged? They are challenged a bit more often for violence than are text-format books (17.5% for graphic novels compared to 13.4% for the OIF database). However, all of the challenges citing violence occurred in school libraries.

Fewer people seem to challenge graphic novels for magic, witchcraft, or occultism (5.0% compared to 7.5%). Perhaps families with objections to these areas do not permit access to comics in any form any more than they welcome fairy tales and fantasy stories.

The triggers for graphic novel challenges seem most often to be sex (60.0% compared to 31.7%), nudity (27.5% compared to 3.3%), and offensive language (12.5%, compared to 26.8%). These are also common triggers for challenges to text-format books, but the patterns are different: far more graphic novel challenges are for sex and nudity, and far fewer are for offensive language. Also occurring occasionally (7.5%, compared to 2.5%) are challenges for unappreciated depictions of an ethnic group, such as showing Polish people as pigs in *Maus*. A vaguer objection, "unsuited to age group" (25.0%, compared to 16.7%), probably implies the sex/nudity/language trio, set into the implicit recommendation that offending items could perhaps be moved rather than removed.

Outcomes

Of the 40 cases, we have knowledge of 26 outcomes. Of these, the title was kept in its original location in 10 cases (25.0%), moved to another location/collection in 4 cases (10.0%; 1 from middle school to high school, 2 from young adult or "YA" to adult, and 1 from adult to YA), and removed from the collection in 9 cases (22.5%). In 2 additional cases, part of the challenged material was retained and part removed. In 1 additional case, the title was removed until the end of the school year and then put back on the shelf. For the removal category, 2 of the cases were objections from a library administrator that did not go through any kind of formal reconsideration process.

Most Challenged Titles

A total of 32 titles were included in the 40 cases. Art Spiegelman's *Maus* and Paul Gravett's *Manga: 60 Years of Japanese Comics* had 3 challenges each, and *Chobits, I Love Led Zeppelin, Ranma 1/2,* and *Watchmen* had 2 each. (The Gravett book is not itself a graphic novel but has substantial illustrative graphic novel–originated content.) All other titles appeared only once. One case involved reconsideration of 14 *fotonovela* series, in which 5 of the titles were canceled and the rest retained.

FORESTALLING COMPLAINTS AND
CHALLENGES: STRATEGIES

Graphic novels are still a relatively new addition to many libraries. But new or old, patrons, library staff, and the collection itself can benefit from keeping everyone informed and involved, maintaining good records, and forming partnerships. Certain logistical factors may also prove crucial. All of these strategies should help minimize problems as well as enhance resources for coping with challenges when they do occur.

Segregate Materials by Age Level

Some public libraries still shelve all graphic novels with YA materials. Unfortunately, this is simply playing along with the "comics are kids stuff" stereotype and invites trouble when adding titles such as the manga *Lone Wolf and Cub* or even the Pulitzer Prize–winning *Maus*. Although available space and tradition always exert traction against change, librarians should plan to eventually morph any single collection into several parts: children's/juvenile, YA/teen, and adult—or similar groupings. Moreover, it is a good idea to locate the three collections at some physical distance apart. If YA is close to children's materials, that limits what can safely be included in YA. If YA is close to adult, that can limit the adult materials. Of course if the library plans to buy only YA titles, then only a YA or teen collection would be needed— which could safely include fare for younger ages. However, this limits the reading of adult comics fans and is in violation of the child's right to read.

Involve and Educate Patrons

The more patrons understand that comics are a format for all types of plots and content and can be done with any level of quality, the more they will understand that graphic narratives can be targeted to children through adults and that a variety of graphic novels belong in the library. In promoting the collection and developing programs around comics, librarians should not hesitate to rely on patrons who are already fans to suggest titles and ideas, participate in advisory groups, and proselytize to their friends.

Advertise the library's commitment to the comics format as well as showcase holdings by creating explanatory signs, handouts, bookmarks, brochure-format reading lists, and displays. (See #2 in the case studies section of this chapter for one approach.) If the adult graphic novels are shelved in the 700s amidst text-format books, extract a rotating display collection in a prominent place to get across the idea that comics are serious as well as exciting fodder for grown-up readers. Feature the different age collections on the library's Web site and newsletters, and invite coverage by local media. Suggested reading lists can be divided by age group, subject, author, or even genre and positioned near the titles themselves. Lists such as these can also give patrons an idea of what they *do not* want to read.

Plan programs around graphic novels for all ages: book clubs, "how-to" classes and draw-a-thons, talks from local artists and experts, and trivia contests. Hold workshops for parents introducing them to graphic novels and showing them how and why to select them for their kids. Tell parents how graphic novels are being used to improve literacy and get more children and teens to read—the average comic book has twice the vocabulary of the average children's book and three times the vocabulary of an average adult–child conversation (Krashen 2004). Assure them that the library has and will buy a variety of well-reviewed graphic novels that are okay for their child, whatever restrictions that the parent wants to impose on their offspring's reading matter. Tell them about the different collections, where they are located, and why. Assure them they can always ask a librarian for help in finding titles acceptable to them.

Involve and Educate Staff

Some librarians, support staff, and administrators may be as uncertain about graphic novels as members of the public. One way to head off objections and stonewalling is through education—not just about graphic novel formats but also more broadly about intellectual freedom and the right to read. (See #3 in the case studies section.)

If a library is planning on introducing or expanding their graphic novel collection, or if confusion is detected anywhere among colleagues, pull together some examples and discuss them with staff—in formal workshops or in more informal sessions. Such staff can include individuals in collection development, technical services, and reader services, but do not overlook administrators and trustees. Also, be sure to prepare staff whose responsibility is handling the media. Assure everyone that reviews are used for selection the same as with text-format books and other materials. With the knowledge that graphic novels are not just comic books and are not always appropriate for children, library staff who are unfamiliar with graphic novels will be able to evaluate them on the same criteria as they do other materials. They will also be more able to catalog and shelve graphic novels in the appropriate places. Those involved in readers' advisory functions for different age groups will have a clearer idea of which patrons should or should not have graphic novels recommended to them and what titles to steer them to—and away from.

Part of educating staff as well as patrons is to do your homework. Find out about these matters:

- How and why graphic novels are used to promote literacy and encourage reluctant readers to make leisure reading a habit. (See Krashen 2004 and "To Read or Not to Read," National Endowment for the Arts, http://www.arts.gov/research/ToRead.pdf.)

- Which library magazines feature graphic novel reviews (there are quite a few).
- The age-level classification systems of various graphic novel publishers.
- How graphic novel and comics publishers are courting libraries as customers by exhibiting at library conventions and including special sections for librarians on their Web sites.
- How general principles of intellectual freedom apply to books and, beyond books, to all media.
- How the library is purchasing a variety of graphic novels, from traditional, conservative, and "safe" to more intellectually and artistically challenging titles.
- What procedures are in place for ensuring that challenges are given careful and informed reconsideration, including procedures for handling staff issues.

Stock a Wide Variety of Titles and Genres

Be sure to stock plenty of non-controversial comics titles: collections from well-known newspaper strips, adaptations of literary classics, and historical collections from the Golden Age and Silver Age of superheroes. For all the different age groups, buy graphic novels with religious themes and viewpoints, treated in a respectful manner and published or endorsed by religious publishers and organizations. (See #1 in the case studies for how one library is doing this.) Besides heading off complaints, this approach could have the additional benefit of recruiting Christian parents to support graphic novels and the library. (See Appendix B-4 for collection-development tips relating to religious-viewpoint titles.)

Ask patrons who are aficionados of different types of titles to pre-review new items and rate them on the criteria of your or their choice. Create reading lists of religious and "safe" titles for patrons, and make sure staff are familiar with them, both for readers' advisory and for showing to those with questions about the format. Contact a local comics shop for suggestions and expert advice.

Build Your Case on Paper

You should be prepared to underscore the library's commitment to graphic novels by including the format in normal library paperwork. For example:

- Keep good circulation statistics to show how popular graphic novels are and how they can attract new patrons. Many libraries report that graphic novels out-circulate other formats and drive the total circulation numbers way up. When a California library reorganized their graphic novels into separate and easily accessible format-based collections, the children's titles were all checked out within days.

- Get reviews or similar background information for new titles, especially if possibly objectionable. Nearly all major book-reviewing sources, such as *Booklist* and *Library Journal,* regularly include graphic novels in their reviews. Some even go so far as to devote entire issues to spotlighting the year's best. If you use patron advisors to pre-review titles, or if librarians pre-review, have them fill out forms to keep on file.

- Have an up-to-date collection-development or materials-selection policy that explicitly includes graphic novels, either as part of a general policy or addressed separately. (See chapter 7, "A Place in the Library," which discusses collection development policies.) It is crucial that graphic novels be evaluated along the same criteria as the rest of the collection. The policy should include the statement that the possibility of an item being challenged or found controversial does not preclude its purchase.

- Make sure the library has an up-to-date reconsideration policy that can accommodate complaints and objections concerning graphic novels. Either this policy should apply to objections from staff, or there should be a separate process that staff at whatever level must follow. We have accounts of staff from technical processors up through directors objecting to graphic novel titles. When it was the director, the items were removed with no formal process although the titles had been selected by a degreed, qualified librarian. The process for internal and external objections need not be the same, but some type of process should be in place for both types.

Cultivate Friends and Allies

Develop good relationships with local comics advocates and enthusiasts in other libraries, schools, comics shops, art organizations, the media, and online communities. The Los Angeles Comics Professionals Monthly Dinner is an informal confab that includes comics creators, publishers, librarians, and anyone professionally involved with comics. Find out if such a networking group exists in your area, and if not, think about starting one. Allies can help with any graphic novel need or issue, from planning programs, finding speakers, and locating reviews to coping with challenges. Online, the Graphic Novels in Libraries discussion group is always ready with expert opinion, suggestions, and referrals. (See http://groups/yahoo.com/group/ GNLIB-L.)

DEALING WITH OBJECTIONS AND CHALLENGES

In theory, dealing with challenges to graphic novels is no different from dealing with challenges to all-text material. In practice, however, it is important to keep in mind the text/graphics double standard: many people consider an image to be far more powerful in its impact than any written description of that image. That said, the following tips will help you prepare to cope with challenges to graphic novels.[4]

There is no way to predict complaints, but good groundwork can establish a "library culture" for ensuring fair treatment of both challenged items and the people reacting to them. Make sure all library staff and board members understand the how and why of intellectual freedom as well as the library's policies and procedures for dealing with challenges. Provide customer service and other human relations training that will help staff deal effectively with sensitive matters. Role-playing several hypothetical complaints, at least one involving an angry parent, would be a good exercise and help staff get past the instinct to panic. A formal procedure benefits both library and initiator by allowing all to be heard and diffusing emotional reactions. But once developed, a formal procedure should actually be followed rather then side-stepped when a high-ranking initiator (such as a board president or county official) comes to call.

The Challenge Process

An objection or complaint may be made in person, over the phone, by e-mail, or by mail. In handling any type of complaint about graphic novels, and about library operations in general, staff should always take a courteous and calm approach. Above all, initiators must be assured that their interest in the library is welcome and that their objections will be given serious consideration through a formal complaint procedure. (Any written material relating to complaints should be acknowledged promptly.)

A first step is simply hearing out the initiator and having an informal discussion one-on-one, over the phone, or by e-mail, depending on how the complaint is made. Complaints received by mail can trigger an invitation to call or meet with staff. The librarian can take the approach of providing information at this beginning stage, such as how graphic novels are selected and how the same standards are applied to selecting all materials, what a broad range of graphic novels is available today, how manga reflect Japanese cultural assumptions, what similar non-graphic materials the library may have, the age-graded areas where materials are shelved (if that is the case), and alternative titles that may be more acceptable. Staff should have ready access to collection-development and reconsideration policies to answer questions at this stage. Often simply taking the time to talk to the patron can put his or her mind at ease. Many people just want to be heard.

If the problem cannot be resolved through informal discussion, invite the initiator to file a complaint in writing, normally through a prepared reconsideration form or questionnaire. (See sample form, Figure 1.) At this stage also, things may simply stop because an initiator may not always return the reconsideration form. Upon having the selection process explained and seeing the form, the individual may feel that his or her concerns have been dealt with.

There are some, however, who will wish to follow through and file a formal challenge in writing. In fact, the reconsideration policy should state that, to best serve the interests of all concerned, anonymous or unwritten complaints will **not** be honored—review and action occurs only when the reconsideration form has been returned. Moreover, the policy should also state that a challenged item should remain available on the shelf until and unless a final decision has been made to relocate or remove.

The formal challenge process begins when a reconsideration form is received and filed. At that time, a reconsideration committee is formed, according to the reconsideration policy. Committee members may be all staff or involve some community members; the actual composition of the committee is up to the individual institution. The committee should then proceed as follows:

1. Read the graphic novel in its entirety.
2. Review the selection process and the criteria for selection.
3. Check reviews and recommended lists to determine opinions of experts and critics.
4. Consider other relevant information such as where the item has been shelved and any related prior incidents or feedback.
5. Meet to discuss the challenge.
6. Make a recommendation to the administrator on retention, relocation, removal, replacement, or other strategy.

The initiator should then be notified about the outcome.

Key Messages about Libraries

When responding to a challenge, focus on several key points:

- Libraries provide ideas and information across the spectrum of social and political views.
- Libraries provide choice for all people.
- Parents are responsible for supervising their own children's library use.
- Collection does not imply endorsement.
- Graphic novels, as do books, deal with all subjects for all ages and show a wide variety of styles and skill levels.

When the Initiator Is a Library Staff Member

Libraries should be prepared to field questions, objections, and serious complaints relating to graphic novels from library staff and administration. Ideally, educating staff about this format can defuse such situations before they develop into festering sore spots or outright conflict. However, a section in the reconsideration procedures should address this possibility, to ensure both staffer and materials are given fair treatment.

If the staffer is not a degreed librarian, simply "pulling rank" can override the objection, asserting the expertise and authority of those who are MLS-endowed over the lower-ranked staffer. However, this leaves the staffer feeling unheard and misunderstood. Such reactions can undermine the staffer's morale as well as job performance and potentially infect an entire department with distrust. A complaint should be heard in a fair manner regardless of the source, and the staffer deserves to be heard as respectfully as would be done for a concerned parent.

A different situation exists if the initiator is a supervisor, manager, or director. Such a situation can be very tricky if degreed librarians disagree with the boss. A process in place beforehand, whether similar to or different from the process for patron challenges, may be able to make such situations more manageable and fair to all. In any case, there should not be any retribution or censure directed to the initiator on account of the complaint, regardless of the initiator's rank and the rank of the individual(s) making the decision.

Talking with the Media

A challenge may attract media attention. How effectively you work with the media may well determine how big the story becomes and will help shape public opinion.

- Designate one or more people to speak for the library, and make it clear that no other staff should talk with the media.
- Ask about the story the reporter has in mind. If you do not feel qualified to address the questions or are uncomfortable with the approach, say so. Suggest other angles ("The real issue is freedom of choice . . . ").
- Ask about the reporter's deadline. Even if it is "right away," you can call back in 15 minutes.
- Remember, nothing is "off the record." Assume that *anything* you say could end up on the front page or leading the news broadcast.
- Prepare carefully for any contact with the media. Know the most important message you want to deliver and be able to deliver it in 25 words or less. You will want to review your library's borrowing and

collection-development policies and the American Library Association's Library Bill of Rights.

- Practice answering difficult questions out loud. You may wish to invest in a session with a professional media consultant or role-play sample questions with someone else (see Sample Questions and Answers following this list).
- Be prepared to tell stories or quote comments from parents and children about how the library has helped them.
- "I don't know" is a legitimate answer. Tell reporters that you will get the information and then call back.
- Never say "No comment." A simple "I'm sorry, I can't answer that" will suffice.

Sample Questions and Answers

The following questions provide sample language for answering questions from parents, the media, and others. You will want to personalize your remarks for your library and community. Remember, keep it simple. Keep it human.

Why Do Libraries Buy Graphic Novels?

Graphic novels are very popular with many readers and cover a range of topics for all ages. Graphic novels can attract new readers and help with literacy. As with books, the library has a responsibility to buy graphic novels to serve the community—your neighbors—including those who may not agree with you. All materials you find in your library were selected by librarians, trained to select materials based on library policies.

Aren't Graphic Novels Mostly Trash, Light Reading, or Kids' Stuff?

Comics are a format, not a genre. Although for many years comics were mostly superhero stories, teen comedies, or newspaper strips, comics can handle any topic and be targeted to any audience. In the last 10 years, American-published comics in the form of longer graphic novels have expanded to cover any topic and level of audience that text-format books do. And like books, some graphic novels attract wide notice and win awards.

Shouldn't I Be Able to Control What My Kids Are Exposed To?

You can control what your children read by going with them to the library or by looking over what they bring home. If there are materials you do not approve of, talk with your children about your objections. We will be happy to provide you and your children with suggestions for other graphic novels that may be more acceptable.

What Should I Do if I Find a Graphic Novel I Do Not Approve of in the Library?

If you have a concern, simply speak to a librarian. We take such concerns very seriously. First, we listen. We also have a formal review process in which we ask you to fill out a special form designed to help us understand your concerns more thoroughly. Anyone who makes a written complaint will receive a response in writing.

CASE STUDIES

The following nine examples of complaints and challenges come from the files of one of the coauthors and illustrate a variation in process and outcomes. Details are reported anonymously unless information was obtained from the media. In those cases, the sources are cited. The order of presentation is roughly benign to problematic.

1. Informal Objection, Not Pursued, Title Retained

Title/author: Dragon Ball, by Akira Toriyama, shelved in YA
Organization: Public library, Minnesota, 2007
Initiator: Parent
Basis of complaint: Sexual situations.
What happened: The parent complained by e-mail, and the librarian responded
 by e-mail. First the librarian did research about reviews and ratings, includ-
 ing getting input through the GNLIB-L discussion group. The information
 was e-mailed to the parent, and the parent was invited to fill out a Request for
 Reconsideration Form if not satisfied. There would then be a more detailed,
 formal response that could be appealed to the library board if the parent wished.
 There was no further communication from the parent.
Comments: There was some indication that the parent was conservative Christian,
 so the library decided to add some Christian-viewpoint graphic novels to the
 collection. "My experience is that if we have alternatives in our collection, it
 diverts a lot of anger." For some time, this library has maintained a Christian
 Press Bibliography: a list for patrons who ask about Christian books for their
 children.

2. Formal Challenge, Not Pursued, Title Retained

Title/author: Ranma 1/2, by Rumiko Takahashi, shelved in YA
Organization: Public library, New York State, 2006

Initiator: Grandparent

Basis of complaint: Sexual situations and nudity

What happened: The patron filled out a complaint form, and the director tried to contact the patron to discuss the situation. The patron never called back, and there was no further contact on the matter. The book was retained in YA.

Comments: Subsequently, a sign was posted in YA, with the following text. There have been no complaints since the sign was put up.

If you are unsure about the age appropriateness of a graphic novel, please note that most manga-Japanese-style graphic novels have an age designation on their back covers. If you are still unsure, please check with the reference librarian. Thank you.

3. Staff Complaint, Formal Process, Title Reviewed and Relocated

Title/author: Showcase, an anthology of three stories by different creators, shelved in adult

Organization: Public library, Ontario, Canada, 2006

Initiator: Library staff member

Basis of complaint: Disgusting subject matter, offensive language

What happened: The staff member used the standard library reconsideration form. A librarian discussed the book with the staff member, showed reviews, and explained the principles of intellectual freedom. Based on review of the content and considering that at least two of the stories deal with coming of age, the book was relocated from the adult to the YA collection.

Comments: In this library, the standard reconsideration form has been used for staff as a matter of process because the library had received staff comments previously about DVDs. Recently, the library began staff development talks about intellectual freedom as relates to the entire collection. Since May 2006, the graphic novel collection has grown considerably, and there have been no further complaints.

4. Informal Objection, Title Reviewed and Relocated

Title/author: Daddy's Girl, by Debbie Dreschler, shelved in YA

Organization: Public library, Pennsylvania, 2007

Initiator: Parent

Basis of complaint: Unsuited to age group.

What happened: Three librarians read the book and gathered reviews and expert comments. Results plus librarian evaluation led to a decision to move the title to the adult collection.

Comments: At the time the book was purchased, there was only a teen graphic novel collection.

5. Formal Challenge, Title Reviewed and Relocated

Title/author: Blankets, by Craig Thompson, shelved in teen section
Organization: Marshall Public Library, Missouri, 2006
Initiator: Parent
Basis of complaint: Nudity and sexual situations
What happened: The title was removed from circulation until the library created
   written guidelines for collection development. A new material-selection policy
   was developed and approved March 2007. This included a reconsideration
   process. The title was then restored and moved to the adult section.
Comments: The title had been shelved with "new arrivals," and there was concern
   that children might stumble onto the explicit illustrations after being attracted
   to the comic-book style of the title. At this library, there are no separate graphic
   novel sections: books and graphic novels are interfiled. *Fun Home,* another
   graphic novel, was challenged in the same incident (Associated Press 2006;
   Goldberg 2006; Olin 2007).

6. Formal Challenge, Title Reviewed, Book Removed

Title/author: Akira, vol. 2, by Katsuhiro Otomo
Organization: Rice Middle School Library, Texas, 2005
Initiator: Parent
Basis of complaint: Violence, offensive language, and sexual situations inappropri-
   ate for middle school readers.
What happened: The reconsideration committee upheld the challenge, and the title
   was removed (Associated Press 2006; ACLU Foundation of Texas 2005).

7. Objection, Government Intervention, Title Removed

Title/author: Manga: 60 Years of Japanese Comics, by Paul Gravett, shelved in adult
Organization: Victorville Public Library, San Bernadino Library System,
   California, 2006
Initiator: Parent
Basis of complaint: Sexual situations
What happened: The parent complained to the library, and she was told that she
   was the only person complaining about the book, and it would not be removed.
   The press then entered the picture as well as county officials. A county official
   ordered all 13 copies of the book removed from the library system, and the
   library complied. The library agreed to look into the concept of a special
   juvenile library card that offers restricted access to materials.
Comments: It was not reported whether a challenge procedure was in place or
   followed; however, the jurisdiction of such a procedure over a county official is
   unclear. The adult section of the library contains other comics material
   acceptable for teens, such as *The Hulk, Calvin and Hobbes,* and *Peanuts*
   (Oder 2006; Olin 2007; Reid 2006).

8. Administrator Objection, No Formal Process, Title Removed

Title/author: I Love Led Zeppelin, by Ellen Forney, bought for adult section but not
  yet added
Organization: Public library, Illinois, 2007
Initiator: Library director
Basis of complaint: Sexual depictions
What happened: Librarian and manager discussed book with director and
  showed book reviews, as well as suggesting various ways to remove or
  mask objectionable content. But the director still felt that the title and
  cover might attract a non-adult to check it out. The book was not added
  to the collection.
Comments: The librarian expressed dismay that so many libraries do not have
  procedures for internal challenges.

**9. Staff and Administrator Objection, No Formal
Process, Title Removed**

Title/author: I Love Led Zeppelin, by Ellen Forney, bought for adult section but not
  yet added
Organization: Public library, Ohio, 2007
Initiator: Technical services staff, then library director
Basis of complaint: Sexual situations
What happened: The librarian met with director and showed reviews and a list of
  Ohio public libraries that own the book, and also pointed out that the library has
  sexually frank films, art books, and contemporary fiction. But the director still
  felt that the title would cause trouble because a child might get a hold of it, and
  a parent would cause a fuss.
Comments: There had been no graphic novels collection-development policy, and
  the director formed a committee to develop one. A policy was developed and
  approved, excluding graphic novels that are "primarily erotica." The committee then recommended to the director that a staff member objecting to an item
  should follow the same steps for challenging it as a member of the public. The
  director never addressed that issue.

COMMENTARY AND CONCLUSIONS

What can we learn from these case studies? Each library will put its own
spin on interpreting the details, but let us offer some general comments.

"Challenge" as an English word suggests both difficulty and opportunity.
Indeed, challenges to graphic novels offer both. The difficulties we can see in
the case studies: librarians have expended considerable time and effort supporting challenged titles, and sometimes the titles are removed regardless.

However, opportunities arise also. The events and aftermath of a challenge may do the following:

- Show a library what is missing in internal procedures—no collection-development document for graphic novels or no reconsideration procedure—and then spur librarians to fill the gaps.
- Reveal lack of information, in the community and also among staff, providing an opportunity to develop educational programs for both groups.
- Show what may be lacking or less obvious in the collection, such as "safe" and/or Christian-friendly graphic novels. Expand collection holdings in these areas, offer them to patrons, and advertise their existence with finding aids and workshops. Expanded materials may not bring back banned titles, but ties with the community will be strengthened, and more readers will be served. And as patrons get used to the format, more varied titles can be gradually reintroduced.
- Help a library form alliances, with local comics groups, advocates, and educators.
- Help correct misplacements—sometimes librarians will agree that a title should indeed be relocated.
- Offer a reality check and help correct purchasing decisions. Libraries serve communities, and just because a title is well reviewed and popular does not mean it is the best thing for this particular library, in this particular community, at this point in time. Libraries and communities grow into new ideas, new titles, and new synergies. In the meantime, there is always interlibrary loan.

Challenges to library materials are inevitable because in a free society people will always disagree to one extent or another. Moreover, challenges show that people care deeply about their community, their children, and their library. They feel empowered—they want to get involved, and they want to fix things. *Voice of Youth Advocates* editor Stacy Creel wrote recently that parents despairing of controlling the sexually freewheeling Internet may focus their wrath on closer-to-hand books (Creel 2008). Like the Internet, graphic novels are relative newcomers on the scene and, like the Internet, are highly visual—so no surprise that they can present an especially inviting target.

Libraries serve communities, and those who challenge are part of them. Challenges create problems for libraries but also opportunities to reconnect with staff and with the community, to improve internal operations, to respond with information and a wider variety of collection materials—and to make new friends and fans. Says CBLDF Executive Director Charles Brownstein, "I look at the challenges as a painful development process, like puberty."[5]

Figure 1: Sample Request for Reconsideration of Library Resources

[*This is where you identify who in your organization has authorized use of this form—Director, Board of Trustees, Board of Education, etc.—and to whom to return the form.*]

Example: The school board of Mainstream County, U.S.A., has delegated the responsibility for selection and evaluation of library/educational resources to the school library media specialist/curriculum committee and has established reconsideration procedures to address concerns about those resources. Completion of this form is the first step in those procedures. If you wish to request reconsideration of school or library resources, please return the completed form to the Coordinator of Library Media Resources, Mainstream School Dist., 1 Mainstream Plaza, Anytown, State, Zip.

Name: _____ Date: _____

Address: _____

City: _____ State: _____ Zip: _____

Phone: _____ E-mail: _____

Do you represent yourself? _____ An organization? _____

1. Resource on which you are commenting:

____ Book   ____ Textbook   ____ DVD

____ Magazine   ____ Library Program   ____ Audio Recording

____ Newspaper   ____ Display

____ Graphic Novel   ____ Electronic information/network (please specify)

____ Other _____

Title: _____

Author/Producer: _____

2. What brought this resource to your attention?_____

3. Have you examined the entire resource?_____

4. What concerns you about the resource? (use other side or additional pages if necessary)
_____

5. Are there resources you suggest to provide additional information and/or other viewpoints on this topic?_____

Source: Office of Intellectual Freedom, Intellectual Freedom Manual *(Chicago: American Library Association, 2006), 360.*

NOTES

1. The coauthors thank the staff in the American Library Association's Office for Intellectual Freedom (especially Deborah Caldwell-Stone, Don Wood, and Bryan Campbell), the Graphic Novels in Libraries e-mail list (GNLIB-L), Kristin Fletcher-Spear, and Stacy Creel for providing information and assistance. We greatly appreciate your help.

2. "Graphic Novels: Suggestions for Librarians" is posted at http://www.cbldf.org, http://www.ncac.org, and http://www.ala.org.

3. OIF's survey of public libraries is described in "Graphic Novels: Suggestions for Librarians" (see note 2). Counts for external and internal objections/challenges were reported to Martha Cornog in an e-mail from Bryan Campbell of OIF, January 24, 2008.

4. Tips were based on those found in OIF's "Coping with Challenges: Strategies and Tips for Dealing with Challenges to Library Materials," "Workbook for Selection Policy Writing," and "Libraries and the Internet Toolkit." These guidelines are available along with a great deal of other useful material at http://www.ala.org/oif. (See links at left for Challenge Support and Intellectual Freedom Toolkits.) Other material was excerpted from "Graphic Novels: Suggestions for Librarians"—see note 2. See also the *Intellectual Freedom Manual* (OIF 2006).

5. Brownstein's remark was made as part of a panel discussion, "Dealing with Challenges to Graphic Novels in the Library," during SPLAT!, a graphic novel symposium presented by the New York Center for Independent Publishing, New York City, March 15, 2008.

REFERENCES

American Civil Liberties Union Foundation of Texas. *Free People Read Freely: An Annual Report on Banned and Challenged Books in Texas Public Schools 2004–2005*. Austin: ACLU Foundation of Texas, 2005 (accessed at http://www.aclutx.org, link to Banned Books and then Banned Books Reports, December 1, 2007).

Associated Press. "As More Graphic Novels Appear in Libraries, So Do Challenges." *International Herald Tribune*, November 14, 2006, http://www.iht.com (accessed November 28, 2007)

Comic Book Legal Defense Fund. "History: About the CBLDF." http://www.cbldf.org/about.shtml. 2006–2007 (accessed November 24, 2007).

Creel, Stacy L. "Editorial: The View from VOYA." *Voice of Youth Advocates,* April 2008, 5.

First Amendment Center. First Amendment Topics: Winters v. New York [Findlaw]. www.firstamendmentcenter.org/faclibrary/case.aspx?case=Winters_v_NY (accessed November 24, 2007).

Goldberg, Beverly [BG]. "Graphic Novels Draw Controversy." *American Libraries,* November 2006, 13.

Hajdu, David. *The Ten-Cent Plague: The Great Comic-Book Scare and How It Changed America*. New York: Farrar, Straus and Giroux, 2008.

Krashen, Stephen D. *The Power of Reading: Insights from the Research*. 2nd ed. Portsmouth, NH: Heinemann, 2004.

Lavin, Michael R. *Comic Books in the '50s: The Comics Code Authority*. 2002. http://libweb.lib.Buffalo.edu/comics/cca.htm (accessed November 24, 2007).

Lent, John A., ed. *Pulp Demons: International Dimensions of the Postwar Anti-Comics Campaign.* Madison, NJ: Fairleigh Dickinson University Press; London: Associated University Presses, 1999.

McWilliams, James. "Comic Books." *First Amendment Center,* www.firstamendmentcen ter.org/speech/arts/topic.aspx?topic=comix. 2006 (accessed September 26, 2007).

Oder, Norman. "Manga History Pulled from Public Library." *Library Journal,* May 15, 2006, 14.

Office for Intellectual Freedom. American Library Association. *Intellectual Freedom Manual.* 7th ed. Chicago: ALA, 2006.

Office for Intellectual Freedom. American Library Association. *OIF Censorship Database 2000–2005: Challenges by Initiator, Institution, Type, and Year.* http://lita.org/ala/ oif/bannedbooksweek/bbwlinks/challengesbyinitiator20002005.pdf (accessed July 18, 2008).

Olin, Anita. "Banned Books Week." *Sequential Tart,* September 24, 2007. www.sequential tart.com/article.php?id=665 (accessed July 18, 2008).

Reid, Calvin. "Manga Work Pulled from Libraries." *Publishers Weekly,* April 24, 2006. http://www.publishersweekly.com/article/CA6327161.html (accessed July 18, 2008).

Wertham, Fredric. *Seduction of the Innocent.* Laurel, NY: Main Road Books, 2004. [Originally published 1953, 1954.]

Wertham, Fredric. *The World of Fanzines: A Special Form of Communication.* Carbondale: Southern Illinois University Press, 1973.

Appendix A

GRAPHIC NOVELS AND GAMES

Robin Brenner

Games and gaming have been rising in popularity in the United States more visibly than have graphic novels and Japanese manga, but all are experiencing booms in popularity and diversity. While games and graphic novels fight for acceptance as valid formats for libraries to collect, the two media offer enticing alternatives to traditional prose storytelling.

Video games and graphic novels suffer from many of the same negative stereotypes. It has been claimed that they are all violent, they have negative effects on their consumers, and they have little redeeming value in terms of learning, emotional intelligence, or social interaction. Fans of both are portrayed as outsiders and nerds who are awkward socially. With the rise of graphic novels and the format gaining traction in literary circles, and given current statistics showing how widespread gaming actually is, these assumptions are no longer accurate if they ever were.

Gamers are everywhere. In preparing their 2008 report, the Entertainment Software Association discovered that 38 percent of households owned a video game console. Although only 25 percent of U.S. gamers were under 18, a whopping 85 percent of the 267.8 million video games sold in 2007 were rated from "Early Childhood" (EC) to "Teen," showing the wide popularity of games aimed at youth (Entertainment Software Association 2008). According to the Pew Internet and American Life Report on Teens, Games, and Civics from 2008, 97 percent of teens play games. A total of 86 percent play console games such as the Xbox or Wii, 73 percent play computer games, and 60 percent play on portable gaming consoles such as the Nintendo DS Lite. Moreover, 99 percent of teen guys and 96 percent of girls play games, and 65 percent of teens play games with other people present in the same room (Lenhart, Madden, and Hitlin 2008). From these statistics, it is obvious that gaming has become an integral part of teen entertainment and family life.

GAMING: A DEFINITION

Within the library world, gaming includes card games, board games, role-playing games, online games, and video games. Video games are currently the most visible, but card games include cribbage, Pokémon, and Magic, and board games may range from Scrabble to strategy games such as chess and Go. Role-playing games, including Dungeons and Dragons as well as live-action role-playing (LARP), also fall within the sphere of gaming in libraries. Online games combine role-playing games with social networks, and the most common (and addictive) form of these is the Massively Multi-Player Online Role-Playing Game (MMPORG), such as *World of Warcraft* or *RuneScape*. All of these types of games present information and stories to a varying degree and thus fit with a library's mission to educate and entertain. Each type attracts different audiences: video games of all sorts split along age and gender divides, and patrons with a wide range of skills and interests may be attracted to console games (that is, games played on dedicated platforms such as the Playstation 3, Wii, or Xbox 360), board games, or both.

GAME PLAY AND COMICS LITERACY

Games, from tabletop to video game adventures, use a lot of the same elements to tell their stories as do comics. The majority of titles in each format require the reader to piece together images and text to create a narrative, and both allow the reader to set the pace and focus their attention as they move through the tale. (However, strict strategy games like chess do not quite demand constructing a narrative in the same way.) Games include more creative interactions because players write their own dialogue and direct the plot of their own participation in the game. Nonetheless, the multiple and often simultaneously engaged literacies involved, from processing visual data to parsing text to investigating the history or background of a story, are skills shared by graphic novel readers and game players. In fact, the younger generation's ease in reading graphic novels can be attributed to the fact that most grew up playing some sort of video game, making connections between text and visuals a more ingrained connection. The problem solving used by comics and manga fans to parse graphic novels and manga, taking into account all of the cultural references that must be mastered as well as the panel connections, is not unlike the problem solving that gamers master during game play. Both mediums encourage research and creativity.

THREE WAYS TO GET A STORY

Fans of both formats can find three major types of connections within the games and graphic novel/comics worlds: graphic novel series inspired by games, games inspired by graphic novel series, and graphic novels that feature gaming and game play without referencing specific games. Often the most successful, story-wise, are the graphic novel series not based on specific games. Such titles are not as limited by the source material or fans' high expectations and thus are in less danger of getting it wrong. But they can still evoke the fun, adrenaline rush, and puzzle-solving satisfaction of game play. Certainly, an accomplished graphic novel based on a game will lead curious readers to the game, and an engaging game may well inspire the player to pick up the related comics series. The *Halo* graphic novel from Marvel Comics is one of the best examples of a stand-alone comic that succeeded in satisfying skeptical fans of the game series, and it consistently ranked number two on the graphic novel sales charts from Diamond Comic Distributors, months after it debuted.

In today's world, no one need be a fan of only one format or medium: in fact, the cross-pollination among formats encourages people to interact with their favorite world of choice in as many ways as they can. Films and television spin off into games, games spin off into comics, and novels spin off into comics. Because many of today's top games, from video games to MMPORGs, are based in Asia and specifically Japan, more and more gamers become manga and anime fans to delve deeper into their favorite game's background. For their part, manga and anime fans become gamers to participate more in their favorite tale, from *Bleach* to *Naruto*. Comics-related series may lead to release of multiple fighting games, as with Naruto, or the many movie tie-in games, as with Spider-Man and Batman. Pokémon, credited with inspiring a whole generation's obsession with anime and Japanese pop culture, was a game first and then an anime and manga series, and Yu-Gi-Oh!, best known as a trading card game, was in fact a manga first and then spun out into anime and games. Kingdom Hearts, which combines anime-style characters with favorite Disney protagonists, became a game favorite first and then conquered the manga market with two hit series. One of the most highly anticipated games of 2009 is the MMO (massively multiplayer online) DC Universe Online, featuring favorite heroes and villains from the DC Universe's 60-plus years of comics history.

For most of these linked products, there is no overarching structure or plot except familiar characters and settings, and games excel at putting the reader—now player—in active control so that they *become* Spider-Man or Naruto and are sent on missions. There are a few series that over time engage different levels of one story through multiple media: the .hack series was famously launched as an anime series and as video game at the same time; in order to fully understand the world presented, fans had to both watch the series and play the game. The .hack series, through many incarnations of

Japanese manga, anime series, and game incarnations, continues to illuminate the same world through different lenses. Other games not directly related to a specific character or universe appeal to fans by bringing to life comics-inspired activities or missions, as with MMPORGs such as City of Heroes, populated with player-created super-powered heroes.

INTERSECTIONS

Although games are the domain of comics fans and non-comics fans alike, gaming's influence on fandom is most visible in relation to manga and anime, especially at conventions. When fans get involved in cosplay (costume play) of their favorite characters, these creative homages are just as much from games as they are from manga or anime series. Because Japanese manga and a large proportion of video and online games are currently made in Japan, the consistent character design across media allows fans to leap from game to comic and back again for inspiration. One of the favorite inspirations for creative cosplayers is Final Fantasy, a long-running series of games that has spawned a number of computer-animated films in a style that is a hybrid of photo-realism with anime touches. Similarly, no anime- or manga-themed convention is complete without gaming programming and events, from the colorful cosplay chess (human chess enacted by characters cosplaying each piece) to halls filled to the brim with consoles offering everything from Dance Dance Revolution to card games and role-playing games.

The connections among gaming and graphic novels are likely to become more intertwined, and finding the links among graphic novels, games, and traditional storytelling can only help libraries attract users and engage their communities.

RECOMMENDED READING ON GAMING

Everything Bad Is Good for You: How Today's Pop Culture Is Actually Making Us Smarter, by Steven Johnson (Riverhead, 2005). An engaging read that explores how today's dominant pop culture media, television and video games, are more intellectually stimulating than consumers may realize.

Game On: Gaming at the Library, by Beth Gallaway (Neal-Schuman, forthcoming). A highly anticipated book from *Voice of Youth Advocates'* Game On columnist and founder and co-chair of ALA's Teen Gaming Interest Group, this title promises to be a substantial primer on everything related to gaming, from how to integrate games into your collection to how to defend game collections and run top-notch game-related programs.

Gamers . . . at the Library? The Why, What, and How of Video Game Tournaments for All Ages, by Eli Neiberger (ALA Editions, 2007). A primer for any library hoping to host gaming tournaments.

Grand Theft Childhood: The Surprising Truth about Violent Video Games and What Parents Can Do, by Lawrence Kutner and Cheryl Olson (Simon and Schuster, 2008). For all of those who are curious about the truth in the stereotypes about violent video games and what players take away from them, this is the latest study with young teenagers.

The Kids Are Alright: How the Gamer Generation Is Changing the Workplace, by John Beck and Mitchell Wade (Harvard Business School Press, 2004). Although Beck and Wade highlight how gamers influence the corporate world, their discoveries and portraits of the gamer generation are enlightening for librarians, educators, and parents as well.

What Video Games Have to Teach Us about Learning and Literacy, by James Paul Gee (Palgrave McMillan, 2003). A valuable work that zeroes in on connections between literacy and gaming.

RECOMMENDED FOR LIBRARIES

Graphic Novels and Manga Featuring Games and Gaming

.hack//Legend of the Twilight, by Tatsuya Hamazaki, Art by Rei Izumi (TOKYOPOP, 2004)

.hack//GU+, by Tatsuya Hamazaki, Art by Yuzuka Morita (TOKYOPOP, 2004)

Culdcept, by Shinya Kaneko (TOKYOPOP, 2004)

Hikaru no Go, by Yumi Hotta, Art by Takeshi Obata (TOKYOPOP, 2004)

Megatokyo, by Fred Gallagher (Dark Horse Comics, 2004–2005; CMX/DC Comics, 2006–)

Penny Arcade, by Jerry Holkins and Mike Krahulik (Dark Horse, 2006)

Portus, by Jun Abe (VIZ Media, 2007)

PvP, by Scott Kurtz (Image Comics, 2004)

Yggdrasil, by Lay Mutsuki (Go Comi! 2008)

Graphic Novels and Manga Inspired by Games

> *Halo,* by Lee Hammock (Marvel Comics, 2006)
> Based on Halo series
> *Kingdom Hearts,* by Shiro Amano (TOKYOPOP, 2005–2006)
> *Kingdom Hearts: Chain of Memories,* by Shiro Amano (TOKYOPOP, 2006)
> Based on the Kingdom Hearts series
> *The Complete Metal Gear Solid,* by Kris Oprisko (IDW Publishing, 2006)
> *The Complete Metal Gear Solid: Sons of Liberty,* by Alex Garner (IDW Publishing, 2008)
> Based on Metal Gear Solid
> *Ragnarök,* by Myong-Jin Ti (TOKYOPOP, 2002–2004)
> Based on Ragnarök (MMPORG)
> *Tomb Raider,* by Andy Park (Bandai Entertainment, 2006)
> Based on the Tomb Raider series
> *Warcraft: The Sunwell Trilogy,* by Richard Knaak (TOKYOPOP, 2004)
> Based on World of Warcraft (MMPORG)

Games Inspired by Graphic Novels and Manga

> *Batman: Arkham Asylum,* Eidos Interactive (Play station 3, XBox 360, PC) (announced for the end of 2009)
> Inspired by the Batman universe, DC Comics
> *Bleach: Blade of Fate,* Sega, 2007 (Nintendo DS)
> Inspired by *Bleach,* by Tite Kubo, VIZ Media
> *The Incredible Hulk: Ultimate Destruction,* VU Games, 2005 (Playstation 2, XBox, Gamecube)
> Inspired by the Hulk, Marvel Comics
> *LEGO Batman,* Warner Brothers Interactive Entertainment, 2008 (Nintendo DS, PC, Playstation 2, Playstation 3, PSP, XBox360, Wii)
> Inspired by the Batman universe, DC Comics
> *Marvel Ultimate Alliance,* Activision, 2006 (Gameboy Advanced, Nintendo DS, PC, Playstation 2, Playstation 3, PSP, XBox, Wii)
> Inspired by the Marvel Universe, Marvel Comics
> *Mortal Kombat vs. the DC Universe,* Midway, 2008 (Playstation 3, XBox 360)
> A crossover between the original game Mortal Kombat and the DC Universe, DC Comics
> *Naruto: Ultimate Ninja Storm,* Namco Bandai Games, 2008 (Playstation 3)
> Inspired by *Naruto,* by Masashi Kishimoto, VIZ Media

Spider-Man 2, Activision, 2004 (Gameboy Advanced, Game-
   cube, Nintendo DS, PC, PSP, XBox)
Inspired by Spider-Man comics from Marvel Comics
X-Men Legends I, Activision, 2004 (Gamecube, PC, XBox)
X-Men Legends II, Activision, 2005 (Gamecube, PC, Playstation
   2, XBox)
Inspired by the X-Men Universe, Marvel Comics

REFERENCES

Entertainment Software Association. "2008 Essential Facts about the Computer and Video
   Game Industry." 2008. http://www.theesa.com/facts/pdfs/ESA_EF_2008.pdf.
Lenhart, Amanda, Mary Madden, and Paul Hitlin. "Teens, Games and Civics." 2008. http://
   www.pewinternet.org/~/media//Files/Presentations/2008/TechSource%20Games%20
   and%20Libraries%20110208finalNN.ppt.ppt.

Appendix B

GUIDE TO GRAPHIC NOVELS IN SPECIAL TOPICS

Martha Cornog

APPENDIX B-1: AFRICAN AMERICAN–INTEREST GRAPHIC NOVELS: RESOURCES

African American–interest comics include those with African American themes, main characters, and/or creators—"by, for, and about people of color." African American writers and artists have had a notable presence in American comics since the 1940s and 1950s (Hajdu 2008), when prejudice often kept them out of other publishing and art careers. Pioneers whose work is recognized now include E. Simms Campbell (1908–1971), who drew glamour gals for *Esquire* and *Playboy,* and Jackie Ormes (1911–1985), the first known woman African American comics creator and who penned several popular newspaper strips in the 1930s through the 1950s. George Herriman (1880–1944), creator of the widely admired *Krazy Kat,* had black ancestry, although this was not generally known during his lifetime. His work pushed the format, both art and content, into new directions and inspired numerous others—and still does.

Today, a lively community supports African American comics creators, some working for the large comics companies and many others working with small presses, on the Web, or self-published. Increased ethnic sensitivity and interest has led to increases in mainstream titles over the last decade or so. However, most African American comics seem to be written primarily for adults. More work would be greatly welcome for teens and younger readers—there seem to be almost no kids' titles with African American main characters. Also, women creators are less common, especially in mainstream publishing. (See information on the Ormes Society later in this appendix.)

To increase representation of minorities in comics, Milestone Media was founded in 1992 by a group of black American cartoonists with backgrounds mostly in the mainstream superhero industry. Despite good intentions and some nine series published through DC Comics—*Static* was made into the animated television series *Static Shock*—the comic books did not sell as well as expected (Brown 2001; Strömberg 2003), and the company shut down its comic book division in 1997. But at the 2008 San Diego Comic Con, both Milestone and DC announced a rebirth: Milestone characters will be folded into the DC Universe and appear routinely in high-profile titles such as *Justice League of America* and *Teen Titans.* Moreover, the old Milestone issues will be collected into graphic novels (Brady 2008).

Rich Watson's blog and the Glyph Awards (see later description) are the best ways to check on trends and identify titles within and outside mainstream publishing. Mainstream African American–interest graphic novels are often reviewed by *Publishers Weekly,* other review journals, and the more serious fan Web sites; but Web comics and small-publisher graphic novels and comic books may not receive much coverage.

Conventions

In addition to the following conventions, there are usually African American-themed panels at the large New York Comic Con and the San Diego Comic-Con.

Black Age of Comics Convention
    http://dablackage.blogspot.com
    Held since 1993 in Chicago, now annually in the fall. The 2008 convention
    included an exhibit, marketplace, signings, and a press conference. Seems to
    focus mostly on indie, small-press, and self-published titles.
East Coast Black Age of Comics Convention (ECBACC)
    http://www.ecbacc.com
    Held since 2002 in May. Small, intimate convention for comics creators and
    fans, with a special program for kids. Goals are to promote literacy, provide
    a venue and networking opportunities for black comics creators, and promote
    "positive black images." Includes exhibits, marketplace, panels, and workshops.

Awards

Glyph Comics Awards
    http://ecbacc.com/wordpress/glyph-comic-awards/
    Recognizes "the best in comics made by, for, and about people of color."
    Presented yearly since 2005 at ECBACC in 10 categories.

Titles and Series Worthy of Consideration

Aya, by Marguerite Abouet and Clement Oubrerie (2 vols., Drawn & Quarterly, 16+)
Black Panther, by Reginald Hudlin and various (series; Marvel, 13+)
Blokhedz, by Mark and Mike Davis and Brandon Schultz (series? Pocket Books,
    2007– 13+)

Bluesman, by Rob Vollmar and Pablo G. Callejo (NBM/ComicsLit, 18+)

Days Like This, by J. Torres and Scott Chantler (Oni, 10+)

Deogratias: A Tale of Rwanda, by J. P. Stassen (First Second, 16+)

Incognegro, by Mat Johnson and Warren Pleece (Vertigo, 16+)

King: Complete Edition, by Ho Che Anderson (Fantagraphics, 16+)

King David, by Kyle Baker (Vertigo/DC Comics, 16+)

Lucifer's Garden of Verses, by Lance Tooks (4 vols., NBM/ComicsLit, 18+)

Luke Cage, by various (series; Marvel, 16+)

Luke on the Loose, by Harry Bliss (Raw Jr./Toon Books, 4–8)

Malcolm X: A Graphic Biography, by Andrew Helfer and Randy DuBurke (Hill and Wang, 13+)

Me & The Devil Blues: The Unreal Life of Robert Johnson, by Akira Hiramoto (series; Del Rey, 18+)

Method Man, by Method Man, Sanford Green, and David Atchison (Grand Central Publishing, 16+)

Narcissa, by Lance Tooks (Doubleday, 16+)

Nat Turner, by Kyle Baker (Abrams, 16+)

Pitch Black: Don't Be Skerd, by Youme Landowne and Anthony Horton (Cinco Puntos, 13+)

Ororo: Before the Storm, by Marc Sumerak, Carlo Barberi and Scott Hepburn (Marvel Comics, all ages)

Satchel Paige: Striking Out Jim Crow, by James Sturm and Rich Tommaso (Hyperion, 10+)

Sentences: The Life of M. F. Grimm, by Percy Carey and Ronald Wimberly (Vertigo, 16+)

Stagger Lee, by Derek McCullough and Shepherd Hendrix (Image, 16+)

Newspaper Strips, Available in Collections

Boondocks, by Aaron McGruder (Andrews McMeel, Three Rivers Press, 13+)

Candorville, by Darrin Bell (Andrews McMeel, 13+)

Explore Black History with Wee Pals, by Morrie Turner (Just Us Books, 8+)

Jump Start, by Robb Armstrong (Andrews McMeel, 13+)

The K Chronicles, by Keith Knight (Manic D Press, Fantagraphics, self-published, 18+)

Mama's Boyz, by Jerry Craft (Mama's Boyz, Inc., 10+)

Online Resources

Digital Femme
> http://www.digitalfemme.com
> Blog of Cheryl Lynn Eaton, comics journalist for *Publishers Weekly* and other outlets and founder of the Ormes Society.

Glyphs: The Language of the Black Comics Community
> http://www.popcultureshock.com/pcs/blogs/glyphs
> Blog of Rich Watson, comics journalist and founder of the Glyph Awards

(which were named after this blog). Frequently updated with news of the black comics community and titles; contains many links.

The Museum of Black Superheroes

http://www.blacksuperhero.com

Articles, gallery, list of superheroes with capsule vignettes, forum, and links.

The Ormes Society

http://theormessociety.com

An organization dedicated to supporting black female comics creators and promoting the inclusion of black women in the comics industry as creators, characters, and consumers. Named after the legendary pioneering cartoonist of color Jackie Ormes. News of African American women cartoonists plus forum and links.

Salute to Pioneering Cartoonists of Color

http://web.mac.com/tim_jackson/iWeb (click on the link for the phrase)

African American newspaper strip cartoonists c. 1920s through 1960s, listed by name of cartoonist, name of cartoon strip, and name of main character(s), with vignettes for many entries.

The Urban Voice in Comics Online Magazine

http://www.uvcmag.com

Articles, features, and news relating to African American and urban themes and personalities connected with comics as well as with derivative games, films, and other media. Includes chat room and a comprehensive calendar of comics conventions nationwide. Sells back issues of the print magazine, issues #1–#5.

Other Resources

Brown, Jeffrey A. *Black Superheroes, Milestone Comics, and Their Fans.* Jackson: University Press of Mississippi, 2001.

Cartoons and Ethnicity; The 1992 Festival of Cartoon Art. Columbus: Ohio State University Press, 1992. Published in conjunction with the exhibition "Illusions: Ethnicity in American Cartoon Art," curated by Lucy Shelton Caswell, and the 1992 Festival of Cartoon Art, Ohio State University, Columbus.

Foster, William H. *Looking for a Face Like Mine: The History of African Americans in Comics.* Waterbury, CT: Fine Tooth Press, 2005.

Goldstein, Nancy. *Jackie Ormes: The First African American Woman Cartoonist.* Ann Arbor: University of Michigan Press, 2008.

Other Heroes: African American Comic Book Creators, Characters and Archetypes. Art Exhibition Catalog. Morrisville, NC: Lulu, 2007. Published in conjunction with the exhibition "Other Heroes: African American Comic Book Creators, Characters and Archetypes," curated by John Jennings and Damian Duffy, Jackson State University, Jackson, Mississippi.

Strömberg, Fredrik. *Black Images in the Comics: A Visual History.* Seattle: Fantagraphics, 2003.

REFERENCES

Brady, Matt. "SDCC '08—Milestone Is Back, and in the DCU." *Newsarama,* July 26, 2008. http://www.newsarama.com/comics/080726-comiccon-mileston-DCU.html.

Hajdu, David. *The Ten-Cent Plague: The Great Comic-Book Scare and How It Changed America.* New York: Farrar, Straus and Giroux, 2008.

APPENDIX B-2: LATINO-INTEREST GRAPHIC NOVELS: RESOURCES

Latinos, those with heritage originating in the Spanish-speaking countries of Europe and Latin America, are the largest and fastest-growing U.S. minority. According to a 2008 study, some 54 percent of U.S. Latinos use library services for information and entertainment (Flores and Pachon 2008). Information needs often center on learning English; entertainment can mean stories in a familiar language and cultural setting—such as with Spanish-language graphic narratives. Also, both needs can be served by English-language comics with themes and main characters relating to Latinos and Latino culture. Of course, graphic novels with Latino themes and characters as well as titles in Spanish will appeal in addition to many Anglos, including those learning about Spanish-speaking countries and cultures or studying Spanish as a foreign language.

Unfortunately, English-language titles with Latino themes or characters are not easy to identify given that no single site or organization seems to track this. You just have to pick them out from the usual review sources; sometimes an ethnic-sounding creator surname will give a clue. You can find countries of creators in the Lambiek Comiclopedia (http://www.lambiek.net), either by checking an individual's name or by inputting a country in the search field to produce a list and then looking up the names to see whose work has appeared in English.

Spanish-language graphic novels are easier to identify, and the following sources can help. Also, you can search Amazon.com. Use Advanced Search and select "Comics and Graphic Novels" in the subject box, plus "Spanish" in the language box. For vendors that handle Spanish-language materials, see the Online Resources section in this appendix as well as those in the table of foreign language vendors provided in *Library Journal* (Hoffert 2008).

Conventions

Guadalajara International Book Fair
http://www.fil.com
Large and prominent book fair for the Spanish-language publishing world, held yearly in Guadalajara, Mexico, by the University of Guadalajara. Attendees number around 400,000 and exhibitors around 2,000, including Norma, Planeta, and other Spanish-language comics publishers located in Latin America and Spain.

Buenos Aires International Book Fair

http://www.el-libro.org.ar

Reported to be the largest Spanish-language book fair in the world, held yearly in Buenos Aires, Argentina, by the Fundación El Libro. Attendance reaches about one million, and there are around 1,400 exhibitors.

Awards

La Catrina Cartoon Prize

http://www.fil.com.mx/ingles/i_catrina/i_catrina.asp

A single award given annually at the Guadalajara International Book Fair.

Haxtur Awards (Premios Haxtur)

http://www.elwendigo.net/haxtur/haxturframeset2.htm

http://www.elwendigo.net/quiniela.htm (gives finalists for current year's awards)

These awards have eight categories and are given to titles worldwide, not just Latino-centric. Many awards have gone to U.S.-originating titles. Given out yearly at the International Comics Convention held in the Principality of Asturia, Spain.

Titles and Series Worthy of Consideration (English Language)

Araña, by Fiona Avery and others (Marvel, 13+)

Bardín, the Superrealist, by Max (real name: Francesc Capdevila Gisbert) (Fantagraphics, 18+)

Battle Gods: Warriors of the Chaak, by Francisco Ruiz Velasco (Dark Horse, 16+)

Blue Beetle, by various creators (DC Comics, 13+)

Che: A Graphic Biography, by Spain Rodriguez (Verso, 16+)

Chicanos, by Carlos Trillo and Eduardo Risso (IDW, 18+)

The Last Knight: An Introduction to Don Quixote by Miguel de Cervantes, by Will Eisner (NBM, 10+)

Love and Rockets, by Jaime and Gilbert Hernandez (Fantagraphics, 18+): Locas series (also called the Hoppers 13 series), Palomar series (also called the Heart-break Soup series)

Pedro and Me, by Judd Winick (Holt, 13+)

La Perdida, by Jessica Abel (Pantheon, 16+)

Sloth, by Gilbert Hernandez (Vertigo, 16+)

White Tiger: A Hero's Compulsion, by Tamora Pierce, Timothy Liebe, and Phil Briones (Marvel, 13+)

Newspaper Strips, Available in Collections (English Language)

Baldo, by Hector Cantú and Carlos Cantellanos (Andrews McMeel, 13+)

La Cucaracha, by Lalo Alcaraz (Andrews McMeel, 13+)

Titles and Series Worthy of Consideration (Spanish Language)

Argentina, Mexico, Cuba, and Spain have had long comics traditions and are home to a substantial comics industry. In addition, hundreds of American, other European, and Japanese series have been translated into Spanish. See the Online Resources section in this appendix for sources of titles and series in print. What follows are only a few suggestions.

Bone (Public Square Books)

Buffy Cazavampiros (series; Norma)

Capstone Press: Graphic Biography series, Graphic History series

Condorito: La Aventura Comienza, created by Pepo (real name: René Ríos) (Rayo/ HarperCollins, 10+)

Fidel, by Nstor Kohan and Nahuel Scherma (also in English; Seven Stories, 16+)

Gareth Stevens Publishing: Graphic Biographies series, Graphic Histories series

Hellboy (Norma)

Lerner Publishing: Graphic Myths and Legends

Love and Rockets (La Cúpula)

Mujeres Alteradas, by Maitena (real name: Maitena Burundarena) (Editorial Lumen, 18+)

Spider-Man (DK Children, Marvel)

Star Wars (Dark Horse)

Strangers in Paradise (Norma)

Tintín (Public Square Books)

Watchmen (Planeta)

X-Men (Marvel)

Fotonovelas

The unapologetically pulp comics variously called *novelas, fotonovelas,* or *novelitas,* small Mexican-produced booklets of soap opera–type stories, have wide appeal to Latino adults. Libraries tend to treat these like mass market paperbacks without cataloging. *Novelas* are sold on subscription from several North American vendors, and popular series include *El Libro Semanal* and *El Libro Sentimental.* Tucson-based Latin American Periodicals offers subscriptions to Spanish children's comics as well as *novelas* and will e-mail libraries an attractive PDF catalog (800-634-2124, lapmagazines@att.net). Some libraries use Novelas Popular in Yonkers (914-337-4434), and others order from local Latino bookstores. Note that these are adult titles, and libraries will want to preview samples to make sure content is appropriate for their communities. (See Logan and Ospina 2005 for more information.)

Online Resources

La Casa del Libros (Spanish-language site)

http://www.casadellibro.com

The online sales site for a bookstore chain based in Spain, founded in 1923 and now part of the large Spanish publishing group Grupo Planeta. On the Libros por Temática drop-down menu, select "Infantil, Juvenil y Cómic" and then choose a subcategory. Lists thousands of titles, including manga, superheroes

American and otherwise, and other Spanish-language graphic novels from
Europe, the United States, and Latin America.

Críticas: An English Speaker's Guide to the Latest Spanish-Language Titles
http://www.criticasmagazine.com
Monthly review e-journal, in English, of Spanish-language books from the U.S.
and international Spanish-language publishing world, produced jointly by *Publishers Weekly, Library Journal,* and *School Library Journal.* (Two print issues
are published per year, in June and November, and can be ordered through the
Web site.) Covers some graphic novels: put "graphic novel" into the search field.

Guía del Cómic (Spanish-language site)
http://www.guiadelcomic.com
A Web site with a good deal of information about selected comics in Spanish,
mostly from Spanish creators and publishers but some listings for U.S. titles that
have been translated. Sections include titles and publishers, with annotations and
links, and creators, with brief biographies and links. Some Argentina titles, also.

Mercado Libre (Spanish-language site)
http://www.mercadolibre.com
Mercado Libre is eBay's Latin American partner, and this is the hub site for
versions in 13 countries. All except Ecuador and Uruguay seem to sell
comics—look for the category on the left that includes the word "comics."
(Note: the Brazil site is in Portuguese.) These sites are good sources for identifying Spanish-language graphic novels from Latin America creators. Spanish
translations of American, Japanese, and European titles are also listed.

Norma Comics (Spanish-language site)
http://www.normacomics.com
Spanish publisher and distributor of Spanish-language graphic novels: hundreds
of European series (including from Spain), manga series, and U.S.-originating
series are listed. Useful for finding out what has been published in Spanish,
especially manga. However, does not seem to include any Latin American titles.

Public Square Books (English-language site)
http://www.publicsquarebooks.com
Vendor for around 300 Spanish-language volumes (within fewer series), many
of which are translations of American comics such as *Bone* and *Hellboy,*
and manga, including *Fruits Basket* and *¡Ah, Mi Diosa!* (*Oh My Goddess!*).
A smaller number of original Spanish volumes. Works with the major book
wholesalers such as Baker & Taylor (PSB's parent company) and Ingram as
well as some of the specialty distributors of Spanish-language books, such as
Bilingual Publications and Chulainn.

Other Resources

Flores, Edward, and Harry Pachon. *Latinos and Public Library Perceptions.* Los
Angeles: Tomás Rivera Policy Institute, 2008. http://www.trpi.org/PDFs/Latinos_&_Public_Library_Perceptions_Final.pdf.
Lent, John A., ed. *Cartooning in Latin America.* Cresskill, NJ: Hampton Press, 2005.

Pilcher, Tim, and Brad Brooks. *The Essential Guide to World Comics.* London: Collins & Brown, 2005. ("Spain," in Chapter 6, "Continental Comics" 192–95; Chapter 7, "South of the Border")

REFERENCES

Hoffert, Barbara. "Immigrant Nation." *Library Journal* 133, no. 14 (September 1, 2008): 34–36.
Logan, Robert, and Carmen Ospina. "Focus on Special Literature: Fotonovelas; How to Bring Fotonovelas into Your Library. *Críticas,* September 15, 2005. http://www.library journal.com/article/CA6257851.html.

APPENDIX B-3 LGBT-INTEREST GRAPHIC NOVELS: RESOURCES

"There is a huge gay audience in comics as well as a big contingent of creators," says Marc Andreyko, who writes for DC Comics (Furey 2007). Comics with lesbian, gay, bisexual, and transgendered main characters have been around since the 1940s as an underground or parallel universe, and in the 1960s such comics began sometimes appearing as strips in gay-audience periodicals; more recently, they have appeared as Web comics (Dynes 1990; Greyson 2007). Perhaps the most prominent currently, Alison Bechdel's *Dykes to Watch Out For* began in 1983 and is now up to some dozen collected volumes, picking up numerous fans outside the queer communities. Then Bechdel's autobiographical graphic novel *Fun Home* was named to "best of 2006" lists from *Time* magazine and the *Village Voice* and won an Eisner Award. Previously, *Pedro and Me* as well as *Stuck Rubber Baby* had attracted favor from educators and librarians for their sensitive and educational portrayal of living with AIDS and growing up gay. *Skim,* about a teen's crush on her teacher, and *12 Days,* about healing from grief, have also received favorable notice from librarians.

LGBT graphic novels such as these center on serious issues. Others such as *Jane's World, Dykes to Watch Out For,* and *Curbside Boys* star a cast of people who just happen to be gay living usual lives of comedy, drama, and problems.

Many librarians have heard of *yaoi* and *yuri,* genres of Japanese manga that deal respectively and usually romantically with guy–guy and gal–gal love. (See chapter 2, "Japanese Manga," and chapter 3, "Girls, Women, and Comics.") Do these comics appeal to LGBT readers? That question has sparked some debate because it has been widely reported that yaoi and yuri are written by women for women and are subsets of the romance genre with wide heterosexual appeal. Robin Brenner conducted an online survey in 2008 through gay-interest Web sites and concluded that many LGBT readers do like yaoi and yuri, but the majority are women (Brenner and Wildsmith 2008). In other words, some gay male readers may enjoy yaoi and maybe yuri but are not the biggest fan group, but women read both regardless of sexual orientation. Yaoi being quite a popular market segment now does mean that titles appear prominently in many bookstores, quite unlike most previous—and most other current—titles with same-sex themes.

"Gay comics" may be a hot button for some librarians in conservative communities as potential censorship magnets. Some titles have no sexually related content at all, but it is true that most do, implied to explicit. Apart from that, the sexual relationship dynamic conveyed by simply having characters who identify as homosexual usually leads librarians to shelve most LGBT graphic novels in adult collections. However, a few titles in the Titles and Series Worth of Consideration section of this appendix are correctly rated teen, and in more liberal communities, some mild yaoi and yuri series such as *Gravitation* or *Kashimashi,* as well as other graphic novels labeled 16-plus, can be shelved in high school libraries.

Conventions

Prism Comics (see description in "Online Resources") hosts a booth at various comics conventions. In 2007, for example, Prism exhibited at the New York Comic Con where Prism members moderated a panel on LGBT comics and at the San Diego Comic-Con—which featured two LGBT panels. Prism also exhibited at San Francisco's Wondercon, at the Emerald City Comic-Con in Seattle, and at Alternative Press Expo (APE).

Awards

Prism Comics awards a Queer Press Grant each September to a comics creator who is publishing a work of interest to an LGBT audience. The program began in 2005. For submission information and a list of past winners, access http://www.prismcomics.org/grant.php.

Titles and Series Worthy of Consideration

With LGBT Leading Characters and Themes

12 Days, by Kim June (Tokyopop, 18+)
The Book of Boy Trouble, edited by Robert Kirby and David Kelly (series of anthologies; Green Candy Press, 18+)
Charm School, by Elizabeth Watasin (Slave Labor Graphics, 16+)
Cavalcade of Boys: Complete Collection, by Tim Fish (Poison Press, 18+)
Fun Home: A Family Tragicomic, by Alison Bechdel (Mariner Books, 18+)
Jokes and the Unconscious: A Graphic Novel, by Daphne Gottlieb and Diane DiMassa (Cleis, 18+)
Pedro and Me, by Judd Winick (Holt, 13+)
Skim, by Mariko Tamaki and Jillian Tamaki (Groundwood Books, 16+)
Steady Beat, by Rivkah (series; Tokyopop, 13+)
Stuck Rubber Baby, by Howard Cruse (DC Comics, 16+)
Top 10: The Forty-Niners, by Alan Moore and Gene Ha (DC/America's Best Comics, 18+)

With Major LGBT Characters/Content (many more series exist)

Explicitly gay characters in mainstream comics go back at least to *Doonesbury*'s Andy Lippincott in 1977 but by implication long before that, such as in *Terry and the Pirates* from the 1930s (Applegate 1994). Among superheroes, *Alpha Flight*'s Northstar is reported as the first superhero to come out, in 1992 (Greyson 2007). A few noteworthy series are listed here. LGBT characters are given in parentheses.

52 (Batwoman, Renee Montoya; DC Comics)
Gotham Central: Half a Life (Renee Montoya; DC Comics)
The Authority (Midnighter and Apollo; Wildstorm/DC Comics)
Countdown (Batwoman and The Question; DC Comics)
Love and Rockets (Maggie and Hopey; Fantagraphics)
Runaways (Karolina and Xavin; Marvel Comics)
Strangers in Paradise (Katchoo and Francine; Abstract Studio)
Young Avengers (Wiccan and Hulking; Marvel Comics)

Newspaper Strips and Web Comics, Available in Collections

Curbside Boys, by Robert Kirby (Cleis, 18+)
Dykes to Watch Out For, by Alison Bechdel (Firebrand, Alyson; 18+)
Jane's World, by Paige Braddock (Girl Twirl Comics, 16+)
Jayson, by Jeff Krell (Ignite! Entertainment, 16+)
Tough Love: High School Confidential, by Abby Denson (Manic D Press, 13+)

Online Resources

The Gay League
> http://www.gayleague.com
> "The fan site for gay comics readers and creators." News, articles, profiles, reviews, resources, fan fiction and art, message board, and links.

Homosexuality in Comics
> http://www.comicbookresources.com
> Four-part series of articles by Emmett Furey in July 2007, with input from nine comics industry professionals about the portrayal of LGBT characters and themes in comics, past and present.

Prism Comics
> http://www.prismcomics.org
> A nonprofit organization that supports lesbian, gay, bisexual, and transgendered comics, creators, and readers. Prism's goal is to promote the work of LGBT creators, artists, and employees in comics as well as LGBT issues in comics in general. News, articles, interviews, profiles of over 300 creators, message board, online store (heavy on comic books), and links.

Yaoi Con
> http://www.yaoicon.com
> Headquarters site for Yaoi-Con, an annual convention for all things yaoi.

Definitions, news, conference information, forums, and links to publishers of translated titles.

Yowie! The Stateside Appeal of Boy-Meets-Boy YAOI Comics
http://www.afterelton.com/print/2008/1/yaoi
Article by Lyle Masaki, January 6, 2008, about the content, appeal, and readership of yaoi, including reactions of gay comics fans.

Yuricon
http://www.yuricon.org
Headquarters for a virtual yuri fan and creator community, which has held conferences and events as well as published several titles. Information, news, lists of characters and series, and links. Founder is librarian Erica Friedman.

Other Resources

Applegate, David. "Coming Out in the Comic Strips: Out of the Closet, into the Newspapers." *Hogan's Alley* 1, no. 1 (Autumn 1994): 75–78. http://cagle. msnbc.com/hogan/features/out/out.asp.
History of LGBT themes in newspaper comic strips, from *Terry and the Pirates* in the 1930s to *Beetle Bailey* in 1993.

Greyson, Devon. "GLBTQ Content in Comics/Graphic Novels for Teens." *Collection Building* 26, no. 4 (2007): 130–34.
History of LGBT themes in strips and comic books, with recommended titles for library collections.

Prism Comics: Your LGBT Guide to Comics. 2008 edition. Edited by Jonathan Riggs. Atlanta: Prism Comics, 2008.
Articles, news, profiles, and dishing about the LGBT comics scene, with 100 pages of short stories and excerpts. Published annually.

REFERENCES

Brenner, Robin, and Snow Wildsmith. "Gender and Sexuality in Graphic Novels & Manga." Presented at the annual meeting of the American Library Association, Anaheim, CA, June 26–July 2, 2008. http://www.presentations.ala.org/images/4/4d/GenderSexuality Manga.pdf.
Dynes, Wayne R. "Comics." In *Encyclopedia of Homosexuality: Volume 1, A-L,* 250–51. New York: Garland, 1990.
Furey, Emmett. "Homosexuality in Comics—Part I." *Comic Book Resources,* July 16, 2007. http://www.comicbookresources.com/print.php?type=ar&id=10795.

APPENDIX B-4 RELIGION-THEMED GRAPHIC NOVELS: RESOURCES

Throughout history, every art form has retold the compelling stories of faith. Two Jewish youngsters created Superman, who has been compared to that mythical Jewish avenger, the Golem (Garrett 2008, 18–19). Indeed, the Bible's superpatriarchs and supermatriarchs called upon special powers to protect their people. A healthy number of graphic novels feature Judaism themes, characters, and cultural history—quite a few, for example, treat the Holocaust alone, such as Art Spiegelman's *Maus,* Pascal Croci's *Auschwitz,* and Joe Kubert's *Yossel.* Much of the work of the late Will Eisner relates to Jewish history and culture.

Christian Bible comics date back to at least the 1940s (Hajdu 2008, 72–73). A fairly complete current version is *The Lion Graphic Bible,* but other Bible-based titles exist—including several manga versions. Christian comics creators, publishers, and enthusiasts have a close-knit community of their own with resources, vendors, organizations, and Web sites (see details later in this appendix). Much rarer are comics based on Buddhism, Islam, or Hindu-related themes: there are only a handful of titles, and it can be difficult to identify new material.

Why collect graphic novels with religious themes? Such titles can offer literacy and entertainment opportunities to patrons uninterested in secular material. Many are tied to the classic stories of faith, retold through contemporary cultural lenses as they have been for centuries. Many are simply good stories and may be evaluated as such the same as other graphic novels. Beyond these reasons, religious-themed graphic novels can offer corrective diversity when parents or community leaders offer objections to any of the other graphic novels in the library's collection. Librarians should consider maintaining lists, pathfinders, and flyers relating to religion-based titles to assure patrons and the community that the collection reflects a diversity of interest along the conservative–liberal and religious–secular continuums. (See chapter 10, "Censorship of Graphic Novels in Libraries.")

Several interesting Islamic and Christian series exist only in comic book form, not as graphic novels. See the Online Resources section of this appendix for details and ordering information.

Conventions

Christian Comic Arts Society (CCAS)
> http://www.christiancomicarts.com
> Holds a meeting, staffs a booth, and plans several panels at the annual San Diego Comic-Con. CCAS may also staff a booth at other large conventions such as Wizard World and holds smaller meetings of its own members.

Awards

In 2004, a set of 10 "Hartley Awards" (http://jangofettclone.tripod.com/id5.html) were given in the name of Al Hartley, a pioneering Christian comics artist who drew for Archie Comics and worked on series with Christian appeal for several other publishers. But no further information seems to be available about these awards. The Christian ministry group Comix35 has held two International Christian Comics Competitions, the second in 2007 (see http://comix35.gospelcom.

net/intcompetition2.html). Winning submissions for both have been published in anthologies—see following list. In 2008, Comix35 held a Manga Messiah Video Competition (http://www.comix35.org/manga_messiah.html) and plans a Christian "Manga-ka Contest" in Japan (http://www.comix35.org/mangaka.html).

Titles and Series Worthy of Consideration

The Adventures of Rabbi Harvey: A Graphic Novel of Jewish Wisdom and Wit in the Wild West, by Steve Sheinkin (Jewish Lights Publishing, 10+)

Buddha, by Osamu Tezuka (series; Vertical, 13+)

Christian Comics 2005 (international anthology from the first International Christian Comics Competition, COMIX35/ROX35 Media, 13+)

Eye Witness, by Robert James Luedke (4 vols., Head Press, 13+)

Hoppel Poppel Kosher Comix, by Ken Eichenbaum (Litterati Books, 13+)

ICCC2 (international anthology from the second International Christian Comics Competition, COMIX35/ROX35 Media, 13+)

"Introducing" series (Icon Books/Totem Books, 16+)
   Introducing Buddha
   Introducing Christianity
   Introducing Hinduism
   Introducing Islam

Jews in America: A Cartoon History, by David Gantz (Jewish Publication Society, 16+)

King David, by Kyle Baker (DC Comics, 16+)

The Life of John Paul II . . . in Comics! by Alessandro Mainardi and Werner Maresta (Papercutz, 10+)

The Lion Graphic Bible, by Mike Maddox and Jeff Anderson (Lion Hudson, 13+)

Manga Bible, by Young Shin Lee and others (series; Zondervan, 10+)

Manga Messiah, by Hidenori Kumai and Kozumi Shinozawa (NEXT/Tyndale, 10+)

Marked, by Steve Ross (Seabury/Church Publishing, 13+)

Megillat Esther, by J. T. Waldman (Jewish Publication Society, 13+)

Ramayan 3392 AD, by various creators (Virgin Comics, 13+)

Serenity, by RealBuzz Studios (series, Barbour Publishing, 13+)

The Story of the Jews: A 4,000-Year Adventure, by Stan Mack (Jewish Lights Publishing, 13+)

Testament, by Douglas Rushkoff and Liam Sharp (series, Vertigo, 18+)

Online Resources

Christian Book Distributors' Christian Comic Book Store
   http://www.christianbook.com
   Plug "Comic Books" into the keyword search feature for the main site. Sells quite a number of Christian-themed and Christian-friendly graphic novels, manga, and comics from a variety of publishers, with brief descriptions and age-ratings.

Christian Comic Arts Society

http://www.christiancomicarts.com

Organization of Christian comics "fans, pros, and amateurs." Puts out an annual guide to Christian comics (see the Other Resources section of this appendix) and holds meetings and panels at the San Diego Comic-Con and some other large conventions. Maintains a related social networking site.

Christian Comics International

http://www.christiancomicsinternational.org

Major online guide to Christian comics around the world: history, notable titles, pioneers, international projects, catalog of "more than 165" titles for purchase, and links.

ChristianComics.net

http://www.christiancomics.net

A "place for Christian comic writers, artists, and fans to [share] fellowship and yak it up." Also sells some 100 titles through the site.

The Guardian Line

http://www.theguardianline.com

A line of four multiethnic Christian-based series available as comic books from Urban Ministries: *Code, Joe & Max, Genesis 5,* and *Seekers.* Previews are available on the Web; no graphic novel compilations. The comic books may be ordered through a link to the Urban Ministries Web site.

Jewish Comics

http://www.jewishcomics.blogspot.com

Blog and news site from Toronto librarian Steven M. Bergson, with links to other blogs and some older lists of titles.

Jews in Comics

http://http://groups.yahoo.com/group/jewishcomics/

Newsgroup "for announcements of new stories in comic books or strips that have a Jewish character in them, announcements about events related to Jewish comics and for discussion about the Jewish comics themselves."

Teshkeel Media Group

http://www.teshkeelcomics.com

A Middle East–based company with offices in Kuwait and New York that publishes *The 99,* a multiethnic Islamic-based superhero series available as comic books. Previews available on the Web; no graphic novel compilations. Subscriptions to the comic books in English may be ordered through http://the99.org.

Other Resources

Christian Comic Arts Society. *2008 Guide to Christian Comics.* Temple City, CA: New Creation Entertainment, 2008.

Fifth annual guide to the Christian comics industry, with 64 pages of news, lists of current and forthcoming comics, Web comics, company information, articles, excerpts, and reviews. Order via http://www.newcreationnow.com/shop.html.

Garrett, Greg. *Holy Superheroes! Exploring Faith & Spirituality in Comic Books.* Louisville, KY: Westminster John Knox, 2008.

Weinstein, Simcha. *Up, Up, and Oy Vey! How Jewish History, Culture, and Values Shaped the Comic Book Superhero.* Baltimore: Leviathan Press, 2006.

REFERENCE

Hajdu, David. *The Ten-Cent Plague: The Great Comic-Book Scare and How It Changed America.* New York: Farrar, Straus and Giroux, 2008.

Appendix C

BIBLIOGRAPHY OF BOOKS: GRAPHIC NOVELS, LIBRARIES, AND LITERACY

Martha Cornog

GRAPHIC NOVELS IN LIBRARIES

These books were written by librarians unless otherwise indicated.

Brenner, Robin E. *Understanding Manga and Anime.* Westport, CT: Libraries Unlimited, 2007. Extensive background about manga and anime visual conventions and prevalent genres, Japanese versus American cultural expectations, plus working with fans and patrons. Briefer coverage of collection development and recommended titles with annotations and age levels (333pp).

Crawford, Philip Charles. *Graphic Novels 101: Selecting and Using Graphic Novels to Promote Literacy for Children and Young Adults; A Resource Guide for School Librarians and Educators.* Salt Lake City: Hi Willow Research & Publishing, 2003. Recommends an assortment of G3–12 titles with annotations and age levels and briefly covers background, collection development, and processing issues (76pp).

Goldsmith, Francisca. *Graphic Novels Now: Building, Managing, and Marketing a Dynamic Collection.* Chicago: ALA Editions, 2005. Broad if concise coverage of background, collection development, processing, programming, and promotion. Some recommended titles with brief annotations but no age levels (113pp).

Gorman, Michele. *Getting Graphic! Comics for Kids.* Columbus, OH: Linworth, 2008. Collection development/readers advisory resource: recommended titles with annotations and grade levels for ages 4 through 12 (84pp).

Gorman, Michele. *Getting Graphic! Using Graphic Novels to Promote Literacy with Pre-teens and Teens.* Columbus, OH: Linworth, 2003. Comprehensive if brief coverage of comics history, role and value in the library and classroom, collection development, bibliographic control, promotion, programming, and recommended titles with annotations and grade levels (100pp).

Kannenberg, Gene. *500 Essential Graphic Novels: The Ultimate Guide.* New York: Collins Design, 2008. Collection development/readers advisory resource: lavishly packaged collection of plot summaries together with reviews, ratings, color cover images and sample panels, age-grading, and further reading lists. Arranged by genre with indexes by age level, creator, title, and publisher. The author is a PhD-level comics scholar rather than a librarian (527pp).

Lyga, Allyson A. W., and Barry Lyga. *Graphic Novels in Your Media Center: A Definitive Guide.* Westport, CT: Libraries Unlimited, 2004. Covers how comics work, collection development, processing, working with comics shops, lesson plans using comics, censorship, and recommended titles for elementary through high schools with grade levels. Some annotations (180pp).

Miller, Steve. *Developing and Promoting Graphic Novel Collections.* New York: Neal-Schuman, 2005. Broad if concise coverage of background, collection development, processing, programming, and promotion. Some recommended titles with very brief annotations, all-ages and teen (130pp).

Pawuk, Michael. *Graphic Novels: A Genre Guide to Comic Books, Manga, and More.* Westport, CT: Libraries Unlimited, 2007. Collection development/readers advisory resource: extensive guide to titles organized by genre, with annotations and age levels. Awards and media tie-ins are also indicated. A brief introduction in comics format reviews background, collection development, processing, programming, and promotion issues (633pp).

Rothschild, D. Aviva. *Graphic Novels: A Bibliographic Guide to Book-Length Comics.* Westport, CT: Libraries Unlimited, 1995. Collection development/readers advisory resource: guide to titles organized by genre, with long annotations and age-levels. Dated: many titles may not be available, but interesting as a list of what was available at that time (245pp).

Scott, Randall W. *Comics Librarianship: A Handbook.* Jefferson, NC: McFarland, 1990. For academic librarians: covers background, collection development, and processing issues. A classic, even if quite dated and focused on comic books (188pp).

Serchay, David. *The Librarian's Guide to Graphic Novels for Adults.* New York: Neal-Schuman, forthcoming. Expected to provide comprehensive coverage of background, genres, collection development, processing, programming, and promotion, for patrons aged teen through adult. A substantial appendix of recommended titles with annotations.

Serchay, David. *The Librarian's Guide to Graphic Novels for Children and Tweens.* New York: Neal-Schuman, 2008. Comprehensive coverage of background, genres, collection development, processing, programming, and promotion, for patrons roughly ages 8 through 12. A substantial appendix of recommended titles with annotations (272pp).

Thompson, Jason. *Manga: The Complete Guide.* New York: Del Rey/Ballantine, 2007. Collection development/readers advisory resource: comprehensive list of over 900 series with annotations and age levels. Separate sections for yaoi and adult (that is, erotic) titles. Sidebars throughout address genres and background issues. Not a librarian, the author has long-term experience as a manga editor at VIZ and has written widely about manga (556pp).

Weiner, Stephen. *The 101 Best Graphic Novels.* New York: NBM, 2005. Collection development/readers advisory resource: concise annotations with age-grading, arranged by author. Includes cover images, occasional sample panels, bibliography, and title index. This is the third edition of this "best of" list that was first published in 1996 (60pp).

GRAPHIC NOVELS AND LITERACY

Beyond the individual focus of each title, all of these books supply excellent background for times when patrons, administrators, other library staff, or the media ask why on earth the library is collecting comics. They also may serve as a resource for those writing grants to start or enhance a graphic novel collection.

Carter, James Bucky, ed. *Building Literacy Connections with Graphic Novels; Page by Page, Panel by Panel.* Urbana, IL: National Council of Teachers of English, 2007. Suggested approaches primarily for middle and high school students and undergraduates. Useful as background for school and academic librarians serving these age groups (164pp).

Cary, Stephen. *Going Graphic: Comics at Work in the Multilingual Classroom.* Portsmouth, NH: Heinemann, 2004. Background, tips, and ideas for teachers working with elementary school through adult levels where students are learning a second language. Useful for librarians serving multilingual patrons (218pp).

Krashen, Stephen D. *The Power of Reading: Insights from the Research.* 2nd ed. Westport, CT: Libraries Unlimited, 2004. Summarizes a large number of academic studies on the benefits of reading and how to encourage reading. One section covers studies showing the value of reading comics (199pp).

Thomas, James L., ed. *Cartoons and Comics in the Classroom: A Reference for Teachers and Librarians.* Littleton, CO: Libraries Unlimited, 1983. Ideas and strategies for using graphic novels in G3 to high school classes. Some information is dated, but many of the suggestions remain useful and interesting (181pp).

Thompson, Terry. *Adventures in Graphica: Using Comics and Graphic Novels to Teach Comprehension, 2–6.* Portland, ME: Stenhouse Publishers, 2008. Background, tips, and ideas for elementary school teachers. Also good as background for elementary and middle school librarians as well as public librarians working in children's services (188pp).

Appendix D

SELECTED ONLINE RESOURCES

Martha Cornog

ENCYCLOPEDIAS AND REFERENCE SITES

Anime News Network
  http://www.animenewsnetwork.com
  Large and well-regarded site for news, reviews (under the "Views" link), and reference information on manga and anime. The Encyclopedia section contains data on hundreds of titles and authors as well as a glossary ("lexicon").
AnimeCons.com
  http://www.animecons.com/events
  Calendar of upcoming U.S. manga/anime conventions up through about 10 months ahead, in date order, plus capsule profiles and links to convention Web sites.
Comic Book Awards Almanac
  http://www.hahnlibrary.net/comics/awards/index.html
  Extensive catalog of U.S. and international comics awards and award winners, arranged by award and then year. Compiled and maintained by librarian Joel Hahn.
ComicBookConventions.com
  http://www.comicbookconventions.com/conventions.htm
  Calendar of numerous upcoming U.S. comics-related conventions, large and small, up to roughly 13 months ahead in date order, with links to convention Web sites. Virtually none relating to manga or anime. (See entry for AnimeCons.com.)
Comic Shop Locator Service
  http://www.comicshoplocator.com
  Directory of comic shops in the United States, Canada, and the UK, searchable by ZIP/postal code. Several in Europe are listed also, searchable by country/city. The site is run by Diamond Comics, the major U.S. distributor of comics-format publications.

Don Markstein's Toonopedia

http://www.toonopedia.com

Concise encyclopedia-type profiles of hundreds of comics-related topics, especially American and classic/older material. "A 'toon' [is] anything that's done in cartoon form, such as animated films, comic books, etc."

Lambiek Comiclopedia

http://www.lambiek.net

Brief profiles of over 10,000 comics artists from around the world; stronger on international creators than Americans. Lambiek is "Europe's first comics shop," located in Amsterdam.

Wikipedia

http://en.wikipedia.org/

Wikipedia has thousands of entries relating to comics titles, characters, creators, detailed plot lines (especially for series set in the DC Universe or Marvel Universe), and related popular culture concepts. Often, it is the only easy-to-find source for a "first stop." But *beware:* the content can change hourly as factionista struggles continually reshape the text to suit preferences and personal agendas. Use the links at the bottom of the entries to verify and broaden the search. Also, never depend on Wiki to provide exactly the same information twice. Copy or print out information to preserve it. For manga and anime, always start with Anime News Network, a more consistently reliable source.

NEWS, ARTICLES, REVIEWS, AND RESOURCES

The Beat

http://pwbeat.publishersweekly.com/blog/

Heidi MacDonald's exhaustive, entertaining, and irreverent blog on all things comics (and related media spin-offs), a link off the Web site of *Publishers Weekly.*

Comic Book Resources

http://www.comicbookresources.com

Extensive site covering mainly American comics, superheroes and otherwise. News, columns, reviews, blogs, resources, and previews.

The Comics Journal

http://www.tcj.com

The Web site for *The Comics Journal,* a hefty magazine that "covers the comics medium from an arts-first perspective." Features excerpts from the magazine, a blog, and some Web-only material, including reviews.

Comics Reporter

http://www.comicsreporter.com

"Tom Spurgeon's Web site of comics news, reviews, interviews and commentary." A large site with wide focus spanning American comics (superhero and not), manga, and other international works, with a good bit of background information, resources, and links.

ComicsResearch.org

http://www.comicsresearch.org/

A large and rich collection of bibliographies and resources relating to comic art and narrative, plus other scholarly information and links. Managed by Gene Kannenbaum.

Comics Worth Reading

http://www.comicsworthreading.com

News and lengthy reviews/commentary on all genres of comics and graphic novels. Managed by Johanna Draper Carlson.

Gilles' Service to Fans Page

http://www.koyagi.com

Invaluable resources for librarians, educators, and others about manga and anime. Guide to the format, recommended core titles, bibliographies, and many other resources and links. From librarian Gilles Poitras.

GraphicNovelReporter

http://graphicnovelreporter.com

Wide coverage of the format with news, reviews, interviews, blog, and newsletter. Considerable content of interest to educators and librarians as well as to comics industry professionals and educated fans. Part of the Book Report Network along with Bookreporter.com and several other Web sites.

Graphic Novels: Resources for Teachers & Librarians

http://library.buffalo.edu/libraries/asl/guides/graphicnovels/

"Designed to introduce librarians (as well as teachers and parents) to the rich, diverse offerings from today's comics book publishers, and to encourage the acquisition of graphic novels in libraries serving young adults." Includes information on formats, publishers, core lists, and collection-development considerations. Compiled and maintained by librarian Michael R. Lavin.

Great Graphic Novels for Teens

http://www.ala.org/yalsa/ggnt

Web page with links to lists of recommended graphic novels for ages 12–18, selected yearly by the Young Adult Library Services Association (YALSA).

ICv2: Inside Pop Culture

http://www.icv2.com

Major news site about popular culture, updated daily. Click on the "comic news by date" link in the sidebar. An invaluable source for sales and market data, including lists of the top-selling manga, graphic novels, and comic books by month, quarter, and year. Some reviews. The organization sells the *ICv2 Insider's Guide,* a useful publication of reviews and market insights covering manga, anime, graphic novels, and games. The reviews are written by librarians. To subscribe, plug "icv2 guide" into the site's search feature.

Manga Life

http://www.mangalife.com

A substantive site of manga news, reviews, and features. "Our aim is to guide you through the masses of manga appearing on the shelves of your book store, to pick out *THE* essential books to own."

Newsarama

http://www.newsarama.com

News, opinion, and previews covering superheroes and other American titles. Substantial coverage of other media (film, games, television) based on comics properties.

No Flying No Tights

http://www.noflyingnotights.com/

Background information about graphic novels in libraries plus core lists for teens, children (Sidekicks), and adults (The Lair). From librarian Robin Brenner.

PW Comics Week

http://www.publishersweekly.com (select from the Newsletters drop-down at the top of the home page)

Weekly newsletter with articles, reviews, interviews, news, and preview panels from new titles. Edited by Calvin Reid and Heidi MacDonald.

Read About Comics

http://www.readaboutcomics.com

Site for reviews written by Greg McElhatton. Many perceptive and lengthy reviews of a variety of titles: superheroes, manga, and others.

Sequart Research & Literacy Organization

http://www.sequart.com

"Sequart Research & Literacy Organization is a non-profit organization devoted solely to the study and promotion of the artistic and literary medium alternately known as comics, comic strips, comic books, graphic novels, manga, sequential art, and sequart." Site resources range from news to a large database of comic book issues, creators, and publishers.

GRAPHIC NOVEL REVIEWS

Most of the major library-interest review periodicals cover graphic novels, including *Publishers Weekly, Library Journal, School Library Journal, Booklist,* and *VOYA.* If your library has a subscription, you can usually arrange for a password and use the periodical's Web site search feature to locate back reviews. You can also try Googling the title in quotes, author in quotes, name of periodical in quotes, and the word "review," which can pick up reviews reprinted or quoted on other sites.

Another source for reviews are publishers' Web sites, which will sometimes provides long quotes or links to reviews in connection with the titles.

Beyond these, many of the sites listed earlier run reviews, including the dependable Anime News Network for manga. In addition, you can usually find reviews of a sort for nearly everything by Googling the title in quotes, author in quotes, and the word "review." Note, however, that this can retrieve anything from highly competent *Time* magazine and *New York Times* reviews to entertaining but infuriating rants from fans with too many words and too little insight. The brief reader reviews for Amazon.com listings fall into this category: some perceptive and knowledgeable, others vague and useless. Yet in the aggregate, even these "reviews" may be able to help a librarian decide whether to consider a title further or write it off right then.

As an alternative to reviews, collection-development librarians can check titles and brief descriptions included in core lists provided by the books listed in Appendix C as well as sleuth out award-winners—see the Comics Book Awards Almanac and Great Graphic Novels for Teens, earlier in this appendix. For best-seller lists, see ICv2. In addition, *Publishers Weekly* periodically prints a list of the 10 top-selling graphic novels, and the *New York Times* includes "graphic books" in its best-seller lists. (See www.nytimes.com/pages/books/bestseller/.)

ELECTRONIC MAILING LISTS

Anime and Manga Research Circle (AMRC-L)

http://www.cjas.org/~leng/amrc.htm

A diverse community of scholars involved in the "academic study of anime and manga, their associated (sub)cultures worldwide, and (tangentially) Japanese popular culture in general. We welcome all professionals, students, and fans who have conducted anime and manga-related research, are in the process of conducting such research, and/or would like to conduct such research in the future."

Comix-Scholars Discussion List

http://www.english.ufl.edu/comics/scholars/

Academic forum about research, criticism, and teaching as related to comic art. Open to theoretical and critical approaches from all disciplinary perspectives. Includes scholars in academia, other institutional frameworks, and working independently.

Graphic Novels in Libraries (GNLIB-L)

http://groups.yahoo.com/group/GNLIB-L/

Forum for discussion of graphic novels and comics, primarily by and for public and school librarians, with some academic librarian participation. Membership is open to librarians, industry professionals, and creators to share reviews and resources for graphic novel collections.

LIBRARIES WITH SPECIAL COLLECTIONS IN COMICS

These lists overlap somewhat but not completely. Not all may be up-to-date.

Comics Research Libraries

http://www.lib.msu.edu/comics/otherlib.htm

Directory of 55 collections in academic and public libraries, U.S. and international. Annotations, contact information, and some (not all) links.

Library of Congress, Caroline and Erwin Swann Collection of Caricature and Cartoon http://www.loc.gov/rr/print/coll/230_swan.html

Scroll down to Related Collections at the Library of Congress and then to Related Collections and Sources Outside the Library of Congress. Includes addresses, contact information, and links for 29 U.S. and international collections total.

Library Research Collections of Comics

http://www.comicsresearch.org/academic.html#libraries

List with links to 22 U.S. and international collections. Part of ComicsResearch. org (see earlier description).

INDEX

About the Editors and Contributors

MARTHA CORNOG has written the graphic novel column for *Library Journal* since 2006 and has published several books, winning an Eli M. Oboler Award from the ALA and a Benjamin Franklin Award from the Independent Book Publishers Association. She sat on a panel about manga in libraries at the 2006 New York Comic Con and has written and reviewed for *Library Journal* for over 30 years. She holds an MLS from Drexel University and an MA from Brown University and has worked in academic and public libraries.

TIMOTHY PERPER is the Review and Commentary Editor for *Mechademia: An Academic Annual for Anime, Manga, and the Fan Arts* and a former book review editor for several scholarly journals. He has written and presented on manga and anime for scholarly journals and conferences and holds a PhD from City University of New York.

Martha and Tim are married and share their house with a large collection of manga and graphic novels.

ROBIN E. BRENNER is the Teen Librarian at the Brookline Public Library in Massachusetts. She has chaired the ALA/YALSA Great Graphic Novels for Teens Selection List Committee, was a judge for the 2007 Eisner awards, reviews manga for Teenreads.com and anime for *Video Librarian,* and regularly gives lectures and workshops on graphic novels, manga, and anime. Her guide, *Understanding Manga and Anime* (Libraries Unlimited, 2007), was nominated for a 2008 Eisner Award. She also hosts a Web site on graphic novels, http://www.noflyingnotights.com, and two sub-sites: Sidekicks, for children through age 12; and the Lair, for adults. She holds an MLS from the University of Illinois at Urbana-Champaign.

Originally from Oklahoma, ERIN BYRNE was a children's librarian for seven years before going on to be Associate Director of the Office for Intellectual

Freedom at the ALA. She is currently a writer living in Chicago. She holds an MLIS from the University of Oklahoma in Norman, Oklahoma.

FRANCISCA GOLDSMITH has worked in collection management, reference, and teen services in U.S. public and academic libraries. She is currently Director of Branch Services at Halifax Public Libraries, Nova Scotia. Author of numerous reviews of graphic novels as well as *Graphic Novels Now* (ALA Editions, 2005), she teaches staff development workshops and online courses related to graphic novels in libraries. Since receiving her MLIS from Simmons College, she has written for a variety of professional publications, including *Library Journal, Booklist, VOYA,* and *KLIATT.*

MICHAEL R. LAVIN is Coordinator of Electronic Collections for the University Libraries at SUNY Buffalo, where he also manages the graphic novel collection and is adjunct instructor in Library and Information Studies. Over his 30-year career, he has worked at several other academic and public libraries. Mike is a lifelong comics fan, has written extensively about graphic novels for libraries, and maintains a frequently cited Web site, Graphic Novels: Resources for Teachers and Librarians (http://library.buffalo.edu/libraries/asl/guides/graphicnovels/). He received the ALA/BRASS award for Excellence in Business Librarianship and the SUNY Chancellor's Award for Excellence in Librarianship. He holds an MBA from Canisius College as well as his MLS from SUNY Buffalo.

Professor JOHN A. LENT is founding publisher and editor-in-chief of *International Journal of Comic Art,* founding chair of the Asian Popular Culture Group within the Popular Culture Society, chair of the Asian Cinema Studies Society, and editor-in-chief/publisher of *Asian Cinema.* He is author or editor of 70 books, including a few on comic art, and a lecturer on comics and animation on every continent. He has been a university professor since 1960 and has taught in the United States, China, Malaysia, and the Philippines. In 2007 and 2008, he was a member of the Pulitzer Prize selection board for editorial cartoons. He holds a PhD from the University of Iowa.

CHRIS MATZ is the Library Director for Christian Brothers University in Memphis, Tennessee. Prior to that, he was the Collection Development Librarian at the University of Memphis. He has earned a BS in political science from the University of Oregon, an MLS from the University of North Carolina-Greensboro, and an MA in English from the University of Memphis. He believes comics and libraries are two great tastes that taste great together.

MICHAEL NIEDERHAUSEN is an adjunct faculty member at Cuyahoga Community College. His master's thesis applies the signifying literary theory to *The Sandman* by Neil Gaiman. He has also written on the works of Grant Morrison for *International Journal of Comic Art,* in which he was a panel member for the Ever-Ending Battle Symposium at the Comics Arts

Conference in 2006. He is currently working on a book about the significance and importance of the Justice Society of America, the first superhero team. Michael is happily married with two children and currently resides in a suburb of Cleveland.

LORENA O'ENGLISH is the Social Sciences Reference and Instruction Librarian at Washington State University in Pullman, Washington, focusing on political science, sociology, and criminal justice. She enjoys promoting scholarly and popular interest in comic books and graphic novels at WSU and often incorporates them into the library classes and technology workshops she teaches. She is a strong advocate for recreational reading on her campus. Lorena coauthored an article on graphic novels in academic libraries published in *The Journal of Academic Librarianship* in 2006. A librarian since 1999, Lorena shares both her profession and her 30-plus-year interest in comics with her husband, Mark. She holds an MLIS from the University of Washington.

GILLES POITRAS is a writer on anime, manga, and Japanese culture and a librarian in the San Francisco Bay area. He has published *Anime Essentials* and two volumes of *The Anime Companion,* he wrote the "Below the Surface" column for the now-defunct *Newtype USA,* and he writes for *Otaku USA* magazine. He serves as an invited guest speaker at many anime and manga conventions and does a popular "Anime for Parents" panel. Gilles maintains a large Web site of information about manga and anime (http://www.koyagi.com), which includes a useful "Librarian's Guide to Anime and Manga" as well as updates to *The Anime Companion* and a supplement for teachers. He holds an MLIS from the University of California at Berkeley.

Herstorian and writer TRINA ROBBINS has been writing graphic novels, comics, and books for over 30 years. Her subjects have ranged from *Wonder Woman* and *The Powerpuff Girls* to her own teenage superheroine, *GoGirl!,* and from women cartoonists and superheroines to women who kill. She has provided English-language rewrites for shōjo manga graphic novels and has lectured and taught comics and graphic novels throughout the United States and Europe.